AMERICA AND THE LAW

Challenges For
The 21st Century

Stephen J. Herman

GRAVIER HOUSE PRESS
An Independent Publishing Company
New Orleans, Louisiana
1999

Library of Congress Publication Data:
Herman, Stephen.

America and the Law: Challenges for the 21st Century / Stephen Herman.
Includes bibliographical references.
ISBN 978-1-7335181-5-4

(Original GNP Paperback ISBN 0-9671179-1-7)
1. Law - U.S. 2. History - U.S. 3. Political Science - U.S. 4. Philosophy.

Library of Congress Catalog Card Number: 99-94312
© Copyright by Stephen Herman, 1996, 1998.

Gravier House Press, LLC
Post Office Box 50337
New Orleans, Louisiana 70150-0337
http://www.gravierhouse.com

Introduction

I wrote this book, over 20 years ago, at the very beginning of my legal career, with the hope that it might be appreciated by practicing attorneys and general interest readers alike. (I also wanted to provide a centralized reference for lawyers, judges, consumer advocates, and academic or political commentators to key studies, quotes, and citations of legal authority which refute the *Contract on America,* the Louisiana tort reform wave of the 1990s, and the other trickle-down economic type arguments that continue to haunt us to this day – in the form of an extensive and exhaustive bibliography.) Of course, a few of my views have changed during the intervening decades, and there is always the urge to go back and make revisions to what you have previously written. Particularly with this type of a book, one could supplement with developing caselaw, legislative enactments, additional statistics, and other relevant commentary, on an almost-daily basis. So once you start, where would you stop? I have generally wanted, or needed, to get on with other things. Moreover, and in any event, I think and would hope that the essential truths (or lack thereof) in what I have attempted to capture would largely remain unchanged.

At the same time, whenever I think back on this book, two chapters stand out. Most notably, the end of the O.J. Simpson chapter, in which I seem to suggest that the murders may have been committed by his son. It now, of course, seems almost silly to entertain the notion that it might not have been O.J.

I think it's a part of, or at least related to, the Confirmation Bias, that people are likely more certain today that they were certain on the day of the verdict that Simpson was guilty than they actually were at the time. Which probably happens naturally in a lot of different contexts. But is particularly acute here, because of the events and information which have only cemented our belief in his guilt over time. First, there is the civil judgment, along with a good bit of evidence that was not admitted during the criminal trial. Second, is the disturbingly imaginative, if not outright confessional, *If I Did It,* which Simpson penned, or at least dictated, in 2007. And, finally, the armed robbery conviction in Las Vegas.

I also think that, while as a matter of science and technology I am sure that anyone who understood DNA testing in 1994 would have scoffed at the idea that a son could have been confused with his father, in the popular consciousness, the discipline still felt new, and therefore fraught with some degree of unreliability.

In this particular instance, however, there were two other dynamics at work. First, although I remember being pretty firmly convinced of Simpson's guilt by the time I did the revised Gravier House Press edition in 1999, I was undoubtedly motivated, from a political and philosophical perspective, to defend and protect the jury. Secondly, from a more "literary" perspective, I didn't really see the point in saying the same thing everyone else was already saying. What would be interesting, or thought-provoking, about that?In 2016, there were a couple of television series revisiting the O.J. Simpson trial. One was a five-part documentary, which aired on ESPN, called *O.J.: Made in America.* The other was a ten-part dramatized series, which ran on FX, called *The People v. O.J. Simpson: American Crime Story.* While each was entertaining in its own right, what made them particularly interesting was the way in which they were framed, in compliment of and contrast to one another. The dramatized series focused on the individual narratives of the primary trial participants, and left you with the sense that the outcome could have

and would have been different, but for the instincts of op-
portunistic defense lawyers combined with the colossal
mistakes made by the prosecution. The documentary, on
the other hand, started with the Watts Riots, and the Rod-
ney King incident, placing the O.J. story largely within
the context of broader racial and political tensions plagu-
ing Los Angeles for some time. Watching this version of
events, you get the sense that the jury was going to strike
some measure of what it believed to be Justice, in a larger sense, irrespective of who the attorneys were, or what
they did or said.

The second part of the book that I frequently recon-
sider, when I'm thinking about it, is the chapter on crime
and punishment. While, from a purely rational perspective, I continue to believe that drugs should be legalized,
it gives me a lot of emotional and psychological angst.
The thought of my kids getting hooked on something like
coke, or heroine, or meth, scares the hell out of me – even
if, as a legal product, the consequences of such addiction
might not be as bad. (Either from a societal standpoint
or for them.) Making something "illegal" does have a
deterrent effect. And there will be some percentage of the
population that is spared a lot of personal and economic misfortune by continued criminalization – even if it
doesn't square with our notions of individual liberty or
results in an overall negative impact to society as a whole.

Nor was I ever quite comfortable with my treatment
of the death penalty. From a purely practical standpoint,
I feel a lot more strongly than I did in the 1990s that the
death penalty is just not worth it. An absurdly disproportionate amount of time and money is devoted to this
single infrequently imposed sentence. Those resources
could be invested much more productively, even within
the criminal justice system, if not other projects and pro-

grams. But, as I note in a footnote, there is a fundamental difference between the practical application (or mis-application) of the death penalty, on the one hand, and the moral or philosophical question of whether the punishment itself is an appropriate sanction. While I still tend to believe, for the same reasons, that the answer is no, I find that I become inordinately aggravated when people take the time and energy to fight, and protest, and hold candle-light vigils for the condemned, not because they believe in a possible innocence, but as a matter of principle, even where there is no question that the perpetrator has committed a terrible crime. When I was a judicial law clerk, Justice Lemmon had a death penalty case I was assigned to, involving a young man, (who happened to be white, although I don't think that really should matter), who raped a college girl, unsuccessfully tried to strangle her with a rope, and then finally killed her by placing a board on her neck and jumping up and down on it. I will probably get some of the details wrong, but what I remember is that when he was an already-disturbed little boy, the defendant took some type of an air or water hose and Superglued it to a little girl's privates. Indeed, I think the rape-murder for which he was executed occurred within weeks of his being released from prison. Why was he in jail? Because he held his 14-year-old sister at knifepoint and raped her on their parents' bed.

When my wife, Karen, was a prosecutor, she was involved in a death penalty trial, and I came to watch her closing. The defendant had already been convicted of five first-degree murders. (As I recall, he didn't get the death penalty during the first trial because you need a unanimous verdict, and the vote was only 11-to-1 for death.) He was now on trial for an additional three murders. Two of the victims were a mother and child. The child was a little boy, only two years old. The defendant shot him eight times. When the police arrived, he was still in his mother's arms, clutching her hair – along with a scrap of scalp, torn loose. In all, the defendant had killed eight people, (that we knew about), using 64 bullets. An average of eight bullets per victim. Sister Helen Prejean, of *Dead Man Walking* fame, was allowed to testify as an "expert" on the bereavement of both the death penalty perpetrator's and victim's families. She testified that the victim's family would, in time, come to regret the death sentence, subjected to further reminders, guilt, frustration, and pain. The jury apparently did not find her testimony very compelling, imposing the ultimate penalty anyway.

To find God's light, or even just a bit of humanity, in these killers, is likely an experience of grace. But we are only on this planet for a limited time. And if someone is going to dedicate a part of his or her life to helping others, it just seems to me that they could probably find a lot of desperate people with more worthy needs and aspirations.

In any event, and on a brighter note, the chapter I always thought about possibly adding was a chapter on intellectual property issues. Some of my general attitudes are captured in a piece called "Who Owns the Rights to That?" which I posted on the gravierhouse website in March of 2009. But there was a case all the way back to 1994 that I thought was interesting, and always wanted to write on. The question was whether highly specialized software should be classified as "tangible property" or "intellectual property" for sales tax purposes. Some taxing authorities had drawn a distinction between "canned" software, which was taxable, and "custom" software, which was not. The Louisiana Supreme Court rejected this distinction, and held that "once the 'information' or 'knowledge' is transformed into physical existence and recorded in physical form, it is corporeal property." (*South Central Bell v. Bartholemy,* 643 So.2d 1240 (La.

1994)) I thought that what the Court should do is look to the costs of the software's components to determine what the purchaser was actually paying for. When someone bought a compact disc, for example, the object of the purchase was largely "intangible" (*i.e.* music), but what he or she was paying for was mostly the cost of the physical disc itself, (as they pretty much all cost $14.95, irrespective of whether you were buying a No.1 artist in high demand or a regional performer who didn't even make the charts). Here, by contrast, the telephone company had paid over $100,000 for software stored on a magnetic tape that probably cost less than $100; so what they were really paying for was the intangible professional service provided by the programmer, and not the tangible corporeal tape that it happened to be delivered on. But whatever the "correct" answer on the sales tax issue, what struck me was the inadequacy of a law from the 1940s to anticipate or accommodate the advances in technology. And, of course, as we have moved into the 21st Century, issues of intellectual property law have only become more complex, more controversial, and more challenging.Another addition which might be warranted is a chapter on the effect and import of Behavioral Economics. I have a paper from 2014 called "Legalnomics" attempts to summarize the basic principles from books like *Thinking, Fast and Slow* and *Predictably Irrational,* as well as some thoughts in a September 2017 piece I did on *The Fourth Turning,* which talks about Jonathan Haidt's similar application of psychology (and associated fields such as evolutionary biology and history/anthropology) to the realm of politics and religion, in his seminal work, *The Righteous Mind.* One of his central themes, in this regard, is that moral decisions, like economic decisions, are largely made on an intuitive basis, and then self-justified by strategic reasoning after-the-fact. These philosophies, central as they are to perception and belief, seem more directed towards advocacy and persuasion strategies. While I see a lot of "arbitrary coherence" in the area of criminal sentencing guidelines, for example, I am not sure that I have any truly original ideas and perspectives here, and it would take a good bit of work (and some creativity) to synthesize these principles into substantive notions of justice.Maybe some day ....

In the meantime, I have only added to the 1999 edition this introduction and a poem I wrote for the Herman Herman & Katz 70th Anniversary celebration in November of 2012. Being as objective as I can be, I still think the book might be appreciated by practicing attorneys and general interest readers alike, and I hope that you find it interesting or useful to you in some way.

~ Stephen J. Herman
New Orleans, Louisiana
June 1, 2018

AMERICA AND THE LAW
Challenges for the 21st Century

Table of Contents

Holding Wrongdoers Accountable

The Million-Dollar Cup of Coffee

Making the Case Against Cigarettes

The English Rule

Clear and Present Danger

The People vs. O.J. Simpson

The Oklahoma City Bombing

The Social Contract

Crime and Punishment

A Nation of Victims

The Private Attorney General

The Betrayed Profession

What The Future Holds

A Few Lines for the Trial Lawyer

Acknowledgments

Bibliography of Sources and References

About the Author

For My Father

Those who won our independence believed that the final end of the State was to make men free to develop their faculties; and that in its government the deliberative forces should prevail over the arbitrary. They valued liberty both as an ends and as a means. They believed liberty to be the secret of happiness and courage to be the secret of liberty. They believed that freedom to think as you will and to speak as you think are means indispensable to the discovery and spread of political truth; that without free speech and assembly discussion would be futile; that with them, discussion affords ordinary adequate protection against the dissemination of noxious doctrine; that the greatest menace to freedom is an inert people; that public discussion is a political duty; and that this should be a fundamental principle of the American government.

- Justice Louis Brandeis and Oliver Wendell Holmes
  Whitney v. California, 274 U.S. 357, 375 (1927).

. . . one wonders when all industries will recognize their obligation to voluntarily disclose risks from the use of their products. All too often in the choice between the physical health of the consumers and the financial well-being of business, concealment is chosen over disclosure, sales over safety, money over morality. Who are these persons who knowingly and secretly decide to put the buying public at risk solely for the purpose of making profits and who believe that illness and death of consumers is an appropriate cost of their own prosperity!

- Judge Sarokin, District Court of New Jersey
Haines v. The Liggett Group, 140 F.R.D. 681 (1992).

Holding Wrongdoers Accountable

Fundamental to any social, economic, or moral system of laws, is the notion that wrongdoers must be held
accountable for their actions, and that injured persons are
entitled to just compensation when wronged. It is essential to the economic and societal growth of any nation to
provide the security that men and women derive from the
knowledge that their physical and intangible possessions,
as well as the health and welfare of their families, shall
be guarded with vigilance by a government which has
pledged to preserve life, liberty, and property, for all of its
citizens. Without such protections, people will cease to
endeavor in common labor and industry. They will cease
to strive for new technologies and inventions. And they
will cease to engage in the daily business of affairs which
form the common threads and fabrics of our society.

People are not going to write books without the protections of a copyright. No one is going to create a new
furnace, or a new engine, or a new medicine, without the
protections of a patent. No one is going to build a house,
or a skyscraper, if someone else can come along and
steal it, by force or by fraud, or disrupt its foundation, or
burn it down. People are not going to engage in hazardous or dangerous employment if they can't be sure that
their spouses and children will be protected. And no one
is going to enter into a commercial transaction if he or
she cannot go to the courts to have it enforced. Economic
and cultural stagnancy is the end result of any society in

which might makes right, and it is therefore fundamental
to our capitalistic system that America be governed as a
nation of laws, and not as a nation of men. There are historically two theories by which our society has held wrongdoers accountable for their actions,
and at the same time attempted to provide just compensation for those who have been wronged. One theory is
a moral theory, based on the "fault" of the wrongdoer.
The other theory is an economic theory, which is based
on the risk created by the defendant's enterprise. Most
of our criminal and many of our civil law systems are
fault-based. They focus on the blameworthiness of the
wrongdoer, and attempt to prevent further injury by punishing the defendant and thereby deterring such persons
or corporations from engaging in the same type of negligent, reckless, or intentionally destructive conduct in the
future.

Originally, however, civil law systems were not
concerned with the moral responsibility or fault of the
wrongdoer, but focused on the stability of an ordered society, by providing individuals with a remedy that would
be accepted by the victim in lieu of private vengeance or
retribution.[1] Over the past century, these principles have
re-emerged in the form of "enterprise" or "strict" liability,
which places the economic burden on the defendant, who
is in a better position to detect, evaluate, and eliminate
the danger, and who can best bear the loss by distributing
such costs, through prices, rates, or liability insurance,
to society at large. Thus, when there is no recognizable
blame, or fault, which is readily attributable to either party, the burden for those damages which arise in the ordi-

---

1   Under Roman Law, for example, there were a series of quasi-criminal penalties, which were paid by the wrongdoer to the injured party. When the value of
currency in Rome fell so that it was no longer worth the victim's while to pursue the
specified penalty, the praetor began to provide the alternative remedy of damages.
See Stone, Civil Law Treatise, Tort Doctrine §123 (1977). See also: Oliver Wendell
Holmes, The Common Law, Lecture I (1881).

nary course of human events is incurred by the enterprise, as a cost of doing business.

In this way, employers are routinely held liable for the conduct of their employees. Parents are held liable for the conduct of their children. Landowners are held liable for the hazards and defects in their property. And manufacturers are held liable for the goods and services they provide.

While it may seem unfair, at times, to bestow liability on a party who, in simplest terms, has done nothing wrong, there is a social and moral justice which emerges out of the underlying economic realities. Assume, for example, that Bestrubber tire company manufactures 100,000 tires in a year, and that 99,999 of those tires are excellent products, which hold up well on the road. There is one tire, however, which is defective, and could blow out at any time. Assume that the company has not been in any way negligent in allowing the tire to be sold to the public; it was inspected and tested, but the defect was internal, and could not be reasonably detected prior to sale. Yet the tire was nevertheless sold to the Johnson family, who is driving down the interstate one day, when the tire blows out, and Beverly Johnson is dead. In such cases, Bestrubber is not blameworthy. Bestrubber is not at fault. But Bestrubber has profited from the sale of its 99,999 well-constructed tires, and in accepting those benefits, should also be deemed to accept the responsibilities for the one that failed. This, after all, is the foundation of a free market economy. If you make a good product, you profit. If you make a harmful product, you don't. When a corporation or other defendant is insulated from suit, society has artificially subsidized an imperfect or even harmful product, and tampered with the delicate balance between providers and consumers which is absolutely essential to our free market economy.

Why the Courts

There are essentially two governmental means through which the people hold wrongdoers accountable to the public at large: legislatively and judicially. Legislative regulation is typically prospective in nature, and enforced by public bodies or agencies. Judicial regulation is typically remedial in nature, and enforced by private persons or companies.

In 1994, politicians launched a massive campaign to remove many regulatory functions from the courts, and place them in the hands of state and congressional legislators. The proposed reforms promised to "reduce the threat of runaway jury verdicts, promote settlements, and promote certainty in commercial transactions by establishing reasonable boundaries for awards."[2] Such proposals, however, fail to recognize the basic fact that the courts are a far superior regulator of injurious conduct than a legislative body or administrative agency.[3]

Efficiency

The Federal Government and most state governments are too big. There are too many laws. There are too many regulations. And there are too many agents and officials, secretaries and clerks, accountants and engineers, who add to the bureaucracy. The courts, by contrast, are infinitely less taxing on the nation and its economy. Less than 1% of the Federal Budget is dedicated to the entire Federal Judiciary, with less than half that amount in many

---

2   Gingrich, Armey, and House Republicans, Contract With America, p. 154 (1994).

3   Administrative agencies serve various roles, including investigatory functions, which are executive, rule-making functions, which are legislative, and fact-finding functions, which are adjudicatory. In this context, a distinction is being drawn between the administrative agency as a rule-making legislative body and the administrative agency as a fact-finding cousin of the judiciary.

states.[4] Despite claims of "litigation explosions" and "back-logs" in the courthouse, it is remarkable to consider the fact that one-third of our government requires less than one percent of our resources.

This phenomenon is due, in large part, to the tremendous amount of support provided to the court system through the private sector. When criminal or quasi-criminal proceedings are instituted by the District Attorney or the U.S. Attorney's Office, for example, or by OSHA, or the EPA, the costs are taxed at the expense of the public at large. Yet when civil suits are instituted by private attorneys, on behalf of private citizens, the costs of those proceedings are borne almost exclusively by the parties and the attorneys involved. The civil litigation system, therefore, provides a way of privatizing criminal and regulatory enforcement of wrongdoing, which contributes to an overall system that is undoubtedly more efficient and cost-effective than it would be if left to a bureaucracy of public officials, public employees, and public funds.

Reliability

Despite complaints that trials are nothing more than highly-choreographed battles between competing attorneys and expert witnesses, a legislative or administrative hearing is generally an even bigger show. So-called "experts" are paraded before the committee or administrative agency, each with his or her own personal and political agenda, while "hired gun" lobbyists meet with the lawmakers in expensive restaurants and behind closed doors, trying to convince the legislators to vote with their side. The decisions in a courtroom are made by judges and juries, who are, for the most part, impartial, disinterested, and fair. The fact-finder is required to review

4   In Louisiana, for example, only 0.5% of the entire 1994 budget was spent on the judiciary. See Annual Report of the Judicial Council of the Supreme Court of Louisiana, pp. 22, 30 (1995).

and to consider the evidence which is introduced during the proceeding, and is bound to such evidence by law, by conscience, and by appellate review. Decisions within the legislative process, on the other hand, are made by politicians, who have cronies, and lobbyists, and party alliances, who feed them with disinformation, money, and the promise of votes. The lawmakers are not required to listen to the testimony or review the evidence, (if there is any evidence), and are free to base their conclusions upon passion, prejudice, personal interests, economic interests, friendships, party alliances, disinformation, money, and the promise of votes. With respect to the appellate judiciary, it is interesting to note that in the 1993-1994 session, the United States Supreme Court delivered some 90 opinions. Of these, almost 40 were unanimous. In almost half the cases, then, the most conservative member of the court and the most liberal member of the court voted the same. While the social and ideological beliefs of each judge may lead him or her to separate conclusions, judges, for the most part, will vote the same way on an issue when they happen to agree with one another, (and will vote separately when they happen to disagree). Their ultimate goal, by and large, is to reach a decision that is lawful, reasonable, and just.

Legislators, on the other hand, are motivated by an entirely different set of considerations. They vote for and against measures based on who proposed them, who's supporting them, and which party will get the credit if they succeed. Legislators routinely, therefore, vote against measures that they believe in, and for bills that run contrary to their own ideological and social beliefs.

The reliability of judicial decisions is further enhanced by the fact that the judge and the jury have the opportunity to view the matter in the context of a specific set of facts and circumstances. They see the real-life effects of a defendant's product or activity on real-life people, in re-al-life settings.[5] In a judicial context, moreover, the court is generally looking at the situation retrospectively, with an added insight into how the events and the conduct in question would develop and unfold. There is no way, by contrast, for a legislative or administrative body to fore-see all of the many consequences that can possibly result from the use of a given product or questionable business activity. Certainly a law which is tailored to one specific case, arising in the context of one specific set of facts and circumstances, will be more appropriate than a broad-based policy designed to placate a number of competing interests. In this way, legislative and administrative reg-ulation is often shortsighted, inflexible, and an invitation to injustice and anomalies.

Justice

When criminal or quasi-criminal proceedings are brought by the government for the violation of a statute or regulation, the goals of punishment and deterrence are often achieved. But the benefits of such enforcement are distributed and diffused across society as a whole. When civil proceedings are instituted by the victim of some-one else's conduct or business activity, there is a justice which emerges as the innocent party is compensated for that harm.

In shipyards and chemical plants, for example, em-ployers routinely violate standards set by OSHA and other governmental agencies. Such violations often lead to the pollution of the environment, and the disability of employees. The threat of regulatory action by the govern-

---

5   While real-life or "lay" witnesses are sometimes called to testify before legislative or administrative bodies, these witnesses are generally selected by a group or party attempting to advance a specific agenda, and therefore tend to have life his-tories or experiences which fall into the extremes. The legislators, in addition, have usually made up their minds, prior to, and independent of, this evidence, which is ultimately symbolic, and anecdotal.

ment may deter such companies from violating standards, but once the damage has occurred, the levying of a fine or penalty against the shipyard is not going to help an employee with asbestosis pay his medical bills, or make his mortgage payments, or clothe and feed his family. A sanction by the EPA against a chemical plant is not going to help neighboring property owners clean up their land. When a corporate executive, likewise, uses unfair trade practices to stifle the competition, the government sometimes has the power to bring criminal proceedings against him under the anti-trust and consumer protection laws. But incarcerating that corporate executive in federal prison for a few months is not going to help the small businessman who has been cheated and slandered get his company off the ground. When people have access to the courts to hold the wrongdoer accountable, corporations are encouraged to act responsibly, and deterred from engaging in conduct which may cause the public harm. But civil suits, unlike criminal or administrative proceedings, are also means of obtaining justice, by providing specific redress to those unfortunate people who have been wronged.

The Failure of Legislative Reforms

Virtually every legislative movement has been counter-intuitive to the security of property rights and individual freedoms, by allowing corporations and other private interests to avoid being held accountable for the damages they cause. Products Liability Acts are designed to make manufacturers and distributors less accountable for the goods they sell. Medical Malpractice Acts are designed to make doctors less accountable for the health care services they furnish. Recently adopted reforms in the area of securities law are designed to make corporations less accountable to their shareholders. And sovereign immunity provisions are designed to make the government less accountable to the public for the services they provide.

Accountability in the Marketplace

Perhaps the most powerful method of regulation originates, not from the government, but from the people, as goods and services are regulated on a daily basis in the marketplace. Essential to this type of regulation, and essential to the health and welfare of every American family, is the free flow of information concerning products, services, and other business or recreational activities. America is currently facing a period of widespread attacks on the free flow of information, rapidly emerging from all sources, both liberal and conservative, Democrat and Republican, as various groups cry out for the censorship of everything from cable television to record albums, on-line computer systems to international communications networks, talk radio to the motion picture industry. Some of the most common threats to the free flow of information in the context of holding wrongdoers accountable and in the area of public health and safety, however, arise on an ad hoc basis in the form of protective orders, and have begun to surface in wider venues in the form of congressional and other legislative statutes, which are specifically designed to shield corporations from disclosure, while packaged as attempts by the government to encourage self-examination by the industry.

Protective Orders

Under the Federal Rules of Civil Procedure and under the procedural rules of most states, corporations involved in lawsuits are entitled to limited protective orders, which, among other things, keep trade secrets out of the hands of that company's business competitors. While such protections do serve a legitimate purpose for many businesses, numerous companies abuse the process and attempt to conceal vices in their products on the basis that the design is a "trade secret" and therefore subject to protection.[6] If the case goes to trial, the information may become public. But where, as in most cases, the dispute is settled out of court, the documents produced in litigation remain under seal. The company's secrets are buried, and the public is never warned.

The most insidious use of such protective orders arises in the form of what are commonly referred to as "secrecy agreements", by which the defendant will offer the plaintiff what is essentially a bribe, in exchange for his or her promise not to disclose anything which has been discovered in the course of litigation. In the summer of 1984, for example, Rickey Lee Antley was playing with the next door neighbor, Keith Warford, when Mrs. Warford suggested that Rickey go over and check on his grandfather, who was alone. The twelve year-old boy jumped on the neighbor's all-terrain vehicle, and motored off down a gravel road toward his grandfather's house, when the ATV flipped over, and the boy was crushed. During the course of litigation, it was discovered that there had been a number of injuries and deaths involving the very same model, and that there was a design defect present in the ATV's construction which caused it to flip, despite its outward appearance of stability.[7] The manufacturer

6   Following the trial of a wrongful death action against a cigarette maker, for example, the trial judge noted that "after the trial began, certain factors, hidden at the pretrial stage, began to emerge and it appeared that the protective order was serving the defendant well in areas unrelated to the protection of its trade secrets. The court was witness to a spectacle wherein the defendant, rich in resources, maintained complete freedom of association and consultation, including courtroom conferences with other attorneys experienced in the trial of similar cases, while plaintiff's counsel, already disadvantaged by the limited resources available to them, were prohibited from doing likewise by a blanket protective order obtained by the defendant early in the case on grounds which later proved largely illusory." Thayer v. Liggett & Myers No. 5314 (W.D.Mich. Feb. 19, 1970).

7   Much of the problem with the ATV design stems from the absence of front

of the model obviously doesn't want the public to find out about this information, because: (a) they will never sell another ATV, (b) it might encourage customers who have purchased the model to demand their money back, or force a recall, (c) it might encourage other people who have been injured in ATV accidents to file suit, and (d) it might increase the chances that the injured parties who do file suit will be successful in the prosecution of their claims. The manufacturer, therefore, will sometimes go to people like the Antley family, and say: "We know that your case is only worth a hundred thousand dollars, but we will settle the case for a million if you promise not to disclose anything which has come to light over the course of litigation." A non-disclosure provision is then incorporated into the settlement agreement, and the court, by way of a protective order, ensures that the court record and all related documents are sealed. If a member of the Antley family or their attorney attempted to reveal any of the relevant information, the manufacturer would have the right to obtain an injunction and/or damages against them.[8] This kind of agreement places the plaintiff's at-

or rear mechanical suspension, and from a solid rear axle, (*i.e.* no "differential"), which means that both rear tires turn at the same rate all the time. The driver, therefore, must use his or her weight to lift the outside wheel off of the ground to make it turn, which combined with the high center of gravity, causes the ATV to flip over. Companies like Yamaha, nevertheless, have marketed these machines as inexpensive, tricycle-like, all-terrain toys, which could be maneuvered safely by people of all ages, without helmets, and without regard to the weight or experience of the driver. The Consumer Products Safety Commission released a report in 1986 which indicated that ATVs pose an unreasonable and eminent risk of death and serious injury, especially among young and inexperienced drivers, that manufacturers should immediately halt production of such vehicles, and that the government should have them recalled. By 1987, there had already been over 690 deaths and 300,000 injuries. Included among those were the deaths of over 300 children under the age of sixteen, and 130 deaths of children under twelve. While the Ford Pinto was recalled after 61 deaths, the Dalkon Shield after 20 deaths, and Reply brand tampons after 25 deaths, ATVs have yet to be recalled. There are an estimated 2.1 million ATVs in the United States being operated by over 5 million riders. See generally: "Consumer Product Safety Commission's Response to Hazards of Three-Wheel All-Terrain Vehicles" 40th Report by Committee on Government Operations (July 16, 1986).

8   In the actual Rickey Antley case, there was no secrecy agreement. The case went to trial, and the jury found that the ATV manufacturer was liable for the

torney in an impossible dilemma, because he or she has
a professional and a fiduciary obligation to his client, in
conflict with his or her moral obligation to the public at
large. In many states, therefore, the plaintiff's bar has
introduced legislation which would make it illegal and
unethical for any attorney to offer or accept a settlement
conditioned on a vow of secrecy. This type of measure
would accomplish two important goals. In the context
of civil litigation, it would level the playing field, by enabling individual plaintiffs to share information and trial strategy which is common to their cause.[9] In a larger
context, such measures protect the public from dangerous
goods and services by ensuring that people receive adequate information about those things which pose a threat
to their health and safety. Asbestos manufacturers, for
example, became aware of the adverse effects of exposure in the 1930s. Rather than informing the public of
such dangers, or ceasing production of asbestos insulation, however, companies like Johns-Manville concealed
the evidence, even from their own workers.[10] As late as

child's death. The court of appeal affirmed, likewise concluding that the ATV is an
unreasonably dangerous product, especially with regard to use by children. Antley v.
Yamaha, 539 So.2d 696 (La. App. 3rd Cir. 1989).

9   In general, the defendant begins every lawsuit with a tremendous advantage. In addition to the fact that defendants are usually large corporations that can afford to expend a lot of time and resources on litigation, the defendant is also frequently
defending other similar lawsuits involving the same issues, and therefore has easy
access to a wealth of information. Yamaha's attorneys in Mississippi, for example,
have access to all of the information from all of the cases that have been tried against
Yamaha in Texas, Delaware, or Vermont. The plaintiffs, on the other hand, must spend
thousands and thousands of dollars and hours "reinventing the wheel" in each separate
lawsuit, unless their attorneys are able to share in relevant information and trial strategy.

10   A letter from the editor of "ASBESTOS" dated September 25, 1935, for
example, acknowledges that "we have written to you on several occasions concerning
the publishing of information, or discussion of, asbestos and the work which has been,
and is being done, to eliminate or at least reduce it. Always you have requested that
for certain obvious reasons we publish nothing, and, naturally your wishes have been
respected." An attorney from Johns-Manville responded that: "I quite agree with you
that our interests are best served by having asbestosis receive the minimum of publicity. Even if we should eventually decide to raise no objection to the publication of
an article on asbestosis, I think we should warn editors to use American data on the

1973, the executive secretary of the Asbestos Information Association presented a Good News/Bad News report to an asbestos trade organization in Arlington, Virginia. The bad news was that workers were dying at an appalling rate due to exposure; the good news was that the American public was still ignorant about the dangers, and the manufacturers could therefore continue to profit from the sale of asbestos products.[11] As a result of such deliberate concealment, over two million people in this country have x-ray evidence of asbestos exposure. The lung diseases associated with such exposure are permanent, irreversible, progressive, and ultimately fatal. It is estimated that at least 200,000 to 300,000 people will die in the next two decades from asbestos related disease. The Dalkon Shield, similarly, was marketed by A.H. Robins in 1970, despite the fact that it had not been adequately tested or proven safe in clinical trials. A confidential Orientation Report circulated two weeks after the Dalkon Shield hit the market acknowledged that "the string or 'tail' situation needs a careful review since the present 'tail' is reported to have a 'wicking' tendency." By August 1971, there had been verification that the string "wicked" bacteria into the uterus causing pelvic inflam-

---

subject rather than English. Dr. Lanza has frequently remarked, to me personally and in some of his papers, that the clinical picture presented in North American localities where there is an asbestos dust hazard is considerably milder than reported in England and South America."

11 "First, there is no doubt that the inhalation of substantial amounts of asbestos can lead to increased rates of various types of lung disease, including two forms of cancer. These are facts which cannot be denied. I have on file over 2,000 medical papers dealing with the health risks of asbestos and hundreds more are published every year. The insulation workers Dr. Selikoff has been studying for more than a decade were and still are dying from asbestos related disease at an appalling rate. The good news is that despite all the negative articles on asbestos-health that have appeared in the press over the past half-dozen years. Only 22 per cent of the American public are aware of the health hazards of asbestos, and 80 per cent of these consider it a hazard only to those who are occupationally exposed. These results should be reassuring to those industry customers who fear that the general public will stop buying their products because they contain asbestos." Matthew Swetonic, Why Asbestos? Asbestos Textile Institute, June 7, 1973.

matory disease, sterility, and even death.[12] A.H. Robins, nevertheless, continued to market the product through 1974, and maintained, for an additional ten years, that the product could be safely worn.[13]The courts are public institutions, supported by public funds, for the benefit of all. It is therefore somewhat inequitable that citizens should be denied access to court records, particularly when such documents may contain compelling evidence of a threat to public health and safety. The United States Supreme Court, nevertheless, has determined that neither a litigant's right to disseminate information nor the public's right to receive it justifies a First Amendment restriction on the courts' ability to issue and enforce protective orders. The Court reasoned that the function of the judicial system is to resolve private disputes, not to generate information, and that the pre-trial process would be impaired by cumbersome or repeated review.[14]In the

12 Walt Schoenberger from A.H. Robins' medical department wanted to know in March 1971 what the Dalkon "string" is made of. "Competition (ORTHO)is telling my doctors that it will break, it will fray easily, and that it is 'multilayered' so that the inner core acts as a wick to induce infection into the uterus." Five months later, Dr. Fred Clark reported that there were "a couple of problems about which the Medical Department should be aware. The sheath is a problem (I do not know exactly how) but I believe there is a problem with its stripping off if the cut ends are handled excessively. Mr. French says the reason given for the sheath is that it provides protection against bacterial invasion. He points out, however, that both ends of the string are cut and left open. It has been shown that the open ends will wick water. It seems to him that if this is so that the ends will wick bodily fluids containing bacteria. In working with the small Shield, the membrane tends to split when the Shield is placed on a peg and the necessary pull applied to tie the second knot."

13 Eventually, A.H. Robins used the U.S. Bankruptcy laws to stave off over six thousand lawsuits, and to limit liability, permanently, for any and all of the damages arising from the injury and death of hundreds of thousands of women. By 1987, A.H. Robins was the highest rated stock on the New York Stock Exchange, even though the company was still in bankruptcy. By the time the reorganization plan was confirmed, the shareholders had quadrupled their money, as the stock rose to four times its pre-bankruptcy value. See generally: Richard Sobol, Bending the Law (1991).

14 Commentators have noted, however, that the Supreme Court's decision in the Seattle Times case does not completely foreclose the issue of First Amendment challenges to protective orders in all cases. Indeed, there might be some information which is so significant to the process of self-governance, that it would be unconstitu-

meantime, while prohibitions against secrecy agreements have been enacted in a minority of jurisdictions,[15] most of these proposals have been defeated by lobbying interests in the state legislatures and in Congress,[16] and the American Bar Association has failed to adopt an ethical rule on this issue as part of its Rules of Professional Conduct, which forms the basis of our lawyers' ethical cannons and codes.

Legislative Restraints

In 1987, Congress passed a law which protects reports, surveys, schedules and data pertaining to highway and railroad development from being discovered by the injured party or admitted into evidence in the course of litigation. If, therefore, Robert Army is traveling down the highway at 30 mph, when he makes a turn onto a four-lane avenue and, without warning, is struck by an oncoming train; and Mary Beth Army is now a young widow, while their daughter, Valerie, suffers from constant nightmares and will experience a void for the rest of her life; this rule prevents both the Army's and the public from discovering that there had been 17 collisions in the past ten years at that very same intersection, that a curve in the highway prevents the driver from seeing the crossing, and that a safety inspector had indicated seven years before Army's death that the crossing needed to be upgraded, while the

---

tional to keep the press and the public from that knowledge. See, for example: Cohen, Access to Pretrial Documents Under the First Amendment, 84 Colum.L.Rev. 1813, 1833 (1984).

15 In Florida, for example, the court is prohibited from sealing documents which may contain evidence of some threat to public health and safety, and any private contract or agreement which would prohibit a party from disclosing such information is against public policy, and cannot be enforced. Fla. Stat. Ann. §69.081. See also: La. C.C.P. 1426; Tex. R. Civ. Pro. 76(a).

16 States which have rejected such legislation include Alaska, Arkansas, California, Colorado, Connecticut, Hawaii, Idaho, Illinois, Iowa, Kansas, Maine, Massachusetts, Minnesota, Mississippi, Montana, Nevada, New Hampshire, New Mexico, Oregon, South Dakota, and Washington. See Arthur Miller, Confidentiality, Protective Orders, and Public Access to the Courts, 105 Harv. L. Rev. 427, 445 (1991).

railroad company and the highway department had nevertheless failed to put up adequate cross-arms, with flashing lights, and warning signs.

Congressional restraints such as this not only frustrate the First Amendment and undermine the principles of civil justice by concealing information and helping wrongdoers to avoid responsibility, but they also do violence to our traditional notions of Federalism, by restricting such information in state court suits. In doing so, Congress has overstepped its bounds and impermissibly interfered with the rights of states to govern themselves, free of undue influence from the politicians in Washington.[17] Even the most conservative members of our Supreme Court, in fact, have recently commented that it is indeed "extraordinary for Congress to attempt to proscribe procedural rules for *state* courts."[18]The greatest threats to the free flow of information, nevertheless, stem not from Congress, but from our own state legislatures. Several states, for example, have recently enacted "environmental audit bills" which allow chemical companies and oil and gas producers to designate their business records as "privileged" and keep them secret from the public. Other states have passed legislation which allows banks to keep their internal documents hidden from the public, even where the violation of state or federal banking laws might be involved. While such measures, like the Congressional legislation on railroad and highway information, are rationalized on the basis that they will promote self-investigation and self-examination, these laws protect not only self-generated audits, but also the underlying facts or data which an audit might contain. If a private citizen were

17 Each State, as an independent sovereign, has a primary interest in the exercise of authority over individuals and entities within its jurisdiction, including the establishment and enforcement of a body of laws, both criminal and civil. Alfred L. Snapp v. Puerto Rico, 458 U.S. 592, 601 (1982).

18 Justice Thomas, joined by Justice Scalia, dissenting, Allied-Bruce Terminix v. Dobson, 115 S.Ct. 834, 846 (1995).

to reveal any information contained in such documents, he or she would face up to $10,000 in fines to the "privileged" company, even if the information proved to be true. Public officials or employees would face jail time for a misdemeanor and up to $1,000 in fines for disclosure, even if the official or employee didn't know, but should have known, that the information was protected by the company under the bill. Not only are these measures patently unconstitutional,[19] but they also fail to serve any legitimate purpose, (other than to protect the reputation and the revenue of a few selected industries). If, in this regard, a corporation is immune from all civil and criminal liability – because the evidence necessary to establish such liability has been deemed undiscoverable and inadmissible by the state – there can certainly be no legitimate government interest in preventing, at the very least, disclosure to the public about the potential for danger or fraud. Fortunately, these types of measures were defeated in several states prior to the close of the 1995 and 1996 legislative sessions. Unfortunately, these types of proposals will continue to surface as long as big business and other private interests attempt to avoid bearing the responsibility for the damages they cause.

---

19 The First and Fourteenth Amendments to the Constitution clearly prohibit a State from punishing a private individual for speaking truthfully, (or even untruthfully, so long as the allegations are made without malice), on matters of public concern. See, for example: Garrison v. State of Louisiana, 379 U.S. 64, 73 (1964); New York Times v. Sullivan, 376 U.S. 254, 269 (1964).

The Million-Dollar Cup of Coffee

In February of 1992, Stella Liebeck got a cup of coffee at a McDonald's drive-thru. Her grandson pulled over to the side of the road so that she could add some cream and sugar to make it sweeter. She accidentally spilled the coffee in her lap, and a jury awarded her almost three million dollars in punitive damages. Jay Leno told jokes on the Tonight Show. The talk radio lines were flooded with calls. And the Republicans in Congress latched on to this decision as symbolic of a civil justice system out of control. Americans now face the loss of fundamental rights due to restrictive legislation. Victims will have no access to the courts, and the wrongdoer will go free. In disputes that do find their way to the courts, judges and juries will be more reluctant to compensate the injured party at the expense of big business. Because the "McDonald's case" was lost by the plaintiffs, in the courts of public opinion.

The News Media and Its Effects on the Courts of Public Opinion

Walter Cronkite recently observed in a television interview that news is the reporting of aberrations. Things only get reported if they're different, he said. If they are the kinds of things that happen every day, if the events are commonplace, nobody cares.

In the context of court cases, the news media does not,

by and large, report the great majority of decisions, which are generally reasonable and fair. The news media tends to focus, rather, on those one or two exceptions which, when reduced to a single sentence or paragraph, appear to be illogical or excessive in their result. If there are 10,000 cases, then, for example, which are decided by juries across the country in a given day, and 9,999 of those cases have results which seem appropriate, the public will only find out about the one case that does not. In the court of public opinion, therefore, that one case becomes representative of the entire system. Even though, in reality, that case is the exception to the system. That case is an aberration.

In Michigan, for example, there was a recent court decision in which an unmarried mother was accepted to college, and the father was awarded custody of their child. The news media reported the holding, and various political groups touted this case as representative of the sexism and injustice that pervade the entire legal system. "This case means" they told us, "that any time a woman goes back to school following a divorce, and tries to better herself, she is going to be punished by society, by losing custody of her child." No. It doesn't. Because this was just one case. In one court, in one city, in one state, in the midst of thousands and thousands of divorce and custody proceedings that get decided in this country every day. The only thing that this case stands for is the proposition that this judge, in this proceeding, presented with these two competing parents, and given this particular set of facts and circumstances, decided that it would be better for the child to live with her dad.[20] The fact that

---

20   The father apparently introduced evidence which showed that the mother, having placed the baby in foster care, left the child with her mother, (the child's grandmother), for extended periods of time, and showed little interest in raising the child. The mother apparently testified that she did not want to take her daughter to the University of Michigan, and moved the child back and forth between the dorms at Ann Arbor and her mother's house in Clemens, Michigan, abdicating the majority of

the decision was even reported to the public is likely an indication that the result was atypical, and probably indicates that this kind of sexism and injustice does not pervade the court system in most cases.[21]In other cases, only half of the story is presented, in order to garner support for an agenda or reform. It was widely reported, for example, that the Girl Scouts had to sell over 80,000 boxes of cookies just to pay their liability insurance premiums for one year. These reports failed to mention, however, that there are over 2.5 million Girl Scouts in this country, which means that if every Girl Scout sold just one box of cookies, the scouts would have enough money to insure the organization for more than 25 years. In another such instance, the local New Orleans newspaper told readers that judges should be appointed, rather than elected, as evidenced by a recent multi-billion dollar verdict that was rendered against a large railroad corporation and other defendants who caused a massive chemical explosion and fire. The editorial failed to mention, however, that the trial judge who presided over that case was not elected, but appointed, to the bench. It is interesting to note, in this respect, that despite widespread claims about the "liberal media", when it comes to civil lawsuits, the mainstream media, for the most part, has abandoned the underdog, and befriended the corporation. Perhaps this is due to the fact that the mainstream press is comprised of big busi-

responsibility to the child's day care center. The mother claimed that the father was delinquent in paying child support, and argued that he was going to abdicate responsibility to his own mother, who would raise her while he himself went to college. In any event, without being present in the courtroom, or knowing the parties involved, it is impossible to say whether the result was proper or just. But if, indeed, the judge's ruling in the case was an unconscionable abuse of discretion, that decision has no precedential value in terms of other cases, nor any far-reaching effects with respect to any other working mothers, or those pursuing education to better themselves.

21 In fact, it could be argued that the back-lash to this decision is actually indicative of the occasional sexism that runs the other way in our society, by sending a message that any judicial system that would allow a child to be placed in the care of his or her father must be defective, because everyone knows that, in the absence of extenuating circumstances, the father is not as qualified as the mother to be a parent to his child.

ness. NBC is owned by General Electric, for example. CBS was bought by Westinghouse, while ABC was recently purchased by Disney for 19 billion dollars. Multimedia, Time-Warner and Turner Broadcasting Company are all, likewise, parts of major corporations.[22] These companies cloak themselves behind the First Amendment to avoid accountability when they injure people through negligent and sometimes even intentional misreporting of the facts, and seem genuinely offended when an individual recovers against a corporation.[23] The public, therefore, is never informed any time that a plaintiff's case is unsuccessful. The media never reports that John Doe sued Giant Company X, and lost.[24] Nor does the media tend to scrutinize suits among giant corporations. Five years ago, for example, an oil company in Texas sued another oil company and recovered 263 million dollars, including over 100 million in punitive damages. But that case did not generate one fraction of the public outcry as Stella Li-

---

22   "In all the years I've worked for newspapers, [including *The Washington Star, The San Francisco Examiner,* and *The New York Herald Tribune*], I have never worked at a liberal newspaper. Not one. There's only about half a dozen in America. There are some 1,700 daily newspapers and they're all run by Republicans. Why? Because Republicans are the kind of people who own things, that's why. And I don't know one of them who's going to let some off-the-wall liberal run his newspaper." David Burgin, editor-in-chief of the *Oakland Tribune.* See "Interview With Ken Kelley" East Bay Express, April 8, 1994.

23   Perhaps this is due, in part, to the fact that advertisers generally feel more comfortable with pro-business journalists and commentators pushing their products. "Certainly Nike would rather have a talk show host who believes in unrestricted world trade selling its shoes than hear its commercials adjacent to Jim Hightower as the talk show populist draws attention to the company's factories in Malaysia, saying working conditions there violate baseline health and safety standards and workers make in a day less than the minimum hourly wage in the United States." Peter Laufer, "The Myth of the Liberal Media" Inside Talk Radio p.208 (1995).

24   One study, for example, found that newspapers report plaintiff victories in punitive damage cases 20 times more often than defendant victories. The study also found that the reduction of such awards on appeal is rarely reported. "Punitive Damages 'Crisis' a Myth, Scholars Say" Trial, Dec. 1996, p.14. In another recent study of verdicts from the 45 largest counties in the U.S., the researchers noted that the absence of any large, headline-grabbing awards in such a broad sample "suggests that the punitive damage cases emphasized in the media are newsworthy precisely because they are so rare." Theodore Eisenberg, The Predictability of Punitive Damages (1996).

ebeck's 2.7 million dollar punitive damage award. This is due in part to the fact that "commercial litigation" is portrayed by the media in an entirely different light. When Penzoil sues Texaco for billions of dollars, or when Shell mounts a ten-year third-party lawsuit against Travelers, it is portrayed as just another part of that company's business. But when the little guy stands up against the big guy, in a true David and Goliath situation, the little guy and his attorney are portrayed as social parasites who are attempting to "hit the lottery" with an undeserving award. The McDonald's case, in many ways, is therefore an aberration. There were 700 other complaints levied by burn victims against McDonald's over the past ten years.[25] But the only complaint that was ever brought to the public's attention was the unusually successful one. On the other hand, in many ways, the McDonald's case was not an aberration. As in many reports, the evidence was edited and manipulated by insurance companies, journalists, and politicians, to make a reasonable jury verdict appear irrational and unjust. The public was never informed about all of the evidence that was presented to the jury. The newspapers and television stations merely reported: "Woman Spills Coffee on Herself Results in $3 Million Award."[26]

----

25 In fact, McDonald's had paid more than $500,000 in claims related to scalding injuries, including injuries to infants and children, as well as other third degree burns.

26 See, for example: Rosen, "Coffee and $2.9 Million to Go" Denver Post, Aug. 26, 1994, p.B-11; "Hot Coffee and a Paint Job" Washington Post, Oct. 18, 1995, p.A-18. As noted by Larry Drivon: "Headlines like: 'WOMAN WINS $200,000 FOR SLIP ON A BANANA PEEL' appear frequently, usually with little or no explanation of what actually happened or what the woman's real injuries were. And the articles never mention the fact that a jury of 12 citizens actually sat through an entire trial, knew exactly what happened, knew who was at fault, knew what the real extent of injuries was, and, after hearing all of the arguments and evidence on both sides of the issue, rendered its verdict." Laurence E. Drivon, The Civil War on Consumer Rights, pp.41-42 (1990). See generally: Galanter, An Oil Strike in Hell: Contemporary Legends About the Civil Justice System, 40 Ariz.L.Rev. 717 (1998); Rustad, Nationalizing Tort Law: The Republicans Attack on Women, Blue Collar Workers, and Consumers, 48 Rutgers L. Rev. 673 (1996).

The Facts of the McDonald's Case

Stella Liebeck woke up early one morning to drive with her son to the airport in Albuquerque, New Mexico, from Santa Fe. They didn't have time to eat breakfast, so after dropping her son at the airport, she and her grandson pulled into a McDonald's drive-thru, where she ordered a McBreakfast and then asked her grandson to pull over so that she could add some cream and sugar to the coffee she was served. Ms. Liebeck had trouble removing the top, and because the dashboard was slanted and there was no cup-holder in the car, she placed the cup in her lap as she tried to pry the top open. Ms. Liebeck tugged at the lid, and the coffee gushed out over her legs, when she was burned.

The coffee McDonald's served her was 180 degrees, and Ms. Liebeck, who was 79 years-old at the time, suffered from second and third degree burns. These burns were severe, and covered her labia, buttocks, and thigh. Ms. Liebeck was hospitalized for seven days, and spent another three weeks recuperating at home. She had to be re-hospitalized later to receive skin grafts in order to repair some of the damage from her burns. The pain from the grafts, according to Ms. Liebeck's daughter, was almost as severe as the original burning, and she did not think that her mother would survive. Ms. Liebeck was practically immobilized, and had lost twenty pounds. She suffers from permanent scarring over sixteen percent of her body. The family was looking for their out-of-pocket medical and other expenses, about $20,000. McDonald's offered $800.

It was revealed at trial, however, that McDonald's had received at least 700 complaints of severe burning due to the scalding temperatures of the coffee they serve. While other establishments sell their coffee at 135 to 140 degrees fahrenheit, McDonald's actively enforced a 185-degree rule. A McDonald's quality assurance manager testified to this, and admitted that a burn hazard exists over 140 F, stating that the McDonald's coffee, as served, was not fit for consumption, because it would burn the mouth and throat.

Though aware that burns would continue to occur, the company refused to change their policy, insisting that "that's the way the customers want it."[27]

The more likely motivation is the fact that hot coffee prevents people from getting free refills. By the time the customer is through eating, the coffee is still too hot to drink, so the customer takes it with him. Therefore, by keeping the liquid they serve at excessive temperatures, McDonald's saves millions in refills every year. The jury ultimately awarded $200,000 in compensatory damages, (*i.e.* medical expenses, loss of earnings, pain and suffering),[28] which was capped off by a 2.7 million dollar punitive damage award. "It was our way of saying, 'Hey open your eyes,'" recalls one juror. "'People are getting burned.'" Betty Farnham, who at first believed the case to be frivolous, was offended by the fact that McDonald's failed to respond to the 700 complaints, and the statement by a corporate safety consultant that one injury in 24 million cups of coffee is "basically trivially different" from zero. "Each statistic is somebody badly burned" responded the juror. "That really made me angry." By the time the jurors concluded their deliberations, Ms. Farnham, who originally thought the claim was frivolous, wanted to send a message to McDonald's corporate executives with a 9.6 million dollar award.

---

27 The morning drive-thru customers want it that way, according to the company, so that when they get to work, the coffee is still warm enough to drink. McDonald's own marketing research, however, indicated that the great majority of drive-thru customers begin to drink the coffee while still inside their automobiles.

28 The reasonableness of the jury's verdict in this respect is bolstered by the fact that an impartial court-appointed mediator looked at the evidence and recommended that McDonald's pay $225,000 prior to trial.

While the judge reduced the $2.7 million punitive damage award to $480,000, even he believed that punitive damages were appropriate in this case to punish the defendant for its "callous" and "willful" conduct, and to deter McDonald's from serving coffee at 185 degrees. Judge Scott, who describes himself as a conservative Republican, insists that the jury's verdict was "not a runaway. I was there."

She Spilled It On Herself

Everyone spills coffee. Whether it's due to clumsiness, or inattentiveness, or because the container is slippery, human beings are imperfect, and they spill things. But in general, when people spill things, they get wet, or they get sticky, or perhaps their clothes get stained. People don't ordinarily have to spend seven days in the hospital with third degree burns. In this sense, it was McDonald's intentional conduct, and not Ms. Liebeck's momentary inattentiveness, which contributed most to the harm.

In a similar recent court case, Eugene Frazier was travelling in the backseat of an automobile when the driver accidentally drifted onto the shoulder of the road. The driver attempted to jerk the car back onto the roadway, but the right front tire caught a soft spot in the shoulder, and the car was shot into a concrete abutment at the base of a highway bridge. The driver and another passenger were injured in the collision, and Mr. Frazier was killed. According to the evidence submitted at trial, the bridge was supposed to have guardrails. In fact, fourteen of the fifteen bridges on this particular strip of highway had guardrails, but for some reason, this one bridge did not. In any event, the evidence showed that if the roadway had been equipped with guardrails, the car would have been knocked back safely onto the highway, and the injuries would not have been severe. But because there were no guardrails, the car smashed head-long into the concrete abutment, and the plaintiff was killed. The highway department argued that the accident was the driver's fault, because the entire collision could have been avoided had he not wandered from the road. The court found, however, that while the driver's inattentiveness caused the car to veer off the highway, it was the absence of guardrails which resulted in the fatal collision at the base of the bridge. Stated another way, it was the driver's fault that he wandered off the highway, but it was the highway department's fault that Eugene Frazier was killed.

In the McDonald's case, Stella Liebeck spilled the coffee on herself. The jury recognized this and reduced her damages accordingly under the doctrine of comparative fault. Ultimately, however, it was the temperature of the coffee, not the coffee itself, which resulted in the harm. Had the coffee in that styrofoam cup not been 180 degrees, Ms. Liebeck would have gotten wet, she might have gotten sticky, and she probably would have stained her clothes. But she would not have been hospitalized for a week with second and third degree injuries.[29] Stated another way, it was Ms. Liebeck's fault that she spilled the coffee on herself, but it was McDonald's fault that she got burned. People spill things on themselves. It's a fact of life. Accidents happen. It is the responsibility, therefore, of those who are in control of a given situation, to ensure that the damages which naturally arise from such mishaps are as minimal as possible. McDonald's sells millions of cups of coffee each and every day. They know that, in the ordinary course of human experience, some of that coffee is going to get spilled onto its customers, especially when many of those cups are sold to drive-thru customers

---

29 In fact, it was demonstrated at trial that human skin becomes exponentially more susceptible to burning as the temperature rises above 155 degrees fahrenheit. If, therefore, McDonald's had kept its coffee at 135-140 degrees, like other establishments, or even 155 degrees, the coffee would have cooled, and given her time to avoid serious burns.

on their way to work at drive-thru windows.[30] They also know, (certainly after seven hundred complaints), that if the coffee inside those cups is 180 degrees, their customers will suffer from second and third degree burns.

Even absent any fault or blameworthiness on the part of McDonald's, (and therefore the absence of any punitive damage award), Ms. Liebeck would still have been entitled to compensatory damages under the doctrine of strict or enterprise liability. After all, McDonald's was in a better position than Ms. Liebeck to detect and eliminate the danger. McDonald's is in the better position to spread the risk through prices or insurance. And McDonald's accepts the purported benefits of selling extremely hot coffee, and should therefore accept the responsibilities. According to McDonald's safety consultant, only one of their customers is severely injured for every 24 million cups of coffee they serve. McDonald's profits from the 24 million good cups; they should pay for the one that burns.

---

30 According to testimony at trial, McDonald's sells 500 million cups of coffee to drive-thru customers each year. The original $2.7 million punitive damage award represents just two days of coffee sales.

Making the Case Against Cigarettes

In the last forty years, there have been over eight hundred lawsuits against the tobacco industry. Of these, only twenty-six have been tried, only three were successful, and two of them have been reversed on appeal. But when reports that the cigarette companies had been concealing scientific information from the public since the early 1960s surfaced in the spring of 1994, the single largest lawsuit in American history was filed by a group of prominent attorneys in the federal district courthouse in New Orleans. The suit was a class action against the major cigarette manufacturers, alleging that they had concealed the addictive effects of tobacco from the American public, while targeting young children with massive advertising campaigns and manipulating the levels of nicotine. The U.S. Fifth Circuit Court of Appeals eventually decided that the claims were too numerous and diverse to be resolved in one lawsuit. Yet these same attorneys, and a legion of others, have instituted more than twenty statewide class actions, numerous individual cases, and over thirty State Attorney General lawsuits for the reimbursement of smoking-related health care costs paid by Medicare and Medicaid. Critics claim these suits are nothing more than get-rich schemes concocted by attorneys, and that actions of this nature pose a dangerous threat to our notions of personal choice and personal responsibility. Others recognize the fundamental injustice of any system that would allow corporations to prey on the health and the resources of the American public and its governmental bodies with impunity.

The Evidence

Tobacco products kill an estimated 420,000 Americans every year. Countless others suffer from the daily effects of shortness of breath, high blood pressure, peptic ulcers, strokes, lung cancer, lip cancer, esophagus cancer, throat cancer, bladder cancer, emphysema, bronchitis, arteriosclerosis, and heart disease. Studies have linked cigarette smoking with birth defects, retarded fetal growth, carcinogenicity in animals, and a shorter life expectancy. The Surgeon General has reported that at least one in every six Americans will die of a tobacco-related illness. "Smoking remains" he has stated, "the single most important preventable cause of death in our society." The typical cigarette has 700 chemical additives, including at least five which have been designated by the Federal Government as "hazardous substances", and the Environmental Protection Agency has recently classified cigarette smoke as a class-A carcinogen. The Surgeon General has reported that cigarettes and other forms of tobacco are addicting substances, that nicotine is the drug in cigarettes that causes addiction, and that the pharmacological and behavioral processes at work in a nicotine addiction are the same forces at work in addictions to heroin and cocaine.[31]

By the early 1960s, the tobacco industry knew that cigarettes were extremely harmful products. They had

---

31   Studies show, for example, that 70% of smokers want to quit, and that 34% attempt to quit each year, but only 2.5% are successful. "Cigarette Smoking Among Adults in the United States" Journal of the American Medical Association, Vol. 273, pp.369-370 (1996).

proven in their own laboratories that cigarette tar causes cancer in animals, and that nicotine was a pharmacologically addictive chemical.

Nevertheless, the cigarette companies have maintained to this date that they are committed to uncovering the scientific truth concerning the health effects of tobacco, that nicotine is not addictive, and that there is no conclusive proof that smoking causes illnesses such as cancer and heart disease.

The cigarette companies created the Council for Tobacco Research in 1954, claiming that it would be an independent health organization, designed to uncover the truths about tobacco and its effects on the body through impartial scientific discovery.[32] The actual research projects conducted by the Council, however, were aimed at proving that smoking did not create health risks, and that, among other things, nicotine was not addictive. All potentially damaging research projects were secretly funneled off to a "special projects" division, controlled by lawyers, who could then shield the results from both the American public and private litigants behind the attorney-client privilege. This allowed the cigarette companies to accomplish several important objectives. While presenting themselves to the public as an industry genuinely concerned with the welfare of its customers, the companies managed to stave off governmental and other scrutiny,

---

32 In a public advertisement labelled A Frank Statement About Tobacco and Health, for example, the Tobacco Institute represented that: "We recognize that we have a special responsibility to the public – to help scientists determine the facts about tobacco and health, and about certain diseases that have been associated with tobacco use. We accepted this responsibility in 1954 by establishing the Tobacco Industry Research Committee, which provides research grants to independent scientists. We pledge continued support of this program of research until the facts are known.... We shall continue all possible efforts to bring the facts to light. In that spirit we are cooperating with the Public Health Service in its plan to have a special study group review all presently available research." The stated purpose of the Council is to make information available to the public, and the tobacco companies have repeatedly promised full disclosure of all Council sponsored research. "The Tobacco Institute believes that the American public is entitled to complete, authenticated information about cigarette smoking and health."

by assuring people that the Council would uncover any potential health hazards and disclose them in a timely fashion. The Council also accomplished a great deal with respect to lawsuits, by using the public research to develop scientific witnesses and expert testimony, while burying potentially harmful information beneath layers of attorneys who guarded the results behind strained and tortured interpretations of the attorney-client privilege and work product rule.[33] With respect to the health effects of cigarettes, the tobacco industry's research indicated that smoke was carcinogenic by the early 1960s, while they represented to the public that "science does not yet know enough about any suspected factors to judge." In the 1970s, scientific studies conducted by the cigarette companies compelled industry researchers to conclude that carbon monoxide will become increasingly regarded as a "serious health hazard" for smokers, and that while such substances as lithium hydroxide can be effective in reducing the levels of carbon monoxide, such effects are "coupled with an increase in tumorigenic activity." In statements to the public, nevertheless, a Tobacco Institute spokesman represented that "there is still no basic answer to why people who smoke fall victim to some diseases in greater numbers than people who don't smoke." Brown & Williamson stated that there was "sound evidence to conclude that 'cigarettes cause cancer' is not a statement of fact *but merely a hypothesis.*" And Philip Morris represented to the public that, with respect to "the lack of

---

33   An internal memorandum proves that the Council "was set up as an industry 'shield' in 1954." The memo goes on to explain that the Council "has helped our legal counsel by giving advice and technical information, which was needed at court trials. CTR has provided spokesmen for the industry at Congressional hearings. The monies spent on CTR provides a base for introduction of witnesses. Bill Shinn feels that 'special projects' are the best way monies are spent. On these projects, CTR has acted as a 'front'." The memorandum concluded by saying that, "It is extremely important that the industry continue to spend their dollars on research to show that we don't agree that the case against smoking is closed. There is a 'CTR basket' which must be maintained for 'PR' purposes."

research on the 'harmful' effects of smoking, the fact is
there is good reason to doubt the culpability of cigarette
smoking in coronary heart disease." The tobacco industry
started performing research on environmental smoke hazards in the 1970s, and discovered that secondary smoke
contained toxic substances, including N-nitrosamines,
and that it was "biologically active" (*i.e.* carcinogenic) in
laboratory tests. Following the publication of the first scientific article linking second-hand smoke to lung cancer
in 1982, however, the tobacco industry launched a massive advertising campaign which attacked the credibility
of the scientist who performed the study, and therefore
called into question his results. Privately, of course, tobacco industry scientists acknowledged that Hirayama,
the researcher who published the study, was correct, that
the Tobacco Institute knew that Hirayama was correct,
and that the Tobacco Institute published its statements
about Hirayama anyway. With respect to nicotine, the
cigarette companies conducted research as early as 1963
which showed that nicotine is a pharmacologically active
substance, that it is an addicting agent, and that cigarettes
are, essentially, nicotine delivery devices. One study concluded that "chronic intake of nicotine tends to restore
the normal physiological functioning of the endocrine
system, so that ever-increasing dose levels of nicotine
are necessary to maintain the desired action. This unconscious desire explains the addiction of the individual to
nicotine." While, in that same year, the vice-president
and general counsel of Brown & Williamson acknowledged privately that nicotine is addictive, as recently as
June 1994, the chairman and CEO of the nation's largest cigarette companies maintained before the Health and
Environmental Subcommittee that "I do not believe that
nicotine is addictive; nicotine is a very important constituent in the cigarette smoke for taste." In the early

1970s, it was discovered that low-tar/low-nicotine cigarettes were just as dangerous, if not more harmful, than
ordinary tobacco products, because the smoker would
puff more frequently, increase the depth and duration of
smoke inhalation, smoke the cigarette to a shorter butt
length, and smoke more cigarettes per day, in order to
satisfy his or her addiction to nicotine. By marketing low-
tar/low-nicotine cigarettes, the tobacco industry could
sell more cigarettes, while at the same time advertising
an ostensibly safer product.[34] In actuality, of course, the
smokers of these cigarettes were being exposed to more
"tar" and harmful chemicals, while the cigarette companies lulled them (and other would-be customers) into a
false sense of security.

One recent article from the *Washington Monthly* char-
acterized the tobacco industry's strategy as follows: "Tar
is what gives cigarettes flavor and causes disease; nicotine is what makes them addictive as heroin or cocaine.
So back in the 1960s, when the public began connecting
cigarettes to cancer, the tobacco industry started marketing low-tar, low-nicotine brands. Since then, these low-
yield varieties have steadily captured more and more of
the market – from two percent in 1967 to more than 60
percent today – and have continued to help make smoking the nation's leading cause of preventable deaths.
You'd think, as the cigarette companies would have you
believe, that smoking low-tar is safer. A 1993 Gallup survey found that 48.6 percent of adults do think so. But a

34   As early as 1974, the tobacco industry's research showed that the smoker
of low-tar/low-nicotine cigarettes "adjusts his smoking habits to duplicate his normal
cigarette nicotine intake" and that "whatever the characteristics of cigarettes the smoker adjusts his pattern to deliver his own nicotine requirements." Vintage nevertheless
ran an advertisement which depicted a smoker saying: "I like to smoke, and what I like
is a cigarette that isn't timid on taste. But I'm not living in some ivory tower. I hear
the things being said against high-tar smoking as well as the next guy. And so I started
looking. For a low-tar smoke that had some honest-to-goodness taste...." Lorillard
advertised: "All the fuss about smoking got me to thinking I'd either quit or smoke
True. I smoke True."

wealth of scientific evidence contradicts this. Scientists, and the Surgeon General, believe low-yield cigarettes can be a *greater* hazard. How can this be? First, low-tar cigarettes give smokers an excuse not to quit. Second, the tobacco companies are marketing cigarettes that deliver vastly more tar and nicotine than a smoker may realize. The problem is 'compensation', the tendency to make up for reductions in tar and nicotine with stronger inhalations. Rather than settling comfortably into their reduced levels of tar and nicotine, most low-tar smokers draw on their cigarettes harder – a lot harder. By pulling harder into their lungs, smokers of low-tar cigarettes can actually raise their risk of disease. Yet the tobacco industry spends upward of $4 billion every year on the advertising and promotion of products such as 'low tar' cigarettes.[35] One magazine ad for Vantage read: 'If "tar" and nicotine has become a concern to you, you may consider changing to Vantage.' A Carlton ad pleaded more simply: 'If you smoke, please try Carltons.'"[36] Two-thirds of all smokers, consequently, buy cigarettes which claim to have reduced levels of tar and nicotine. The tobacco industry, at the same time, enhances nicotine delivery to the smoker by adding ammonia and other chemical compounds which increase the effective levels of the nicotine. A 54-page handbook for leaf blenders and product developers from Brown & Williamson, for example, explains how ammonia compounds convert nicotine into a "free" form, which is absorbed more rapidly into the blood stream. Scientists and marketing specialists have, in this regard,

---

35 Varying accounts report the annual expenditures to be anywhere from $4 billion to $6 billion. See, for example, U.S. Dept. of Health and Human Services, Preventing Tobacco Use Among Young People: A Report of the Surgeon General, Feb. 24, 1994, p.160 (FTC reported expenditures of $4 billion in 1990); Pierce and Gilpin, "Looking for a Market Among Adolescents" Scientific American, May 1995, p.50 (expenditures of $5 billion reported in 1992); Shankar Vedantam, "Ads, Not Peers, Recruit Young Smokers, Study Says" Times Picayune, Oct. 18, 1995, p.A-10 ($6 billion per year).

36 David Segal, "The Unfiltered Truth" Washington Monthly Sept. 1993.

identified ammonia-treated bandcast as "the soul of Marl-boro." In this way, the addition of ammonia "helped the industry lower the tar and allowed smokers to get more bang with less nicotine." Humectants, such as glycer-ine and propylene glycol, also work to enhance the nic-otine's impact by ensuring that the nicotine content does not become diminished, and by making the smoke easier to inhale. Changes in ventilation, at the same time, enable the manufacturer to reduce the levels of tar while pro-viding a higher percentage of nicotine. Finally, evidence has surfaced which indicates that the cigarette companies have actually been adding concentrated extracts to their cigarettes, and strategically manipulating the levels of nicotine. The cigarette industry has always claimed that nicotine is a natural ingredient of tobacco leaves, whose levels rise and fall in direct proportions to the amount of "tar". But when the companies started to market their low-tar/low-nicotine products, the amount of tar in the cigarettes was reduced by much greater proportions than the amount of nicotine. Based on studies which show that low-tar cigarettes actually tend to have proportionately higher concentrations of nicotine, some researchers have concluded that lower-yield cigarettes are enriched with nicotine by the tobacco companies so that people be-come, and remain, addicted. This is supported by internal memoranda from Philip Morris and the American Tobac-co Company, which refer to a series of studies designed to access various techniques of blend manipulations and increases in alkalinity for increasing "smoke impact" (*i.e.* nicotine) in low-tar cigarettes. In an internal memoran-dum from the Philip Morris Company, for example, a scientist asked the reader to "think of the cigarette as a dispenser for a dose unit of nicotine." Reports from in-dustry research conferences further demonstrate that, as early as 1970, Brown & Williamson's parent company,

British American Tobacco, was instructing its subsidiaries to experiment with high-nicotine extracts from various different kinds of tobacco leaves. This concept of blending concentrates to achieve the desired nicotine levels is consistent with the FDA Commissioner's recent charges that some of the companies have used tobacco that was genetically engineered to contain about twice the amount of nicotine. An internal memorandum from the American Tobacco Company, for example, dated June 1974, refers to experimentation with high-nicotine sun-cured tobacco from Malawi. In a Federal lawsuit brought by plaintiffs against five tobacco companies in the late 1980s, the District Court Judge concluded that the plaintiffs had presented evidence "from which a reasonable jury could conclude that the tobacco industry, in general, and defendants in particular, were aware of the risks of smoking; were concerned about the publication of those risks by others and the consequent impact upon cigarette sales; and sought to discredit or neutralize the adverse information by proffering an independent research organization, the Council for Tobacco Research, which purportedly would examine the risks of smoking and report its finding to the public. The evidence presented by plaintiff supports a finding that the industry research which might indict smoking as a cause of illness was diverted to secret research projects and that the publicized efforts were primarily directed at finding causes other than smoking for the illnesses being attributed to it. A jury might reasonably conclude that the industry's announcement of proposed independent research into the dangers of smoking and its promise to disclose its findings was nothing but a public relations ploy – a fraud – to deflect the growing evidence against the industry, to encourage smokers to continue and nonsmokers to begin, and to reassure the public that adverse information would be disclosed. Despite the industry's promise to engage independent researchers to explore the dangers of cigarette smoking and to publicize their findings, the evidence clearly suggests that the research was not independent; that potentially adverse results were shielded under the caption of 'special projects'; that the attorney-client privilege was intentionally employed to guard against such unwarranted disclosure; and that the promise of full disclosure was never meant to be honored, and never was."[37]

Accountability

The tobacco industry in America takes in approximately $48 billion in revenue each year. At the same time, however, the sale of tobacco products causes over four hundred thousand deaths, generates billions of dollars in health care costs, and accounts for approximately $8.4 billion dollars of corporate loss due to smoke-related employee absenteeism and disease. There is scarcely one person in this country who has not experienced the pain of watching a loved one die from prolonged tobacco use, or a friend who has been inflicted with illness and chronic suffering. And yet, to this day, the cigarette companies have refused to accept any responsibility for the damages they cause.

Lawsuits brought by private individuals do not seek to ban or outlaw products. The objective is not to take cigarettes, or alcohol, or guns, or any other product off the shelves; the objective is merely to force the manufacturer to pay for the real and provable damages which those products are known to cause.

It may be true that tobacco products offer the benefits of taste, pleasure, relaxation, stress reduction, and weight control. But the use of tobacco products also results in shortness of breath, high blood pressure, peptic ulcers,

---

37   Haines v. Liggett Group, Inc., 140 F.R.D. 681, 683-684 (D.N.J. 1992).

lung cancer, lip cancer, throat cancer, emphysema, bronchitis, arteriosclerosis, and heart disease. Even absent any blameworthiness or fault on the part of cigarette companies, the tobacco industry accepts 100% of the profits, and should bear at least some of the responsibility. We live in a free society, with a free market economy, where people and companies make business choices each and every day. The cigarette companies choose to sell cigarettes. Even though they know that cigarettes are harmful, even though they know that cigarettes are addictive, and even though they know that the consumption of cigarettes by their customers will eventually lead to illness and death. Those companies nevertheless make the conscious decision to place those products on the shelves. In doing so, the cigarette companies reap an average of $48 billion each year in revenue, yet assume none of the liabilities. The tobacco industry has embraced a rising sentiment among our nation of victims that refuses to accept any responsibility for the choices they make. Claiming that they are the innocent "victims" of an overzealous medical community, a politically motivated Congress, a power hungry Food and Drug Administration, and a legion of greedy and opportunistic plaintiffs lawyers, these companies place all of the blame on the smoker, telling individual juries and the American public that the illness and death which occurs naturally as the result of their product should be attributable solely to the actions of their customers. Smokers, they say, know that cigarettes will kill them, they know that nicotine is addictive, and therefore, the smoker assumes the risk for any damages they cause.

Assumption of Risk

It can be safely said, in this day and age, that every adult in this country is probably aware of the fact that smoking is dangerous and that nicotine is addictive. But millions of smokers became addicted to cigarettes in the forties, and fifties, and sixties, before the harmful effects of tobacco use were well-publicized, and therefore did not "assume the risk" of their own addictions to illness and disease. Second of all, the people whom cigarette companies now allege "assume the risk" of tobacco use are not adults. They are children.

It may be easy to say that a forty year-old is able to understand and appreciate the fact that he or she will become addicted to tobacco products, and that those cigarettes will eventually lead to his or her death. But no one starts to smoke when they're forty. They start smoking when they're twelve, or thirteen, or fourteen. When they're young, and invincible, and immortal, and can't really understand or appreciate the concept of having emphysema or lung cancer when they are old and gray. There are over three million smokers under the age of eighteen in this country who consume over a billion packs of cigarettes each year. Studies show that the average smoker begins smoking when he or she is 14 years old, and that 91.3% of all smokers are addicted by their twentieth birthday. The tobacco companies, knowing that they have to hook their customers while they're young, spend billions each year on advertising. Studies show that 91% of all six year-olds know Joe Camel, and that 69% of all teen smokers smoke Marlboro, the most advertised brand.

In this way, the tobacco industry targets children, gets them addicted when they are too young to appreciate the dangers, so that when they grow up, and start to be able to understand and appreciate the risks of smoking, and want to quit, it's too late.[38] In a report prepared for the Imperi-

38 In 1970, the assistant creative director for a promotional firm hired by Lorillard sent a letter to the head of the art department at a school in New York, seeking assistance in the formulation of an ad campaign targeted for kids. "We're adults" he wrote, "You've got a group of talented kids. Hence this letter. We have been asked by our client to come up with a package design, a design that is attractive to kids. The assignment is as follows: To design a cigarette package and cigarette carton that has

al Tobacco Company, for example, researchers acknowledged that, "however intriguing smoking was at eleven,
twelve, or thirteen, by the age of sixteen or seventeen
many regretted their use of cigarettes for health reasons
and because they feel unable to stop smoking when they
want to."[39] The researchers noted that "starters no longer
disbelieve the dangers of smoking, but they almost universally assume these risks will not apply to themselves
because they will not become addicted." The desire to
quit seems to come earlier, they reported, even prior to
the end of high school. "However, the desire to quit, and
actually carrying it out, are two quite different things."

A recent study by the Institute of Medicine further indicates that most adolescent smokers either plan to quit
before they reach adulthood, but fail, or have already attempted to kick the habit unsuccessfully. A recent Gallup
poll likewise confirms that 64% of adolescent smokers
have tried to quit, and that 70% regret their decision to
start smoking. Other studies show that 85% of high school
seniors who smoke believe that they will not be smoking
in five years. Of course, five years from now, only half
of those who are now occasional smokers will manage to
quit, while almost 40% will actually increase their consumption, and 70% of those who are now heavy smokers
will still be going through at least a pack a day.Some cig-

selling appeal to the 'youth market.' The new product name is 'Kicks' (a new cigarette). Guidelines that must be followed include.... Note: While the cigarette is geared
to the youth market, no attempt (obvious) can be made to encourage persons under
twenty-one to smoke. The package design should be geared to attract the youthful
eye, not the ever-watchful eye of the Federal Government." Philip Morris went so far
as to conduct a study on whether hyperactive children would be good targets for prospective customers. The research tracked over 6,000 hyperactive children, beginning
with 3rd graders, to see if they were more prone to smoke. Noting that such children
were often treated with stimulants, the researchers looked for "whether such children
may not eventually become cigarette smokers in their teenage years as they discover
the advantage of self-stimulation via nicotine."

39 The report indicates, with respect to the youth of target smokers, that play-
ful experimentation with cigarettes can begin as early as five years of age, though most
often around seven or eight, while serious experimentation begins in most cases from
12 to 13.

arette smokers have been successful in kicking the habit, just like drug users have been successful in defeating their addictions to cocaine. But for others, it is more difficult. For them, smoking is not a choice, but an addiction. They start smoking when they are twelve or thirteen years old. They hear the news reports that they will become addicted to the substance, but they tell themselves that it won't happen to them. Their parents tell them that they will end up with cancer and heart disease when they're in their fifties and sixties, but that's a million miles away. They tell themselves that they'll quit when they go to college, or when they get married, or when they have kids. But when they grow up, and they start to get married and have children, and start to feel responsible; when the future gets a little bit closer, and they start to understand the bounds of their own mortality; millions of smokers, at that point, try to quit. Again and again. But by that time, they are physically, psychologically, and medically addicted to the cigarettes. They can't stop. It's too late. It could be said, therefore, that the smoker assumes the risk of smoking from the time that he or she starts, until the time that he or she tries to quit – at twenty, or twenty-five, or twenty-seven years of age. But the smoker does not assume the risk of smoking from that point forward, because it's an addiction, not a choice, which compels that person to smoke, against his will.

While experimenting with dangerous activity is a part of growing up for most Americans, noted Wayne Hearn in a recent article on smoking among adolescents, it is the addictive nature of nicotine which makes experimentation with cigarettes particularly dangerous to the child. "Skateboarding behind a truck, for example, may be more immediately dangerous to one's health" he observed, "but it's an activity unlikely to hook someone for life."[40]

40 Wayne Hearn, "Adolescence and Addiction: War on Smoking Has New Front" Times Picayune, March 5, 1995, p. D-13.

Even if, however, the average smoker were not addicted to any substance in the tobacco product, and could therefore quit if he or she wanted to at any time, it is undeniable that the cigarette companies know that their product is harmful, they know that their product kills people, and thus, by choosing to sell that product to the American public, the cigarette companies have assumed the risk for any damages they cause.

Who Pays

The harmful effects of smoking are not confined to those who choose to smoke, or those who, by no choice of their own, are addicted to nicotine. Studies show that approximately 9,000 nonsmokers die each year as a result of second-hand smoke, including an estimated 3,000 who die from lung cancer alone. The typical cigarette has 700 chemical additives, including at least five which have been designated by the Federal Government as hazardous substances,[41] and the Environmental Protection Agency has recently classified cigarette smoke as a class-A carcinogen. While the full extent of the environmental impact from smoking is still, in many ways, a mystery, the economic and societal impact may be more profound.

Nonsmokers do not, in any way, assume the risks of smoking. Nor do nonsmokers in any way profit from the sale of tobacco products such as cigarettes. Nevertheless, when such products result in illness and death to countless Americans, it ultimately becomes the burden of millions of nonsmokers to pay for this loss.

Everyone pays the costs of smoking. Everyone pays in the form of higher health insurance premiums, and life insurance premiums. Everyone pays in the form of medical research, and increased hospital expenses, and other health-related fees. Everyone pays in the form of higher

---

41   Cigarettes have been found to include ammonia, arsenic, butane, cyanide, DDT, asbestos, formaldehyde, Polonium 210, and lead.

disability benefits, and workers compensation benefits, for people who cannot work as a result of tobacco-related illnesses. Everyone pays in the form of Social Security benefits, and welfare benefits, and Medicare and Medicaid. Everyone pays in the form of farm subsidies, which are awarded to the tobacco growers. And everyone pays in the form of employee absenteeism due to sickness and lost productivity due to cigarette breaks, which can amount to one work-month for every employee smoker per year. Despite this, the tobacco industry, which profits from the sale of cigarettes in excess of $8 billion annually, has not been required to contribute one cent.[42] The tobacco companies are social vultures and economic parasites. They prey on the stress and the anxiety of their customers, exploiting the vulnerable nature of their fears and insecurities. They prey on their wallets and their pocketbooks, and then, when the costs of those transactions begin to surface, they demand that the American public and its governmental bodies foot the bill, abdicating all responsibility. The cigarette companies, in this way, are preying on our social and economic institutions, and it

42 The University of California and the Center for Disease Control have reported an estimated $50 billion per year in total health care costs, with the Federal Government spending $20 billion each year on Medicare and Medicaid alone. Other studies have shown a loss of $8.4 billion annually to corporate employers as a result of employee absenteeism due to smoking-related illness and disease. Based on these and other figures, it has been estimated that the United States economy loses as much as a total of $100 billion due to cigarette consumption each year. See generally: Glantz, Fox and Lightwood, "Tobacco Litigation: Issues of Public Health and Public Policy" Journal of the American Medical Association, Vol. 277, No. 9, March 5, 1997, p.752; Bartecchi, MacKenzie, and Schrier, "The Global Tobacco Epidemic" Scientific American, May 1995, p.46; Center for Disease Control and Prevention, "Medical Care Expenditures Attributable to Cigarette Smoking–U.S." Morbidity and Mortality Weekly Reporter, Vol. 43, pp.469-472 (1994); Brownlee and Roberts, "Should Cigarettes Be Outlawed?" U.S. News and World Report, April 18, 1994, p.35; Anthony Lewis, "Just Say No" The New York Times, Oct. 16, 1995. In one of the few cases which has actually been tried to verdict, the jury concluded that the industry was responsible for 20% of the consequences, while the smoker was responsible for 80% of the harm. While it can be argued that the cigarette makers' fault is considerably greater, even at only 10%-20% of the fault, when you consider purely economic damages of almost $100 billion annually, the American public has effectively been subsidizing the profits of the tobacco industry to the tune of $10 billion to $20 billion per year.

has therefore become the role of the civil justice system
to demand accountability.

Tobacco and the American Way

Tobacco, on its own merits, cannot be defended. The
cigarette industry, therefore, attempts to tap into the fears
of the American public with "what's next" and "where
will it end" arguments, in an effort to link the use of tobacco products to freedom of choice and the American
way.

For a number of reasons, however, the production and
sale of cigarettes is legally, morally, medically and socially very unlike the production and sale of other potentially dangerous products such as alcoholic beverages,
firearms, or fatty foods.

Cigarettes, first of all, are inherently dangerous when
used as they are intended. Alcohol, firearms, and fatty
foods, by contrast, are only dangerous when abused. It
is important to note, in this respect, that unlike the great
majority of people who can be described as "social drinkers", when it comes to cigarettes, the overwhelming majority of smokers are physically and pharmacologically
addicted to nicotine.[43]Makers and distributors of alcoholic beverages, moreover, take reasonable steps to prevent

43 Dr. Russell has noted, for example, that only 2% of people who smoke can
be described as "social smokers" who smoke only occasionally. Social use of alcohol
is just the opposite, with only 2% of people who drink actually dependent on the alcohol. M.A.H. Russell, Meeting of Experimental Pathology Club, at the Imperial Cancer
Research Fund, June 27, 1975. For other varying accounts of alcohol dependency,
(1.5% to 12%), and nicotine dependency, (90% to 98%),see generally: Carl Sherman,
"Kicking Butts" Psychology Today Vol.27, No.5, Sept. 1994, p.40; Warren King, "The
Puzzle of Alcoholism" Seattle Times, July 2, 1990, p.A-6; Nancy Shute, "The Drinking Dilemma" U.S. News & World Report, Sept. 8, 1997, p.58. It is interesting to
note, in this regard, that when asked whether the American public could expect to see
the States begin to file similar (i.e. health care expenditure recovery) lawsuits against
other industries, New York Attorney General Vacco replied that he "was ultimately
convinced of the propriety of this strategy based primarily upon two factors: the addiction of kids and the deadliness of the addiction. That, I think, distinguishes the
tobacco industry from virtually any other industry that produces consumer products in
America." See "Vacco: Tobacco Deal Unique" National Law Journal, Sept. 8, 1997,
p.A-6.

the types of abuses which cause the greatest harm, such as "Friends Don't Let Friends Drive Drunk" and "Know When To Say When" campaigns. Cigarette makers, by contrast, not only refuse to take efforts to warn the public of their inherent dangers, but make conscious attempts to intentionally conceal and mislead their customers about the serious health risks involved. McDonald's, unlike Philip Morris, provides safer alternatives, such as a reduced-fat hamburger, grilled chicken sandwiches, and an assortment of salads. Gun manufacturers sometimes install safety-latches and other protective devices. Beer companies offer lite beers and even non-alcoholic beverages.

Fast food franchises additionally provide lists of ingredients and nutritional information, while beverage makers are required to identify the specific levels of alcohol.

These industries do not add harmful chemicals to make them more addictive or unnaturally powerful. And an analogy, therefore, cannot be drawn between a McLean Burger or a Lite Beer from Miller, on the one hand, and Camel Lights, on the other. A low-tar/low-nicotine cigarette, rather, is like a "lite" beer which actually has more alcohol or calories than a regular beer, or a sandwich which is marketed and sold as a "healthy" burger, but, in fact, has more fat or cholesterol than the ordinary Whopper or Big Mac.

As a legal matter, finally, it would be impossible to prove causation against any one specific food or beverage company. An obese person, for example, likely does not purchase all of his or her food from a single Popeyes or Burger King. He or she acquires foods from a host of sources, including grocery stores, fast food restaurants, sit down restaurants, diners, delis, parties, picnics, and home-cooked meals. An alcoholic, likewise, probably drinks, over the course of his or her lifetime, wines, beers and liquors produced and distributed by a plethora of different, (many of them foreign), companies. The tobacco industry, by contrast, is essentially just six companies: Philip Morris, RJR, Brown & Williamson, Lorillard, Liggett & Myers, and U.S. Tobacco. There is generally a high level of brand loyalty among individual smokers, and, by virtue of their conspiratorial efforts to manipulate and conceal information from the public, the tobacco companies can likely be held jointly liable, as they have acted as one.

It is true that America was founded, in large part, by tobacco farmers. But America was also founded, in large part, on slavery. At some point in our history, men of moral courage and social responsibility determined that tobacco farmers could no longer profit at the expense of others who fell trapped and oppressed beneath the weight of their greed.

Freedom of choice, of course, is integral to the American way of life. But standing behind your product, standing behind your word... that, too, is the American way.

Cigarette sales should not be banned, nor should tobacco use by the public become criminalized activity. In a free society, it is paramount that individuals, and not the government, be permitted to weigh the risks and the benefits of commercial transactions, and of the goods and services they consume.

But fairness requires that people, when making these decisions, have access to the free flow of information which is necessary for a proper evaluation of the dangers associated with such conduct, and justice demands that the suppliers of those goods and services remain accountable for their part in the commercial transaction, and responsible for at least some of the harm.

People have the right to choose things that are bad for them. But when companies choose to profit from the sale of products or the promotion of activities which are addictive and harmful, they should bear at least some of the responsibility for those addictions, and for the damages they cause.

The English Rule

When injustice arises in this nation, people turn to the courts. The courts protect ideas and inventions, by enforcing copyrights and patents. The courts protect property and incorporeal rights, by enforcing contracts and business transactions. The courts protect entrepreneurs and small businessmen, by enforcing laws against monopolies and unfair competition. And the courts protect the consumer, by enforcing warranties, whether express or implied. Society comes to the courts to have those who pose a danger to the public incarcerated, while the wrongly accused rely on courts to protect life, liberty and property by due process of law. Regulations that protect the environment are effected through the court system, while corporations go to the courts to challenge regulations that are overly burdensome or unfair. It is the courts which ensure basic liberties, like freedom of speech, and equal protection, and it is the courts which see that rights of privacy and protection from governmental intrusion are enforced. The courts serve as the instrument by which the government protects society from individuals and corporations, and at the same time by which individuals and corporations secure protection from the government itself. The Constitution does not exist without the courts to defend and to define it. Without the courts to enforce them, laws are just words on a page. When someone has been wronged in this country, he or she cannot go to the President. Executives have neither the time nor the inclination to encumber themselves with the redress of individual grievances. Legislators, likewise, respond only to lobbyists and campaign contributions, and are reluctant to act on behalf of individuals unless a political advantage can be obtained. Without access to the courts, the average American will lose economic and individual freedoms, facing increased threats to the health and welfare of his family, and unable to achieve any type of justice when wronged.

Despite claims of litigation explosions, frivolous lawsuits, and runaway jury verdicts, measures of so-called "tort reform" are ultimately engineered to deprive the average American of his or her access to the courts, so that corporate interests can avoid accountability for their wrongdoing, and insurance companies can profit by avoiding millions and millions of claims. Doctors, lawyers, manufacturers and energy companies will be free to provide goods and services that are defective and even harmful, while polluting the environment with poisons and hazardous substances. More people will suffer from sickness and injury, and those persons who do suffer will have no hope of achieving justice, which has been guaranteed to them by their Constitution, and under principles of Natural Law.

The "Litigation Explosion"

Civil filings have decreased a total of 6% over the past three years, and while there has been a dramatic increase in domestic disputes, suits against asbestos manufacturers, and employment discrimination cases, there are no more civil lawsuits *per capita* today than there were in

1959.[44]   Of these, tort cases, which include auto accidents, medical malpractice cases, legal malpractice cases,
railroad-crossing cases, plane crashes, explosions, unfair trade practices, and products liability suits, account
for less than two percent of the total caseload, and only
six percent of all civil claims.[45]   Around three-fourths of
these cases are settled by the parties, while 23% are dismissed by the court and only 3% go to trial. A new study
conducted by Tillinghast Towers Perrin, whose studies
have traditionally been cited by manufacturers and other
defense interests, shows that more than 50% of all pain,
suffering and economic loss goes uncompensated, and
that the gross annual costs of tort suits have not increased
in proportion to the general growth of the economy since
1985. Robert Sturgis, who conducted the study, concluded that "both the propensity to sue and the willingness
of defendants to settle questionable liability claims have

---

44   In Louisiana, for example, civil filings decreased in 1994 by 3.7%, while
civil jury trials decreased by 13.6%. In the Eastern District of Louisiana, civil filings
are down 45% since 1984, while filings in Federal Court across the country decreased
by 36% between 1985 and 1991. Domestic cases are increasing at approximately
three times the rate of civil filings, while the General Accounting Office has determined that the "litigation explosion" is largely attributable to suits involving just one
product – asbestos. With the exception of asbestos cases, product liability filings in
federal court have decreased dramatically since 1980. For these and other figures,
see: General Accounting Office, Product Liability: Extent of "Litigation Explosion"
in Federal Courts Questioned (1988); National Center for State Courts, Examining the
Works of State Courts, 1994, Pub. No. R-178 (1996); Annual Report of the Judicial
Council of the Supreme Court of Louisiana (1995); American Bar Association, Facts
About the American Civil Justice System; Reuben, "Putting the Brakes on Torts" ABA
Journal Jan. 1997, p.39; "Painful Decisions" ABA Journal, Aug. 1995, p.67; Alpert,
"Federal Bench Is Case Poor" The Times Picayune, March 7, 1996, p.A-1; Galanter,
"Public View of Lawyers" Trial, April 1992, p.72; "Someone Hear An Explosion?"
Newsweek, March 20, 1995, p. 34; "The Litigation Explosion is a Myth" Business
Week, March 10, 1986.

45   From 1984 to 1994, the civil caseload increased only 24%, while criminal
filings increased 35%, juvenile cases 59%, and domestic cases 65%. By 1994, civil
filings accounted for only 22% of the total caseload in state courts, while juvenile
(2.2%), criminal (15.6%), and traffic and municipal cases (60.2%), made up the rest.
Tort cases, moreover, comprise only 6.2% of civil filings, while domestic relations
(25%), property (17.2%), small claims (20.5%), contract (8.6%), and other (22.5%),
make up the rest. National Center for State Courts, Examining the Works of State
Courts, 1994, Pub. No. R-178 (1996).

actually declined."[46]Advocates of change in the judicial system, nevertheless, emphasize the fact that America is the most litigious society on earth. They point out that two-thirds of the world's lawyers live in this country, while Americans account for only 6% of the population. While there were already 355,000 lawyers in 1970, that number doubled by 1990, and is growing steadily at a rate of approximately 40,000 per year. This amounts to 2.67 lawyers for every thousand people, while in our nation's capital there is one lawyer for every sixty women and men.[47]

Despite such figures, however, the legal system demands little of our resources. Last year the Federal Government devoted less than one percent of its annual budget to the entire federal court system, while states spent less than half that on their respective judiciaries. In all, the courts consume less than three-fifths of 1% of all government expenditures. This includes the cost of judges, prosecutors, public defenders, courthouse operation and maintenance, judicial administrators, and clerks. Even if, however, the demands of our court system were more taxing, such expense would pale in comparison to the good which is achieved. America may very well be, in this respect, the most litigious society in the world. But America is also the most productive society in the world. America is the most innovative society in the world. And America is the most interesting society in the world. The courts are the safeguard of such freedoms. The courts are the safeguard of democracy. The courts protect our thoughts and

46 Jay Matthews, "Payment Rates Ease in Jury Awards and Liability Settlements, Survey Shows" Washington Post, Nov. 13, 1995, p. A-5.

47 Actually, more recent estimates suggest that American lawyers, in fact, make up only 25 to 35 percent of the world's attorneys, including judges, in-house counsel, and government employees. This is roughly proportionate to the United States' share of the world's gross national product, and far less than the U.S. expenditures on scientific research and development. See Galanter, "The Public View of Lawyers" Trial April 1992, p.71.

our beliefs, our ideas and our inventions, our properties and our lives.[48] "If our tort system is expensive" noted one law professor in a recent interview, "it's because we have lots of torts. We should be thinking of ways to reduce the number of torts, not the number of recoveries."[49]

The "Lottery" System

The median award for plaintiffs who win jury trials is approximately $51,000, while the average bodily injury payment under an auto liability policy is only around $8,000. Million-dollar verdicts are awarded in only 8% of jury trials won by plaintiffs, (*i.e.* one-tenth of one percent of all tort cases). The median punitive damage award is just $38,000.[50]Nevertheless, some legislative bodies have deemed it necessary to institute caps or limitations on recoverable damages. While proponents allege that such limits are designed to eliminate excessive or arbitrary jury verdicts, these measures are primarily intended to prevent the typical plaintiff from being able to find an attorney who is willing to handle his or her claim. The

48 It has been noted, for example, that "the number of lawyers in a country seems to relate directly to the level of individual rights and freedoms their citizens possess. China's 1.1 billion people have a mere 50,000 lawyers, almost all of whom work for the government. East Germany, with 16.6 million people, had about 3,500 lawyers and judges, only 600 of them private attorneys. The Soviet Union, with more than 280 million people, had only 230,000 lawyers, most, again, working for the government. There are few, if any, lawyers in Rwanda." American Bar Association, Facts About the American Civil Justice System, p.4.

49 Professor Richard Abel, "Public Discontent" ABA Journal, Aug. 1995, p.71. Studies show, for example, that there are more than 21,700 deaths and 28.6 million injuries each year from the use of unsafe products alone. Consumer product injuries account for one out of every six hospital days, and the loss from personal injury, property damage, and death, amounts to over $200 billion per year. "Sellers of Unsafe Products Are Treated as Criminals" Times Picayune, Aug. 15, 1995, p.C-3.

50 In the 25 years between 1965 and 1990, only 355 punitive damage awards were rendered in product liability cases. Excluding asbestos cases, which accounted for 25% of these awards, there were an average of only 11 awards per year. See Rustad Demystifying Punitive Damages in Products Liability Cases, The Roscoe Pound Foundation, p.23 (1991). See also: Erik Moller, Trends in Jury Verdicts Since 1985, Rand Institute for Civil Justice (1996); Daniels and Martin, Civil Juries and the Politics of Reform (1995); National Center for State Courts, Examining the Work of State Courts, 1994, Pub. No. R-178 (1996).

typical plaintiff is injured and poor. He has lost a loved
one, or has suffered from a physical infirmity, been dispossessed of his house, or terminated from his job. The
typical plaintiff has hospital bills, and medical expenses,
and either rent or a mortgage to pay. He has water bills,
and electric bills, and food and clothes to provide for his
child. The typical plaintiff, accordingly, cannot afford to
pay court costs, expert witnesses, copying costs, court reporters, paralegals, or filing fees; nor can he afford to pay
the attorney even a nominal hourly charge. The typical
plaintiff therefore agrees to a contingency fee arrangement with his attorney, by which the attorney will be paid
from a percentage of the client's award. The attorney, in
doing so, is accepting a certain risk, and as with any businessman or investor, the attorney's willingness to accept
such risk is dependent upon the time and money which he
or she must invest in his client's cause of action, coupled
with the likelihood and amount of any potential recovery.
If defendants, therefore, make the business proposition
for the plaintiff's attorney so undesirable that the investment is not worthwhile, the plaintiff will be denied his or
her access to the courts.

Caps and limitations on recoverable damages are engineered accordingly, to make the investment of litigation
so unprofitable for the average American's attorney, that
the average American will not be able to file a claim.

A medical malpractice case, for example, generally
takes years to develop and costs an average of $75,000,
while only 26% are successful.[51] If the damages are lim-

51 These cases are particularly expensive to prosecute because the attorney
needs to hire at least one medical expert who charges a sizeable fee to screen the case
and decide whether it has merit; then the case must, in many states, be presented to
"medical review panel" of experts, which is purposely designed to make the process
more lengthy and expensive, before suit can even be filed; the attorney must spend a
tremendous amount of time learning the science of the case from his expert, (who may
charge up to $1,200 per hour or $20,000 per proceeding), and developing exhibits and
other demonstrative evidence so that the attorney and his or her expert witnesses can
educate the jury or the judge. These costs are added to the customary costs which are

ited to $250,000, the attorney would only be entitled to a $70,000 fee.[52] Few businessmen would place $75,000 and five years of their lives completely at risk for a 26% chance to earn a maximum of $70,000. Plaintiff's attorneys, nevertheless, are criticized for "hitting the lottery" with these types of investments every day. The effect of such measures, moreover, is that those who are most severely injured will bear the entire burden of the reform. Several years ago, for example, a young television producer was sitting alone in her quiet Arizona residence, unaware that a nearby public service utility line was leaking natural gas. She went to light a cigarette, and the apartment exploded in a tremendous fireball. Her delicate body was charred, except for a small area on the top of her head. Once she had stabilized, the doctors cut dead skin from her body, and replaced it with the skin from her scalp. As it healed, the skin tightened, thickened, and scarred. After four years of surgery, at a cost of $850,000, she was left with the face of a monster, hooked up to a respirator, deaf from the antibiotics, and unable to speak. The doctors, at that point, had done all that they could. This woman will spend the rest of her life wearing a wig, to cover her mutilated scalp, and to soften the areas where her ears once were. The simplest of household chores will require assistance, and she will never work again. Whenever she limps into a room, people will stop what they are doing and stare at her. She will be the subject of laughter and ridicule. And she will never walk in a normal way again. This woman has suffered pain and will continue to suffer pain, both physical and emotional, that is unimaginable. Yet, with a $250,000 limitation on the recovery of

associated with the typical suit.

52 If the award were $250,000, the client would reimburse the attorney his $75,000 in costs and expenses, leaving 40% of $175,000, a $70,000 fee. (Because of the substantial time, expense and difficulty in handling medical malpractice cases, they are generally taken on a 40% contingency fee basis. On a traditional 33% contract, the maximum fee would be only $58,300.)

non-economic damages, (while someone suffering from a broken arm will be entitled to full recovery), she will be limited to less than $25 per day. What is most interesting to note, in this respect, is that the overwhelming majority of research in this area indicates that most consumers who are injured or defrauded are actually undercompensated for their injuries. Most potential plaintiffs, studies show, are already intimidated by the current legal system, and are generally convinced that the possibility of recovering damages is not worth the financial and psychological expense of going to court. In many cases, moreover, when a consumer is defrauded, he or she does not even know that he has been the victim of fraud. It has been estimated, consequently, that less than 3% of people who are injured or defrauded outside of the workplace or their automobile ever make a claim for damages in a court suit, or even an informal demand against the insurance company.[53]

"Gotcha"

Over the past century, most states have adopted a form of "strict" or "enterprise" or "vicarious" liability, which renders employers responsible for the conduct of their employees, parents responsible for the conduct of their children, landowners responsible for the hazards and defects in their property, and manufacturers responsible for the goods and services they provide.

While, at first blush, such responsibility may seem

53 A 1991 survey of people who suffered injuries serious enough to require medical attention found that 80% never even considered trying to collect money from someone else. Of the remaining 20%, only half take any action, (*e.g.* talking to an attorney, threatening to sue), while only one-fifth, (*i.e.* 2 in 100), actually filed suit. See Deborah Hensler, Compensation for Accidental Injuries in the U.S., Rand Corporation (1991). Another study conducted by Harvard University concluded that only one out of every seven or eight hospital patients who are injured as a result of malpractice actually file malpractice claims, while only half of these claimants actually recover. The legal system, therefore, is paying just 1 malpractice victim for every 15 or 16 torts committed by hospitals and physicians. Harvard Medical Practice Study, Patients, Doctors and Lawyers: Medical Injury, Malpractice Litigation, and Patient Compensation in New York (1990).

peculiar or unfair, the foundations of strict liability are actually rooted in three sound public policies. First, the employer, or parent, or owner, or manufacturer, is generally in a better position to detect, evaluate, and eliminate the danger. Second, the employer, parent, owner, or manufacturer, is generally in a better position to bear the loss, by spreading the risk, through prices, rates, or insurance, to society at large. And finally, it is the employer, parent, owner, or manufacturer, that benefits from the services, life, ownership, or sale, of its employees, children, property, or goods, and in accepting those benefits, should also be deemed to accept the responsibilities.[54]Recently, however, there has been an appeal by corporate and other interests to retreat from such legal advances, and to return to a fault-based model of responsibility. These appeals, in all cases, view the issue from a one-sided perspective, posing questions in a vacuum, and without due appreciation for the alternative model they propose. When strict liability was repealed in Louisiana, for example, the question was frequently asked: "Suppose your sick tree falls on your neighbor's car, but you didn't know anything was wrong with it, should you get sued?"

Of course, when viewed solely from the perspective of the person that owns the tree, the natural reaction is: No.

One must consider, however, the alternative: "Suppose your neighbor's sick tree falls on your car, should you have to pay for the damages?"

And of course, when viewed from the perspective of the person that owns the car, the obvious reaction is: No.

One must therefore consider the issue from an objective viewpoint, with due regard for the social and economic policies involved. When viewed in this way, one can only reach the conclusion that, of the two innocent parties, the property owner should be the one to bear the

54 This principle derives from the old legal maxim: "He who derives the advantage ought to sustain the burden."

responsibility for that harm. The property owner, after all, is in a better position to detect and eliminate the danger, and, by purchasing a simple homeowner's policy, to spread the risk of loss. It is the property owner, moreover, who derives the fruits or other benefits of ownership, and should therefore also accept the responsibility.

The property owner, nevertheless, is being increasingly immunized from liability, while the neighbor with the tree plowed into his fender either has to pay to get his car fixed, or, assuming that he has insurance, watch his premiums rise while paying the deductible.

In the area of products liability, likewise, many states are retreating from strict liability, with the introduction or re-introduction of a risk-benefit analysis, sometimes referred to as "BPL". The "B" typically refers to the burden to the manufacturer, while the "P" is the probability of injury, and "L" is the gravity of the harm. If the burden is greater than the probability of harm times the gravity of harm, (*i.e.* if B>PL), the defendant is not held accountable.

The problem is: Where the burden is greater than the probability of harm times the gravity of the harm, the burden on the manufacturer is effectively zero. Or, stated another way: Where a company has reasonably determined that it will be more cost-effective to let people become injured, or killed, or economically damaged, rather than correct a problem, it is relieved of all responsibility for that harm. Justice and fairness, as well as simple logic, compel the opposite result: Where a company has already profited from the decision to allow people to become injured, killed, or economically damaged, rather than correct the problem, (because such a decision is economically beneficial to the company), that company should, at the very least, pay for harm.[55]Otherwise, the

55   In the Ford Pinto case, for example, Ford calculated that the cost to society of allowing people to become injured and killed by defective gas-tanks would be $49.5

manufacturer, which has already received the benefit of its bargain, so to speak, is rewarded with a windfall, while the entire burden falls upon the innocent shoulders of another, who is forced to effectively subsidize the benefits to the landowner, or businessowner, or manufacturer, and society at large.

The eroding concept of strict liability, in this way, lies at the heart of a free market economy. If you make a good product, you profit. If you make a harmful product, you don't. Even without "fault", the party who stands in the best position to detect, evaluate, and eliminate the danger, must bear the responsibility for the harm that his products, property, employees, animals or children, may happen to cause.

"Deep Pockets"

When two or more wrongdoers contribute to a single event or injury, they were traditionally held to be "jointly and severally" or "solidarily" liable for that harm. This allowed a plaintiff to recover all of his or her damages from a single defendant, and placed the burden on the defendant to collect from other parties who might be bankrupt, insolvent, unknown, immune from liability, or beyond the jurisdiction of the court. Like the doctrine of strict liability, it was grounded in the old equitable principle that, where two innocent parties must suffer a loss at the hands of another, the loss should be borne by the party who has most contributed to the injury by allowing it to occur.

Large corporations and insurance companies, however, want to avoid such "deep pocket" litigation, and have

---

million, while the cost of correcting the problem, (at $11 per vehicle), would have been $137 million. Under a cost/benefit analysis, therefore, Ford argued that, because the Burden was greater than the Probability of Loss, it was not liable for the harm. Yet, accepting Ford's calculations, the company had already saved $87.5 million by deciding to sacrifice the lives of its customers. At the very least, then, Ford should be required to compensate those victims the $49.5 million for their loss.

therefore lobbied for the end of joint and several liability, which has been modified or abolished in 41 states. The result, in many cases, is that a wealthy defendant who has been negligent or even reckless in its conduct will evade additional liability, at the expense of an innocent plaintiff who did not contribute in any way to the harm.

In 1989, for example, an ambulance was traveling west down Highway 407, called to the scene of an accident, with lights flashing and sirens on. The ambulance driver had the sun in his eyes, and didn't know that he was about to cross paths with an oncoming train. The train engine was obscured by a line of trees, which were supposed to be cut back by the railroad, but which the company had failed to maintain. There were no cross-arms at the intersection, nor flashing lights, nor bells. The train itself was speeding, and did not blow its whistle at the designated time. The railroad had failed to man the train with appropriate lookouts, and though the train's engineer did eventually see the approaching ambulance, he did not put on the emergency brakes, or even slow down. The ambulance driver finally saw the train engine approaching, slammed on his brakes, and skidded 285 feet into the intersection, colliding with the speeding train. Patrick Landry, a 21 year-old emergency medical technician who was riding in the passenger seat of the ambulance, is now a quadriplegic, who will suffer from paralysis and severe brain damage for the rest of his life. He will never have children. He cannot feed himself. He cannot clothe himself. He cannot go to the bathroom. And he may never walk again.

Even if Patrick Landry were entitled to recover from the ambulance driver, the ambulance driver himself is severely injured and has no money, nor any way of earning a living. But Patrick Landry cannot recover from the driver, nor from the ambulance service, because of statutory immunities. Patrick Landry's only available recourse, therefore, is against the railroad, for its failure to properly maintain the intersection and for its negligent operation of the train. In the absence of joint and several liability, Landry will be forced to argue, disingenuously, that the railroad company is solely responsible for his injuries, while the railroad will be permitted to defend its case by shifting the blame onto the ambulance driver, who is not there to defend himself. The judge or jury deciding the case will get a distorted view of the evidence, and Landry will have to bear the loss for any fault which is ultimately attributed to the driver. If, for example, the jury were to assess the railroad company with 80% of the fault, and the ambulance driver with 20%, and the damages were found to be one million dollars, the judgment for Patrick Landry against the railroad company would be $800,000. On the surface, this seems fair. The railroad company was responsible for 80% of the injuries, and is therefore liable for 80% of the damages. But the real focus of inquiry, in such cases, is not the overall verdict, but only that portion of the loss which is not recoverable by the injured party because one or more of the wrongdoers involved is immune, unknown, insolvent, or beyond the jurisdiction of the court.

The question, therefore, is not who should be liable for the million dollar jury verdict, but who should be responsible for that $200,000 in hospital bills, physical therapy, nursing care, lost wages, pain, and suffering, which Patrick Landry cannot recover from the ambulance driver because he doesn't have any money, and because he is also immune. In the absence of joint and several liability, the railroad company, who was 80% at fault in causing the plaintiff's injuries, is relieved of all liability with respect to these damages, while the injured victim, who was 0% at fault, is required to bear 100% of that loss.[56]The repeal of joint and several liability, moreover, tends to lead, ironically, to the filing of more and more suits. Rather than simply proceeding against the "major" defendant, the plaintiff is forced, in the absence of joint and several or solidary liability, to file suit against absolutely everyone who may be liable for the damages sustained. This naturally results in a substantial increase of lawsuits against individuals and small businesses – those precise parties whom the reforms are alleged to protect. The end result, therefore, is that large corporations who are partially at fault in causing injuries to another are relieved of liability, at the expense of small businessmen, the injured party, and the uninsured. The other effect of the repeal of joint and several liability is the windfall it produces for the "major" defendant corporations. While, ostensibly, each defendant is responsible for its degree of fault in the matter, the reality is that many types of cases will be impossible to prosecute, from an economic perspective. Negligent, reckless, or otherwise responsible industries will be effectively immune from prosecution, at the expense of an innocent third party who has been injured as a result of the defendant's negligence, recklessness, or other conduct or activity.[57]

56 In cases where the plaintiff is partly at fault, the fault of an absent or insolvent party can be reallocated among the remaining parties, (including the plaintiff), so that the plaintiff and the defendant share proportionately in absorbing that loss. If, then, the plaintiff is 20% at fault, the defendant is 40% at fault, and the remaining 40% of fault is attributable to a third party, who could not be joined in the lawsuit because he or she was either immune, insolvent, or beyond the jurisdiction of the court, then the plaintiff would be required to absorb one-third of that loss, while the defendant would be accountable for the other two-thirds. In the end, the plaintiff would absorb 33.3% of the loss, while the defendant would be liable for 66.7% of the recoverable damages. This approach avoids the unfairness of the traditional common law rules of joint and several liability, which would cast the total risk of uncollectibility upon the solvent defendants, and of a rule abolishing joint and several liability, which would cast the entire risk of uncollectibility upon the plaintiff. See Uniform Comparative Fault Act, §2(a) (1977).

57 In an inadequate security case, for example, where a hotel guest is robbed, or raped, or otherwise assaulted, due, in part, to the negligence of the hotel or motel owner, a reasonable jury might conclude that the hotel was 20% at fault in causing the plaintiff's injuries, with 80% attributable to the assailant. Traditionally, where

Some deep pockets are negligent or even reckless in their conduct. Others derive an economic benefit from the goods and services they provide. When such conduct or business activities result in harm to the public, deep pockets should bear the responsibility for that harm.

Frivolous Claims

Mary Ann Maselli lost her husband to cancer as a result of exposure to asbestos over a number of years. The typical plaintiff in Mrs. Maselli's position is an elderly woman whose retirement savings have been exhausted on her husband's hospital bills, part of which she still owes. She is in debt to her bank, and to various doctors, and has no means but her monthly Social Security check to support her from day to day. She, like most plaintiffs, cannot afford to pay court costs and other expenses, nor can she afford to hire an attorney for even a nominal sum. This is generally not a problem, because Mrs. Maselli can likely find a an attorney who would be willing to handle her claim on a contingency fee basis. If the case is successful, Mrs. Maselli will pay a portion of her award to her attorney for the time and money he or she has expended in pursuing her claim. If Mrs. Maselli's case is unsuccessful, on the other hand, that cost is absorbed by the attorney, and Mrs. Maselli is in no worse a situation than when she began.

Under the "English rule" however, Mrs. Maselli and other plaintiffs who are already injured, who are already

the hotel owner and the assailant were jointly and severally liable, the innocent plaintiff could be fairly compensated. In the absence of such a mechanism, however, the time and expense of developing a case against the hotel would not be justified by the prospect of recovering just 20% of the loss. Effectively, therefore, the negligent hotel owner is relieved of all responsibility, while the innocent hotel guest – who played no part in causing the injuries; who favored the hotel with her patronage; and who relied upon the hotel's representation as a safe and comfortable place to stay – is required to bear the entire burden, cost, and pain, of her loss. The auto industry, likewise, is effectively relieved of virtually all responsibility for making un-crashworthy vehicles, while highway departments are absolved of virtually all responsibility for inadequate maintenance or negligent design.

cheated, who are already struggling, and who generally have little or no resources to spare, would face the proposition of becoming liable for the asbestos manufacturer's legal fees. Because few plaintiffs are in a position to assume such liability, the measure works like a fine or a penalty, which punishes the average citizen like Mrs. Maselli for exercising her constitutional right to petition the government for redress, seeking only the opportunity to have a jury listen to her story, and a bit of justice for her family.[58]

The English rule which has been proposed in Congress on the heels of Newt Gingrich's *Contract With America* is particularly punitive, because it imposes attorney's fees on a plaintiff who rejects the defendant's settlement offer, and then recovers less than the amount offered by the defendant at trial. This provision allows the defendant to strong-arm a plaintiff into accepting a low settlement offer, because the plaintiff will face the additional risk of having to pay a team of high-priced defense lawyers' exorbitant fee. Ultimately, the provision would allow a wrongdoer who is guilty of negligent or even reckless or intentionally harmful conduct see his or her liability to the injured victim offset by the cost of his or her own attorney's fees. The rule would encourage defendants to make litigation as lengthy and as expensive as possible, while at the same time deterring the ordinary citizen from having his day in court. The courts of England, it is interesting to note, are in fact moving away from their traditional loser-pay system, and adopting an "American

---

58   Even if a plaintiff like Mrs. Maselli were willing to accept the responsibility, the risks weigh so disproportionately in favor of the defendant in a typical situation, that the result is bound to be unjust. In Mrs. Maselli's case, for example, the asbestos manufacturer would be able to hire a team of high-priced attorneys who could afford to drag out the litigation as long as possible, while the plaintiff's representation would consist of a one or two person operation, who has to personally furnish all of the client's expenses and costs. Because the defendant will typically hire more attorneys, who will charge the client more money, the risk to the plaintiff may be three or four times as great as the risk to the asbestos manufacturer.

rule" whereby each party is responsible for his or her own legal fees. The English have begun to make such changes in their system because "they no longer believe," as one author put it, "that you can achieve civil justice, changes in unsafe products, safe workplaces, and a clean environment, without the American-style contingent fee system where people have access to the courts."[59]Despite claims that the loser-pay system is necessary to weed out frivolous lawsuits, the courts already have devices by which such lawsuits may be summarily dismissed, and by which sanctions can be imposed. Rule 11, for example, in Federal Court and analogous provisions in state courts require the attorney to certify, in any pleading, that he or she has conducted a reasonable investigation into the facts and the law relevant to the matter, and that there is a reasonable basis to the claim. Sanctions can and should be imposed by the court if a claim or defense is frivolous, and either the attorney or the client, or both, can be required to pay the opposing attorney's fee.

Frivolous claims are further "weeded out" by the economic realities of practicing law, and the nature of the contingency fee. Attorneys, many of whom begin their careers with thousands of dollars in undergraduate and law school bank loans, have to pay for office space, libraries, secretaries, paralegals, telephones, faxes, word processors, research services, investigators, court reporters, copying expenses, depositions, experts, court costs, and filing fees. The great majority of attorneys are therefore unwilling to waste their time and money pursuing a frivolous claim.

Despite complaints that "in many cases, defendants know that the suit would not stand on its own merits, but agree to settle out of court just to avoid the endless

59 G. Marc Whitehead, "Public Discontent" ABA Journal, Aug. 1995, p.71.

and expensive claim and appeal process,"[60] there are just as many, if not more cases, in which the plaintiff knows that the suit would stand on its own merits, but agrees to settle out of court for a fraction of what he or she is entitled, because the defendants threaten to hire a team of attorneys who will file hundreds of court pleadings, mounting defense upon defense, with appeal after appeal, to make the litigation as long and as expensive as possible. In general, this presents more problems for the plaintiff than the defendant, because the plaintiff needs the money to pay hospital bills, or in lieu of compensation, while the defendant can easily afford to wait out a potentially adverse result. Such strategy is also more problematic for the plaintiff's attorney, who must pay all of the expenses out of his own pocket, while the defense attorneys are generally reimbursed by the corporation or insurance company on a monthly basis. Measures to reduce frivolous lawsuits should be directed at frivolous lawsuits, and measures to reduce the costs of litigation should be directed at frivolous defenses, as well as frivolous claims. Yet corporations and insurance companies are not truly concerned with frivolous lawsuits. In addition to Rule 11 and corresponding state court procedures for attacking such filings, the defendants also have the weapons of summary judgment, no cause of action, no right of action, lack of subject-matter jurisdiction, lack of personal jurisdiction, prescription, preemption, statutes of limitations, statutes of repose, involuntary dismissals, directed verdicts, and judgments not withstanding the verdict, which can often affect suits which have merit as well as frivolous lawsuits, and which, together, result in the dismissal of approximately one-fourth of all claims.[61]

---

60 Gingrich, Armey, and House Republicans, Contract With America, p.145 (1995).

61 A study conducted by the Civil Trial Court Network in 1991, which was sponsored by the Justice Department, indicates that 23.7% of tort cases are dismissed

Sometimes these measures are inadequate, and the defendant will have to settle the claim for its "nuisance value". But by strong-arming one vulnerable plaintiff who has a legitimate half-million cause of action into a $250,000 settlement, the insurance company or other corporation can make up for twenty-five or thirty of its "nuisance" settlements based on allegedly frivolous claims.

The purpose of tort reform is not to deter frivolous lawsuits. The purpose of tort reform is to stave off legitimate lawsuits, and thereby avoid accountability, by throwing out the baby with the bath. While it may seem unfair, at times, for a defendant to pay thousands of dollars in defense of a contestable lawsuit, that is the cost of living in a free society. That is the cost of doing business in a free economy. That is the cost of living in a country where property rights and individual liberties are protected by due process, trial by jury, and open access to the courts.[62]"The fear that courts may be flooded with litigation is not a sufficient justification to disallow those claims that are legitimate," writes Louisiana Supreme Court Chief Justice Pascal Calogero. "It is the duty of the courts to discern valid claims from the fraudulent ones."[63]

Voodoo Economics and the "Trickle Down" Theory of Tort Reform

summarily by the courts. See "The Big Picture" ABA Journal, Aug. 1995, p.65.

62   "Over the course of centuries, our society has settled upon civil litigation as a means for redressing grievances, resolving disputes, and vindicating rights when other means fail. There is no cause for consternation when a person who believes in good faith and on the basis of accurate information regarding his legal rights that he has suffered a cognizable injury turns to the courts for a remedy. That our citizens have access to their civil courts is not an evil to be regretted; rather, it is an attribute of our system of justice in which we ought to take pride." Zauderer v. Office of Disciplinary Counsel, 471 U.S. 626, 643 (1985).

63   LeJune v. Rayne Branch Hospital, 556 So.2d 559, 563 (La. 1990). The United States Supreme Court has similarly noted that most frivolous and vexatious litigation is terminated at the pleading stage, or on summary judgment, and that the threat of sanctions provides a significant deterrent to baseless litigation that is asserted merely to harass the defendant, or for some other political or monetary gain. Clinton v. Jones, 117 S.Ct. 1636, 1651 (1997).

A few years ago, sixteen year-old Kristen Knowles was in the hospital visiting a family member who was ill. Kristen's grandmother was complaining about the fact that the hospital was charging six dollars for every tablet of Tylenol. Kristen said something to the nurse, who told her that it's because of the greedy lawyers with all of their frivolous lawsuits; that's what makes everything so expensive. Of course, hospitals spend less than 1% of their resources defending lawsuits, which includes the cost of malpractice insurance, legal expenses, and the payment of settlements and awards.[64] So if a hospital is charging its patients six dollars for a tablet of Tylenol, less than six cents are attributable to the malpractice of physicians, the profits of insurance companies, the fees of the attorneys, (both plaintiff and defense), and both frivolous and nonfrivolous claims. Linda Muller, in that same hospital, had a cesarean a few years ago. During the procedure, the doctor felt a nodule on her liver. Following the surgery, Mrs. Muller consulted her internist, who was informed of the nodule, and decided to run an ultrasound in order to locate and identify the problem. The CAT scan is a more accurate test for locating and identifying such growths, but the ultrasound is cheaper, and easier to perform. In Mrs. Muller's case, the ultrasound was insufficient, and despite continued abdominal pain, the doctor let the problem go untreated. A year and a half later, it was finally discovered that the nodule had been a malignant tumor, but by this time the cancer had progressed to an incurable stage. If Mrs. Muller's doctor had performed the CAT scan, instead of or in addition to the ultrasound, the growth would have been located, and Linda Muller might have been saved. But obviously, the doctor was not

64 It is interesting to note, in this regard, that awards, settlements and litigation costs account for no more than 60 cents of every premium dollar, with the insurance companies pocketing at least 40%. Jamie Court "Malpractice Reform is Harmful" San Diego Union-Tribune, Aug. 24, 1994, p.B-5; Patrick Salvi, "Malpractice Award Limits Hurt Victims" Chicago Tribune, Oct. 12, 1993, p.18.

worried about lawsuits; he was not worried about being held accountable for the treatment he was prescribing; and therefore he failed to use "preventive" medicine.[65] The truth is, preventive medicine makes physicians more cautious and careful. Preventive medicine improves treatment. Preventive medicine saves lives. If Linda Muller's doctor had used preventive medicine, Linda Muller might be alive today. Every proposal of tort reform is advertised as a method of saving the average American money, which "trickles down" from doctors, lawyers, insurance companies, and other businesses and corporations. Every proposal of tort reform is promoted as a way of creating jobs, lowering the costs of goods and services, and cutting the price of insurance premiums. When insurance companies make money, however, they don't lower their premiums. They get on television and say that we are in the midst of an "insurance crisis", while the CEO of Travelers Insurance Company earns $68 million per year. In 1975, the insurance companies claimed that there was a "medical malpractice crisis". They convinced legislators around the nation to pass Medical Malpractice Acts, which now prevent many patients from filing suit due to restrictive statutes of limitations, make the costs of litigation higher by forcing plaintiffs to submit their cases to medical review panels, and limit the amount of damages that can be recovered.[66] Meanwhile, the insurance companies, who were already earning around $18 million a year in Louisiana alone, continued to charge the doctors

65 "Preventive medicine" is used to refer to treatment and testing which is alleged to be medically unnecessary, but performed by physicians nevertheless, to protect themselves from medical malpractice claims.

66 The Louisiana Medical Malpractice Act, for example, does not allow a plaintiff to institute a claim after three years, even if the plaintiff did not or could not have known that he or she was the victim of any malpractice, (if, for example, a patient was negligently infected with the HIV virus in 1990, but doesn't find out until he gets tested for AIDs in 1994); forces the plaintiff to submit the case to a medical review panel of doctors before he or she can file suit; and limits recoverable damages to $500,000. See La. Rev. Stat. 9:2800.40, et. seq.

excessive premiums. In the five years following the passage of the Louisiana Medical Malpractice Act in 1975, insurance carriers continued to charge doctors over $86 million in premiums, while paying out less than $9 million in claims.[67]

The absence of any "trickling down" to patients is further evidenced by a 1992 General Accounting Office study which showed that *per capita* health costs approximately doubled in every state of the union between 1982 and 1990, irrespective of whether the state had adopted caps on damages, or other legal reforms. Data collected by the National Association of Insurance Commissions likewise shows that profits from medical malpractice insurance increased in almost every state between 1985 and 1992, regardless of whether there was a cap on damages.[68] Physicians are among the most honorable and most valuable of all professions. They deserve our respect, they deserve our esteem, and they deserve to be well paid for the services they provide. But doctors are not perfect, and like all of us, they make mistakes.[69] Insurance com-

[67] According to the Insurance Commissioner's records, the recapitulation of medical malpractice insurance business transacted in Louisiana from 1976 through 1980 is as follows:

Year	Premiums Earned	Losses Paid
1976	$18,554,650	$785,138
1977	$16,120,237	$1,935,898
1978	$17,192,407	$1,192,137
1979	$16,325,980	$2,208,535
1980	$18,022,394	$2,486,516
TOTAL:	$86,215,668	$8,606,224

[68] In fact, it is interesting to note that six of the top ten states in medical malpractice insurance profitability did not have caps on damages, and that two of the states which have implemented some of the most limiting restrictions on damages, (California and Indiana), have enjoyed no comparative savings in health care expenditures. Wencl & Brizzolara, "Medical Negligence: Survey of the States" Trial, May 1996, p.22; General Accounting Office, Health Care Spending – Nonpolicy Factors Account for Most State Differences (1992).

[69] A neurosurgeon at Sloan-Kettering, for example, recently took the wrong person's diagnostic films into the operating room, and began searching through the healthy part of his patient's brain. Another surgeon, in Long Beach, California, re-

panies have effectively argued that, because doctors do perform such an important role in our society, they should be held to a lesser degree of accountability. But when a person goes to a doctor, that patient is generally nervous or even scared about his health, and naive with respect to the treatment that may be required. That patient is relying on that doctor's skill and experience. That patient is relying on the doctor's professionalism and care. That patient, or his employer, or the government, is paying that doctor a lot of money. And that patient is placing his most valuable possession, his health, in that doctor's hands. There is a special relationship which develops between the doctor and his patient, consequently, a special trust. If anything, therefore, a doctor should be held to a higher standard of responsibility. Nevertheless, an exhaustive study conducted by Harvard Medical School concluded that less than 5% of all medical malpractice victims receive any type of compensation, and those who do wait an average of seven years to collect a single dime. This phenomenon is pervasive, not only in the area of medical malpractice insurance, but throughout the entire insurance industry. Auto insurers, for example, experienced five years of profits before beginning to pass any savings along to their customers. Even though such savings were attributed primarily to cautious driving among aging baby boomers, safer cars, an increase in seatbelt usage, and stricter enforcement of drunk driving laws, the auto insurers continue to complain about frivolous lawsuits

cently performed an operation which sought to remove Harry Jordan's cancerous kidney, but the doctor removed Mr. Jordan's healthy kidney instead. Alex Muro, from Pelham, Alabama, describes his experience as follows: "The doctors had told us my father had a bug and would be home in a couple of days. When I voiced concern about my father's worsening condition, the doctor took offense. He suggested we were subjecting him to 'intense scrutiny.' Two days later, I was asked to decide whether to 'no code' (not resuscitate) our father. According to the medical report, the 'only complication' during my father's final days was the conflict caused by 'one particular son' who persisted in 'second guessing' the care my father was given. Some of us do not sue doctors for failing to be gods. We sue them for failing to be human." Newsweek, April 22, 1996, p.18.

and the need for "no fault" insurance schemes. No-fault reforms, like reforms in the area of medical malpractice law, generate profits for the insurance companies, yet little or no savings to consumers in the form of premiums.

In 1989, for example, the majority of the ten states with the highest premiums were no-fault states, while seven of the ten states with the lowest premiums were not. In 1993, likewise, the average insurance premium in no-fault states was $792, while only $667 in states with traditional tort liability. In 1994, the premiums in no-fault states were an average of 15% higher than those with fault-based systems, while four of the five states with the highest insurance premiums were states which had adopted no-fault schemes.[70]

With respect to product liability litigation, the number of claims per dollar of product liability insurance premiums fell by almost 50% from 1984 to 1988 nationwide. As in the area of medical malpractice liability, the potential savings to be passed along to consumers is relatively insignificant, as the direct costs of all product liability litigation, including the costs of defense and loss prevention activities, accounts for less than 1% of retail sales. Nevertheless, and in any event, insurers have experienced significant gains. State Farm Fire & Casualty's total assets, for example, have increased by 28.1%, State Farm Mutual Auto Insurance Company's by 34.2%, and Allstate Insurance Company's by 42.7%, from 1989 to 1993, while *Forbes* has reported that CIGNA made $234 million, Progressive $267 million, and the Travelers $950 million, in 1993 alone. Property and casualty insurers, as a whole, experienced a 127% increase in total assets, (and

---

70 No-fault fails to address the number of accidents, serious injuries, and car thefts, which are among the principal factors in calculating auto insurance premiums, explains Amica's general counsel. "What people want is the same coverage for less money," noted New Jersey Republican Majority Leader Paul DeGaetano, "not less coverage for less money." See Howard Twiggs, "No-Fault Means No Choice and No Savings" Trial March 1997, p.9.

a 163% increase in policyholder surplus), between 1982 and 1991.[71] In 1995, property and casualty insurers experienced an 85% increase in profits, with a net income of more than $20 billion. Even if the insurance carriers, moreover, were to pass along this revenue to their customers, those businesses would then have to pass on their savings to the American public in the form of lower prices or greater jobs. But companies like IBM are not going to lower the prices of their computers with the money they save from lower insurance premiums; they're going to pay that out to stockholders in the form of higher dividends. Companies like McDonnell-Douglas and Boeing are not going to go out and hire a bunch of workers with the money they save on lawsuits; they are going to give raises to their directors and their executives.

While earnings are up dramatically and the stock market is at an all-time high, the average worker has seen nominal advances, while job loss and lay-offs are in record proportions. Exxon and Shell have replaced thousands of workers with computer-automated collection devices at the gas pumps, and companies like Ford and GM build factories in other countries, so that they can save money on labor, while taking American jobs.[72]The choice

71 Even after adjusting for inflation, the industry experienced a 61% increase in total assets and an 86% increase in policyholder surplus over that same period of time. The Fact Book: Property/Casualty Insurance Facts, Insurance Information Institute, pp.17-18 (1993).

72 In 1995, the Dow Jones rose 35.5%, the NYSE composite rose 31.3%, the S&P 500 rose 34.1%, and the NASDQ composite rose 39.9%, while the bond markets jumped by over 25% as well. At the same time, however, wages and benefits rose just 2.8%, the smallest increase since 1981. It was reported that 85,000 manufacturing jobs were lost in July 1995, while firms laid off 41,335 in October, which saw an additional loss of 10,000 jobs in the apparel industry. Mobil, which earned $523 million in the fourth quarter of 1994, cut 500 jobs in January, while ATT, which earned $2.82 billion during the first quarter of 1995 and whose stock was up 46.3% from its yearly low, cut 40,000 jobs in 1996. It was additionally reported that the Union Bank merger in California cost 850 jobs, that U.S. job losses were up by 43% in August, and that, in addition to the ATT job cuts, the Baby Bells had cut an additional 130,000 jobs since 1984, (plus 20,000 more by GTE), with an additional 50,000 projected for the next year. In all, despite the tremendous economic recovery, IBM has cut over 100,000 jobs, GM 74,000, Sears 50,000, and Digital 20,000, since 1993.

that legislators are making, therefore, is not a trade-off between consumer rights on the one hand, and lower prices or increased employment on the other. The choice that legislators are making, rather, is between the rights of the American people to due process, trial by jury, and access to the courts, versus the wealth of insurance companies and multinational corporations. The underlying design to such plans is kind of a "reverse Robin Hood" theory: Give to the rich, while taking from the injured and the poor.

Even assuming, however, that the savings of tort reform measures did "trickle down" to the American public, it would hardly be worth the price. If a doctor, for example, made $500,000 per year, and paid $50,000 annually in medical malpractice insurance premiums,[73] and with the passage of a Malpractice Act restricting the patients' rights to recover, the doctor's premiums were immediately reduced to $10,000,[74] then the doctor would need to make only $460,000 to maintain the same level of income. Assuming that all of these savings were passed on to the patient, then a procedure that now costs the patient a thousand dollars, would only cost the patient nine hundred and twenty; a one hundred dollar office visit would only cost the patient ninety-two dollars. And for 8% in savings, the doctor would be relieved of all accountability for the care that he or she provides to the patient, and the patient would lose all of his or her rights to any kind

---

73   Actually, the Harvard Study found that the average physician spends considerably less, (*i.e.* an average of only $15,000), on malpractice insurance premiums each year. For some specialists, however, such as anesthesiologists and obstetricians, the rates are considerably more. See Harvard Medical Practice Study, Patients, Doctors and Lawyers: Medical Injury, Malpractice Litigation, and Patient Compensation in New York (1990).

74   This, of course, would never happen. As shown above, the insurance companies maintain the same level of premiums, telling the doctors that the constitutionality of the measure has to be tested; that the measure could be repealed; that, despite the reforms, their claims have risen; or any other excuse they can think of to keep the doctors paying exorbitant malpractice insurance premiums.

of compensation if the doctor makes a mistake and the
patient is harmed.

The American government was established as a safeguard against tyranny. The tyranny of military force, the
tyranny of lords and barons, the tyranny of the king. But
the American people today face a different species of tyranny. Referring to the passage of the Sherman Anti-Trust
Act of 1890, Justice Harlan noted that: "The Nation had
been rid of human slavery – fortunately, as now we all
feel – but the conviction was universal that the country
was in real danger from another kind of slavery thought
to be fastened on the American people, namely, the slavery that would result from aggregations of capital in the
hands of a few individuals and corporations controlling,
for their own profit and advantage exclusively, the entire
business of the country, including the production and sale
of the necessaries of life. Such a danger was thought to
be then imminent, and all felt that it must be met firmly and by such statutory regulations as would adequately
protect the people against oppression and wrong."[75]Since
that time, however, statutes and regulations have become
the very tools by which a minority of individuals and
corporations have begun to deprive the people of their
fundamental safeguards against oppression and wrong.
The slavery which has resulted has become a tyranny of
lobbyists, a tyranny of insurance companies, a tyranny
of the corporation. In the early part of this century, for
example, states adopted Workers Compensation statutes,
by which the injured worker would be paid according to a
legislative scale depending upon the nature of his injury,
while the employer would be immune from liability in
tort. "It was an interesting spectacle" trial attorney Gerry
Spence once noted, "rock hard in their commitment to
the free-enterprise system, socializing, of all things, jus-

75 Standard Oil v. The United States, 221 U.S. 1, 83-84 (1910) (Harlan, J.,
concurring).

tice itself. Businessmen are not regulated to receive the same profits, nor is the sale of their products regulated to bring the same price; nothing else is regulated except justice for the worker. The employer could still sue anybody, for anything, for any amount. Only the workers were required to give up their right to sue their employer, no matter how gross the employer's negligence, and they would also have to agree to a uniform pittance for their injuries. True, employees would now be compensated even if the boss was not negligent or even if the employees were negligent themselves, but that was to concede little, for, in reality, what worker lays himself open to injury or death on the job except as the job requires?"[76]

These decisions, however, are legislative choices. They are policy decisions. Whether such measures are safe or unsafe, wasteful or cost-effective, good or bad. But before our legislators can begin to decide such political issues, there is first an issue of power, an issue of function, an issue of role. The first question in any measure of "reform" is a constitutional question, and if the proposal is unconstitutional, then neither Congress nor any of our state legislators have the right to make such policy decisions on behalf of the American public whom they were elected to serve.[77]

Our Federalism

Our Federal Government is a government of limited, enumerated powers. Article I of the Constitution outlines those few and defined subjects over which Congress exercises its jurisdiction, while all non-enumerated powers are reserved to the people, under the Ninth Amendment, or to the States, under the Tenth. The American system

---

76 Spence, With Justice for None, pp.69-70 (1989).

77 "If we are to keep our democracy, there must be one commandment: Thou shalt not ration justice." Learned Hand, Address to the Legal Aid Society of New York, Feb. 16, 1951.

thereby added an additional layer of protection to the traditional republican forms of government, by creating another series of checks and balances between the Federal Government and the States. This design, known as Federalism, was adopted to ensure the protection of individual rights and fundamental liberties.

For over two hundred years, the judicial bodies of the several states have been governed according to the exclusive jurisdiction of each state's procedural, remedial and evidentiary laws. In the past several years, however, Congress has begun to propose and to enact a plethora of measures which would have a preemptive effect upon the orderly administration of justice as defined and conducted by the states.

The Constitution gives Congress the power to "regulate Commerce with foreign Nations, and among the several States, and with the Indian Tribes." Congress, therefore, has the power to establish rules of trade, for example, pertaining to goods and services that are bought and sold across state lines. Congress has the power to establish unfair trade practice and consumer protection laws for those people and companies that purchase goods and services from other states by mail or by phone. Congress has the power to establish uniform laws of redhibition, or warranty. But a state court lawsuit between two parties is not the regulation of interstate commerce.[78]If Christopher Hanchey, for example, a citizen of Illinois, goes to see an attorney in Illinois, who commits legal malpractice, in Illinois, and Mr. Hanchey therefore brings a lawsuit against the attorney in an Illinois court of law, that legal action is not the regulation of interstate commerce.[79]Even

---

[78] Alexander Hamilton, for example, noted that the administration of private justice is better provided by local legislation, and "can never be the cares of a general jurisdiction." The Federalist Papers, No.17 (1788).

[79] In the context of employment disputes, likewise, the Supreme Court had once ruled that: "Much stress is put upon the evils which come from the struggle between employers and employees over the matter of wages working conditions, the

in a products liability lawsuit, where, for example, an automobile is manufactured in Michigan, sold in Oregon, and causes injury or death due to brake failure in California, the subject of the lawsuit may be associated with interstate commerce, but the procedural and evidentiary rules by which an injured party may recover against the car manufacturer is not the regulation of interstate commerce.[80]

Newt Gingrich's *Contract With America* insists that the states are better equipped to manage their own affairs than are the politicians in Washington, yet when it comes to the court system, the *Contract* takes the contrary position that Congressmen are better able to provide justice than are our local lawmakers and judges. The *Contract* insists that the regulation of business and industry is better maintained by local and state-wide legislative and administrative bodies, yet when it comes to civil justice, the *Contract* proposes a uniform set of regulations which

right of collective bargaining, etc., and it is insisted that interstate commerce is greatly affected thereby. The conclusive answer is that the evils are all local evils over which the Federal Government has no legislative control. The relation of employer and employee is a local relation. And the controversies and evils, which it is the object of the act to regulate and minimize, are local controversies and evils affecting local work undertaken to accomplish local results. Such effect as they may have upon commerce, however extensive it may be, is secondary and indirect. An increase in the greatness of the effect adds to its importance. It does not alter its character." Carter v. Carter Coal, 298 U.S. 238, 308-309 (1936). A year later, however, the Court was "packed" by F.D.R. and the import of this decision was effectively overruled. The Court established a new standard by which Congress was permitted to legislate all areas which, in the aggregate, have a "substantial affect" upon interstate commerce, and the Commerce Clause, for 50 years, became an ever-expanding stamp of approval for any and all action that Congress has deemed fit to take. See, for example, NLRB v. Jones & Laughlin Steel, 301 U.S. 1 (1937); United States v. Darby, 312 U.S. 100 (1941); Wickard v. Filburn, 317 U.S. 111 (1942). Recently, nevertheless, there has been an effort by the Supreme Court to protect States' rights, and to reign in such federalized power. See, for example: United States v. Lopez, 514 U.S. 549 (1995); Printz v. United States, 117 S.Ct. 2365 (1997).

80   "One cannot replace 'commerce' with a different type of enterprise, such as manufacturing. When a manufacturer produces a car, assembly cannot take place 'with a foreign nation' or 'with the Indian Tribes.' Parts may come from different States or other nations and hence may have been in the flow of commerce at one time, but manufacturing takes place at a discrete site. Agriculture and manufacturing involve the production of goods; commerce encompasses traffic in such articles." Justice Thomas, concurring, United States v. Lopez, 115 S.Ct. 1624, 1643 (1995).

emanate from Washington. The *Contract* seeks to limit the corporation's accountability to its shareholders, while at the same time making the government more accountable to corporations. The *Contract* limits the access of the average American to his or her court system to address wrongs at the hands of business enterprises, while expanding the access of those enterprises to challenge government regulation. Suits brought by average Americans, according to Gingrich and the Republicans, have become a national crisis which have to be curtailed, while corporations, on the other hand, may be trusted to decide for themselves whether suing the government in an attempt to sidestep lawful regulation is sound. If a defective product poses a danger to the public, that is a local matter, but when someone is injured by that product, and tries to hold the manufacturer accountable, it suddenly becomes a matter of national concern. All of these measures are ultimately designed to benefit corporations and other business interests, by insulating them from suit, and by allowing insurance companies to avoid millions of dollars in claims. Not only will this lead to more financial exploitation and personal injury at the expense of the American public, but it also infringes on the rights of states to provide adequate justice for their citizens, in violation of the Tenth Amendment, and contrary to the well-founded principles of Federalism.

Fundamental Rights

Even if Congress had the authority, under our Constitution, to make such legislative decisions on behalf of the American public, neither Congress nor any state legislature has the power to make any law which deprives the people of fundamental rights. Rights such as due process, trial by jury, and equal protection, are specifically enumerated in the Bill of Rights and in the Fourteenth

Amendment, but the Ninth Amendment makes it clear that there are fundamental rights which are not expressly enumerated, but which exist as a matter of Natural Law.[81]The United States Supreme Court has additionally recognized that the specific guarantees in the Bill of Rights have "penumbras" which emanate from such personal freedoms, and which give them the life and substance they require. In the context of our court system, the First Amendment's right to petition the government for redress, the Fifth Amendment's rights of due process of law and to just compensation, the Seventh Amendment's right to trial by jury, and the Fourteenth Amendment's rights to due process and equal protection, create a penumbra of fundamental rights on behalf of each citizen to seek justice in a court of law.

Access to the Courts

From the time of *Magna Carta,* the laws of England embodied the principle that all of the King's subjects, "for injury done to him by any other subject, may take his remedy by the course of law, and have justice and a right for the injury done him, freely without sale, fully and without any denial, and speedily without delay."[82]

81 The Ninth Amendment provides that: "The enumeration in the Constitution of certain rights, shall not be construed to deny or disparage others retained by the people."

82 See Blackstone, Commentaries on the Laws of England, Vol. I, p.137 (1765). Locke, in fact, believed that the right of reparation was an inalienable right, guaranteed by Natural Law: "The state of nature has a law of nature to govern it" he wrote, "which obliges everyone. And reason, which is that law, teaches all mankind who will but consult in that, being all equal and independent, no one ought to harm another in his life, health, liberty, or possessions. Besides the crime which consists in violating the law, there is commonly an injury done to some person or other, and some other man receives damage by his transgression, in which case he who hath received any damage has besides the right of punishment common to him with other men, a particular right to seek reparation from him that has done it. And any other person who finds it just may also join with him that is injured, and assist him in recovering from the offender so much as may make satisfaction for the harm he has suffered. From these two distinct rights, the one of punishing the crime for restraint, and preventing the like offense, which right of punishing is in everybody; the other of taking reparation, which belongs only to the injured party, comes it to pass to the magistrate, who

In our country, the right of open access to the courts is basic to our system of government, and one of the fundamental rights protected by the Constitution. The First Amendment provides that Congress shall make no law abridging the right of the people "to petition the Government for a redress of grievances" and the constitutions of several states have specific provisions that address the right of open access to the courts.[83] The United States Supreme Court has recognized that "the right to sue and defend in the courts is the alternative of force. In an organized society it is the right conservative of all other rights, and lies at the foundation of orderly government."[84]For many groups, in fact, litigation is not merely a technique for resolving private differences, but a method of holding the government accountable. In this sense, the right of access to the courts is a form of political expression. The dispossessed and disenfranchised, who are unable to achieve their objectives through election ballots, must often turn to the court system, which is the only avenue available to petition the government for the redress of harms.

The right of access to the courts is additionally rooted in the Constitution's guaranty that no person shall be deprived of life, liberty, or property, without due process of law. "Perhaps no characteristic of an organized and cohesive society," wrote Justice Harlan, "is more fundamental than its erection and enforcement of a system of

---

by being magistrate hath the common right of punishing put into his hands, can often, where the public good demands not the execution of the law, remit the punishment of criminal offenses by his own authority, but yet cannot remit the satisfaction due to any private man for the damage he has received." Locke, Second Treatise on Government, Chapter II, §§6,10-11 (1681).

83 In Pennsylvania, for example, Article I, Section 11 of the Constitution provides that: "All courts shall be open; and every man, for injury to him in his land, goods, person, or reputation, shall have remedy by due course of law, and right to justice administered without sale, denial, or delay." See also, for example: Ohio Const. Art. I, §16; N.H. Const. Pt. I, Art. 14; R.I. Const. Art. I, §5; Va. Const. Art. III, §17.

84 Chambers v. Baltimore & Ohio Railroad, 207 U.S. 142, 148 (1907).

rules defining the various rights and duties of its members, enabling them to govern their affairs and definitively settle their differences in an orderly, predictable manner. Without such a 'legal system' social organization and cohesion are virtually impossible; with the ability to seek regularized resolution of conflicts individuals are capable of interdependent action that enables them to strive for achievements without the anxieties that would beset them in a disorganized society. It is to courts, or other quasi-judicial official bodies, that we ultimately look for the implementation of a regularized, orderly process of dispute settlement. Within this framework, those who wrote our original Constitution, in the Fifth Amendment, and later those who drafted the Fourteenth Amendment, recognized the centrality of the concept of due process in the operation of this system. Without this guarantee that one may not be deprived of his rights, neither liberty nor property, without due process of law, the State's monopoly over techniques for binding conflict resolution could hardly be said to be acceptable under our scheme of things. Only by providing that the social enforcement mechanism must function strictly within these bounds can we hope to maintain an ordered society that is also just."[85]When someone believes that he or she has been wronged at the hands of another, the natural reaction is anger. But if society's members spend all of their time engaged in acts of vengeance and retribution, observed Judge Miriam Waltzer, they will have neither the time nor the motivation to acquire or to create knowledge, or things. If every time man A creates a new item, for example, man B steals it, pretty soon man A will stop working to create the item and start trying to get even with man B. This will lead to a new cycle of ever-increasing violence and retribution, causing society to lose man A's knowl-

---

85 Boddie v. Connecticut, 401 U.S. 371, 374-375 (1971).

edge of creation, as well as the items he had begun to make. The removal of revenge from the hands of angry persons, therefore, is one of the major purposes of the judiciary. "If the members of our society do not believe that the wrongs which they may suffer are righted by our judicial process, then they take revenge into their own hands in their own time, place, and manner, and a functioning society ceases to exist."[86]

The Right to Trial by Jury

At the foundation of any democratic society is the fundamental belief that people are good, that people are honest, that people are intelligent, and that people can and should therefore be trusted to govern themselves. In a republican government, such as our own, the affairs of state are governed by those who we elect as our representatives, yet in our own communities, democracy is preserved in the form of the jury trial, for the resolution of our common and daily affairs.[87]

When twelve members of our society are chosen at random to decide the facts of a case, that jury has a collective intelligence of nearly five hundred years. They bring twelve different sets of knowledge and life experiences, twelve different canons of technical and professional skills, twelve different points of view. Their passions and their prejudices will be tempered by common deliberation, while the beliefs and morays of the community will be reflected in the body they compose. The

---

86   Jones v. City of New Orleans, No. 94-0172 (La. App. 4th Cir. Dec. 15, 1994).

87   "We of the United States think experience has proved it safer for the mass of individuals composing society to reserve to themselves personally the exercise of all rightful powers to which they are competent. Hence, with us, people being competent to judge of the facts occurring in ordinary life have retained the functions of judges of facts under the name of jurors. I believe that action by the citizens in person, in affairs within their reach and competence, and in all others by representatives chosen immediately and removable by themselves, constitutes the essence of a Republic." Thomas Jefferson, Letter to Pierre S. DuPont, April 4, 1816.

jury members do not know the parties, nor the attorneys involved, nor do they have any political or personal interests in the outcome of the case. A judge's appreciation of the evidence, on the other hand, will be limited by his or her own life experience and beliefs. The judge will often know the lawyers, and even the litigants involved. Judges who are elected naturally feel indebted to those who have supported them, and are ultimately answerable to the public, whose uneducated view of the case may demand an unjust or improper result. Appointed judges are likewise indebted to those who have helped them attain their positions, and must be ever-mindful of the political forces that have the power to see them promoted (or not promoted) to a higher court. Even if only subconsciously, the judge will be influenced by his own passions and prejudices, which will not be tempered by eleven other jury members, and may be unduly swayed by his or her own personal interest in the outcome, political motivations, or social and economic beliefs. From the time our Constitution was founded, therefore, it was believed that the jury system embodied the most direct and most noble form of democracy, more essential even than the right to vote. Men like Madison and Jefferson believed that trial by jury was fundamental to the security of liberty for the people, and the only anchor by which a government could be held to the principles of its constitution.[88] In today's so-

---

88 "Trial by jury in civil cases is as essential to secure the liberty of the people as any one of the pre-existing rights of nature." James Madison, In Defense of Trial by Jury, Vol. I, p. 8 (1789).

"I consider trial by jury as the only anchor ever yet imagined by man, by which a government can be held to the principles of its constitution." Thomas Jefferson, The Writings of Thomas Jefferson (1788).

"The friends and adversaries of the plan of the convention, if they agree in nothing else, concur at least in the value they set upon the trial by jury; or if there is any difference between them it consists in this; that the former regard it as a valuable safeguard to liberty; the latter represent it as the very palladium of a free government." Alexander Hamilton, The Federalist Papers, No. 83 (1788).

ciety, the only instances where a person's vote has a direct and truly democratic bearing on the outcome of a public issue are local referenda, constitutional amendments, and a jury's decision with regard to the facts of a case. To change legislation, the public must vote for people whom they have never met, based on fifteen-second television commercials and thirty-second radio spots, or possibly an occasional debate. Once elected, the legislators, who have been elected for thousands of different reasons by thousands of different people, must propose or be presented with the desired legislation, and properly motivated to vote the way the public wants, despite lobbying efforts, campaign contributions, party alliances, pork-barrel projects, promises of votes on other issues, and the personal or political objectives of the legislator.

In a courtroom, on the other hand, the jury is introduced to the parties involved, presented with evidence that forms the factual basis of the lawsuit, educated as to the scientific and technical aspects of the dispute, and then creates, by direct vote, the specific law of the case. In the absence of a jury system, these laws will be

"The jury system has come to stand for all we mean by English justice, because so long as a case has to be scrutinized by twelve honest men, defendant and plaintiff alike have a safeguard from arbitrary perversion of the law." Winston Churchill, A History of English Speaking Peoples, Vol. I, pp.218-19 (1956).

"Maintenance of the jury as a fact-finding body is of such importance and occupies such a firm place in our history and jurisprudence that any seeming curtailment of the right to a jury trial should be scrutinized with utmost care." Dimick v. Schiedt, 293 U.S. 474, 486 (1935).

"We are good friends of the jury trial. We believe in it as the best system of trial ever invented for a free people in the world's history. In spite of all suggestions to substitute a trained judge of fact, the system of trying facts by a regular judicial official, known beforehand and therefore subject to the arts of corruption and chicanery, would be fatal to our system of justice. The grand solid merit of the jury trial is that the jurors of fact are selected at the last moment from the multitude of citizens. They cannot be known beforehand, and they melt back into the multitude after each trial." John Wigmore, To Ruin Jury Trial in the Federal Courts 19 Ill. L. Rev. 98 (1924).

"Trial by jury" Wigmore continued, "must and shall be preserved! Amidst the throng of cruel sacreligisms that assail us nowadays in the legal sanctuary, none is more dangerous, than the proposal to abolish trial by jury."

made by legislators and judges, scientists and business executives, panels of experts and anonymous bureaucrats. They will be influenced by lobbyists, lawmakers, and campaign contributions; by party alliances, business alliances, and professional alliances; and by the social, economic, and political interests at stake.

Critics of the jury system allege that juries cannot be trusted to sift through convoluted evidence to arrive at a decision which is both reasonable and just. But whom can we trust, if not ourselves, to make such decisions?

In the Karen Silkwood case, for example, a nuclear energy company was contaminating its workers with plutonium. Ms. Silkwood was concerned about the effects of such contamination, and had discovered that photomicrographs had been touched up by the company to conceal defects in the welds of fuel rods, which had been constructed for an experimental "breeder reactor" that was designed to manufacture plutonium. Ms. Silkwood went to the *New York Times* with such information, but her Honda was run off the road and into a ditch, where she died. The jury awarded Silkwood's family over $10 million in compensatory and punitive damages,[89] but the court of appeal reversed, finding that the jury's verdict was preempted by the exclusive jurisdiction of the Nuclear Regulatory Commission – an agency composed of anonymous bureaucrats, who are neither elected by nor accountable to the public, and which had repeatedly refused to enforce its own rules and regulations for the benefit of the American people. Silkwood's attorney, who was ultimately successful in overturning the court of appeal decision and having the verdict reinstated, was faced with numerous questions about whether juries can be trusted to regulate such a sophisticated and perilous endeavor as nuclear energy. "If the judges won't trust the jury" he responded, "would

---

89 This was just 0.5% of Kerr-McGee's annual two billion dollar income.

they rather trust Kerr-McGee? Or how about the Nuclear
Regulatory Commission, which has habitually betrayed
its trust to the American people? Should we trust the bureaucracy one more time, but distrust our own citizens? It
is not that juries occasionally go wrong. It is that judges
too frequently reveal the haughty conceit that has surely
done us in – the idea that judges are wise but that ordinary people are not, that judges know, but that the people
do not."[90]People should not have to depend on politicians
to protect their property rights and fundamental liberties.
People should not have to depend on the FDA to reject all
of the drugs that may be harmful or dangerous, nor upon
the EPA to determine whether a chemical company is dis-
charging hazardous wastes. People should not have to depend on the attorney generals to find and to prosecute all
unfair trade practices and anti-trust violations, nor upon a
group of bank executives to determine whether customers have been defrauded by lending institutions. People
should not have to depend on lawyers to decide whether
an attorney has mishandled a lawsuit, nor upon doctors to
determine whether a physician is guilty of malpractice.
People should not have to depend on corporate directors
to decide whether they have engaged in activities that
are potentially harmful to the public, nor upon manufacturers to decide whether they have marketed goods and
services that are potentially unsafe.[91]Trial by jury is not
only the fundamental right of every plaintiff and every
defendant to have a decision which is reasoned, impartial,
and just, but it is also the right of the American public to

90 Spence, With Justice for None, p.81 (1989).

91 "All power tends to develop into a government in itself. Power that controls the economy should be in the hands of elected representatives of the people,
not an industrial oligarchy. Industrial power should be decentralized. It should be
scattered into many different hands so that the fortunes of people will not be dependent on the whim or caprice, the political prejudices, the emotional stability of a few
self-appointed men." Justice Douglas, dissenting, in United States v. Columbia Steel
Co., 334 U.S. 495, 536 (1948).

participate in the administration of justice, to be a part of their government, and to represent the community in a way that no judge, nor congressman, nor executive, nor administrative official, nor panel of experts, can.[92] "The sacred privilege of trial by jury" as one author put it, "is the unadulterated voice of the people which should be heard in the sanctuaries of justice as fountains springing fresh from the laps of the earth."[93]

Equal Protection

The guarantee of equal protection is axiomatic to any republican system of government designed to protect individual freedoms by the separation of powers among several different bodies which govern one another through a series of checks and balances. In such a system, courts do not generally interfere with the legislative process. When presented with a law that is either challenged or sought to be enforced, the courts will generally give deference to the legislative decisions of Congress and the States, because weighing competing political, economic and societal interests in order to formulate a policy or rule of law is the function of legislative, not judicial, bodies. If the legislative branch makes a law which is inefficient, impractical, or unwise, the electorate has the power to voice objection, forcing their representatives to go back and draft the law correctly, or vote them out of office. The courts, therefore, do not invalidate "bad" laws, but only those laws which either threaten constitutionally protected freedoms, or are not subject to the political check.[94]The people, acting

---

92 "Juries, above all civil juries, help every citizen to share something of the deliberations that go on in the judge's mind; and it is these very deliberations which best prepare the people to be free." Alexis de Tocqueville, Democracy in America (1840).

93 Henry Hallam, The Constitutional History of England (1827).

94 If, for example, Massachusetts were to prohibit Vermont maple syrup from being sold in Boston, that law is not subject to the political check, because the residents of Vermont, whom the law effects, have no political influence over Massachu-

through their representatives, generally have the right to determine that the benefits of a given proposal outweigh the costs, so long as those costs are distributed equally over society at large. The courts, in this instance, will not invalidate the provision, even if it turns out to be a "bad bargain", because the majority can always come back and have the measure revoked or changed. What the people cannot do, however, is accept various benefits, at the expense of a limited group of individuals, because that proposal is bound to be a bad bargain for the minority, who are powerless to effectuate political change.[95] The guarantee of equal protection, in this way, is closely related to the takings clause, which prevents the majority from taking or expropriating the property rights of individuals, without paying just compensation.[96] It works like a constitutionally issued license, which allows the courts to step in and nullify rules of law which would otherwise be left to the legislative prerogative. In the context of "tort reform", those measures, on their face, appear to affect everyone equally, because everyone is ostensibly giving up his or her right to just compensation, in exchange for the promise of reduced insurance premiums, lower prices, and increased jobs. But actually, in a true sense, the

setts lawmakers, because they don't vote in Massachusetts elections. These kinds of laws are therefore invalidated by the courts under what has come to be known as the "Dormant Commerce Clause". See generally: Philadelphia v. New Jersey, 437 U.S. 617 (1978).

95 This is why affirmative action programs do not require the same level of judicial scrutiny as laws which discriminate against minorities. In the former case, the majority can always come back and say we were wrong, this isn't working, this isn't fair, and the program will be abolished or changed. What the majority cannot do, however, is say we are going to accept these advantages at the expense of greeks, or at the expense of blacks, or at the expense of japanese, and if you don't like it, there's not a damn thing you can do about it. Absent equal protection, there is the potential for a tyranny of the majority, whereby the racial, ethnic, or religious minority, is at the mercy of the majority, because the minority alone does not have the votes to bring about political change.

96 " The Fifth Amendment's guarantee that private property shall not be taken for a public use without just compensation was designed to bar the Government from forcing some people alone to bear public burdens which, in all justice and fairness, should be borne by the public as a whole." Armstrong v. U.S., 364 U.S. 40, 49 (1960).

majority is accepting the promise of reduced insurance premiums, lower prices, and increased jobs, at the sole expense of that minority of innocent victims who have been wronged at the hands of another, and have lost their right to sue. Because few people see themselves as the future victims of fraud or injury, while everyone, by contrast, perceives the realities of unemployment, the purchase of goods and services, and the expense of insurance premiums, in a *de facto* sense, there is no political check. Even though tort reform is undoubtedly a "bad bargain" for anyone who is injured or defrauded at the hands of another, there's really nothing they can do about it, because they will always be in the minority, and the legislative process will therefore be unresponsive to their pleas.[97]

If there were, in fact, a medical malpractice insurance crisis, and if that crisis could, in fact, be solved by limiting recoverable damages to $250,000 and by enacting a three-year peremptive period or statute of repose,[98] then the burden of those remedial measures would fall exclusively and entirely on those few innocent victims of mal-

---

[97] There are many legislative measures that apply to everyone, on their face, but in a *de facto* sense, only effect certain minority segments of the population. Criminal laws, for example, apply to everyone, but only ultimately effect people that commit murder, or theft. Commercial fishing regulations apply to everyone, but only effect commercial fishermen. Patent laws apply to everyone, but only effect people and corporations who invent things. These provisions, however, generally involve an element of choice on the part of the individuals or groups who bear the costs and the burdens they impose. Criminals choose to kill or to steal things, commercial fishermen choose to earn a living by fishing, and inventors are seeking to profit by the protections that a patent provides. No one, on the other hand, chooses to be the victim of medical malpractice. No one chooses to be the victim of an explosion. No one chooses to be the victim of deception or fraud. Just like no one chooses to be black. No one chooses to be jewish. No one chooses to be a woman or man. In this sense, the victim of social or personal wrongdoing is analogous to the member of a minority ethnic group, or race, or religion. The guarantee of equal protection for tort victims, therefore, should be no less vigilantly guarded or ensured.

[98] Under a prescriptive period, or statute of limitations, the plaintiff is given a certain time period in which suit must be filed; however, that period is suspended if the plaintiff does not know, and could not reasonably know that he has a cause of action. With a peremptive period, on the other hand, or statute of repose, the established time period is absolute; and therefore a person's cause of action can be extinguished before he or she is ever aware that it exists.

practice who are so severely injured that their recoverable damages would have been greater than $250,000, and by those who have been injured in such a way that the results of medical malpractice do not manifest themselves within three years. In 1980, for example, Lorraine Whitnell went to a urologist with a bladder condition. Over the course of her treatment, the urologist performed a biopsy, which revealed evidence of cancer. For the next four years, Mrs. Whitnell suffered from continuing bladder pains, which she believed to be part of a recurring infection. During this time, she was never informed by her doctor of the biopsy results, nor did he perform any follow-up tests or procedures to rule out or to eliminate the cancer. Unsatisfied with her treatment, Mrs. Whitnell went to a new doctor, who informed her that a tumor had developed in her bladder and that immediate surgery would be required. The next day, he removed Mrs. Whitnell's bladder and her appendix, as well as all of her reproductive organs, leaving her permanently disabled, and in constant fear that the cancer would return. Because her state's Medical Malpractice Act extinguishes the plaintiff's cause of action after three years, without exception, Mrs. Whitnell was deprived of any right to go to the courts and seek redress for her injuries, even before she ever knew that she had any reason to sue. Such measures are not only inequitable with respect to all tort victims, but result in further discrimination among the tort victims themselves. When legislators seek to cut the costs of insurance by placing limits on recoverable damages, those who are injured less severely are entitled to full recovery, while those who suffer from catastrophic losses bear the entire burden of the reform.[99] When legislators seek to make insurance

---

99 The Supreme Court of New Hampshire, for example, has recognized that: "It is simply unfair and unreasonable to impossible burden of supporting the medical care industry solely upon those persons who are most severely injured and therefore most in need of compensation." Carson v. Maurer, 424 A.2d 825, 837 (N.H. 1980).

claims more predictable by placing absolute restrictions on the time periods in which a suit may be filed, those people who suffer from deafness or amputated limbs are entitled to recovery, while others such as Mrs. Whitnell who develop bladder cancer or AIDs over a number of years have no right to seek justice in a court of law.[100]The fundamental rights of the American people are being held hostage by insurance companies and multinational corporations. Justice has become subordinate to economic interests, while property rights and individual freedoms have been sacrificed on the altars of political favoritism and corporate greed. If our lawmakers cannot be trusted to protect our rights from the social and economic parasites who will stop at nothing in order to accumulate wealth and to avoid accountability, then our courts must ensure that the costs and the burdens of maintaining such wealth in the hands of corporate America do not fall exclusively on the shoulders of those people among us who have been injured and wronged.[101]

---

[100]   It is interesting to note, in this regard, that the most common form of malpractice occurs when doctors fail to diagnose breast cancer. There have been around 2,450 reported cases of such failure to diagnose since 1985. The most common occurrences arise when a woman has detected a lump through self-examination, but that physical finding is overlooked or ignored by the physician, where the doctor either fails to detect the lump himself, or assumes, perhaps because of the woman's age, that it is benign. In such cases, the doctor is supposed to insist on re-examination within two months, while some may even order a mammogram, just to be safe. The failure to follow-up physical examinations or inconclusive mammogram was found to be present in over 30% of the cases.

[101]   "Therefore" wrote Aristotle, "this kind of injustice being an inequality, the judge tries to equalize it This is why, when people dispute, they take refuge in the judge; and to go to the judge is to go to justice. Justice is that in virtue of which the just man is said to be a doer, by choice, of that which is just, and one who will distribute either between himself and another or between two others not so as to give more of what is desirable to himself and less to his neighbor, (and conversely with what is harmful), but so as to give what is equal in accordance with proportion; and similarly in distributing between two other persons. Injustice on the other hand is similarly related to the unjust, which is excess and defect, contrary to proportion, of the useful or hurtful. In the unjust act to have too little is to be unjustly treated; to have too much is to act unjustly." Nicomachean Ethics, Book V, Chapters 4-5.

Clear and Present Danger

The most valuable of all natural resources is the idea. Ideas are commodities in the marketplace, building blocks in the world of science, and the lifeblood of human emotion that feeds our intellect and forms the bread of our daily lives. And this country, more than anything else, has been a nation of ideas. From the genius of its Constitution, to the wealth of its culture, to the invention of the computer, the television, the telephone, the airplane, the light-bulb, and the automobile. Though misguided at times, America at its heart has always attempted to survive as a nation of rights, not might, of reason, not power, of laws, not men.

To that end, the First Amendment has always held a special place in the unfolding of America, where people continue to believe that the free exposition of ideas is the essence of capitalism, the foundation of democracy, and the first right of man under Natural Law.

People have an absolute right to think, to feel, to imagine, to doubt, to challenge, to believe, and to experience any and every idea or emotion capable to them. This right is singular, and stands alone, where the individual is sovereign, and is not subject to the common laws of men.

While some may fear the harm that can at times arise from hateful, violent, sexual thoughts and images which go unchecked, those very symbols, messages and sounds are capable of evoking anger, and disgust, and counter-reasoning, which stir men to act, and which are necessary to the dialectic of human progression. Such fantasies, moreover, give men and women a spiritual outlet for their passions, emotions, and frustrations, which are better unleashed in the world of books and motion pictures than upon our fellow man.

The democratic ideal itself compels an unfettered distribution of information, while placing implicit faith in the common intelligence of the individual to determine what is good, what is right, what is necessary, and what, on the other hand, can be tossed aside. At the same time, we place faith in the force of ideas themselves, with the quiet belief that truth, in the end, will be victorious over falsehood, that good will vanquish evil, and that right will conquer wrong. For these reasons, and for reasons beyond expression, we should be eternally vigilant against attempts to suppress the communication of images and ideas, even (and especially) those that we come to loathe.

The Absolute

The absolute right of people to think, to feel, to imagine, to doubt, to challenge, to believe, and to experience any and every idea or emotion capable to them begins with a division of the human universe into two physical and metaphysical worlds. In the physical world, men and women have the right, as a community, to restrain and enjoin others for the protection of person and property. In the metaphysical world, on the other hand, the individual alone is sovereign, and beyond the reach of society's laws.[102]

---

102   "The sole end for which mankind are warranted, individually or collectively, in interfering with liberty of action of any of their number is self-protection. That is the only purpose for which power can be rightfully exercised over any member of a civilized community, against his will, is to prevent harm to others. His own good, either physical or moral, is not a sufficient warrant. He cannot rightfully

The necessity of society to protect itself from violence, slander, harassment and other intrusions into one's person and property, therefore, must be directed at such physical and actual intrusions, and does not in any way justify the censorship or prohibition of thoughts and emotions which give life to the world of ideas.[103]Despite the fact, in this regard, that some images and sounds will undoubtedly have a real, and actual, and proximate causal relationship to physical acts of violence, which cannot be justified, in a utilitarian sense, by the societal worth or value of the expression, the issue, however, is not a question of social utility, but a question of the power and authority of a society to subject something which is intangible, and sacred, and personal, to such legislative scrutiny. Even assuming, therefore, that in weighing the positive and adverse ef-

be compelled to do or forbear because it will be better for him to do so, because it will make him happier, because, in the opinions of others, to do so would be wise, or even right. These are good reasons for remonstrating with him, or reasoning with him, or persuading with him, or entreating him, but not for compelling him, or visiting him with any evil in case he do otherwise. To justify that, the conduct from which it is desired to deter him, must be calculated to do evil to someone else. The only part of the conduct of any one, for which he is amenable to society, is that which concerns others. In the part which merely concerns himself, his independence is, of right, absolute. Over himself, over his own body and mind, the individual is sovereign." John Stuart Mill, On Liberty (1859).

103   The United States Supreme Court, regrettably, did not take this approach in *Osborne v. Ohio,* when it held that the government has the right to make criminal the mere possession of child pornography. In this context, the physical conduct from which society seeks protection is the sexual exploitation of children, which, as noted by the dissenting justices, can be combated in other ways. The producers of such pornography, for example, can be prosecuted for kidnaping, sexual exploitation, solicitation, and in some cases, sexual assault. The molestation of children, by the same token, (which is allegedly promoted and encouraged by the consumption of such pornography), is made criminal by child molestation laws, statutory rape provisions, sexual assault, and in some cases kidnaping and aggravated rape. But, because the mere possession of offensive materials is something which in and of itself poses no potential danger or harm to society, such conduct cannot form the substance of a crime. "The Court today" notes the dissenters, "is so disquieted by the possible exploitation of children in the production of the pornography that it is willing to tolerate the imposition of criminal penalties for simple possession." Then, quoting Justice Marshall, from *Stanley v. Georgia,* the dissenting judges remind us that, "if the First Amendment means anything, it means that the State has no business telling a man, sitting alone in his own house, what books he may read or what films he may watch." Justice Brennan, joined by Justice Marshall and Justice Stevens, dissenting, Osborne v. Ohio, 495 U.S. 103, 139-145 (1990).

fects of certain forms of expression (and that such positive and negative consequences can be reliably weighed) there will be some expression whose value is ultimately outweighed by its potential for danger, the government is nevertheless without right to intrude upon something which belongs to the individual, as sovereign, and beyond the laws of men.[104]

Even assuming, for example, that the broadcast of *Beavis and Butthead* or *The Terminator* will have the effect of promoting cruelty and indifference generally, and, in some cases, specific acts of destruction and physical harm, the right of the average person sitting quietly in his or her own living room to view, and to ponder, and to react to such images and ideas, is absolute, such that any incidental harms which may befall person or property are secondary, and must be endured.[105] As a practical matter,

[104]   From a constitutional perspective, it can be said that society, in adopting the First Amendment, has already made a cost/benefit analysis, and determined that the benefits of free expression are so great, they will automatically outweigh any harm which may result, no matter what the cost. As noted by the Supreme Court in *Virginia Board,* "the choice between the dangers of suppressing information and the dangers of misuse if it is freely available is not our choice to make." Virginia Board v. Virginia Citizens, 425 U.S. 748, 770 (1976).

[105]   In 1993, a five year-old boy in Ohio killed his two year-old sister when he set the family mobile home on fire imitating the cartoon characters Beavis and Butt-head. While many argued that the television program should be banned from the airwaves, others wondered why the child was not being supervised by his parents, or some other responsible party, who should have prevented him from starting the fire, or from watching the show. Supporters of the television sitcom additionally attempted to justify the program as a source of legitimate social commentary. The cartoon figures, they note, "are not just any losers, they are our losers; totems of an age of decline and non-achievement. One in five people who graduated college between 1984 and 1990 holds a job that doesn't require a college education. If this is not a hard economic reality for a whole generation, it is psychological reality." Fernanda Moore added that a show like *Beavis and Butthead* is not directed at stupid people, (who are more likely to imitate the cartoon figures), but people who are intelligent enough to appreciate the show on a different level. See Leland, "Battle for Your Brain" Newsweek, Oct. 11, 1993, pp.50-51. While *Beavis and Butthead,* in sum, is probably a legitimate source of social commentary which can be appreciated on many levels, it is hard to say that its social utility, or the utility of any television program, is worth the life of a two year-old child. Such a balancing of interests, however, cannot be left to the scrutiny of politicians, or judges, or even juries. We, as a society, have already determined that, for the sake of the individual, and his right to think and to feel and to imagine, such tragedies, while unfortunate, must be endured.

moreover, the harmful effects of the information will generally be outweighed by the benefits involved. The backlash to outrageous expression, most often, will be greater than the provocation, and censure will be more prevalent than imitation. Apathy, cruelty and indifference, in this way, will be offset by empathy, sympathy and charity, as the thoughts and images which may, in some, give rise to sexual and violent energy, in others will produce reaction and counter-reasoning, disgust and offense, anger and disdain.[106] Emotionally, such expression will stir just and good men to action, while providing conflicted hearts with an outlet for their doubts and frustrations, which are better left to internal conflict and fantasy than to the physical world of men.[107] Intellectually, at the same time, such challenges to the *status quo* will cause one to search for new answers and justifications, forming the dialectic of human progression.

The Dialectic

Since the time of the ancient Greek philosophers, men and women have engaged in a series of dialectics as a means for arriving at truth. Through this process, a hypothesis is suggested, and then challenged, and so on, until the hypothesis, or some later refinement, alternate, or contrary hypothesis, is proven to be true or disproved. This, in many ways, is the method by which science, technology, and knowledge itself evolves: thesis, antithesis, synthesis, and so on.[108] Without antithesis, there can be no

106   "A principal function of free speech under our system of government is to invite dispute. It may indeed best serve its high purpose when it induces a condition of unrest, creates dissatisfaction with conditions as they are, or even stirs people to anger." Terminello v. Chicago, 337 U.S. 1, 4 (1949).

107   "The secret thoughts of a man" observed Hobbes, "run over all things, holy, profane, clean, obscene, grave, and light, without shame or blame." Leviathan Part I, Ch. 8 (1651).

108   "The problem 'What is dialectic?' is ancient and complex; this question, which has been a concern of philosophy from the time of Plato, reaches its greatest urgency in Hegel, since it constitutes the core of his system. Hegel's dialectic

synthesis. And the suppression, therefore, of thoughts and ideas which challenge our commonly accepted notions of truth and decency, may, in fact, be an impediment to what lies beyond.[109]There are wonderful lessons to be learned, in this context, through negative examples: learning what not to do, learning from mistakes. Negative examples, in fact, are of particular value in the area of moral development and religious education, where stories and images of cruelty and injustice are often effective tools in the incitement of anger, disgust, and shame.[110]Finally, it is important that people be allowed to experience pain, death and injustice in the metaphysical world (of fantasy and imagination, of books and records, music and art, television and computers), so that we can better understand and appreciate the beauty of our own physical worlds. The Romantic poets, in this regard, often spoke in terms of paradoxes, where people come to appreciate innocence through experience, life through death, and happiness through sorrow and pain. There is no peace without war, they believed, no good without evil, Innocence without Experience, Heaven without Hell. The passion and energy of life is sustained, in this manner, by conflicting

is a ternary structure, in which *thesis* is opposed by the *antithesis* and both are united in the *synthesis*. The synthesis, however, is not a mere *conciliation;* rather, the thesis leads necessarily to the antithesis, and vice versa, and this *movement of being* leads inexorably to the synthesis, in which the thesis and the antithesis are preserved and superseded – *aufgehoben.* Each stage finds its *truth* in the one that follows." Julian Marias, The History of Philosophy, pp.320-321 (1967).

109   "Men feared witches and burnt women. It is the function of speech to free men from the bondage of irrational fears." Justice Louis Brandeis, joined by Oliver Wendell Holmes, concurring, Whitney v. California, 274 U.S. 357, 376 (1927).

110The motion picture *Roots,* for example, may generate a stronger resolve to achieve racial justice and equality than a television sitcom such as *The Cosby Show,* which attempts to, by way of example, portray the races allied in friendship and cooperation. *Platoon* and *Full Metal Jacket,* by the same token, may serve as more powerful and forceful advocates for peace than films such as *Woodstock,* which attempt to portray man and nature in harmony and at one. *The Holocaust* and *Schindler's List,* in this regard, might stir anti-Semitism in a minority of viewers, but will likely cause most people to feel that an intolerable wrong has been committed, and fortify their resolve to see that it never happens again.

and competing ideas and emotions, which alone may be harmful, but in the aggregate, make human existence exciting, intelligent, religious, and ultimately meaningful.[111]

While the temptation, therefore, to protect ourselves and each other from ideas which seem dangerous is often compelling, a world without images and ideas which some may find offensive, distasteful, or even harmful, will ultimately become stagnant, lifeless, and stale.

Information as a Commodity

The free flow of information is essential to the democratic process, and to the success of a free market economy. The people, as the ultimate source of power in a democratic society, must have full and accurate information about the political, social, and economic issues and events in order to make reliable and well-informed decisions about the governance of the state. If, moreover, the government, which is made up of people who are regulated by the public through the political process, has the power to restrict the flow of information about itself, the government and those in government can effectively avoid all accountability for their actions, whether improper, imprudent, or wrong.[112]The economy, likewise, is

111 "What though the radiance was once so bright
    Be now forever taken from my sight,
Though nothing can bring back the hour
    Of splendour in the grass, of glory in the flower;
We will grieve not, rather find
Strength in what remains behind;
In the primal sympathy
Which having been must ever be;
In the soothing thoughts that spring
Out of human suffering;
In the faith that looks through death,
    In years that bring the philosophic mind."
- William Wordsworth, The Immortality Ode (1802-1804).

112 "To persuade others to his own point of view, the pleader, as we know, at times resorts to exaggeration, to vilification of men who have been, or are, prominent in church and state, or even false statement. But the people of this nation have ordained in light of history, that, in spite of the probability of excesses and abuses, these liberties are, in the long view, essential to enlightened opinion and right conduct on

dependent upon the vigorous exchange of information in a free-market system, where the integrity of commercial transactions depends upon the reliable information available to the parties involved. The availability of greater information, therefore, will benefit economically interested individuals, by providing them with the tools to define their goals, calculate their means, and plan their courses of action.[113] Consumers, in this context, must be informed about the quality, quantity, reliability and price of the various goods and services which are available to them, while businesses, at the same time, must be able to effectively promote their products in the marketplace, in order to keep competition alive. The information provided to consumers, as noted in previous chapters, not only provides them with the knowledge to make informed business decisions, but also serves to inform and to warn them of various dangers to their own health and to the environment at large. Aside from the obvious and direct protections accorded by the dissemination of such information, this process provides an additional regulator of goods and activities which are potentially harmful, and for holding the wrongdoer accountable in the marketplace for such harms. When, therefore, the government, through environmental audit bills, railroad and highway anti-discovery measures, and court-protected secrecy agreements, prevents such information from reaching the consumer, the government is not only compromising the health and welfare of the public, but also serves to stifle competition, by subsidizing imperfect, defective, and even harmful goods and services, while preventing po-

---

the part of the citizens of a democracy." Cantwell v. Connecticut, 310 U.S. 296, 310 (1940).

113 "So long as we preserve a predominately free enterprise economy, the allocation of our resources in large measure will be made through numerous private economic decisions. It is a matter of public interest that those decisions be intelligent and well-informed. To this end, the free flow of commercial information is indispensable." Virginia Board, 425 U.S. at 765.

tentially better products from development, introduction, and success in the marketplace. As a commodity, it has been suggested, information will tend to be devalued in the marketplace, because information is a public good. The benefits of information, explains Daniel A. Farber, extend to third parties, but because the producer does not consider these benefits in his production decisions, less information is produced than is socially optimal. There are people who, if they had to, would be willing to pay for the benefits of additional information, but the additional information is not disseminated because the market is unable to translate those individuals' preferences into an incentive for the producer. If the government, therefore, intervenes into this market, it should be for the purpose of subsidizing rather than limiting speech.[114]

The Democratization of Information

As a democracy, we put our faith in our own abilities to assess the value and veracity of information, conflicting opinions, and representations, in order to govern the affairs of state, the affairs of our business, and the affairs of our daily lives.[115] The government, therefore, has no power to "protect" people from information which it perceives to be potentially harmful or dangerous, because the right to make such decisions ultimately resides in ourselves.[116] As one of America's most respected ju-

114 Farber, Free Speech Without Romance 105 Harv. L. Rev. 554, 558 (1991).

115 The nature of a Democracy is designed to assume "that information is not in itself harmful, that people will perceive their own best interests if only they are well enough informed, and that the best means to that end is to open the channels of communication rather than to close them." Virginia Board, 425 U.S. at 770.

116 "I find no merit whatsoever in the Government's assertion that an interest in restraining competition among brewers to satisfy consumer demand for stronger beverages justifies a statutory abridgment of truthful speech. Any 'interest' in restricting the flow of accurate information because of the perceived danger of that knowledge is anathema to the Constitution; more speech and a better-informed citizenry are among the central goals of the Free Speech Clause. Accordingly, the Constitution is most skeptical of supposed state interests that seek to keep people in the dark for what government believes to be their own good. The Government's asserted interest, that

rists, Learned Hand, once noted, the First Amendment "presupposes that right conclusions are more likely to be gathered out of a multitude of tongues, than through any kind of authoritative selection. To many this is, and always will be, folly; but we have staked upon it our all."[117]

Faith

From the genesis of modern political philosophy, courageous men and women have placed their faith in the power of truth and righteousness to emerge victorious from the battlefield of ideas. Such sentiments appear as early as 1644 in the writings of the great English poet, John Milton, when he wrote, "though all the winds of doctrine were let loose to play upon the earth, so Truth be in the field, we do injuriously by licensing and prohibiting, to misdoubt her strength. Let her and falsehood grapple; who ever knew Truth put to worse, in a free and open encounter?"[118] In his First Inaugural Address, Thomas Jefferson invited "any among us who would wish to dissolve this Union or change its republican form, to stand undisturbed as monuments of the safety with which error of opinion may be tolerated where reason is left free to combat it." And Martin Luther King expressed the same enduring belief when he accepted the Nobel Peace Prize in 1964: "I believe that unarmed truth and unconditional love will have the final word in reality. That is why right temporarily defeated is stronger than evil triumphant."

These principles stem not only from a deeply-rooted respect for others, but also from the humble recognition that men are imperfect, and fallible, and frequently fail to

---

consumers should be mislead or uninformed for their own protection, does not suffice to justify restrictions on protected speech in *any* context, whether under 'exacting scrutiny' or some other standard." Justice Stevens, concurring, Rubin v. Coors Brewing Company, 115 S.Ct. 1585, 1597 (1995).

117 United States v. Associated Press, 52 F.Supp. 362, 372 (S.D.N.Y. 1943).

118 Milton, Areopagitica (1644).

recognize truth when it appears.[119] The foolish sentiments
of one era will frequently become the commonly-held beliefs of another, while what seem at first to be enlightened
and revolutionary propositions may turn out to be nothing
but false prophesy. The heretics of one generation may
prove to be the prophets of another, as men and women of
genius like Socrates and Galileo are persecuted and mar-
tyred while living, only to be revered when they are gone.
The evolution of truth and justice, in this way, is a lengthy
and tortuous process, wherein society is best served by
reserving its judgment, in deference to the opinions of
others, while allowing conflicting beliefs to compete and
do battle in the marketplace of ideas.[120] Commitment to

[119]"The beliefs which we have most warrant for, have no safeguard to rest on,
but a standing invitation to the whole world to prove them unfounded. If the challenge
is not accepted, or if accepted and the attempt fails, we are far enough for certainty
still; but we have done the best that the existing state of human reason admits of; we
have neglected nothing that could give the truth a chance of reaching us: if the lists are
kept open, we may hope that if there be a better truth, it will be found when the human
mind is capable of receiving it; and in the meantime we may rely on having attained
such approach to truth, as is possible in our own day. This is the amount of certainty
attainable by a fallible being, and this is the sole way of attaining it." John Stuart Mill,
On Liberty (1859).

[120]   "Persecution for the expression of ideas seems to me perfectly
logical. If you have no doubt of your premises or your power and want a certain
result with all your heart you naturally express your wishes in law and sweep away
all opposition. To allow opposition by speech seems to indicate that you think the
speech impotent, as when a man says he has squared the circle, or that you do not care
whole-heartedly for the result, or that you doubt either your power or your premises.
But when men have realized that time has upset many fighting faiths, they may come
to believe even more than they believe the very foundations of their own conduct that
the ultimate good desired is better reached by a free trade of ideas – that the best test
of truth is the power of the thought to get itself accepted in the competition of the
market, and that truth is the only ground upon which their wishes safely can be carried
out. That at any rate is the theory of the Constitution. It is an experiment, as all life
is an experiment. Every year if not every day we have to wage our salvation upon
some prophecy based upon imperfect knowledge. While that experiment is part of
our system I think that we should be eternally vigilant against attempts to check the
expression of opinions that we loathe and believe to be fraught with death, unless they
so imminently threaten immediate interference with the lawful and pressing purposes
of the law that an immediate check is required to save the country." Oliver Wendell
Holmes, joined by Justice Brandeis, dissenting, Abrams v. United States, 250 U.S.
616, 630 (1919).

"To courageous, self-reliant men, with confidence in the power of free and fear-
less reasoning applied through a popular government, no danger flowing from speech

such principles requires courage and faith, and is necessary to not only the political and economic success of society, but to all scientific, artistic, and moral progression.

The Government and Communication

The Federal Government prohibits the transmission of language which is obscene, indecent, or profane. Such regulation is justified, in part, by the asserted privacy interests of the individual, who should not have to suffer exposure to offensive or indecent expression within the privacy of his or her own home. This reasoning, however, is severely undermined by the countervailing constitutional protection of the individual in the privacy of his own home to receive and experience information, and by the practical reality that an offended viewer or listener can merely change the channel, or simply turn off the tv. The more palatable justification which has been advanced as the basis for such regulation is the protection of the young. Yet, despite rapidly emerging evidence that violent and sexually explicit expression may have a real and actual effect on the psychological development and ultimately therefore the actions of children, the source of our limited government's regulatory power is derived from its authority to regulate "interstate commerce" not

can be deemed clear and present, unless the incidence of the evil apprehended is so imminent that it may befall before there is opportunity for full discussion. If there be time to expose through discussion the falsehood and fallacies, to avert the evil by the process of education, the remedy to be applied is more speech, not enforced silence. Only an emergency can justify suppression. Such must be the rule if authority is to be reconciled with freedom." Brandeis, joined by Holmes, concurring, <u>Whitney v. California</u>, 274 U.S. 357, 377 (1927) .

"There is no such thing as a false idea. However pernicious an opinion may seem, we depend for its correction not on the conscience of judges and juries, but on the competition of other ideas." Justice Lewis Powell, <u>Gertz v. Robert Welch, Inc.</u>, 418 U.S. 323, 339-340 (1974).

"Indeed, it is the measure of the confidence of a society in its own stability that it suffers such fustian to go unchecked." Learned Hand, <u>U.S. v. Dennis</u>, 183 F.2d 201, 212 (2nd Cir. 1950).

the protection of children, and therefore, aside from any limitations imposed by the First Amendment, the government is nevertheless without power to decide what the people can and cannot listen to or watch on tv. Beginning with the first World War, the number of radio stations began to increase so rapidly that, by 1925, every channel in the standard broadcast ban was occupied by at least one station, and there were 175 new stations ready to go on air. The Radio Act of 1927, therefore, authorized the government, through the Federal Radio Commission, to license and regulate the industry. "The plight into which radio fell prior to 1927," explained the Supreme Court in *NBC v. United States,* "was attributable to certain basic facts about radio as a means of communication – its facilities are limited; they are not available for all who wish to use them; the radio spectrum is simply not large enough to accommodate everybody. There is a fixed natural limitation upon the number of stations that can operate without interfering with one another."

The right, however, to restrict the number of parties who can broadcast on the airwaves, does not give the government the right to regulate or interfere with the substance of the communication.[121] Such regulation, if there be any, is reserved to the people, who will choose the communication they deem valuable from a marketplace of broadcasters, who have an economic and commercial incentive to make their programs interesting, informative, and entertaining.

The necessity, moreover, for the licensing of broadcasters, is rapidly eroding, as new channels of communication are becoming more and more available through the use of cable television, fiber-optic technology, and direct

121   "Unlike other modes of expression, radio inherently is not available to all. That is its unique characteristic, and that is why, unlike other modes of expression, it is subject to governmental regulation. But Congress did not authorize the Commission to choose among applicants upon the basis of their political, economic, or social views." NBC v. United States, 319 U.S. 190, 226 (1943).

satellite tv. The Internet, for example, can disseminate information from millions of broadcasters, while the market provides the television viewer with networks dedicated to everything from news, sports, weather, movies and talk shows, to nature and discovery channels, business and finance, music television, arts and entertainment, history, and court tv.[122]Nevertheless, and in any event, the prohibition of offensive communication from the Internet is not the regulation of interstate commerce; the installation of a V-chip in television sets to weed out sexual or violent expression is not the regulation of interstate commerce.[123] The question, again, is not a question of policy. It's not a question of whether such legislation would be good or bad, effective or ineffective, right or wrong. The question, rather, is a constitutional question – a question of power, a question of function, a question of role. And, in this regard, it is not the function of the Federal Government, or

[122]   In striking down provisions of the Communications Decency Act of 1996 which would have criminalized the transmission of "indecent" or "patently offensive" material over the Internet, the Supreme Court noted as follows: "Unlike the conditions that prevailed when Congress first authorized regulation of the broadcast spectrum, the Internet can hardly be considered a 'scarce' expressive commodity. It provides relatively unlimited, low-cost capacity of all kinds. This dynamic, multifaceted category of communication includes not only traditional print and news services, but also audio, video, and still images, as well as interactive, real-time dialogue. As the District Court found, 'the content on the Internet is as diverse as human thought.' We agree with its conclusion that our cases provide no basis for qualifying the level of First Amendment scrutiny that should be applied to this medium." Reno v. American Civil Liberties Union, 117 S.Ct. 2329, 2344 (1997).

[123]   The regulation of interstate commerce, in this regard, is power of the Federal Government to prevent unfair and deceptive trade practices, to make rates or use taxes uniform across state lines, to issue licenses based on objective and content-neutral criteria, to enforce the anti-trust laws where there is competition, and to regulate the monopolies. It may be argued, by some, that "obscene" material – which, taken as a whole, the average person, applying contemporary community standards, would find appeals to the prurient interest; describes, in a patently offensive way, sexual conduct specifically defined by statute; and, taken as a whole, lacks serious literary, artistic, political, or scientific value – is, itself, an unlawful product or commodity, like illegal arms, contraband, or illicit narcotics, which can therefore be removed from the stream of commerce altogether. While others may argue that even obscene material is beyond government, and particularly Federal Government, regulation, the former reasoning would not justify the suppression or censorship of non-obscene, yet violent, indecent, or potentially offensive expression, which is otherwise, and appropriately, protected.

any government, to determine what television programs, or computer programs, or radio programs, or books, or films, or newspapers, that people should watch, or listen to, or read. At the heart of this matter is an abdication of power, an abdication of responsibility. Men and women are abdicating their own power and responsibility to determine what is good, what is right, and what is interesting, by asking the government, or television producers, or automated computer chips, to make those evaluations for them.[124] This, fundamentally, is the antithesis of democracy, which places its faith in the intelligence and the will of the individual, to think, to imagine, to create, to experience, to feel, and ultimately to govern, in terms of society, in terms of the economy, and in terms of the family, throughout the course of our daily lives. Even assuming, moreover, that it were appropriate for the government to assume this role, the government, as a practical matter, could not prohibit harmful expression, because society, at a given point in time, cannot truly know what is harmful.[125] What we now believe to be good, in this regard,

---

124   "Should a slapstick barroom brawl be rated the same as a cop-show shootout?" asks Mark Lorando of *The Times Picayune*. "How does a V-chip distinguish between a responsible movie such as 'The Burning Bed' which conveyed the trauma of domestic violence, and an episode of 'Walker, Texas Ranger' which gets its kicks out of karate? Would 'Schindler's List' make it past the chip? Or 'Forest Gump'? What about the witch-melting scene in 'The Wizard of Oz'? Pro football is pretty violent. So are commercials for R-rated action films. Will they get rated? What about the evening news?" Lorando, "V-Chip Clouds Future of Television" <u>Times Picayune</u> Aug. 13, 1995, p.A-6.

125   Not only is there a question as to whether the government can, theoretically, determine what is harmful, but there is also a question of whether, as a practical matter, it will. Bob Dole, for example, recently unleashed an attack on Hollywood, denouncing movies with allegedly "mindless" and gratuitous violence, like *True Romance* and *Natural Born Killers,* while promoting "family" movies like *The Santa Clause, The Lion King, The Flintstones,* and *True Lies.* Yet, as noted by Richard Schickel, *True Romance,* with brilliant satire, celebrates love (or true romance) above all, while *Natural Born Killers* argues, (ironically, much like Dole), that the tabloid media and other images of television and computer violence are encouraging people to act in violent and destructive ways. *The Santa Clause, The Lion King, The Flintstones,* and *True Lies,* on the other hand, "depict women being locked up and tortured by their temporarily estranged husbands, little animals celebrating the power of bigger animals to devour them, and father figures who are sullenly distracted and moronically inept.

might turn out to be bad, and what we now believe to be bad might turn out to be good. What we now believe to be true might turn out to be false, and what we believe to be false might turn out to be true. Violence and sex, for better or worse, are a part of our society. And while sexual and violent images can encourage harmful and destructive activity, they can also form the basis of, not only passion and imagination, but an essential part of the social commentary which seeks to make society peaceful, prosperous, and respectful of human life.[126]If you take away X, you take away the reaction to X, which might be good. If permitted, the government will take away X, and the dialectic progression of thought and emotion will be lost. Television, music and film producers will take the life out of all powerful, energetic, and potentially innovative sounds and images, and the world of images and ideas will become stagnant, lifeless, and stale.[127]"The rule is," noted radio talk show host, Howard Stern, who has been fined millions of dollars by the FCC, "don't say anything that is 'patently indecent' or offensive to your community. Well, I live in a community where priests rape young

These movies, at their heart, tell the viewer that women need to be kept in their place, that the powerless should gladly acquiesce to their exploitation by the powerful, that privatizing emotions is like privatizing services, and that white males truly are boobs." Perhaps of greater significance is the fact that Dole chose to attack the works of people like Oliver Stone, (who would appear to support Democratic candidates and causes), while notably failing to criticize, (and even complementing), the notoriously graphic works of Arnold Schwartzenegger, Bruce Willis, and Sylvester Stallone, who are all Republicans. See Richard Schickel, "No, But He Reads the Polls" Time June 12, 1995, p.29.

126   "Which is more threatening to America" asks writer John Edgar Wideman, "the violence, obscenity, sexism and racism of movies and records, or the stark reality these music and movies reflect? If a messenger, even one who happens to be black and a rapper, arrives bearing news of a terrible disaster, what do we accomplish by killing the messenger?"

127   "If you think that anything blocked by the V-chip on network television is going to have sponsors" notes Dick Wolf, "you're delusional. Anything that gets blocked for content, sexuality, violence is going to be anathema. And that is de facto censorship, because the networks won't put adult shows on, and you are going to have an amazingly bland landscape of situation comedies." See Lorando, "V-chip Clouds the Future of Television" Times Picayune, Aug. 13, 1995, p.A-6.

boys, where you get shot in your car, where angry black mobs stab Hasidic Jews, and the mayor turns his back, where crack runs free like the River Ganges, and where movie directors fuck their wives' daughters. Now you tell me what I should talk about on the radio!"[128]

Personal Injury and Abuse

The First Amendment prevents the Government from making any law which abridges the freedom of speech or of the press. But when a person or corporation causes injury to another, through defamation, breach of an express warranty, unfair trade practices, or fraud, the Constitution should not be invoked to insulate the wrongdoer from accountability, nor as a barrier to the redress of the individual who has been harmed.

In most cases, such liability is imposed only when the misrepresentation is intentional – when, for example, a business corporation intentionally misleads its customers by fraud. Defamation law, however, poses more difficult questions with respect to whether mere negligence can be actionable by an individual who has been harmed in a court of law.[129]

While, originally, defamation was unprotected by the First Amendment, the landmark case of *New York Times vs. Sullivan* ushered in a new era of protection for the press, and other individuals, by establishing an "actual malice" requirement for recovery in a defamation suit in-

---

128   Stern, Private Parts, pp.420-421 (1993).

129   In cases of negligent misrepresentation, breach of express warranty, detrimental reliance, and in some breach of contract cases, injury can arise by mere negligent acts or omissions; but it can be argued that, in those cases – as with cases of unfair and deceptive trade practices, and fraud – the injury to the consumer arises, not out of the false or misleading representation, but in the failure of the product or service to perform as promised by the service provider, seller, or manufacturer. It should be noted, nevertheless, that a material misrepresentation or omission is an essential element of each cause of action, (whether by purpose, by negligence, by reckless disregard, or without fault), and therefore speech is, to some extent, being regulated, when it, combined with some other action or omission, causes harm.

volving a public official, which has now been expanded to a "public figure", or any matter of public concern.[130] As a result of these and other protections, around 75% of all libel cases are dismissed by the courts prior to trial. Of the cases which do go to trial, the defendant wins almost half, with over 70% of the cases in which a plaintiff is successful reversed, at least in part, on appeal. The U.S. Supreme Court, in this context, has taken the position that a civil action for damages by a private citizen is analogous to a criminal prosecution by the State, and that such Constitutional protections are necessary to give the First Amendment the "breathing space" that it needs to survive. From a historical perspective, however, and as a practical matter, the media and even private individuals have been insulated from real and actual damages which cannot be justified by the First Amendment or the free exposition of ideas.[131]The protection of free speech was designed to ensure that the government could not avoid political (or criminal) accountability for wrongdoing by suppressing the right of the people and their press to freely criticize the actions or failures of public officials, their suitability for office, or the affairs of state. "If we advert to the nature of Republican government" wrote Madison, "we shall find that the censorial power is in the people over the Government, and not in the Government over the people."[132] If a public official, therefore, in his or her

---

130   "Actual malice" is present when a statement is made with the knowledge that the statement is false, or with reckless disregard as to whether the statement is true.

131   The right to bear arms, for example, does not give an individual the right to take out his gun out and shoot someone else without justification. So too, the right of free speech carries certain responsibilities, and is subject to various abuse. This way of thinking is expressed in several state constitutions, such as New York's, which provides that a person has the right to speak, write, or publish his or her sentiments on any subject, but is "responsible for the abuse of that right." N.Y. Const. Art. I, §8. See also, for example: Ohio Const. Art. I, §7; La. Const. Art I, §8; Texas Const. Art. I, §11.

132   Annals of Congress, Vol. 4, p. 934 (1794).

private capacity, can discourage the media from good faith criticism due to the threat of litigation, the official would effectively be able to insulate himself or herself from public scrutiny.[133] While it is not clear whether a prohibition of such action is Constitutionally mandated, as the Supreme Court has suggested, or merely a matter of sound public policy, any such restriction of the right to pursue defamation actions should be strictly limited to suits against public officials who are truly public officials, regarding matters which are truly matters of public concern. The Constitution, after all, only prohibits censorship by the Government. A civil suit, on the other hand, is an action brought by an individual for the redress of some injury to property or reputation against another who is alleged to have caused him harm. The Government, in this type of proceeding, is not prohibiting or regulating any type of speech or publication. The Government, rather, is merely providing a forum for the private dispute.[134]While the Supreme Court has rejected such a government-action/private-action distinction, the Court has drawn a distinction between the communication of factual assertions and the communication of opinions or ideas. "There is no such thing as a false idea" wrote Justice Powell in *Gertz*. "But there is no constitutional value in false statements of fact. Neither the intentional lie nor the careless error materially advances society's interest in 'uninhibited, ro-

---

133   A rule compelling the critic of official conduct to guarantee the truth of all his factual assertions, noted the Supreme Court, leads to inevitable self-censorship. "Under such a rule, would-be critics of official conduct may be deterred from voicing their criticism, even though it is believed to be true and even though it is in fact true, because of doubt whether it can be proved in court or fear of the expense of having to do so." New York Times v. Sullivan, 376 U.S. 254, 279 (1964).

134   "Whatever the outer confines of the Clause's reach may be" wrote the Supreme Court, for example, in the context of the Eighth Amendment, and its proscription on excessive fines, "we now decide only that it does not constrain an award of money damages in a civil suit when the government has neither prosecuted the action nor has any right to receive a share of the damages award." Browning-Ferris v. Kelco Disposal, 492 U.S. 257, 263-264 (1989).

bust, and wide-open' debate on public issues."[135]

The Court has also, in this context, drawn a distinction between the rights of the speaker and the rights of the listener. In the area of commercial speech, for example, businesses can be prohibited from engaging in advertisement which is false or misleading.[136] And in the regulation of television and radio programming, "it is the right of viewers and listeners, not the right of broadcasters, which is paramount."[137]As a practical matter, moreover, the imposition of liability for publication of facts which are false due to the publisher's negligence will not have a significant effect on the free exposition of ideas. This assertion is based on the fact that not all inaccuracies will be defamatory, and that, in fact, most of the information which the public needs to receive on an immediate basis is not. When dealing with traffic, stock quotes, and the weather, for example, there is no time to conduct an in-depth investigation; but there is also no potential for defamation, as a hurricane, or a fire, or a traffic accident, cannot ordinarily be libeled or defamed.[138]

With respect to other matters, even political matters, there is a need for society to receive information, but there is not a need, in general, for society to receive in-

135   Gertz v. Robert Welch, Inc., 418 U.S. 323, 339-340 (1974).

136   "The First Amendment's concern for commercial speech is based on the informational function of advertising. Consequently, there can be no constitutional objection to the suppression of commercial messages that do not accurately inform the public about lawful activity." Central Hudson, 447 U.S. at 563.

137   Red Lion Broadcasting v. FCC, 395 U.S. 367, 390 (1969).

138   There will be some cases in which a public emergency could be accompanied by a potential for defamation. In cases where, for example, there is a chemical leak, or an explosion, some might argue that the press would be discouraged from providing the public with necessary information, for fear that Chemical Company X or Oil Company Y could be negligently implicated as the cause of the situation. In such cases, however, the media would have means to inform the public of the situation, while reserving judgment about the origin of the emergency until a reasonable investigation can be maintained. Negligence, moreover, as a legal principle, generally involves an inquiry into what is reasonable *under the circumstances,* such that the urgency of the situation would undoubtedly be taken into account by any judge or jury member who might be deciding such a case.

formation immediately, before a reasonable investigation into the truth of the factual allegations can be made.[139] The necessity for immediate dissemination of information, in most cases, is not premised on a public need for that information, but on a commercial incentive, which encourages the press to make more money by "scooping" the story before the competition.

"Newspapers, magazines, and broadcasting companies" the Supreme Court has noted, "are businesses conducted for profit and often make very large ones. Like other enterprises that inflict damage in the course of performing a service highly useful to the public, they must pay the freight; and injured persons should not be relegated to remedies which make collection of their claims difficult or impossible unless strong public policy considerations demand."[140] When, accordingly, the burdens of free speech fall exclusively on the shoulders of a minority of wronged individuals, those parties who profit by the negligent dissemination of such false information should bear the responsibility for that loss.

---

139   The fact that Newt Gingrich or Bill Clinton may have cheated on their wives, for example, or that O.J. Simpson may have killed his wife, or that Michael Jackson may have molested a child, may all be of legitimate interest or concern to the public; but there is no need, on the part of the public, to know that information NOW, before there is time for reasonable investigation.

140   Curtis Publishing v. Butts, 388 U.S. 130, 147 (1967); quoting, Buckley v. New York Post, 373 F.2d 175, 182 (2nd Cir. 1967). See also: Gertz v. Robert Welch, 418 U.S. 323, 369-404 (1974) (White, J., dissenting); Rosenbloom v. Metromedia, 403 U.S. 29, 64 (1971) (Harlan, J., dissenting).

The People vs. O.J. Simpson

From the moment O.J. Simpson was arrested, it was clear that, one way or the other, the events which were yet to unfold would have a profound impact on the way in which Americans would continue to view the issues of race, wealth, equal justice, television in the courtroom, the death penalty, the jury, and the criminal justice system as a whole. While it remains to be seen whether *The People vs. O.J. Simpson* will have any lasting effects on the substantive law of this nation, what is clear is that the American people have entered the judicial arena, and have been both amazed and disgusted by what they have seen.

Equal Justice

Perhaps the greatest point of contention with the American people concerning the O.J. Simpson trial was the idea of unequal justice. In the beginning, this discussion was centered primarily on the issue of race. The proceedings were racially motivated, the commentators told us, citing poll after poll which demonstrated the disparity between the attitudes of white Americans and the attitudes of black Americans on the question of O.J. Simpson's guilt. And yet, those polls merely reflected the attitudes of the American public about the criminal justice system in general; they said absolutely nothing about the fairness or propriety of the proceedings themselves. After all, if it were a white athlete, like Joe Namath, or Dan Marino, or Andre Agassi, accused of the same crime, the State would have prosecuted the case no less vigorously.

There is no way, the media experts and legal commentators told us nightly, with all of the publicity surrounding the proceedings, that O.J. Simpson could possibly hope to receive a fair trial. And yet those very same experts and commentators told us nightly that there was no way that O.J. Simpson could possibly be convicted of the crime. Never did any commentator or expert once touch upon the apparent logical inconsistency. Certainly it cannot be said, although it was said often, that a defendant who could not possibly be convicted is being wrongfully deprived of a fair trial. And finally, we were constantly reminded of the fact that the rich, like O.J. Simpson, could afford to buy their freedom with a team of high-priced experts and investigators and attorneys, while kids from the ghetto get "a different kind of justice" provided by appointed counsel who have neither the time nor the resources to properly develop a defense. Yet these people disregard the fact that the prosecution of O.J. Simpson was proportionate to the defense, and that in the typical case, involving "kids from the ghetto", the district attorney's ability, or lack of ability, to delve into the facts, to interview witnesses, and to develop exhibits and testimony, is limited, and generally commensurate with that of the defense. They forget the fact that hundreds of indigent defenders around the country have more first degree murder trial experience than all the members of the "dream team" put together. And that rich people represented by private attorneys get convicted, while poor people represented by public defenders get acquitted every day. The system, moreover, only seems unfair in this regard when the prosecution of a wealthy defendant and the prosecution of an indigent defendant are viewed side by side. The question, however, is not whether the O.J. Simpson trial is inherently more or less fair than the trial of X, but whether the system provides protections which guarantee that both the trial of O.J. Simpson and the trial of X will each be fair, in their own way. Rich people are at liberty to expend their money freely on legal efforts to prove their innocence. That seems fair. Indigent people, who otherwise could not afford an attorney, have counsel provided for them by the public, free of charge. That seems fair too. All defendants, at the same time, are protected by the right to face their accusers, the privilege against self-incrimination, the reasonable doubt standard, and above all, the jury, which is made up of ordinary citizens, from all walks of life, who have no particular monetary or social connections to the prosecution, the victim, or the accused.

Even assuming, however, that wealthy people could always parlay enough well-presented evidence, or at least questions, to assure reasonable doubt, and therefore acquittal, the number of defendants like O.J. Simpson, William Kennedy Smith, and the Menendez brothers, are statistically insignificant.[141] They present no appreciable danger to the community, and whatever danger they do present would be far outweighed by the danger that would arise from the various proposed reforms. An entire justice system cannot be modeled around a small minority of cases. An entire justice system cannot be modeled around an aberration."My biggest concern" said one television commentator on this note, "is not in the end whether O.J. Simpson is found guilty or innocent, but that the American public in viewing what is perhaps the most

---

141   Shortly after the murders, the U.S. Bureau of Justice Statistics reported that very few men charged with murdering their wives, (just over 1%), are acquitted. And virtually none of them are adored celebrities with sufficient assets to justify a civil suit.

bizarre and outrageous of trials in all of American history, will think that this is the way the American justice system works."

From the television coverage, to the sequestration of the jury, to the number of attorneys, to the money expended, to the length of the trial, the O.J. Simpson case was in no way representative of the great mass of criminal proceedings that take place every day in this country, and says absolutely nothing about the criminal justice system as a whole.[142]

Court TV

There was a great German physicist named Heisenberg, who believed that we could never accurately examine any subject or phenomenon, because the process of examination itself has an effect upon the object which is being observed. It is not hard to see, by analogy, how Heisenberg's "uncertainty principle" can be applied to cameras in the courtroom, where observation of the trial by the public will have its own effect upon the proceedings, and their result.

Sunlight is the greatest disinfectant, it has been said. And the presence of television in the courtroom might well eradicate unpopular, unprofessional, dishonest and unfair conduct on the part of lawyers and judges, due to the public scrutiny that television coverage would afford. At the same time, however, the presence of television cameras could also have the effect of making courtroom proceedings more erratic, unpopular, unprofessional, dishonest, and unfair. The jury, in this regard, or even the

142   In an essay regarding the myth that the Simpson trial exposed deep flaws in the American justice system, Ellis Cose, for example, notes that "the justice system may, in fact, be deeply flawed, but Simpson's situation is not much of an indication of that, if for no other reason than that the Simpson case is such an aberration. Screams for reform of the justice system became pervasive after the first jury delivered its verdict. But changing the justice system because of the Simpson results makes roughly as much sense as changing the rules of golf because Tiger Woods hits the ball so far." Cose, "Getting Past the Myths" Newsweek Feb. 17, 1997, p.36.

judge, when acting as fact-finder, is meant to reflect the feelings and the opinions and the experience of the community. It is a democratic process. But the reliability of that process is enhanced by selection, and accountability, and most of all, through education. Television has the power to subvert that process, and to undermine the reliability, because there is nothing to ensure that the "jury" of viewers will be free of partial interests and attitudes, or that they will sit and watch and listen to all of the evidence, throughout the course of the trial. Television cameras in the courtroom vastly increase the risk that not only the jury, but also the lawyers, the witnesses, and the judge, could be held hostage by the courtroom of public opinion, when the general public, save in exceptional circumstances, is not exposed to all of the evidence; when the public is exposed to facts and rumors and unsubstantiated innuendo from which the jury is hopefully insulated; when the public has not taken an oath which binds them to the evidence, and is not in any way accountable for the result; when the public has not been subjected to the scrutiny of *voir dire,* to ensure against bias and personal prejudices; and when the public's impression and evaluation of the evidence will be shaped, in part, by the opinions of so-called experts and commentators, who have no personal knowledge of the facts, who are not bound by the code of professional responsibility, and who have their own personal and political motivations, interests, and beliefs.

More significant, however, is the effect that television coverage will undoubtedly have on the evidence which is presented, or not presented, at trial. Especially in criminal cases, where witnesses are already intimidated, threatened, and reluctant to get involved in the process, the presence of television can only deter them further from testifying. For those that do testify, the television coverage will make witnesses who are already nervous even more nervous and anxious about their testimony; it will encourage and generate even more coaching and preparation by attorneys; and will generally lessen the reliability of the evidence, and ultimately, therefore, the result. The presence of television cameras, at the same time, may also encourage phonies and pranksters to come forward, pretending that they have reliable evidence, just so that they can become famous, or get themselves on tv.

In civil cases, corporations are going to look at the trial as a free advertising opportunity, and the proceedings will therefore cease to be the determination of facts – *i.e.* whether X corporation breached its contract to one of its inventors – and will take the form, rather, of a promotional effort, where the attorneys and witnesses tell the public how good or safe or inexpensive the company's vacuum cleaner really is. This will undoubtedly spawn the propagation of corporate courtroom battles, which will clog the judiciary with legally constructed advertising wars, premised upon frivolous antitrust or patent-infringement or breach of contract claims.

Television coverage, at the same time, may also encourage the prosecution of groundless lawsuits by individuals against corporations, where the plaintiff hopes to force the defendant, though free from liability, into a settlement to avoid the negative publicity.

The Public Has A Right to Know

The public has the right to know. But the prohibition of television cameras from the courtroom does not prevent the public from knowing anything. It does not prevent the public from receiving information. It just prevents television stations and corporate affiliates from profiting off of the trial.

In addition to the illusory "public has a right to know"

argument, the advocates of cameras in the courtroom also tell us about the great "civics lesson" that the American public was exposed to over the course of the O.J. Simpson trial. Even assuming, however, that such an atypical and aberrant proceeding could provide substantial insight into the inner workings of the legal system, the purpose of the O.J. Simpson trial was not to educate the public. The purpose of the trial was to determine whether O.J. Simpson, on the night in question, went to his ex-wife's house, and killed two people with a knife. The integrity of that process, and the reliability of that determination, should not be undermined by a desire to educate the public through tv. To the extent that the print media and reporting from journalists on radio and television fails to adequately educate the American public, court proceedings can certainly be recreated in a true-to-life manner with actors, after the outcome has already been decided, and where there are no real life consequences involved. But the media does not want to expend money for the production costs, and are looking for a low-budget way of turning a profit, by subverting the integrity and reliability of the judicial system to their own economic gains.[143]

Integrity

The American public is alerted daily to the signs of moral bankruptcy and social decay. From talk shows to televangelists, from C-SPAN to the Playboy Channel, with the break-down of family values to the disintegration of our religious beliefs. There is a great search in this country for something that we can look to as sacred. And what is sacred in America is the law. The courthouse. Individual rights and freedoms. The protections of life, liberty, and property. The jury system, democracy, and

143   "It is time for the judiciary to make it clear" said Judge Mary Ann Murphy, "that we are not a part of the entertainment industry." Carrizosa, "Critics Call for Ban on Cameras in the Courts" L.A. Daily Journal, Jan. 9, 1996, p.1.

the right to vote. The Constitution is our Bible, as it were. And there are some things which just shouldn't be on television.

When something is put on television, it is cheapened. It is commercialized. It is promoted. And made somehow plastic, and fantastic, and not real. The search for justice will be undermined by a search for what is controversial, for what is juicy, for what is entertaining.

There are ugly sides to the legal process in America. There are ugly lawyers, ugly litigants, and ugly cases. But the Law itself is the beginning and the end of our society. It is beautiful, and majestic, and noble. It is something that we can look to as sacred, something that we can believe in. It is something worth keeping. And it is something worth keeping off tv.

Bad Cops, Spousal Abuse, and the Dream

One of the most hotly contested issues in the area of criminal law is the admission of other crimes evidence or prior bad acts to prove guilt in a criminal trial. This debate stems from the general proposition that we do not want to convict people because we don't like them personally, or because we don't like their politics, or because we think they are bad.[144] We want to convict people based on the fact that they have engaged in certain criminal conduct from which they should be deterred. There is a rule of

---

144   This problem becomes particularly significant when the prior crimes or bad acts are fairly innocuous in comparison to the crime of which the defendant is currently accused, or when the prior crimes or bad acts involve things to which the public has a particularly visceral aversion. If, for example, a twenty-five year-old man is on trial for killing his lover in a heat of passion, the introduction of evidence that he has been convicted of shop-lifting and theft a few times as a teenager will tend to make us feel that the defendant is a criminal, and therefore guilty, even though, logically, the prior crimes evidence is not likely to be very indicative of the defendant's guilt in terms of the murder in question. Or, where there is, for example, evidence that someone is a member of the Ku Klux Klan, or the Nazi party, there is a good chance that he or she will be convicted, even though that person's affiliation may have absolutely nothing to do with the question of guilt in relation to the crime of which he or she is accused.

evidence, therefore, which prevents the admission of a person's bad acts to show that he or she is a bad person, in order to show that he or she committed the crime in question.[145] This rule hopes to focus the proceedings on the material questions at issue, and to thereby make the determination of facts more reliable.[146]

While this rule is an excellent tool for judging the correctness of an issue, and while it is generally a good tool for deciding civil matters, where the purpose of the proceeding is the redress of a specific injury, this rule of evidence, in a criminal proceeding, is based upon a punishment or fault-based model, rather than a model of public protection, and therefore will always fall prey to criticism and abuse. Society, in this sense, does not have any "right" to punish a defendant for a particular transgression. Society's right to imprison and incarcerate others is to protect society from harm. The whole objective of the criminal proceeding, therefore, should not be to ascertain whether a defendant is guilty or innocent, but to determine whether the defendant is a threat to society, because of a propensity to commit future crimes. Guilt or innocence is just a threshold requirement which: (a) satisfies our notions of due process, and protection of the innocent, and (b) evidences the fact that the person is a danger to society at large. Even assuming, in this regard, that prior bad acts are not indicative of guilt or innocence

---

145   "Evidence of other crimes, wrongs, or acts is not admissible to prove the character of a person in order to show action in conformity therewith." Federal Rule of Evidence 404(b).

"The business of the court is to try the case and not the man; a very bad man may have a very righteous cause." Thompson v. Church, 1 Root 312 (1791).

"It makes no difference whether a good man has defrauded a bad man or a bad man has defrauded a good man, or whether a good or bad man has committed adultery; the law can look only to the amount of damage done." Aristotle, Nicomachean Ethics.

146   The rule also may have some roots in the reinforcement of protections against Double Jeopardy, in order to prevent people from being convicted twice or even more times for the same crime.

in a particular setting, they are certainly relevant in the determination of whether the defendant poses a threat to society, and therefore, should generally be admissible in a criminal trial.

The exclusion, moreover, of other crimes evidence, in many ways infringes on the province of the jury, which should generally be able to decide for itself whether the information is relevant or inflammatory, probative or prejudicial, whether it is indicative of a person's guilt or innocence in a particular case, or whether the defendant is a threat to society at large. If the judge is permitted to exclude the evidence, the law is assuming that the judge is making the proper determination, and at the same time betraying a mistrust of the jury members to properly arbitrate and to judge.

The problem, on the other hand, with free and unfettered admission of evidence, is that we want the jury's attention to be focused on the factual questions involved. We want the jury to be focused on the determination of X, and the further the jury (or the judge, or the appellate court, or the legislature, or the media, or the public) gets from X, the less reliable the determination of X will be. This, in many ways, was the problem with the O.J. Simpson trial.

First, was the sheer volume of evidence, and the sheer length of the trial. The prosecution's evidence, even if it was a "mountain", was introduced in such a piecemeal fashion, over such a long period of time, amidst such scrutiny, interruption, and repetitious cross-examination from the defense, that it undoubtedly lost most if not all of its effect on the jury over the course of the trial. When the public was presented with the prosecution's case, it was done by news reporters, and commentators, who summed up all of the evidence in a nice little package, very short and concise, as if on a single poster-board. The jury, by contrast, saw bits and pieces of the case, separated by long periods of direct questioning, cross-examination, recess, week-ends, and sidebars, so that the force of the evidence was diluted, and its impact less profound. Second, were the collateral matters, which constantly drew the focus away from whether O.J. Simpson, on the night in question, went to his ex-wife's house, and killed two people with a knife. The focus of the trial, rather, was drawn to spousal abuse, the defendant's dreams, problems with alcohol, and the n-word. The evidence of spousal abuse in the O.J. Simpson trial is a classic example of other crimes evidence. The defense argued that it could not be admitted, because it would merely demonize O.J. in the eyes of the jury, who would believe that O.J. is a bad man, and therefore committed the crime.[147] The prosecution argued, on the other hand, that the evidence was relevant to show motive, and intent, and was therefore probative on the issue of whether O.J. Simpson killed his ex-wife on the night in question. The judge allowed this evidence to go to the jury, which, appropriately, was bothered by such evidence, but did not believe it to be dispositive of the defendant's guilt.

The evidence of O.J. Simpson's dream, in which he supposedly dreamed that he killed his wife, was the subject of much commentary at the beginning of the trial. Some commentators argued that people dream about countless things that they would never do in real life, and therefore the evidence was not probative, while others claimed that the report of his dream could have been a veiled confession.[148] The judge again allowed this to go to the jury, which was reasonable, but on cross examina-

147   Or, in the alternative, they would not care whether O.J. was guilty or innocent of killing Nicole, but would feel that, either way, he deserved to be punished for the spousal abuse alone.

148   In *State v. Patricia Van Winkle,* for example, the defendant was convicted, in part, by a confession in which she claimed to have dreamed about killing her son. 635 So.2d 1177 (La. App. 5th Cir. 1994).

tion, permitted the defense to delve into areas where they arguably did not belong. The witness was Ron Ship, an old friend of Mr. Simpson, who claimed that O.J. told him after the murders that he once had a dream of killing his ex-wife, Nicole. On cross-examination, the defense was permitted to solicit evidence of Mr. Ship's alleged drinking problem, even though there was no evidence to suggest that Ship was in any way impaired during his actual conversation with Simpson. The only effect of such evidence could have been to tell the jurors, "don't believe this guy because he is an alcoholic", even though the fact that he is an alcoholic has nothing to do with whether O.J. Simpson told him that he had a dream about killing his wife, and even less to do with whether O.J. Simpson, on the evening in question, went to his ex-wife's house, and killed two people with a knife. While the jury is certainly qualified to deem this evidence irrelevant and to disregard it, such testimony nevertheless takes the focus of the trial away from the determination of X. It dilutes the relevant evidence, and makes the determination of X less reliable.The most striking admission of evidence, in this regard, was the cross-examination of and other testimony concerning Detective Furhman. The fact that Furhman used the n-word, was abusive with suspects, or may have pulled African American drivers over without reasonable suspicion or probable cause, may prove that Furhman is a racist and a bigot, justify his dismissal from the police force, or form the basis of civil or even criminal liability. But the fact that Furhman used the n-word, almost ten years ago, does not, in and of itself, say anything about whether he planted evidence, and even less about whether O.J. Simpson, on the evening in question, went to his ex-wife's house, and killed two people with a knife. While the jury, again, is certainly able to dismiss the evidence as irrelevant, such testimony nevertheless dilutes the evidence, takes the focus away from the factual determinations at issue, and undermines the reliability of the trial.

The Jury

In many ways, it was not O.J. Simpson on trial, but the jury. Most people had a forgone conclusion about O.J. Simpson's guilt or innocence that was solidified before the trial began, and viewed the proceedings as a test of the jury, to see whether the jury would ultimately come to the "right" conclusion.

The "experts" in the media, for example, demonstrated an implicit mistrust of the jury. These experts, assuming that O.J. was innocent, told us that the inherent inequities of a system which was stacked against him would assure his conviction; or, in the majority of cases, assuming that O.J. was guilty, told us that the "song and dance show" put on by the defense team would hoodwink and bamboozle the jury, by playing on their racial biases and emotions, and by obfuscating the truth. Yet, nightly, on every call-in show, at least one lay person would phone in with some insight or observation, and the so-called expert analyst or commentator would say, "That's interesting, I never thought of that before."

In practically every way, the O.J. Simpson trial was atypical. From the fame of the defendant, to the television coverage, to the sequestration of the jury, to the number of attorneys, to the money expended, to the length of the trial. And yet, despite the fame of the defendant, the television coverage, the sequestration of the jury, the number of attorneys, the money expended, and the length of the trial, the things that most of the jurors have said about the case have been perfectly reasonable. They said that the gloves obviously fit, but that O.J. was not putting them on correctly. They said that Johnny Cochran played the race card, but that the prosecution played the race card too by assigning Christopher Darden to the case. They said that neither Furhman nor Vanatter were particularly believable witnesses. They said that they were troubled by the evidence of spousal abuse, but that some of the evidence cut both ways. They said that Johnny Cochran's closing was offensive, because he tried to pressure the jury into acquitting due to arbitrary factors, rather than relying on the merits of his case. And they said that, in a civil case, where the burden is preponderance of the evidence, they would have found against O.J. Simpson, but that the State had not proved his guilt beyond a reasonable doubt. And whether you believe, in your heart, or in your mind, that O.J. Simpson is guilty, that is a reasonable evaluation of the trial.[149]

The Case

The analysis of the O.J. Simpson trial was piecemeal. Each day, the writers and television commentators focused on who made points today, who lost points today, who made advances, and who, in their opinion, was

---

149   "During the criminal trial there was continuous public opinion polling asking whether Simpson was 'guilty' or 'innocent', even before the prosecution had finished its case. Yet the public was not polled about the question the jury had to decide: Do you believe that the State proved Simpson guilty beyond a reasonable doubt?" It is also important to remember, in this regard, all of the evidence that was not presented during the criminal trial, including: testimony that Simpson owned a blue and black sweat suit; Simpson's taped statement from the Bronco chase in which he said "the only person who deserves to be hurt is me"; a photograph of Simpson wearing the Bruno Magli shoes; a reported call from Nicole to a battered wife shelter days before the murder; Nicole's diary, including an entry that he beat the "holy hell" out of her; notes from an interview between Simpson and a spousal abuse expert; a recording of Nicole saying that Simpson got an "animal" look during a fight in 1993; phone records indicating that Simpson got a message from his then-girlfriend, Paula Barbieri, breaking off their relationship, the day of the murder; testimony about Simpson's "getaway" disguise with a toiletry bag and passport in the Bronco; expert testimony indicating that the cuts on Simpson's hands came from fingernails; additional testimony about spousal abuse; and the absence of any testimony from Mark Furhman. "Both juries in the Simpson civil and criminal cases reached reasonable verdicts" concluded attorney Barry Scheck, "given the different evidence before them and the very different burdens of proof they were sworn to apply." Scheck, "Tried and True" Newsweek Feb. 17, 1997. See also: Booth, "Legal Experts Cite Many Factors as Making Difference in Simpson Verdicts" Washington Post, Feb. 6, 1997, p.A-6.

harmed. Many, therefore, lost sight of the big picture, and what a truly interesting case this actually was.

We know that Nicole Simpson and Ronald Goldman were murdered. That is a fact. It cannot be disputed or denied. And given that fact, we know that someone must have killed them. And yet, at the same time, given that fact, and given the surrounding circumstances, it doesn't really make sense that O.J. Simpson killed them; and yet, on the other hand, it makes even less sense that it could have possibly been anyone else.

First of all, how did one person commit the crime; but, on the other hand, how did and why would two people?[150] Why was there blood; but, on the other hand, why wasn't there more blood? If it was a crime of passion by O.J., then why was it so carefully premeditated; but, on the other hand, if it was a robbery, initiated by someone else, why use a knife, instead of a gun? If the target was Nicole, why kill Goldman; but, on the other hand, if the target was Goldman, why do it there? Plus, and perhaps most significantly, with all of the people, and all of the resources, at the disposal of the defense, if it were someone other than O.J. Simpson, wouldn't they have uncovered at least some evidence about who it was? And then, of course, there is the blood. It must have been O.J. Simpson. But beyond a reasonable doubt? Maybe it was his son.

---

150   This question, of course, does not have anything to do with the guilt or innocence of O.J. Simpson specifically, because it doesn't make sense, whomever the killer was, (or killers were).

The Oklahoma City Bombing

The experts said it was a highly organized group of Muslim terrorists from the Middle East; as it turns out, it was a couple of white guys from Michigan. The experts said that they intentionally chose Oklahoma City because it was located in the geographical center of the nation, and in a place where people generally feel safe; as it turns out, it was just because they had happened to have been there before. The experts said that the bomb was detonated from an automobile or truck that was parked inside the courthouse garage; as it turns out, they just drove up and parked it right out in front of the building. The experts said it was a very sophisticated device, probably some sort of plastic explosives; as it turns out, they poured some diesel fuel over a bunch of fertilizer, stuck a fuse in it, and lit it on fire.

Political Posturing
President Clinton used the Oklahoma City bombing as an excuse to attack Republican talk show hosts, arguing that their inflammatory rhetoric was to blame.[151] Re-

151   Clinton spoke of "right wing extremists", "loud and angry voices", and "promoters of paranoia", on the radio, who have created a climate of anger towards, mistrust of, and hostility against, the Federal Government, and are therefore partly responsible for the bombing. See Jonathan Alter, "Toxic Speech" Newsweek, May 8, 1995, p.4; Rush Limbaugh, "Blame the Bombers Only" Newsweek, May 8, 1995, p.39; William Raspberry, "Words Can Push Some Over Edge" Times Picayune

publican Senate Leader Bob Dole responded by attacking television and movie producers supportive of the Democratic cause.[152]

It is one thing for a politician to attack hate speech because it may lead to violence, but it is quite another to attack such expression merely because the critic disagrees with the speaker's political, social, or religious beliefs.[153] Even assuming some causal connection between the media and the bombing, the President was not attacking Rush Limbaugh or G. Gordon Liddy because their rhetoric was responsible for the bombing; he was attacking them because they are his political enemies. Dole, likewise, was not attacking television and film producers because their programming leads to violence; he was attacking them because they are his political foes.[154]The bombing, in this way, brought into focus the political landscape as one of two parties which exist for the sake of their own advancement, rather than any political philosophy; who are devoted to interests, rather than ideas. The Democrats, accordingly, claimed that the terrorists were right-wing whackos; the Republicans called them left-wing anarchists and revolutionaries. What both par-

---

April 27, 1995, p.B-7.

[152]   Bob Dole lashed out against "Hollywood dream factories" who produce "nightmares of depravity" which have created a desensitized climate of violence and hate. "Hollywood Brushes Off Attacks by Dole" Times Picayune, June 2, 1995, p.A-9; Cal Thomas, "Is the Problem Really Hollywood?" Times Picayune June 8, 1995, p.B-7.

[153]   This distinction was touched upon by Justice Scalia in the *RAV* decision, in which he notes that "the power to proscribe particular speech on the basis of a noncontent element (*e.g.* noise) does not entail the power to proscribe the same speech on the basis of a content element. Thus, the government may proscribe libel; but it may not make the further content discrimination of proscribing *only* libel critical of the government. As with the sound truck, so also with fighting words: The government may not regulate based on hostility – or favoritism – towards the underlying message expressed." RAV vs. City of St. Paul, 505 U.S. 377, 383-387 (1992).

[154]   Dole admitted, in fact, that he had never even seen *True Romance* or *Natural Born Killers*, which he condemned as being too violent, while notably failing to voice any criticism for the notoriously graphic works of Arnold Schwartzenegger, Bruce Willis, or Sylvester Stallone, who are all Republicans.

ties ignore is the fact that liberal and conservative are not terms which describe Democrats and Republicans, but philosophies about the nature of government, in relation to the individual, and the structure of society as a whole.

Liberal and Conservative

A liberal has the fundamental belief that people are good, and that, left to their own devices, people have the ability, in general, to govern themselves. Conservatives, on the other hand, tend to believe that people are basically flawed, and that, left to their own devices, people will make the wrong choices, or act in a self-interested manner, which will lead to chaos and despair. To them, the government is there to protect people from each other, and at the same time, to protect people from themselves. The liberal welcomes change, and evolution, while the conservative wishes to protect the *status quo*. The liberal is marked by faith, and hope; the conservative marked by fear. The two-party system that we have in America, by contrast, revolves around issues, not beliefs. The Republicans are in many ways liberal, and the Democrats in many ways conservative.[155] What marks the parties, by and large, is their allegiance to various interests, and not political or social philosophies. The right to bear arms, for example, is generally considered "conservative", because the NRA and other similar groups have traditionally been members of the Republican Party. But as matter of political philosophy, the right to bear arms is a very liberal idea. Conservative thinkers want to avoid revolution and

155   "In America the use of the word 'liberal' by politicians has been used in the same degree of reverence as 'child-molester' to mean a person who believes in big government, lots of taxes and public spending, someone who is willing to infringe economic liberties in pursuit of the common good. In Europe, the word means just the opposite. A European liberal 'will favour limited government and give freedom priority over the supposed interests of society.' So it seems that in America 'liberal' has become detached from its proper meaning." Otis Pike, "The European Take on 'Liberalism'" The Times Picayune, Jan. 1, 1997, p.B-7, (quoting an article in *The Economist*).

anarchy, and therefore believe that a nation's arms should be placed in the hands of the government, to preserve the social order. Liberals, on the other hand, like our Founding Fathers, believed in decentralizing the military, and placing physical power, as well as political power, in the hands of the people. This would protect people from the tyranny of an oppressive government, with the concomitant belief that ordinary citizens could be trusted to carry arms.

The concept of "laissez faire" economics, likewise, is also a liberal idea. It places faith in the concept that people, if properly informed, will make their own wise economic choices, and that the markets, if left to their own dynamics of checks and balances, of investment and consumption, of supply and demand, will succeed, and progress, and evolve.

Environmental protection efforts, by contrast, are generally conservative. The environmentalists believe that corporations, if left alone, will fail to act responsibly. That they will rape the land of its natural resources, and dump their wastes untreated into the waters and air. This is not to say that the Republican Party is really liberal, and the Democratic Party conservative. It is only to say that the parties are not concerned, as they pretend to be, with any political philosophy. They just want to achieve a desired result.

Despite, for example, all of the Republican promotion of social Darwinism, laissez faire economics, and the free-market system, Republicans, by and large, want the government involved in the economy. They want the government to subsidize corporate interests, and to stimulate the economy, through tax credits, tax deductions, tax exemptions, pork-barrel contracts, research grants, farm subsidies, and immunities from government regulation, criminal sanction, and liability in tort. The party, in this way, is not dedicated to a liberal theory of economics. It is dedicated, rather, to the protection and the promotion of the wealthy, big business, and the corporation.[156]

Waco and Weaver

The events which transpired in Oklahoma have be-come inextricably intertwined with two other recent events, the Weaver shooting, and the Waco affair.[157] These events placed both Republicans and Democrats in uncomfortable positions, and, along with the bombing, exposed the parties as mere political animals who care more about furthering their own interests, as parties, than

[156]   The point was well made by George Will, in a column concern-ing the Republican Party's contradictory positions regarding the desire for a limited government in the areas of environmental, anti-trust, or other business regulations, as well as welfare, food stamps, and other "social" expenditures, and yet, at the same time, the desire for big government, in order to promote their "family values", such as censorship, restrictions on abortion, and prayer in public schools: "This could get con-servatives' dander up" he wrote. "A category of small businesses is being subjected to injurious regulation in New York City. That city, the capital of liberalism and hence overbearing government, is disrupting the free market by burdening, with the intent to discourage, a form of commerce involving a legal commodity. The government is do-ing this because it disapproves of the practice of supplying the particular commodity for which there is a demand. Furthermore, the government wants to engage in social engineering, shaping the social climate of neighborhoods by purging this commerce from most places where market forces have produced. It is enough to make conser-vatives' blood boil. Or maybe not. The commodity is pornography and other 'adult' entertainment. Hence the conservatives' conundrum: Can they square their advocacy of smaller, less intrusive government with a more ambitious moral agenda for govern-ment?" Will, "Big Stick Conservatism" Newsweek, Nov. 11, 1996, p.96.

[157]   In 1993, a leader of the Branch Davidian cult, David Koresh, locked himself away with a number of cult members including many children whom Koresh had allegedly molested, with a tremendous amount of weapons, many of which were illegal, and was therefore being pursued by, among others, the ATF. There was a stand-off between the Branch Davidians and Federal Agents in Waco, Texas, which ended when the Federal Agents attempted to take the compound, and Branch Davidians, in a mass suicide effort, set the compound on fire. A year earlier, the ATF was involved in another stand-off in Idaho, when they were led to the farm of a sep-aratist named Randy Weaver. Mr. Weaver, who was rumored to be a Nazi or a Nazi sympathizer, first sold illegal weapons to an undercover ATF Agent in 1986, refused to spy on the Nazis, and was arrested again on illegal weapons charges in 1991. Weaver and his family holed up in their cabin on Ruby Ridge, when Federal Marshals were in-volved in a shootout with Weaver's son, leaving Sammy Weaver and Federal Marshal William Degan dead. The FBI was called in, there was a stand-off, which lasted ten days, and ended when a sharp-shooter killed Vicki Weaver, who was standing in the doorway, cradling her child in her arms.

about the ideas and principles to which they generally ascribe. For the last several decades, Democrats have consistently supported the rights of individuals, even guilty individuals, against potential overreaching and abuse by the police and other law enforcement agencies. Republicans, on the other hand, have consistently taken a hard line on crime. They have supported the police power of both state and federal governmental efforts to investigate criminal activity, accepting as necessary minor incidents of overreaching or abuse.

If the parties had been true to their traditional values, the Democrats would have argued that people, whatever their political or religious views may be, have the right to be left alone. If separatist families, or cults, or anyone else, want to lock themselves up away from society, in the absence of some injury to the property or rights of their neighbors, the police and federal law enforcement officials should respect their privacy interests and leave them alone. The Republicans, on the other hand, would have argued that the government cannot sit idly by while criminals evade prosecution, locking themselves away in compounds, while stock-piling illegal weapons and arms.

The Democratic White House, however, in the wake of the Oklahoma City bombing, immediately requested anti-terrorist legislation, which sought to expand the search and seizure powers of the FBI.

The Republican Congress, at the same time, came to the defense of Weaver and Koresh, and attacked the law enforcement officers for overreaching, while the Democrats, who ironically inherited the situation from a Republican administration, defended them.

This, of course, is just one example of the many contradictory positions which evidence an allegiance to classes and interests, rather than principles or ideas. The Republicans who defended Clarence Thomas, for example, then attacked President Clinton, while the Democrats who lionized Anita Hill then condemned and ridiculed Paula Jones. The Democrats, likewise, who complained that the Iran Contra Hearings didn't go far enough, are the same people who later complained that the Whitewater Investigation had gone too far. When it's poor black people or Hispanics in the projects, Republicans support the government's unfettered right to search, seize, and keep the peace, but when it comes to white right-wing fascists in the mountains, or the privacy interests of corporations, or the expropriation of private lands, Due Process and Just Compensation have no bounds. And finally, Democrats, who support the rights of plaintiffs in civil cases, jump to the defense of the wrongdoer in a criminal proceeding, while Republicans, who lead the fight against street criminals, bend over backwards to protect and to insulate wealthy corporate defendants from accountability under the law.

The Terry Nichols Trial

In the trial of Terry Nichols for the bombing of the Alfred P. Murrah Federal Building, not one prosecution witness saw Terry Nichols with Timothy McVeigh, and only one witness placed Nichols anywhere near Oklahoma City – *i.e.* Herington, Kansas, roughly 250 miles away – during the week before the explosion.[158] There were no confessions or other incriminating statements made by or attributed to Terry Nichols. And the woman who handled the paperwork for the rental of the Ryder truck testified that it was not Terry Nichols who accompanied McVeigh when they came to pick up the truck. The trial of Terry Nichols, therefore, tends to illustrate a dangerous grey line between convicting people based upon their actions, and punishing them for their associations or beliefs.

158   An employee of a surplus store testified that Nichols asked to trade picks and axes for shingles.

The prosecution, for example, introduced evidence that Nichols was the member of a militia, who owned and handled weapons, who was troubled by the events at Waco and Ruby Ridge, and who was generally mistrustful of an overly-expansive government. The prosecution introduced evidence that Nichols owned anti-government literature, including the anti-Semitic novel *Hunter,* which was found at the Nichols home. And finally, the prosecution introduced evidence that Nichols and McVeigh were good friends prior to the explosion. This evidence, of course, complimented a host of other evidence, (all circumstantial), including fingerprints found on the wrapper of a blasting cap in Kingman, Arizona;[159] fingerprints on a contract for a storage shed in Council Gove, Kansas, near Herington, rented under the name "Ted Parker"; fingerprints on a registration receipt for the registration of a room in Pauls Valley, Oklahoma, south of Oklahoma City, in the name of "Joe Kyle" in October of 1994; a receipt for a ton of ammonium nitrate fertilizer with Timothy McVeigh's fingerprints that was found in Nichols' kitchen; coins and guns that were apparently recovered from the robbery of an Arkansas gun collector, (allegedly by Nichols and McVeigh), in November of 1994; hearsay testimony attributing statements to McVeigh, (but not Nichols), that the two of them intended to blow up the Alfred P. Murrah Federal Building; evidence that Nichols lied about what he was doing the day that the bomb was constructed;[160] and, finally, testimony from Nichols'

[159] The prosecution's main witness, Michael Fortier, was a friend of Timothy McVeigh, who lived in Kingman, Arizona. Timothy McVeigh apparently told Fortier that he intended to use explosives that were stored in Kingman to detonate a bomb in Oklahoma City, and that he wanted Fortier to hold on to several blasting caps for safe keeping.

[160] Nichols claimed that he was at a government auction in Fort Riley, Kansas, and produced a receipt which appeared to indicate that he had submitted a sealed bid at 12:37 p.m. on March 18, 1995. The prosecution, however, presented evidence that the time-clock was a month and an hour off, and that the bid, therefore, was actually submitted at 1:37 p.m. on April 18, 1995.

wife that she recalled seeing a letter from McVeigh about a week before the explosion, making references to "shake and bake" and needing "an excuse for your second half." While all of this evidence, together, is likely sufficient to form the basis of a conviction, this strain of prosecution certainly blurs the distinction between action and thought, personal responsibility and guilt by association. It raises questions about at what point can people be held responsible for the books that they own, or the political party they belong to, or the conduct of their friends. To what extent can a person be held responsible, not for his actions, but for his beliefs.

The Social Contract

Without government, there can be no evolution culturally, no scientific progress, no economic growth. Men and women, alone, would live in a constant state of fear. They would hesitate to develop, to cultivate, and to construct, for fear that some other person or group of people would come along and take the products of their labor, or destroy them, and all of their industry would be lost.[161] So we, collectively, by consent, give a part of our autonomy, a part of our authority, a part of our freedom, to the sovereign, for our common benefit and protection, which thereby allows us to grow.[162]

161   "Nature hath made men so equall, in the faculties of body, and mind; as that though there be found one man sometimes manifestly stronger in body, or of quicker mind than another; yet when all is reckoned together, the difference between man, and man, is not so considerable, as that one man can thereupon claim to himself any benefit, to which another may not pretend, as well as he. For as to strength of body, the weakest has strength enough to kill the strongest, either by secret machination, or by confederacy with others, that are in the same danger with himself. It is manifest that during the time men live without a common Power to keep them all in awe, they are in that condition which is called Warre; and such a warre, as is of every man, against every man. In such a condition, there is no place for Industry; because the fruit thereof is uncertain: and consequently no Culture of the Earth; no Navigation, nor use of the commodities that may be imported by Sea; no Building; no instruments of moving, and removing such things as require force; no Knowledge of the face of the Earth; no account of Time; no Arts; no Letters; no Society; and which is worst of all, continual fear, and danger of violent death. And the life of man solitary, poore, nasty, brutish, and short." Hobbes, Leviathan, Part I, Chpt. 13 (1651).

162   "Man being, as has been said, by nature all free, equal and independent, no man can be put out of his estate and subjected to the political power of another without his own consent. The only way whereby anyone divests himself of

There are some things, however, which are not subject to the social contract. Matters which are personal and private, like thought, and speech, and religious beliefs, which do not affect others, nor pose a threat to society at large. Such rights, it has been said, are inalienable, bestowed by Natural Law.[163]There are other rights which are inalienable, because they are corollary to the social contract itself. Such rights, which include due process, equal protection, and just compensation, ensure that the sacrifices demanded by the social contract fall equally and universally on the shoulders of all of its citizens, as well as the benefits which the social contract confers.[164]These rights stand independent of any further constitutional protections which may be incorporated, by the consent of the people, within the fabric of the social contract itself. Those types of rights, such as the right to bear arms, the right to trial by jury, or the right to appointed counsel, are not in and of themselves inalienable, but are, rather, principles to which we are wedded, because we feel, as a nation, that they are integral to our society, and in many

his natural liberty and puts on the bounds of civil society is by agreeing with other men to join and unite into a community for their comfortable, safe, and peaceful living one against another in a secure enjoyment of their properties, and a greater security against any that are not of it. This any number of men may do, because it injures not the freedom of the rest; they are left as they were, in the liberty of the state of nature. When any number of men have so consented to make one community, or government, they are thereby presently incorporated, and make one body politic, wherein the majority have the right to act and conclude for the rest." Locke, Second Treatise on Government, Chpt. VIII, §95 (1681).

163   "There should be some Rights" Hobbes made clear, "which no man can be understood by any words, or other signes, to have abandoned, or transferred." Leviathan, Part I, Chpt. 13.

164   "The commitments that bind us to the social body are obligatory only because they are mutual, and their nature is such that, in fulfilling them, one cannot work for others without also working for himself. Equality of rights, and the notion of justice it produces, stem from the preference that each man gives to himself, and therefore the nature of man.... In order to be truly general, the general will must be general in its object as well as in its essence, that it must come from everyone if it is to apply to everyone.... By whatever direction we approach the principle, we always reach the same conclusion, namely, that the social pact establishes such equality among citizens that they all bind themselves under the same conditions and should all enjoy the same rights." Rousseau, The Social Contract, Chpt. 4 (1762).

ways necessary to guarantee other rights and individual freedoms, which are inalienable, and which are the aims of all human industry, community, and growth.

Our Social Contract

Our social contract is the Constitution. It establishes a limited form of government, with specific enumerated powers, which are vested in the legislative branch, subject to the inalienable and natural rights of men. Congress, within this structure, is held to the provisions of the social contract through a system of checks and balances among the branches of the Federal Government, as well as the Tenth Amendment and those powers reserved to the States. It is the hope that, in maintaining such a separation of powers among the many members of the body politic, individual rights and freedoms will be better protected and preserved.[165]

Inalienable Rights and Corollary Principles

Many people seem to believe that rights and freedoms in America are guaranteed merely by the Bill of Rights, or some other Constitutional protection, and therefore, if the Constitution were changed or amended, such protections could be modified, or abrogated altogether.

Even in a democracy, however, there are limits. Because the democratic process is naturally limited to matters of public concern.[166] Majorities, and even super-ma-

165   "In a single republic, all the power surrendered by the people is submitted to the administration of a single government; and the usurpations are guarded against by a division of the government into distinct and separate departments. In the compound republic of America, the power surrendered by the people is first divided into two distinct governments, and then the portion allotted to each subdivided among distinct and separate departments. Hence a double security arises to the rights of the people. The different governments will control each other, at the same time that each will be controlled by itself." Madison, The Federalist Papers, No. 51 (1788).

166   "Besides the public person, we must also consider the private persons who compose it, and whose life and freedom are naturally independent of it. We must therefore distinguish between the respective rights of the citizens and the sovereign, as well as between the duties which the citizens must fulfill as subjects

jorities, cannot bind individuals to their will on non-social, non-governmental, non-public issues. In a world of one million people, 999,999 cannot force the last to give his or her faith to a certain deity. They cannot make the last marry another, nor prevent her from watching a movie, nor from writing a book. The government, in this regard, has no right, nor power, nor authority, to interfere with choices and activities which are merely private, or which are metaphysical, and have no direct and appreciable effect on the physical, public world.[167]The government, and the people who comprise it, are likewise bound by corollary principles, which are axiomatic to the social contract itself. Majorities, and even super-majorities, in this regard, cannot accept benefits at the sole expense of a minority, nor expropriate property without just compensation, nor deprive any man or woman of life, liberty, or property, without due process of law.

The presence of such unenumerated and inalienable rights is confirmed by the Ninth Amendment, which provides that "the enumeration in the Constitution, of certain rights, shall not be construed to disparage others retained by the people."[168] It is possible, therefore, in this way, for

---

and the natural rights they should enjoy as men. It is acknowledged that the social pact requires each individual to relinquish only that part of his power, possessions and freedom which it is important to the community to control." Rousseau, The Social Contract Chpt. 4 (1762).

167   "The makers of our Constitution undertook to secure conditions favorable to the pursuit of happiness. They recognized the significance of man's spiritual nature, of his feelings and his intellect. They knew that only a part of the pain, pleasure, and satisfaction of life are to be found in material things. They sought to protect Americans in their beliefs, their thoughts, their emotions, and their sensations. They conferred, as against the government, the right to be left alone – the most comprehensive of rights and the right most valued by civilized men." Justice Brandeis, dissenting, Olmstead v. United States, 277 U.S. 438, 478 (1928).

168   "The language and history of the Ninth Amendment reveal that the Framers of the Constitution believed that there are additional fundamental rights, protected from governmental infringement, which exist alongside those fundamental rights specifically enumerated in the first eight constitutional amendments. It was proffered to quiet expressed fears that a bill of specifically enumerated rights could not be sufficiently broad to cover all essential rights and that the specific retention of certain rights would be interpreted as a denial of others that were protected." Justice

a Constitutional provision to be "unconstitutional", in the sense that the text of the social contract itself, if violative of such inalienable rights and principles, could, by nature, be rendered null and void.

The Difference Between Legislative and Constitutional Questions

Many people seem to believe that governmental powers, like individual protections, are subject to the will of the people, and therefore, change. They view constitutional questions in the same way that they view legislative questions – as a balancing of competing interests, of costs and benefits, of public support versus disfavor, and with respect to the actual merits of the governmental action or law.

Constitutional questions, however, are very different from legislative questions. Their focus lies with the function of the government, the power of the government, the authority of the government, and its role. Constitutional questions seek to determine which, if any, governmental body is responsible for taking such action; and whether, in taking such action, that governmental body will be interfering with or abrogating inalienable rights, corollary principles, or other constitutionally established guarantees. The general analysis, in this regard, is: (a) Is it subject to the social contract? (b) Is it part of the social contract? (c) Does it abridge some inalienable right or constitutional protection? (d) And then, finally, is it effective or ineffective, cost-efficient or wasteful, good or bad. To survive both constitutional and political analysis, therefore, a Congressional measure must first involve an issue or an activity which is subject to governmental regulation. Next, the measure must relate to one of the specifically enumerated powers conferred to Congress

Goldberg, joined by Warren and Brennan, concurring, Griswold v. Connecticut, 381 U.S. 479, 488-489 (1965).

in Article I. Then, the law must avoid interfering with
or abrogating rights conferred to the people in the Bill
of Rights, or other corollary principles. And finally, once
those constitutional requirements have been satisfied,
the law should be supported by the people, the benefits
should outweigh the costs, and the means by which the
law is effected should generally be well-tailored to ends
for which the measure was proposed.[169]

The Limits of Governmental Power

As noted above, the government, independent of
the Constitution, is limited to matters which are public
and social by nature, such that the activity or conduct
in question will have a direct and appreciable effect on
other men. If, on the other hand, the matter is personal,
or private, or spiritual, the government, regardless of the
Constitution, has no right to get involved.[170]With an issue
such as prayer in public schools, therefore, the question
is not whether daily prayer by America's children would
instill a sense of value and purpose, or whether it would
help to stop violence or illiteracy or teenage pregnancy,

---

169   When dealing with the action of a State Legislature, the analysis
is: (a) whether the activity in question is subject to governmental action or regulation;
(b) whether the power is conferred to the State under that State's Constitution, (which
generally confers a plenary police power, of unenumerated rights, to act on behalf of
the welfare of its citizens); (c) whether the State action or regulation is preempted by
some Federal action or law; (d) whether the action or regulation would abrogate a right
conferred by the Federal Constitution, the State Constitution, or otherwise reserved
to the people by corollary principles, or other rights of Natural Law; and finally, (e)
whether the law is supported by the people, whether its costs would be outweighed
by its benefits, whether it would be effective, whether it would be cost-efficient, and
whether the means are well-tailored to the ends for which the measure was proposed.

170   "As soon as any part of a person's conduct affects prejudicially
the interests of others, society has jurisdiction over it, and the question whether the
general welfare will or will not be promoted by interfering with it, becomes open to
discussion. But there is no room for entertaining any such question when a person's
conduct affects the interests of no persons besides himself, or needs not affect them
unless they like (all the persons concerned being of full age, and the ordinary amount
of understanding). In all such cases there should be perfect freedom, legal and social,
to do the action and stand the consequences." John Stuart Mill, "Of the Limits of
Authority of Society Over the Individual" On Liberty (1859).

or whether some kids would be uncomfortable, or even whether such a measure would be violative of the First Amendment's Establishments Clause. The question, rather, is whether the government, any government, has the authority to legislate in an area which is private, spiritual, metaphysical, and necessarily personal to the individual involved. The issue of drug legalization, likewise, is not limited to questions about whether the absence of proscriptions on drug use would lead to intolerable levels of addiction, or whether it is ultimately cost-effective to spend money fighting the importation and distribution of narcotics, or whether the criminalization of drug use is actually resulting in the commission of more crime. There is also a legitimate question as to whether the government, any government, has the authority to legislate in an area which is ultimately private and personal to the individual involved.[171]

This is not to say that people have an "inalienable right" to use drugs, or to commit suicide, or to engage in various sexual practices, which are analogous to the rights of free thought, free speech, and free religion. But the limits on society's authority to legitimately interfere with such activity will result in various *de facto* privacy rights, and afford individuals the freedom to engage in such activities, which do not, in and of themselves, cause the public any harm.[172]

Inclusion Within the Social Contract
Assuming that the conduct or activity in question is

---

171   Of course, as soon as an individual's drug use threatens the life or property of another – *e.g.* driving under the influence, distributing to minors, criminal trespass – it will then become a matter of public concern.

172   Viewed in this light, it can be said that *Roe v. Wade* decision does not stand for the proposition that a woman has a constitutional "right" to have an abortion, but rather that, due to the inherent limits on the powers of public bodies, and the inherently private and personal nature of the decisions involved, the State is without right or authority to prohibit such conduct, or make it criminal.

subject to governmental regulation, there arises a question of whether the governmental action or regulation in question is included within the specific enumerated powers conferred by the social contract, in Article I.It is of no moment, otherwise, how good, or effective, or cost-efficient, a measure might seem. It is of no moment how broad, or widespread, or strong the public support. The social contract in America is limited to the terms of the Constitution. And the Federal Government only has the power to establish and to regulate interstate commerce, immigration and naturalization, bankruptcy, patents, copyrights, the post office, the army, the navy, the militia, and the inferior federal courts. In all other matters, the Federal Government is without authority to act, no matter how well-intentioned or popular or apparently effective such action might be.[173]

Corollary Principles and Other Constitutional Protections

As noted above, the Federal Government cannot, even in the areas of interstate commerce, immigration and naturalization, bankruptcy, patents, copyrights, and national defense, make any law which deprives people of inalien-

---

173   As a practical matter, the great majority of Congressional power stems from the commerce clause, which, since the New Deal, has been construed to allow Congress to take action in any area which "affects" or "is affected by" interstate commerce in the aggregate – *i.e.* a broad and expansive interpretation, which has generally conferred on Congress free license to take any action it wishes. However, the Supreme Court has recently recognized some boundaries to Congressional power under the Commerce Clause, which traditionally did not apply to agricultural activities, the production and manufacture of goods, or the sale of goods and services among two people within the same state. "If we wish to be true a Constitution that does not cede police power to the Federal Government" wrote Justice Thomas, "our Commerce Clause's boundaries simply cannot be defined as being 'commensurate with the national needs' or self-consciously intended to let the Federal Government 'defend itself against economic forces that Congress decrees inimical or destructive to the national economy.' Such a formulation of federal power is no test at all: it is a blank check. At an appropriate juncture, I think we must modify our Commerce Clause jurisprudence. Today, it is easy enough to say that the Clause certainly does not empower Congress to ban gun possession within 1,000 feet of a school." Justice Thomas, concurring, U.S. v. Lopez, 115 S.Ct. 1624, 1650-1651 (1995).

able rights, such as free speech and free religion, corollary principles, such as due process and equal protection, or other constitutionally established protections, such as trial by jury and the right to bear arms.

Because constitutional interpretation is entrusted to the judicial branch of the government, the recognition of such protections is closely related to separation of powers doctrine, because the court, itself, to some extent, has the ability to define its own powers.[174]In the legislative arena, the courts appropriately defer to Congress and to the States, because poor legislative decisions can be corrected through the political process. In the constitutional arena, on the other hand, the court will interfere with the legislative process in order to protect individual freedoms, which do not depend on the will of the majority, or in situations where the effects of legislation in question are not subject to the political check.[175]The courts, like legislative bodies, are bound by the constitution and its underlying principles, and are therefore prohibited from

174   An example of the judiciary defining its own powers was illustrated recently in the case of *Clinton v. Paula Jones.* When the plaintiff, Ms. Jones, instituted a sexual harassment claim against the President, he attempted to assert an immunity which would have suspended prosecution of the action until the end of his term. Clinton asserted that such an immunity was implied by the Constitutional structure, and its separation of powers among the several branches of government. While many believed that such an immunity would be in the best interests of the public, in order to protect the dignity of the office, and to prevent interference with his Presidential duties, the Supreme Court held that it was the role of the Congress, not the judiciary, to make such a policy decision. "If Congress deems it appropriate" the Court wrote, "to afford the President stronger protection, it may respond with appropriate legislation." But because Congress had not created such an immunity, the Court was not empowered to stay the civil suit. Clinton v. Jones, 117 S.Ct. 1636 (1997).

175   As discussed previously, the guarantee of equal protection operates along this basis: The people, acting through their representatives, generally have the right to determine that the benefits of a given proposal outweigh the costs, so long as those costs are distributed equally over society at large. The courts, in this instance, will not invalidate the provision, even if it turns out to be a "bad bargain", because the majority can always come back and have the measure modified or repealed. What the majority cannot do, however, is accept various benefits, at the expense of a limited group of individuals, because that proposal is bound to be a bad bargain for the minority, who are powerless to effectuate political change. The doctrine, in this way, works like a constitutionally issued license, which allows the courts to step in and nullify rules of law which would otherwise be left to the legislative prerogative.

engaging in a cost/benefit analysis when fundamental rights are at stake. The judiciary, nevertheless, has traditionally confused constitutional analysis with the legislative process, whereby the right or liberty at issue is treated merely as a factor to be considered against the weight of the governmental interest involved. To remain true to the fundamental principles which underlie the social contract, the courts need to retreat from this balancing approach, wherein inalienable rights, corollary principles and other constitutionally established protections are merely seen as interests to be factored against countervailing social and economic forces, and begin to view them as absolutes.

The Law

Once the foregoing constitutional requirements have been satisfied, and only then, are the elected representatives permitted to engage in the legislative process, wherein the focus of inquiry becomes whether the program or law will produce benefits which outweigh the costs, whether there is public support for the legislation, and whether the measure is well-designed to achieve the intended results. Within our structure of government, such decisions are left to the discretion of legislative bodies, who are free to make such policy decisions on behalf of the people, subject to the political check, in the form of the vote. As a matter of policy, the law should be simple, coherent, consistent, permanent, universal, and fair. Laws should not, in this regard, be made on an *ad hoc* basis. They should not be enacted to satisfy the desires of a particular group or interest, nor address an immediate issue of concern. A good law will still be good in fifty years. A permanent measure should not be employed in an attempt to remedy a temporary concern. Otherwise, the people will be left with a hodge-podge of topical laws that are neither consistent nor coherent, nor complete. They will be out-dated and arcane to their purposes. An invitation to injustice and anomaly.

The Dual Sovereignty of the Federal Government and the States

Our constitution establishes a dual sovereignty wherein the power of the Federal Government is coexistent with the powers of the respective States. Like the separation of powers among the three branches of the Federal Government, a bifurcation of power between the States and the Federal Government would prevent an accumulation of excessive power in any one body, thereby reducing the risk of tyranny, and promoting the preservation and advancement of individual liberties.[176]Under this system of dual sovereignty, the powers of the States are numerous and indefinite, while the powers of the Federal Government are few and defined.[177] While, therefore, the Constitution establishes a hierarchy in favor of the Federal Government which is conferred by the Supremacy Clause, the consideration of whether State Action is usurped by Federal Regulation should begin and end with the presumption that the historic police powers of the States are

---

176   "A confederacy of the people, without exaggeration, may be said to be entirely the masters of their own fate. Power being almost always the rival of power, the general government will at all times stand ready to check the usurpations of the state governments, and these will have the same disposition toward the general government. The people, by throwing themselves into either scale, will infallibly make it preponderate. If their rights are invaded by either, they can make use of the other as an instrument of redress." Alexander Hamilton, The Federalist Papers, No.28 (1788).

177   "The powers delegated by the proposed Constitution to the federal government are few and defined. Those which are to remain in the State governments are numerous and indefinite. The former will be exercised principally on external objects, as war, peace, negotiation, and foreign commerce; with which last the power of taxation will, for the most part, be connected. The powers reserved to the several States will extend to all the objects which, in the ordinary course of affairs, concern their lives, liberties, and properties of the people, and the internal order, improvement, and prosperity of the State." James Madison, The Federalist Papers, No. 45 (1788).

not preempted by Federal Law. The courts, in this regard, have recognized three types of preemption: express preemption, where Congress explicitly provides that State law is to be preempted by Federal statute; implied preemption, where the scheme of Federal regulation is sufficiently comprehensive to reasonably infer that Congress has "left no room" for supplementary regulations by the States; and implied preemption, where there is an actual conflict between the Federal legislation and incompatible State regulation or law.

Given, however, the limited nature of the Federal Government and its powers, it is somewhat disturbing that Congressional action has been afforded such wide preemptive effect by the courts. Congress, in this regard, should not be able to preempt State Action in a given area merely by expressing a desire to do so.[178] Nor should the actions by Congress be construed, in light of the limited and specifically defined limits of its concurrent powers, to have an "implied" preemptive effect.[179] The only instances, thus, in which proposed government action by the States should be deemed to have been preempted by Federal Legislation, are instances where there is an actual conflict between the two mandates, such that compliance with both is impossible. As a practical matter, moreover, in the context of civil litigation, where the effects of Federal Preemption are most prominent, corporations should

---

178   "It merits particular attention that the laws of the Confederacy as to the *enumerated* and *legitimate* objects of its jurisdiction will become the SUPREME LAW of the land. Thus, the legislatures, courts, and magistrates, of the respective members will be incorporated into the operations of the national government *as far as its just and constitutional authority extends.*" Printz v. U.S., 117 S.Ct. 2365, 2373 (1997); Hamilton, The Federalist Papers, No.27 (1788). "The Court [in *Gibbons v. Ogden*] was not saying that whatever Congress believes is a national matter becomes an object of federal control." Justice Thomas, concurring, U.S. v. Lopez, 115 S.Ct. 1624, 1648 (1995).

179   "The right of citizens to recourse in the courts in the event of injury is too important a right to be implicitly pre-empted or overturned." Attorney General Dennis Vacco, *"Medtronic v. Lohr:* Important But Incomplete" New York State Trial Lawyers Institute, p.10 (1996).

not be permitted to evade accountability for their unsafe and defective products merely because they have complied with the minimum requirements of Federal Regulation.[180]In addition to the fact that legislative decisions are often guided by private interests, and that the judgment of regulatory bodies is not infallible, there is also a distinction that must be drawn between positive enactments, which seek to establish minimum standards for the placement of goods and services in the stream of commerce, and civil actions for damages, which seek to redress personal injuries and social wrongs.[181]As noted by Tom Triplett, of South Carolina, during deliberations over the passage of the National Highway Safety Act, "we need a traffic safety agency and we need to research our problem from end to end, but we don't need to relieve the manufacturer

180   "Government regulations provide uniform performance requirements to deter manufacturers from marketing defectively designed products. Design defect litigation, because it is fact intensive, insulated from the political process, and capable of responding to rapid technological advances, provides more individualized remedies for harm caused by defective designs." Ford Bronco II, 909 F.Supp. 400, 409 (E.D.La. 1995).

181   "Unlike positive state enactments" wrote the Ninth Circuit, concerning the preemption of state law products liability actions due to the passage of the Medical Devices Amendments to the Food and Drug Act, "common law imposes only an indirect effect on manufacturers. Defendants in common law damages actions retain the freedom to choose their own response to the legal challenges they face. For example, manufacturers facing common law challenges retain the discretion whether to alter their product or whether to bear the cost of any lawsuits that might result from their decision, whereas, manufacturers bound by positive state enactments are required to conform their product to the law.... State common law damages actions guarantee people who are injured by a manufacturer the opportunity to be compensated for their harm. State regulation of manufacturers directly governs their actions in releasing their goods into the market. Thus, state common law serves a different purpose than state regulation and is unlikely to have been the target of congressional attempts to promote the introduction of safe medical devices onto the market or even curb dual regulation of the medical devices industry. Reading the MDA's preemption provision in the manner advocated by the defendant would result in consumers of Class III devices being left without recourse for any harm suffered. Such a result flies in the face of the congressional intent behind the MDA legislation: consumer protection. The federal law requiring the premarket approval of Class III devices was not enacted in order to free manufacturers from the everyday burdens of the marketplace after they are permitted to enter it. Premarket approval is supposed to benefit consumers, not create a rose garden, free from liability, for manufacturers." Kennedy v. Collagen Corp., 67 F.3d 1453, 1459-1460 (9th Cir. 1995).

of his natural responsibility for the performance of his product. You may think that the manufacturer is afraid of government regulation, but the cry you are hearing may be, 'Brer Fox, please don't throw me into the briar patch!' If the government assumes the responsibility of safety design in our vehicles, the manufacturers will join together for another 30-year snooze under the veil of government sanction, and in thousands of courtrooms across the nation, wronged individuals will encounter the stone wall of, 'Our product meets government standards,' and an already compounded problem will be recompounded."[182]

Taxing

Paying taxes is the most direct and immediate relationship that people have with their government on a continuing basis. The relationship, therefore, between a government and its citizens will in large part be determined by the tax system, in terms of both the structure and the amount of taxes that are paid.

The touchstone requirements of any tax structure are that the system be simple, universal, and fair. Whether a single flat rate, or a series of progressive levels, the entire tax code should be able to be printed on a single page.[183] Everyone should participate.[184] And all income, whether

182   Hearings Before the Committee on Interstate and Foreign Commerce of the House of Representatives, 89th Congress, 2nd Sess. Part 2, 1249 (1966).

183   Simple and progressive are not mutually exclusive. The number of rates does not make the structure any more complicated. A taxpayer would still be able to file a return on a single postcard. It would merely require one more step in the process – i.e. the taxpayer would have to look at a chart to determine what rate he or she is paying, and then use that number as the multiplier, rather than a pre-determined static X percent. It would probably be best, in this regard, to have a progressive series of 3%, 7%, 10%, 13%, 17%, 20%, 23%, 27%, 30%, based on the total yearly income involved. The problem with having such a progressive system, however, is that, while, in a real sense, it is more "fair", something about it seems unfair. People will always tend to believe that they are carrying a disproportionate burden, which will cause resentment and class warfare. Therefore, it may be that, in this instance, the appearance of fairness is more important than actual fairness, and a single tax rate of 19% or 21%, for example, may be preferable to a progressive scale.

184   Even people on welfare, or other social assistance, should be

personal or corporate, salary or wages, dividends or capital gains, should be taxed the same.[185]The code should include three exemptions: one for charitable contributions, one for health care expenditures, and one for expenditures on education. Many of the current exemptions are designed, unlike these, either to protect special interests, or to encourage the American people to manage their money in various ways. The problem is that, by giving an exemption to encourage people to do one thing, the government is effectively punishing people for doing something else. And it is not the proper function of the government to punish people for renting, rather than home-owning, or for saving, rather than spending, or for investing in stocks, rather than purchasing bonds. In a democracy, like America, we assume that people, and not the government, can best decide how to manage their own affairs. The only exemptions which are therefore justified in a tax code are those private expenditures for services which are governmental in form. Charitable organizations, in this regard, are essentially privatized systems of government, which compound resources from their benefactors, and redirect them for the support of common services, uti-

required to contribute. Even if it is only symbolic. People must feel that they have some stake in their government, and its activities, and its expenditures, and should also have an appreciation of the sacrifices that each and every other citizen is required to make.

185   The people who advocate getting rid of the capital gains tax argue that the corporation pays taxes on its income, and therefore, such taxes have already been paid. The corporation, however, is a legal fiction, which is responsible for the payment of its own taxes, as a person, while at the same time protecting the owners of the corporation by limiting their potential loss. The creation of the corporation, in this regard, is a *quid pro quo:* the shareholder pays taxes twice on the income, but is not held personally liable for the debts of the corporation. What the advocates of capital gains exclusions really seek is to "have their cake and eat it too" so to speak. They want the benefits and protections of the corporation, without the concomitant responsibilities.

Those who are able to control their own terms of employment, moreover, would be able to restructure their income so that very little of the money they earn is paid as "salary" while the great majority of their money comes to them in the form of "dividends" or "capital gains". The extremely wealthy, therefore, would pay little or no taxes, with a disproportionate tax burden falling on the middle class.

lized for the public good. There is no reason, therefore, in this regard, to compel people to contribute, twice, to a system to which they are already contributing voluntarily. Education, likewise, is a public system, which is subsidized and supported by the government on a universal basis. There is no reason, accordingly, to tax people on income which is already supporting, even in a private or semi-private setting, a system which is essentially public, and maintained by public funds. With respect to medical expenditures, the health of the individual, like the education of the individual, is in many ways a public concern. The contagious nature of much illness and infection, the potential for epidemics, and the importance of physical well-being to private industry and economic development, make the health of one, in many ways, the health of all. There seems to be, moreover, a broad consensus that the public should be maintaining the health care system,[186] yet without abridging the choice of consumers, nor the professional autonomy of medical providers. While some further public services such as Medicaid might still be appropriate for people who are indigent, and for those who have suffered catastrophic injury or disease, an exemption for all health care and medical expenditures would be a good way for the public to subsidize and support the health care system, while preserving professional autonomy and choice. These three exemptions are appropriate and meaningful, because they are not designed to encourage or discourage people from making economic choices, but rather, to make the taxation of personal expenditures complimentary with the support and maintenance of pub-

---

186   As evidenced by the enactment of the Medicare and Medicaid programs, the establishment and support of charity hospital systems, and the Bill Clinton election process and administration, I think it is safe to say that, even though people are wary and resentful of others who might get a "free ride", the great majority of people in this country have an instinctive belief that necessary health care is something, like food, shelter, or education, which, particularly in the case of children, should, absent extreme circumstances, somehow be provided.

lic needs.

Spending

The purpose of governmental enterprise is to fulfill a common demand, which, as a practical matter, cannot be supplied at a profit by the private sector on an individual basis. Police protection, for example, cannot be provided on a transactional basis. Nor fire protection. Nor a common defense. Nor schools. Nor highways, bridges, and roads. These types of works benefit everyone, and are therefore supported by everyone, through the collection of taxes and a subsequent distribution through appropriations.[187]

The government should not, through that process, be engaged in the advancement of special interests, the stimulation of the economy, the slowing of the economy, the enlargement or constriction of the money supply, high or low interest rates, spending, consuming, investing, saving, social engineering, or a redistribution of the wealth. All of these matters should be left to individual economic choices, the dynamics of the marketplace, and the ordinary cyclical patterns of the economy. The government has the power, with the consent of the people, to support charitable types of programs, such as welfare, medicaid, or the support of arts and sciences.[188] But such spending should only be done with a broad consensus of the population. It should be broad in effect, and not limited to specific projects or specific locations, and should be done on

[187]   Adam Smith, for example, believed in three vital roles for the state: (1) a national defense, (2) ensuring justice and protecting property, and (3) building canals, harbors, and roads. Smith also supported universal education, as an antidote to the numbing effects of economic specialization.

[188]   The distinction is between a right or a duty, on the one hand, and the power or authority, on the other. A person does not have a "right" or an entitlement, in this regard, to receive food, or health care, or other necessities, nor does the government have a "duty" or obligation to provide them. Yet the people, nevertheless, as a community, have the power to provide such services, if, for social, moral, religious, or economic reasons, they desire to do so.

an *ad hoc* basis, without long-term commitments, so that the substance of the funding can be tailored to the level of surplus or deficit of resources at the time. Essentially, however, the responsibility of the government lies with works and services that benefit everyone: Army, navy, police, fire, sanitation, education, parks, and roads.[189]

Accountability

The sovereign is a creature of the people. Its property is the property of the people, held in trust, and managed for the public good. The government, therefore, stands in a fiduciary relationship to its people. It owes its citizens the highest degree of care, and must therefore be accountable to its citizens when the sovereign causes harm. The doctrine of "sovereign immunity" was judicially established in the European monarchies, such as England, founded upon the ancient principle that the King can do no wrong. Over the last century, most of the states have abolished the doctrine of sovereign immunity as arcane, outdated, and unsuited for a republican democracy. In recent years, nevertheless, states have begun to reintroduce the concept of sovereign immunity, which shields the government and its political subdivisions from liability, unless such immunity is expressly waived by legislation.[190]While there may be an acceptable argument for

189   "In order to be truly general, the general will must be general in its object as well as in its essence, that it must come from everyone if it is to apply to everyone, and that it loses natural rectitude when it tends toward a specific individual object, for we are judging something alien to us, with no true principle of equity to guide us." Rousseau, The Social Contract, Chpt. 4 (1762).

190   Ironically, the push for sovereign immunity has been contemporaneous with efforts to make the government more accountable to its citizens, through measures like term limits, election codes, disclosure requirements, new ethics provisions, and campaign finance reforms. Other efforts, at the same time, have sought to make the government more accountable to corporations, by giving them more access to the courts to challenge government regulation, and by creating a new right of action against the government in favor of corporations being investigated by federal agencies. The government, therefore, according to these advocates, (who are typically Republican), should be politically accountable to the people, but not financially accountable, except to corporations. If, therefore, a corporation is wrongly ac-

sovereign immunity in cases of "strict" or "enterprise" liability, because the government cannot really be said to "profit" from its works or activities, there is nothing which justifies the insulation of a State's responsibility to its citizens, when the State or one of its agencies, by its fault, causes harm.

All people, moreover, profit in some way from governmental activity, and, as a corollary to the social contract, the costs of such works and services should not fall exclusively on the shoulders of an injured few. In this way, the doctrine of sovereign immunity, even in terms of a government's strict or enterprise liability, is inconsistent with the corollary principles of equal protection[191] and just compensation.[192]

---

cused of dumping its toxic wastes into the Ohio River, the corporation is entitled to damages; but if the average person loses his sight, or his property, or his child, because the Navy dumps its wastes into the Ohio River, then the government cannot afford to waste its resources on his "frivolous" lawsuit, and is therefore not accountable for the harm.

191   "By whatever direction we approach the principle, we always reach the same conclusion, namely, that the social pact establishes such equality among citizens that they all bind themselves under the same conditions and should all enjoy the same rights." Rousseau, The Social Contract, Chpt. 4 (1762).

192   "The Fifth Amendment's guarantee that private property shall not be taken for a public use without just compensation was designed to bar the Government from forcing some people alone to bear public burdens which, in all justice and fairness, should be borne by the public as a whole." Armstrong v. U.S., 364 U.S. 40, 49 (1960).

Crime and Punishment

The aim of the criminal justice system is not to achieve justice. Its purpose, rather, is to protect society from harm. Because, in many cases, our notions of justice are at odds with the effective protection of society from criminal conduct, it often appears that the system is fundamentally corrupt and unfair.

If the objectives of the criminal justice system were to arrive at justice, society would, for example, punish the wealthy criminal more harshly, because the rich person is generally better equipped with the means to conform his conduct to the rules of society, and can therefore be said to have more "fault" in the commission of a given transgression. As a practical matter, however, the system naturally tends to punish poor people more harshly for the same offenses, even though they are perhaps less morally culpable, due to inadequate preparation, inadequate means, and the pressures of necessitous circumstances. While this is, of course, in an ethical sense, "unfair", because the purpose of the system is actually to protect others from criminal activity, it is nevertheless reasonable, because the poor person is generally less able to conform himself or herself to society's morays, and therefore has more of a propensity to commit further criminal action in the future, presenting, generally, a greater threat to society at large.[193]

Despite the obvious unfairness and prejudice in such a system, a criminal proceeding is by nature prejudicial, because it is designed to prevent anticipated conduct in the future, based solely on the events of the past.

In a civil proceeding, by contrast, it is generally easy to be just, because the judge or jury has the opportunity to remedy a given situation by looking into the past, and knowing, with some degree of certainty, how the events in question would ultimately develop and unfold. In a criminal proceeding, on the other hand, there is no way to know, conclusively, what danger to society a defendant may present, except by the inferences from past conduct which may be drawn. Because of the inherent imperfections within such a judicial process, society has developed a fault-based system of punishing past criminal activity, which is perpetually at odds with the underlying purposes and goals of the criminal law.

Fault, in this regard, is in many ways a legal fiction. Fault is in many ways illusory, and deceptive, and therefore a great source of tension in the public perception of the criminal justice system, and in the way it is administered by the courts. It is impossible to argue that people have no dominion over their actions. People are constantly modifying their behavior to achieve various economic, social, or other personal results. People are constantly making decisions. People are constantly making a choice. But as a matter of logical causation, there is always a way to draw the argument so that the root of the criminal activity is ultimately something over which the actor has no physical control.

Every action is the result of some choice. Every choice

---

193   As an additional matter, moreover, it makes less sense to keep someone who is economically productive incarcerated, as compared with an individual who makes no significant economic contribution to society, or has no basic means of support.

is the result of some motivation. Every motivation is the result of some fear, or respect, or intelligence, or wisdom, which is the result of other events and personal qualities, which are ultimately the result of some unrecognizable, unnameable, unidentifiable characteristic, which is the product of either genetic or environmental factors, or some combination of the two, and which, in any event, is not within the actor's physical dominion or control. Through such an analysis of causation and justification, therefore, it can always be shown that no one is really at fault for anything. But society must nevertheless be protected; so it has created the fiction of "fault" in order to justify the incarceration of individuals who are, by nature, free and equal to us all.[194]

What has been lost, therefore, is the recognition that society has no right to punish others. Society has no right to exact vengeance, or retribution. Society has no right to incarcerate people due to their "fault" in bringing about some harm. The basis, rather, of the criminal justice system, and the authority for the government's power in this regard, is the protection of the social order. It is the protection of life, liberty and property from violence and transgression and intrusion, whatever the source or the cause of such unacceptable conduct may be.As a matter of social psychology, and anthropology, and programs which seek to prevent the development of

194   This is not to say that people do not have control over their actions; that people do not have choice; that people do not have free will. But the reasons why people decide to engage in certain activities, the reasons why people make certain choices, and the various ways in which people exercise their own free will, are ultimately due to the combined effects of nearly infinite societal events and personal characteristics, over which the person in question ultimately has no control. Certainly, in this regard, it can be fairly stated that some people are good and some people are bad; some people are weak while others are courageous and strong; some will take the easy way out while others will take the road less traveled; and for those decisions, as a matter of public policy, people must be held accountable. Yet, from a purely moral standpoint, or scientific perspective, people ultimately do not have any control over why they are good or bad, weak or strong, intelligent or stupid, courageous or timid, eager to take the easy way out or willing to take the road less traveled. And therefore, ultimately, the concept of "fault" is illusory.

criminal activity before it has a chance to evolve, all of
the interesting and important questions lie in why and
how an individual becomes a criminal. But as a matter of
public policy, and police protection, and the social order,
it does not matter how or why the person became a threat
to society. It does not matter whether he or she is uneducated or ill-prepared. It does not matter whether he or
she was abused or molested. It does not matter whether
he or she was the victim of religious prejudice, or gender
bias, or racism. It does not matter whether he or she is
unintelligent or unwise. It does not matter whether he or
she is desperate or poor. Because nothing gives that person the right to interfere with the life, liberty, or property
of someone else. Nothing gives that person the right to
violate the law. Fault, therefore, is not dispositive of the
issue of incarceration. The dispositive issue, rather, is the
threat to society posed by the accused. And the underlying goal of the criminal proceeding, therefore, is not the
determination of guilt or innocence, but the determination of whether the defendant, for whatever reason, poses
a threat to society, and the propensity of that defendant,
to do violence to the health and welfare of others by continuing to break the law.[195]Fault, in this context, may be
good evidence of a threat to society, a good predictor of
future action, because a person who commits a crime intentionally and with malice, or with complete disregard
for the rights and the welfare of others, is likely to engage

---

195   "One might compare imprisonment with quarantine. Regard-
less of any personal culpability, indeed even if the criminal is seen as being ill, incarceration is justified much as enforced isolation of a person with a contagious disease
might be justified." Rychlak, Society's Moral Right to Punish 65 Tul.L.Rev. 299,
312-313 (1990). This type of thinking is reflected in the recent *Kansas v. Hendricks*
decision, in which the court upheld the indefinite involuntary commitment of a person who "suffers from a mental abnormality or personality disorder which makes the
person likely to engage in the predatory acts of sexual violence." While the court held
that a finding of dangerousness, standing alone, is generally not sufficient to justify
confinement, a person can be confined when such predisposition is coupled with proof
of some additional factor, such as mental illness or incapacity. Kansas v. Hendricks,
117 S.Ct. 2072, 2080 (1997).

in criminal activity again. But the purpose of the criminal proceeding is not to punish those who are at "fault" for their criminal activity. It is to protect society from the infliction of future harms. One area in which the underlying goals of the criminal justice system are at odds with its procedures relates to the introduction of prior crimes evidence or other bad acts, in order to prove that the defendant has a propensity towards criminal activity, and is therefore likely to have committed the crime in question. Such evidence is often excluded on the basis that it tends to make the determination of guilt or innocence in a particular setting unreliable, because the determination will be made, in part, by an inherent prejudice to the defendant arising from other matters, rather than solely from evidence which pertains to the actual merits of the case. The problem, however, is that the underlying purpose of the proceeding, as noted, is not to determine guilt or innocence with respect to one specific isolated incident, but to make a determination as to whether the defendant poses a threat to society, due to a propensity for criminal activity, which will likely continue in the future, in the absence of incarceration or some other governmental control. And while the admission of other crimes evidence or prior bad acts may lessen the reliability of a determination of guilt or innocence with respect to a specific crime which has allegedly been committed, the admission of such evidence will tend to make more reliable the determination of the underlying issue – *i.e.* whether the defendant poses a threat of future harm.

When a defendant raises a claim of self-defense, likewise, the focus of inquiry is not whether he or she was "justified" in taking such action. The focus of inquiry, rather, falls on whether the defendant has a predilection towards violence, or whether such action was merely the result of fortuitous circumstances.

The killer of a friend or relative, while morally indefensible, often poses little future threat to the public, while the small-time street criminal who may be convicted of simple robbery will often progress into a menace to society.

Such prejudices and stereotypes must, as a matter of course, permeate into the system if the people are to be adequately protected. And it is therefore with significant, yet understandable, difficulty, that our judges, juries and lawmakers struggle to find a process which can, in some measure, be regarded as just.

Alcohol, Tobacco, and Firearms

There are a whole host of crimes which do not protect society, but rather, advance legislatively proscribed morals, on the basis that people need to be protected from themselves. Such laws include the prohibition of drug use, gambling, prostitution, pornography, sodomy, and other "victimless" crimes.

Many such laws involve activities which are private, and beyond the social contract, because they pose no danger to the public at large. Other victimless or "morality" crimes may have indirect or secondary effects on the community, but are nevertheless offensive to the principles of a free society, in which people, and not the government, are entrusted with the ultimate power and responsibility to decide what is for them.[196]

---

196   "Neither one person, nor any number of persons, is warranted in saying to another human being of ripe years that he shall not do with his life for his own benefit what he chooses to do with it. He is the person most interested in his own well-being: the interest which any other person, except in cases of strong personal attachment, can have is trifling, compared with that which he himself has; the interest which society has in him individually (except as to his conduct to others) is fractional, and altogether indirect; while, with respect to his or her own feelings and circumstances, the most ordinary man or woman has means or knowledge immeasurably surpassing those that can be possessed by anyone else. The interference of society to overrule his judgment and purposes in what only regards himself, must be grounded on general presumptions; which may be altogether wrong, and even if right, are as likely to be misapplied in individual cases, by persons no better acquainted with the

As a practical matter, moreover, these measures often have adverse consequences, by exacerbating and exaggerating the problems which the free consumption of the vice would otherwise cause. With respect to narcotics, for example, it is the criminalization of drugs, rather than the use of drugs, which creates the great majority of the harm. The violent power struggle among mobsters, gang members and drug lords for control of the market poses a greater threat to society than the ills of addiction,[197] and, at the same time, exacerbates the adverse effects of addiction by making the purchase of narcotics more difficult, more dangerous, and more expensive. The sale of drugs could be regulated and monitored by the government to eliminate impurities and to ensure proper warnings and disclosures, while the revenue generated from the sale of the narcotics could be used to combat its societal harms. The tax revenue could be used to fund educational programs, for example, and rehabilitation programs, drug treatment centers, medical screening services, and other health care expenditures, as well as anti-drug promotional efforts and advertising campaigns. The billions of dollars which are currently wasted in our fruitless effort to stave off the importation, distribution and consumption of narcotics could likewise be used for such medical and educational purposes, or to support other law enforcement

circumstances of such cases than those are who look at them merely from without. In this department, therefore, of human affairs, individuality has its proper field of action. In the conduct of human beings toward one another, it is necessary that general rules for the most part be observed; but in each person's own concerns, his individual spontaneity is entitled to free exercise. Considerations to aid his judgment, exhortations to strengthen his will, may be offered to him, even obtruded on him by others; but he himself is the final judge. All errors which he is likely to commit against advice of warning, are far outweighed by the evil of allowing others to constrain him to what they deem his good." John Stuart Mill, "Of the Limits of the Authority of Society Over the Individual" On Liberty (1859).

197   It has been noted, for example, that, unlike victims of car crashes, who are almost always privately insured, four out of five gunshot victims are on public assistance or uninsured, costing taxpayers an average of $4.5 billion per year. See Headden, "Guns, Money & Medicine" U.S. News & World Report, July 1, 1996, p.31.

efforts, or for the prevention of other crimes.[198]Neither potentially harmful substances, therefore, such as narcotics, alcohol, and tobacco, nor potentially harmful activities, such as gambling and prostitution, should be banned nor made criminal.[199] Rather, they should be regulated by the government, to make them as safe as possible, and taxed, to provide resources that can be utilized to fight the harms inherent in such vices, through education, rehabilitation, and contributions to medical screening and care.

The Exclusionary Rule

The exclusionary rule is a judicially created device which renders inadmissible evidence which is obtained by the police in an unconstitutional manner. This practice, which has been justified on the basis that it is ostensibly necessary to prevent governmental overreaching, is not well-tailored to the achievement of its intended purposes, and at the same time produces a great amount of unintended and adverse consequences. The purpose of the Fourth Amendment is to protect the people from arbitrary and inconvenient intrusions by lazy or overzealous law enforcement officials, and particularly to prevent the members of various races, religions or political affilia-

---

198   The so-called "war on drugs" is estimated to cost taxpayers somewhere between $40 billion and $120 billion per year. See, for example: Jim Harrigan, "More Than Just Saying No" L.A. Times, Aug. 27, 1997, p.B-6; John Leone, "A Partnership Blind to Corruption" L.A. Times March 17, 1997, p.B-5. See also: Michael Hedges, "War On Drugs May End" Chicago Sun Times Feb. 9, 1997, p.36.

199   It should be noted that, while guns, in general, should be available products in the market place, (and the right to bear arms is of course guaranteed by the Constitution), guns must be distinguished from other products, such as drugs, or alcohol, or tobacco, because the consumption of drugs, or alcohol or tobacco does not, in and of itself, pose any danger or threat to others. Guns, on the other hand, involve a direct and immediate threat to society, wherein the natural consequence of consumption, even in cases where such use is justified, is to cause another harm. While, therefore, guns are analogous to alcohol, narcotics, and tobacco, in that they are considered to be inherently dangerous products, limitations on gun distribution, possession, and use, unlike prohibitions of the other substances, are not really "victimless" or "morality" crimes, because they are not designed primarily for the consumer's own benefit or protection, but for the protection of society at large.

tions from being subjected to intentional governmental targeting, harassment, or abuse. The exclusionary rule, however, does not really discourage lazy or overzealous law enforcement officials from conducting unparticularized or baseless searches and seizures, because the law enforcement official has no vested interest in whether the defendant is ultimately convicted, and may in fact feel that by locking the suspected perpetrator up temporarily, even absent a conviction, he is serving a public good. The exclusionary rule, likewise, does not do anything to discourage the government, in general, nor an individual law enforcement officer, in particular, from targeting an individual based on his race, religion, gender, sexual orientation, political affiliation, or some other personal reason, because the purpose of such an intrusion is not to collect or gather evidence for conviction, but rather, the harassment or abuse.

The exclusionary rule, therefore, offers little benefit or protection to innocent people who have their rights infringed upon by overzealous or intentionally discriminatory law enforcement officers, because there won't be any evidence of that person's guilt for the court to exclude. What the exclusionary rule most often accomplishes, rather, is the release of guilty people, who are then free to go out into society and cause more harm.

Obviously, the government must be deterred from violating people's constitutional rights to be secure in their privacy, property, and possessions, but that does not mean that the exclusionary rule is a good way to do it.

Rather than "punishing" the police officer for acting improperly, the exclusionary rule punishes society for the police officer's negligence or misconduct, by exposing the public to the potential for future harm.

A more effective measure, rather, would be to impose civil damages, penalties, and fines, for constitutional violations, which would hold the government accountable for its actions, and would therefore serve as a better deterrent against overreaching and abuse.[200] The guilty as well as the innocent could be entitled to such penalties, fines, and damages, through administrative law proceedings conducted by magistrates, (much like civil asset forfeiture proceedings), which would be conducted either independently, in the case of innocent victims, or, in the case of accused persons, ancillary to the prosecution of the alleged crime. At the same time, however, in criminal proceedings, evidence of a person's guilt should only be excluded when it is unreliable – *i.e.* confessions, when there is evidence that the statement was coerced by threats of force or actual physical violence; or physical evidence, when there is evidence that the object in question was actually planted by the police or otherwise compromised.

Punitive Damages

The Nineteenth Century scribe, William Hazlitt, once observed that "corporate bodies are more corrupt and profligate than individuals, because they have more power to do mischief, and are less amenable to disgrace or punishment."

The corporation, after all, is a legal fiction. Society can't throw a corporation in jail. The stockholders are not personally liable for the debts of the corporation, and the officers and directors are generally anonymous and immune. For political and economic reasons, government agencies are reluctant to institute criminal or regulatory proceedings against a corporation, while the penalties or

---

200   The law does currently impose such liability on government officials for constitutional violations, but there are several immunities and special defenses which make recovery impracticable. In addition, because the decisions relied upon in the civil context are for the most part taken from criminal precedent, they tend to be overly protective of the powers of law enforcement officials, because judges in the criminal context are naturally reluctant to let people whom they believe to be guilty of criminal activity out of jail on a technicality.

fines, in the event of successful prosecution, are minimal.[201] The criminal prosecution of individual officers and
directors is rare, not only because such men and women
tend to be wealthy and powerful members of the community, but also because such actions are easily defended on
the basis that any one individual officer or director either
did not participate in the decision, or was not fully aware
of the ramifications, or was just fulfilling his or her legal and fiduciary obligations to act in the best interests of
the company.[202] Yet corporations steal millions of dollars.
And corporations kill thousands of people. With bank
fraud schemes, and insurance fraud schemes, and credit
card schemes. With tobacco, and asbestos, and ammonia.
With the Phen-Fen diet drugs, and the Ford Pinto, and
the Dalkon Shield. At a nitromethane plant in Sterlington,
Louisiana, for example, two chemical companies entered
into an arrangement by which one company would purchase the plant, but the other would maintain it without
a profit for ten years. The chemicals involved were extremely flammable and explosive, and were improperly
piped over a compressor which was old, defective, and in
constant need of repair. Both companies knew that repairs
were necessary, yet the operator, who had nothing to gain,
refused to take necessary precautions, and the owner, who

201   David and Melissa Baucus, for example, studied of the effects
of corporate crime in the *Academy of Management Journal.* In an analysis of 256
major corporations from 1974 to 1983, the researchers looked at the stock price of 68
companies that were convicted of employment discrimination, antitrust violations, or
the sale of harmful products, and found that, despite slightly lagging performance, the
stock price of most convicted companies kept pace with the market over the five years
following a conviction. It was only the stocks of corporations that were assessed with
punitive damages in product liability cases that took a relative bath. Gene Koretz,
"Does Corporate Crime Pay?" Business Week April 14, 1997, p.30.

202   In a criminal proceeding, the government must satisfy the *mens
rea* requirement, which encompasses proof that the defendant has acted with criminal
intent, or guilty mind. In the absence of a "smoking gun" letter or memorandum attributable to a specific officer or director, or the testimony of a whistle-blower willing
to admit that he or she was present when the officer or director was informed of, or
ordered, or consented to the conduct or activity, the conviction of an individual officer
or director would be nearly impossible to obtain.

had $190 million in property damage insurance coverage, was content to let the plant explode. Eight people died and hundreds were injured, which was fortunate. If the brunt of the explosion had been a few hundred yards in either direction, it would have ignited the ammonia production facility, several tanks of propane, or underground storage tanks of nitromethane, which could have taken out the entire City of Monroe. Yet both companies were willing to sacrifice the lives of their own workers, and their neighbors, in order to protect their profits, and to take advantage of the economic potential involved.

In the context of business transactions, fraudulent sales practices not only do injury to the consumers who are directly affected, but tend to subvert the entire free market system, because "in a well-functioning market populated by rational economic actors, voluntary market transactions produce outcomes in which both parties are better off, thus yielding an increase in total social welfare."[203]

Many banks and insurance companies, for example, have instituted various programs involving the purchase of collateral protection insurance, or CPI. The insurance is supposed to protect the interest of the bank in the borrower's collateral, in the event that the borrower's own automobile or other insurance lapses during the course of the loan. Rather than purchasing comparable replacement comprehensive and collision insurance, however, many banks and insurance companies have created a scheme by which the borrower is secretly charged for inflated, unauthorized, and worthless endorsements and excess coverages. The borrower is generally not informed about the charges until the end of the loan period, while the bank receives rebates and kickbacks from the insurance com-

203   "A seller's decision to withhold information from the buyer means that there can be no assurance that there will be an increase in social welfare." Hager and Miltenberg, "Punitive Damages and the Free Market" Trial Sept. 1995, p.30.

pany, and the interest compounds. The borrower, several months or several years later, thinks that he or she has finally paid off his or her note on the automobile, only to discover that he or she owes the bank thousands of dollars in premiums and interest for CPI. In the absence of punitive damages, this kind of conduct can often be taken without much risk, and at a significant profit to the company. "Punitive damages are especially important in cases of consumer fraud" noted one author, "precisely because many consumers never learn that they have been defrauded. Consequently, most perpetrators of consumer fraud escape even the possibility of sanction. Moreover, victims who detect fraud will often be deterred from suing by financial and other obstacles, including the typically overwhelming disparity between the relatively small amount of their loss and the anticipated costs of litigation."[204] There is no reason, in such cases, for a corporation not to commit fraud, because the worst that can happen is that the company will break even, while the great likelihood is that it will avoid all accountability for most if not all of its fraud.[205]Punitive damages, therefore, have evolved as a way of protecting society from the wanton, reckless, or intentionally wrongful conduct of corporations, which are generally beyond the effective reach of our criminal laws.

The Ultimate Penalty
The American public, and most civilized nations, will

204   Hager and Miltenberg, "Punitive Damages and the Free Market" Trial Sept. 1995, p.30.

205   In the CPI cases, for example, it is reasonable for the banks and the insurance companies to predict that, at most, only 10% of the customers whom they have defrauded will ever seek redress through the court system, or even discover that they have been the victims of fraud. Even if one of those borrowers were successful in pursuing the matter as a class action, the worst that can happen is that the banks and insurance companies would just have to give back the money they stole. More likely than not, this will not be the case, and the company can profit from 90% of its fraud.

be perpetually divided over the use of capital punishment, because the issue is not truly a political issue, but a matter of deeply-rooted psychological and moral concern. While people tend to argue about the merits of the death penalty – *i.e.* whether it is an effective deterrent, whether it is cost-efficient, or whether it is racially or otherwise arbitrarily imposed – such arguments are for the most part illusory.[206] By and large, people who oppose the death penalty generally do so because they share the basic fundamental belief that killing is just plain wrong, irrespective of the circumstances, while the people who favor the death penalty generally do so because they share the fundamental belief that if you kill somebody, you deserve to die. The problem with leaving the issue of capital punishment to the political process and majority rule is that, if the State kills someone, everyone is implicated in the killing. On the other hand, we as a society prevent people from taking the law into their own hands, and therefore, it could be argued that by taking away that right (to the

---

206   The death penalty is not a deterrent in most cases, because, to the people committing the vast majority of capital crimes, the threat of death is a constant factor in their lives. Certainly, to a lawmaker, who lives in the suburbs, the threat of being executed for the commission of murder might act as a sufficient deterrent to prevent him from carrying out a contemplated scheme, but a drug dealer, who lives in the ghetto, faces the risk of execution – by law enforcement officials, by other drug dealers, by rival gang members, by armed victims, or accidentally, in drive-by shootings – every day. The added risk, therefore, that he or she might be caught, tried, convicted, and ultimately executed by the government, is probably fairly distant and remote.

The costs to society, whether associated with the trial and appellate process or whether associated with keeping the criminal in jail for life, are so insignificant, in comparison with the government's overall expenditures, that neither the cost of incarceration nor the cost of execution can really be used to justify the maintenance or the discontinuation of an activity which is so deeply rooted in our sense of justice and fundamental beliefs.

Finally, with respect to the argument that the application of the death penalty is racially motivated or otherwise arbitrarily imposed, it should be noted that the people who use this criticism to oppose the death penalty are arguing, in effect, that more people should be executed. If there is a problem with the application of the death penalty, then what needs to be addressed is the application; such alleged procedural defects, however, say nothing about the appropriateness of the punishment itself.

extent that it can be called a "right") from the victim's loved ones, the State thereby assumes the responsibility of exacting such vengeance, when culpability, by due process, has been proved.

There is ultimately, however, in an advanced and civilized nation, no legitimate societal or governmental interest in exacting vengeance, punishment, or retribution. The only legitimate basis in such a nation for criminal law is the protection of society from harm. If the State, in this regard, can lock someone away in prison for life, society is protected, and no further societal interest could be served.

A Nation of Victims

The most powerful victim in our society is the corporation. The perpetual victim of an over-intrusive government, an oppressive tax structure, unduly burdensome safety requirements, unduly burdensome environmental regulations, unreasonable demands by labor unions, unreasonable demands by shareholders, skyrocketing insurance premiums, employee benefits, and lawsuit abuse.

Whenever a corporation is attacked by the government, it blames the legislators or regulators for having political motivations. It blames lobbyists and special interest groups for misrepresenting the facts, or for inflicting undue pressure on the lawmakers. It blames the researchers or scientists for conducting studies that are biased, incomplete, or otherwise flawed.

Whenever a corporation is sued by an individual, it blames the injured victim, for being careless, or for assuming the risk, or, in some cases, for making up or exaggerating the injury, and, in other cases, for being an alcoholic, or a drug addict, or for having an abortion, or committing adultery, or something else which has absolutely nothing to do with the case. It blames, at the same time, the government, which approved the activity, or regulated the conduct, or failed to regulate the conduct, and did not otherwise prohibit the company from

engaging in fraudulent or harmful practices. It blames
other parties, and other victims, and other defendants. It
blames greedy trial lawyers, who bring these allegedly
frivolous claims.[207]What is significant, therefore, about
the "nation of victims" and "personal responsibility" arguments is the corollary notion that, if people are responsible for their own problems, for their own injuries, for
their own conditions, then other people, necessarily, are
not responsible for that harm. If the individual, therefore,
is responsible for his own food, or his own clothes, or his
own education, then society is not responsible. And the
aim, for many, is not the empowerment of the individual,
but the alleviation of any and all responsibility from the
shoulders of everyone else.

The entire "personal responsibility" movement is, in
many ways, a movement towards the abdication of responsibility. An abdication by the government. An abdication by society. An abdication by the corporation.

The underlying and principal objective is not to make
the individual person more responsible, but to relieve big
business, and the government, and society, of their responsibilities. Not only our legal responsibilities, but also
the moral or ethical or religious obligations that we, as individuals, or as a nation, might hold. To feed the hungry,
or clothe the naked. To provide care to the sick, or shelter
to the homeless, or aid to the poor. To educate people. To
protect the environment. To treat others fairly and hon-

---

207   Of course, while corporations claim to be the victims of the
tort system, it is interesting to note that, between 1985 and 1991, almost half of all
federal lawsuits involved businesses suing other businesses. Studies show, moreover,
that big businesses are overwhelmingly the winners in lawsuits, whether plaintiffs or
defendants. When they are plaintiffs, they win 79% of the time, compared to an overall
average of 62%. As defendants, they win 62% of the time, compared with an overall
average of 38%. And despite complaints that plaintiffs are always hitting the lottery
with runaway verdicts, studies show that the average jury verdict is only somewhere
between $19,000 and $30,000. See Dunworth & Rogers, Corporations in Court: Big
Business Litigation in U.S. Federal Courts, 1971-91 (1995); Stephen Adler, The Jury,
pp.147-148, 257-258 (1994); "Suits By Firms Exceed Those by Individuals" Wall
Street Journal, Dec. 3, 1993.

estly in our business dealings. To manufacture and sell
products that are safe. To use our land and our property
responsibly.[208]And ultimately, this movement, from the
modification of the tax structure to the dismantling of
government regulation, from term limits to tort reform, is
designed to take power away from the government, and
to take power away from the people, while placing that
power in the hands of corporations. Where the great majority of this nation's wealth and power can be aggregat-

---

208   "By blaming everything on 'society'" writes Newt Gingrich,
for example, "contemporary liberals are really trying to escape personal responsibility
that comes with being American. If 'society' is responsible for everything, then no one
is personally responsible for anything. But when confronted with a problem, a true
American doesn't ask, 'Who can I blame this on?' A true American asks, 'What can I
do about it today?'" Gingrich, To Renew America (1995).

Yet the same thing can be said of big business and industry. By focusing on the
"personal responsibility" of the employee, the neighbor, and the customer, corporate
interests are really trying to escape their responsibility for the damages they cause. If
the 'individual' is responsible for everything, then the corporation is responsible for
nothing. A responsible businessman, when confronted with a problem, would ask,
"How can I make the workplace, or my products, or the environment, better and safer?" And not, "What individual customer, or worker, or lawyer, or government agency, can I blame this on?"

Robert Wright, in this context, wrote an interesting editorial on Mr. Gingrich and
his nation of victims: "Newt Gingrich is fed up with all of the finger pointing" notes
Wright. "He is tired, he says, of people blaming their problems on one another or on
society at large – rather than taking responsibility for their fates and charging ahead
with a can-do attitude. Having made this point, Gingrich proceeds to survey America's problems and blame them on various people. So exhaustive is the finger pointing
in Gingrich's book that even the tendency to blame others gets blamed on others.
Thus, the victim mentality which encourages people to blame their personal failings
on 'society' is largely the work of 'the countervailing Left.' Indeed, a remarkable feature of American problems, as analyzed in Gingrich's book, is that they are never the
fault of Republicans. Even the slightest misdemeanor, if committed by a Republican,
turns out to originate in some external cause. For example, Gingrich once saw Republicans 'grandstand for the news media.' But it turns out that they had been egged on
by 'liberals in the Washington press corps.' A naive observer might think Republicans
share the blame for the demise of family values. After all, Republicans get divorced
just like everybody else. Gingrich himself left his first wife and their two children for
a younger woman. But in Gingrich's carefully crafted references to family morality,
neither divorcing a wife nor leaving your children draws any criticism. Rather, what's
wrong is for a man not to 'support' his children. Thus the moral of the story is: men
with money (like Republican voters) are free to move from wife to wife, but poorer
men (unlike Republicans) are not. If some underclass man dumps his wife, he's the
cause of America's festering moral crisis. But if Gingrich dumps a wife, he's – well,
Speaker of the House." Wright, "Newt the Blameless" Time July 17, 1995, p.64.

ed, insulated, isolated, protected, and beyond reproach.

Voodoo Economics

The corporation, usually portraying itself as a victim, seeks constant assistance from the government, in the form of tax credits, tax deductions, tax exemptions, pork-barrel projects, government contracts, public monopolies, land grants, research grants, loan protections, subsidies, immunities from government regulation, immunities from criminal regulation, and immunities from liability in tort.[209]

Such assistance is justified by a theory of "trickle down" economics, aptly labeled "voodoo economics" by former President Bush. The theory is that everyone will benefit from the support of big business, because the good fortune of the corporation will "trickle down" to the average American in the form of lower costs and greater jobs. The reality, however, is that corporations, by and large, are not going to lower the prices of their goods and services, or go out and hire new workers, with the added resources that such governmental subsidies may bring. They are going to give raises to their executives and directors, make capital re-investments, or distribute the profits to their stockholders, in the form of higher div-

---

209   In 1995, for example, the Republican-controlled Congress handed out $12 billion in farm subsidies, (including $42 million to tobacco growers), $600 million in merchant marine fleet subsidies, $750 million to Amtrak, over $500 million to power plants, $40 million to GE, Westinghouse and Asea Brown for research and development, $35 million to purchase land from McDonnell Douglas, $2.4 billion to General Dynamics for the construction of a Wolf submarine, an $840 million increase in highway expenditures, and an excess of $6 billion to the Defense Department over and above what the Pentagon asked for. In 1996, such outlays continued, including, for example, $2 billion to subsidize electric power in places like Aspen and Hilton Head, $3 million per vessel to cargo ship owners, and $110 million to promote Uncle Ben's Rice, V8 Juice and Friskies Cat Food overseas, (a budget which is almost 30% higher than it was in 1995). In all, the government spends an estimated $75 billion a year to various business interests, almost half of the Federal deficit. See Goodgamen, "Here Comes the Pork" Time May 17, 1995, p.18; Samuelson, "Surviving the Guillotine" Newsweek, Nov. 20, 1995, p.65; Tumulty, "Why Subsidies Survive" Time, March 25, 1996, p.46.

idends. While earnings are up dramatically and the stock market is at an all-time high, the wages of the average worker have seen only marginal increases, while job losses and lay-offs are in record proportions.

In 1995, for example, corporate profits rose over 40%. The Dow Jones Industrial Average rose 35.5%, the NYSE composite rose 31.3%, the S&P 500 rose 34.1%, the NASDQ composite rose 39.9%, and the bond markets rose 25%. Yet wages and benefits for the average worker rose just 2.8%, the smallest increase since 1981.[210]

From 1990 to 1995, pre-tax corporate profits increased by 45%, while the average hourly earnings for non-supervisory workers decreased by .01%.

Since 1993, IBM, whose CEO makes $4.6 million annually, has cut over 100,000 jobs; GM, whose CEO makes $3.4 million, has cut 74,000 jobs; Sears, whose CEO makes $1.6 million, cut 50,000 jobs; Bell South, whose CEO makes $1.5 million, cut 21,000 jobs; and, Digital, whose CEO makes almost a million, has cut 20,000.

ATT, which earned $2.82 billion during the first quarter of 1995, and whose stock price was up 46.3% from its yearly low, was in the process of cutting 40,000 jobs, while the Baby Bells, who had already cut over 130,000 jobs since 1984, were in the process of cutting another

---

210   The average total compensation of CEOs, by contrast, who were earning approximately 212 times the salary of the average worker, increased by over 10%. In 1992, the Chairman and CEO of Columbia/HCA, for example, received $127 million in total compensation, which is enough to reduce by 10% the hospital bills of over a quarter of a million patients, pay the full hospital bills of 25,400 patients, or pay the salary of about 6,500 Columbia/HCA employees. In 1995, the annual total compensation of top executives included: $8.1 million for the CEO of Aetna, $4.8 million for the CEO of CIGNA, $11 million for the CEO of Transamerica, $27.4 million for the CEO of GE, $10.8 million for the CEO of Pfizer, $9.9 million for the CEO of Exxon, and $41 million for the CEO of Travelers. In 1996, the average total compensation for top executives rose another 54%, to $5.8 million, while ordinary Americans saw pay raises in the 3% to 5% range. See generally: "Executive Pay" Wall Street Journal, April 11, 1996, pp.R16-R17; "Health Care Costs: Executive Compensation" Health Letter, Vol.12, No.4 (April 1996); Reingold, "Even Executives Are Wincing at Executive Pay" Business Week, May 12, 1997, p.40.

50,000.

It was reported that 85,000 manufacturing jobs were lost in July 1995, while firms laid off 41,335 in October, which saw an additional loss of 10,000 jobs in the apparel industry. Mobil, which earned $523 million in the fourth quarter of 1994, cut 500 jobs in January of 1995, while U.S. job losses were up by 43% in August, and the Union Bank merger in California eliminated 850 jobs. In the Wells Fargo takeover of First Interstate Bank of California, the institution has promised to cut 9,000 jobs, as opposed to First Bank of Minneapolis, which only wanted to get rid of 6,000. "This was probably the first big takeover battle" noted one author, "ever decided by how many people Wall Street thought each bidder could fire. Interstate stock closed Friday at more than $40 above its price of $106 before Wells pounced. Wells stock was up almost $20 from its pre-offer price of $207. First Bank has made $190 million. The losers? Guess who? The Interstate and Wells employees who will lose their jobs when the banks are combined. Meanwhile, Wall Street's blood lust for job cuts rages on, looking for its next set of victims."[211] This is not to say that there is an unreasonable distribution of wealth among corporate workers and corporate executives, nor is it to say that corporations or their executives make too much money. A corporation deserves to be rewarded for the goods and services it provides to its customers, and a corporation, and its officers, and its stockholders, are entitled to any and all profits resulting therefrom. But a corporation is not entitled to profit from goods and services that are harmful or defective, nor is a corporation entitled to profit from fraud. A corporation is not, likewise, entitled to be subsidized by the public, in the form of tax credits, tax deductions, tax exemptions, pork-barrel projects, government contracts, public mo-

---

211 Allan Sloan, "Take This Job and Cut It" Newsweek, Feb. 5, 1996, p.47.

nopolies, land grants, research grants, loan protections, subsidies, immunities from government regulation, immunities from criminal regulation, and immunities from liability in tort. A corporation does not have an obligation or a duty to lower prices, increase wages, retain employees who are not cost-effective, or create unnecessary new jobs. But a corporation is, on the other hand, obligated to provide a safe environment for its workers, to refrain from polluting and destroying the environment, to avoid providing goods and services which are harmful and defective, and to refrain from deceptive trade practices and fraud.

The interests of the average American, it is important to recognize, are not synonymous with or even allied with the interests of the corporation.[212] As workers, as consumers, as investors, and as business partners, the American people, to the corporation, are only a means to an end. In the best of businesses, they share, at most, a symbiotic relationship, from which the worker, the customer, the investor, and the business partner will be extricated as soon as the arrangement is no longer mutually beneficial to the corporation. In the worst of businesses, the corporation has nothing but contempt for its customers, its workers, its investors, and its business partners, and will cheat them, rob them, use them, and sacrifice them, any way they can.[213] It is therefore ridiculous for individuals to give up their rights, and their property, in order to subsidize corporations. Not only is this suspect in light of the practical relationships between the individ-

212   "The notion that a business is clothed with a public interest and has been devoted to public use is little more than a fiction intended to beautify what is disagreeable to the sufferers." Oliver Wendell Holmes, Tyson & Brother v. Banton, 273 U.S. 418, 446 (1927).

213   Such contempt was exhibited by an executive at R.J. Reynolds, when he was asked why none of the company's executives seemed to smoke. "We don't smoke that shit" he said. "We reserve that right to the young, the poor, the black, and the stupid."

ual and the corporation, but there are even greater questions with regard to the "trickle down" theory, both as an economic principle,[214] and in terms of the government's proper function and role. The government, in this regard, should not be engaged in the business of stimulating the economy. The government should not be engaged in the business of creating new jobs, or forcing lower prices, or increasing wages. The government should not be engaged in the business of encouraging investment, or encouraging savings, or encouraging spending, or consumption, or anything else. Such dynamics should be left to personal economic choices, and the market forces at play.

Even if, however, it were a proper function of government to stimulate the economy, it would be much more effective, as a matter of economics, to stimulate the economy from the demand side, by encouraging spending and consumption, rather than supply-side "trickle down" economics, because the public is not getting a 100% return on its investment in terms of growth. If you give, for example, a hundred dollars to a corporation, eighty or ninety dollars might get used to expand the business, create new jobs, lower prices, *et cetera,* but at least ten or twenty percent of that money is going to end up sitting around in some bank account, or in cash reserves, or in a pension plan, of either the corporation or its stockholders. If you give a poor person, by contrast, or even a middle class person, one hundred dollars, he or she is likely to spend every cent.[215] Such spending is in the same way going to

214   "'There was no Reagan miracle,' says Herbert Stein, senior fellow of the American Enterprise Institute. Total output in the 1980s ran a tad above that of the 1970s but well below the fat 1950s and 1960s, when marginal tax rates were much higher. Compared with other countries, America is lightly taxed. All levels of government collected 31.5 percent of GDP in 1994, compared with 32.3 percent in Japan and 46.5 percent in Germany." Jane Bryant Quinn, "Politics: Fable vs. Fact" Newsweek, April 1, 1996, p.62.

215   This phenomenon is sometimes called the "consumption function", which describes the general relationship between income and consumption. "As income increases, other things being equal, consumption will increase, though not at

create revenue for the supplier, who can then expand the business, create new jobs, lower prices, *et cetera*. While the trickle down theory, therefore, only gives the public an 80% or 90% return on its investment, the "bubble up" theory gives the public 100%. Such a difference, which may seem small initially, will eventually lead to greater and greater economic stimulation and benefits, which are enhanced by the multiplier effect.[216]

The Abdication of Power

The sad reality of the entire nation of victims and personal responsibility debate is that, at its center, lies an abdication of power, an abdication of freedom, an abdication of responsibility. In a world which is increasingly advanced, and increasingly complex, and increasingly complicated, people are becoming more and more intimidated by the prospect of making decisions. Of governing their own affairs.

People don't seem to trust themselves to make decisions. They don't trust juries. They don't trust elections. They don't trust their government officials and representatives. As a result, people are abdicating the power of decision to experts, to scientists, to economists, and to business executives. We look, increasingly, to others, to

the same rate as income. As income rises, consumers tend to save proportionately more and spend proportionately less and the reverse happens when income falls." The Penguin Dictionary of Economics (5th ed. 1992) p.86.

216   The "multiplier effect" is an economic principle which is used to denote the actual impact of consumption on the economy. If, for example, someone buys a model train from a toy store, the store owner is going to use some of that money to buy groceries, and the grocer is going to use some of that money to pay for his dry-cleaning, and the dry-cleaner is going to use some of that money to pay for gas, and so on. The multiplier, therefore, is determined by the proportionate amount of spending in relation to saving on the part of each economic actor, such that the more money which is dedicated overall to consumption, the greater the multiplier.

In the context of "trickle down" economic measures, therefore, the loss of that ten or twenty dollars which is not infused into the economy by the corporation or its stockholders may result in an overall difference of one hundred or two hundred dollars, depending on the amount of money in circulation, the nature of the economic transactions, and other factors contributing to the "multiplier" involved.

provide us with rating systems that will tell us what is good, or what is educational, or what is harmful, while automated electronic devices like the V-chip tell us what movies to watch, what computer programs to access, what songs to listen to, and eventually what books to read. We look to the schools to provide our children with religious background and moral development. We look to radio talk show hosts and political commentators to tell us which political issues are significant, and who is right, and how to vote. From the *Contract with America* to the Rush Limbaugh radio show to the general sentiments of our time, we are stripping the power away from our government, and at the same time stripping the power away from the people. So where, it may be asked, is all of that power going?

The corporation. A tyranny of nameless, faceless, unrecognizable and wholly unaccountable officers and directors, with wealth and power and decision-making ability, that is cloaked and shielded and insulated by the corporate veil.

The Tyranny of the Corporation
It was prophesied by Justice Harlan in his concurrence to the *Standard Oil* decision, and in the movie *Network,* by Arthur Jensen, the fictional CEO. "You are an old man" he told Howard Beale, "who thinks in terms of nations and peoples. There are no nations. There are no peoples. There are no races. There is no Third World. There is no West. There is only one holistic system of systems: One vast and innate, interwoven, interacting, multi-variate, multi-national dominion of dollars. You get up on your little twenty-one inch screen, and you howl about America, and Democracy. There is no America. There is no Democracy. There is only IBM, and ITT, and ATT, and DuPont, Dow, Union Carbide, and Exxon. Those are the

nations of the world today. We no longer live in a world of nations and ideologies. The world is a college of corporations, inexorably determined by the immutable by-laws of business. The world" he told us, "is a business."[217]

The corporation, over the last century, has become a tyrannical device, which shields, insulates, protects, and immunizes, individuals and their wealth from accountability. Officers and directors of corporations, by and large, are nameless, faceless, anonymous, unrecognizable, and to a great extent unaccountable for the actions, debts, liabilities, and decisions of the corporation. The public is not free to gain access to corporate records, nor can the public vote the officers and directors out of office if they don't like what they see. The shareholders and investors, in most instances, are not even given access to corporate records without making a requisite showing, and are not likely to be concerned about the corporation's treatment of others, as long as the corporation is making money for them. The corporation itself can't be thrown in jail. The shareholders and investors are not personally liable for the debts of the corporation. And the corporation itself can, in most cases, protect its own assets through Bankruptcy and Reorganization. The corporation, unlike the government, therefore, is not subject to the political check. Nor is the corporation bound to respect the rights of free speech, or privacy interests, or other protections afforded by the Constitution. The corporation, finally, while owing a fiduciary duty to its shareholders – which is essentially a duty to itself – is free to profit at the expense of others, and owes no duty to the public good. The only limits on corporate power, consequently, stem either from the regulatory efforts of the government, or from the enforcement of property rights and individual free-

217   Network, © Copyright 1976, by Metro-Goldwyn-Meyer and United Artists, written by Paddy Chayefsky, produced by Howard Gottfried, and directed by Sidney Lumet.

doms by the people in the courts. If the corporation can therefore abridge such checks on its authority, the wealth and the power of the corporation will be absolute, beyond reproach, sovereign. The *Contract with America* and its progeny are in this way crafted to promote, protect, and enhance the wealth, the power, and the autonomy of the corporation, by emasculating government regulation, on the one hand, and at the same time abrogating the people's rights to hold corporations liable for damages in a court of law. The *Contract,* in this manner, makes the corporations less accountable to their shareholders,[218] less accountable to the public,[219] and less accountable to the government,[220] while, at the same time, ironically,

218   The restriction on derivative suits by shareholders for negligent or intentional misrepresentations as to the value of the securities, by stock brokers, lawyers, corporate executives, or CPAs, has already begun to have an adverse effect on the rights of the small investor, since its recent passage. In California, recently, for example, the Chairman of a small high-tech company sold 60,000 shares, along with at least nine other company officials, who sold blocks of stock in November of 1995 to unwitting investors, prior to their announcement that the company would not meet fourth quarter projections, causing the value of the stock to fall by 17%. But, according to legal experts in the area, the newly enacted Congressional tort reform measures will likely prevent the defrauded investors from having their day in court. See Bill Richards, "Shareholder Law Raises Hurdle for Top Killer of Class Actions" Wall Street Journal, Jan. 4, 1996, p.B-1.

219   The *Contract,* as discussed earlier, seeks to restrict the average person's access to the courts by placing economic and substantive legal barriers, such as caps on damages, abrogation of joint and several liability, giving preemptive effect to the presence or lack of government regulation, interference with the contingency fee arrangement, and the imposition of a loser pay rule. Such measures are supported by the erroneous and misleading assertion that "Americans spend an estimated $300 billion a year in needlessly higher prices for products and services as a result of excessive legal costs." This figure comes from an assertion by former vice-President Dan Quayle that was never supported by any social or economic study, summary, or report. In actuality, the total cost of all litigation, including judgments and settlements, attorneys fees on both sides, court costs, and the value of time litigants spend dealing with lawsuits, is only somewhere between $28 billion and $35 billion per year. See Gingrich, Armey, and House Republicans, Contract With America, pp.143-155 (1994). *But see:* Marc Galanter, "The Public View of Lawyers" Trial April 1992, p.71; Testimony of James S. Kalalik, Rand Corporation for Civil Justice, Before the Joint Economic Committee, U.S. Congress, July 29, 1986.

220   Perhaps the most ludicrous series of measures which the *Contract* and its progeny seek to effectuate are the reduction of funds to the FDA, along with a concomitant reduction of the FDA's investigatory and regulatory powers; and yet, at the same time, a blanket protection from liability for any drug or medical de-

making the government more accountable to the corporation.[221]Corporations, above all else, do not want decisions about the safety of their products, the fairness of their trade practices, and the effects of their activities on the environment, to be made by the people, in the forum of the jury trial. "Though a company is typically richer and more powerful than the individual" explains Stephen Adler, "its wealth provides it no particular advantage before a jury that is randomly picked from the community. The company can't buy the jury's protection, as it conceivably might buy the loyalty of an elected state judge who's dependent on campaign contributions. And it can't benefit from social connections at the top of society that's shared by corporate and judicial officials but not by the average juror."[222]At the same time, however, corporations

vice which receives preliminary FDA approval – even in the face of fully-funded and fully-empowered FDA approval of such notorious devices as the Telectronics pacemaker, the Pfizer heart valve, tampons which resulted in toxic shock syndrome, and the Dalkon Shield. In addition to the FDA measures, the *Contract* and its progeny seek to afford the corporation more freedom and autonomy, by placing a burden on the USDA to prove that a new inspection system is cost-effective, on the EPA to choose the cheapest way of reducing pollution hazards, and on the NHSTA to submit proposed auto-safety regulations to a new method of cost-benefit analysis, as well as anti-discovery measures, environmental audit bills, and the granting of an immunity to any company which admits to violations. See generally: Gingrich, Armey, and House Republicans, Contract with America, pp.125-141 (1994); Sharon Begley, "Of Helmets & Hamburger" Newsweek July 24, 1995; Anthony Lewis, "Are Americans Looking Up to the Radical Reality?" Times Picayune, Aug. 1, 1995, p.B-5.

221   Not only does the *Contract* seek to expand a corporation's access to the courts to challenge government regulation, but it also affords the corporation a new right of action against the government, to collect damages incidental to agency investigation. Gingrich, Armey, and House Republicans, Contract with America, pp.134 (1994).

222   Adler, The Jury, p.146 (1994). "The founders of our Nation considered the right of trial by jury in civil cases an important bulwark against tyranny and corruption, a safeguard too precious to be left to the whim of the sovereign, or, it might be added, to that of the judiciary. Those who passionately advocated the right to a civil jury trial did not do so because they considered the jury a familiar procedural device that should be continued. Trial by jury of a layman rather than by the sovereign's judges was important to the founders because juries represent the layman's common sense, the passional elements in our nature, and thus keep the administration of law in accord with the wishes and feelings of the community. Those who favored juries believed that a jury would reach a result that a judge either could not or would not reach." Justice Renquist, dissenting, Parklane Hosiery, 439 U.S. 322, 343-344 (1979). "The broad representative character of the jury should be maintained, partly

don't want those decisions to be made by legislators, nor regulators, nor administrative officials. Who, therefore, one may ask, is going to be in charge of deciding whether products are safe or unsafe, whether business practices are fair or deceptive, and whether corporations are causing excessive damage to the environment?

The executives and directors of corporations.

"What is finished" concluded Howard Beale, "is the idea that this great country of ours is dedicated to the freedom and flourishing of every individual in it. It's the individual that's finished. It's the single solitary human being that's finished. It's every one of you that's finished. Because this is no longer a nation of independent individuals, but a nation of 200 million transistorized, deodorized, whiter than white steel-belted bodies, totally unnecessary as human beings, and as replaceable as pistons and rods."

The American people cannot abdicate their power to the government, nor to the scientists, nor to the economists, nor to the political commentators, nor least of all to the corporation. While, in complex times, it is inevitable that people will look to those who are considered "experts" because of their intelligence and their education to guide us in our decisions, all of the experience and education in the world is of no use when that expertise is held hostage to, or subjected to, or subverted to, the political, economic, and personal interests of the experts, or the interests they serve. Experts, in fact, have the potential to cause even greater damage, because their endorsement of a product, or a course of conduct, or an activity, will lull people into a false sense of security, and allow for the fur-

as an assurance of diffused impartiality and partly because sharing of the administration of justice is a phase of civic responsibility." Justice Frankfurter, joined by Reed, dissenting, Theil v. Southern Pacific, 328 U.S. 217, 227 (1946). "Twelve men in a jury box know more about the common affairs of life, and can draw wiser and safer conclusions." Justice Hunt, Railroad Company v. Stout, 84 U.S. 657, 664 (1873). "One bad Federal Judge can do a lot more damage than a jury who goes crazy in one case." Judge Martin Feldman, Eastern District of Louisiana, It's the Law Oct. 23, 1995.

ther exploitation of the American people, who will suffer even greater harms. The heart of a democracy lies in the faith of its people. Faith in the common intelligence and the ability of the individual to decide for himself or herself what is good and what is bad, what is safe and what is unsafe, what is effective and what is ineffective, what is beautiful and what is grotesque, what is right and what is wrong. Of course, we need experts, and scientists, and social commentators, to give us guidance and direction, to provide us with facts, and to educate us about the nature of the forces and the issues involved. But ultimately, power must lie with the people. And those people who do not have faith in their own abilities to think, to feel, to make decisions, to vote, to sit on a jury and judge, have no place in America. People without faith have no place in a democracy. [''."You know, so much of the time we're just lost" said Paul Newman to the jury playing the fictional character of Frank Galvin in *The Verdict*.[223] "We say, 'Please, God, tell us what is right. Tell us what is true.' And there is no justice. The rich win. The poor are powerless. We become tired of hearing people lie. And after time, we become dead. We think of ourselves as victims, and we become victims. We become weak. We doubt ourselves, we doubt our institutions, and we doubt the law. But today" he told the jury, "you are the law. Not some book. Not the lawyers. Not the marble statue, nor the trappings of the Court. They are just symbols, of our desire to be just. They are, in fact, a prayer. A fervent and a frightened prayer. In my religion, they say, 'Act as if ye had faith. Faith will be given to you.' If we are to have faith in justice, we need only to believe in ourselves."

---

223   The Verdict © Copyright 1982 by 20th Century Fox, written by David Mamet, based on the novel by Barry Reed, produced by Richard Zanuck & David Brown, and directed by Sidney Lumet.

The Private Attorney General

When an individual presents a danger to society, the people have a means for deterring wrongful conduct, by the threat or the actual imprisonment of the individual behind bars. Yet when a corporation presents a danger to society, the people, in general, are powerless to enjoin the corporation from such activities. When serious injury is done to another, the injured party generally has a remedy for compensation in the civil law. Yet when a lot of relatively minor injuries are inflicted upon a great number of individuals, the aggrieved parties will often be precluded from pursuing a remedy, because the costs of prosecuting a legal action would far outweigh the potential return. Two procedural mechanisms, therefore, have evolved within the legal system, to allow such claims to be vindicated and to ensure that corporate wrongdoers are held accountable for their wrongs. These devices are the class action lawsuit and the recovery of punitive damages. While the aims of such litigation can often be pursued by either method, the class action is principally designed to vindicate the rights of a large number of aggrieved parties, while punitive damages are designed to deter a corporation from wrongful conduct, and to thereby protect society from future harm. Both of these mechanisms are similar in that they encourage the litigants and their attorneys to act as "private attorney generals" in the service of the public good.

While a great majority of the attacks on class actions and punitive damages are politically and economically motivated, the confusion of civil law and criminal law in the assessment of punitive damages, like the confusion of legislation and adjudication within the class action procedure, give rise to legitimate concern. Nevertheless, and in any event, the private attorney general is absolutely essential to the vindication of rights, and to the protection of society from harm.

The Class Action

The right to file a class action, which originated in equity, was devised to provide a means of addressing small wrongs that otherwise might go unredressed.[224] Over the years, the device has developed as an effective means for both protecting consumers and promoting judicial economy. Class actions prevent duplicative proceedings and endless repetition of common issues. Class actions allow plaintiffs to combine their resources and thereby obtain adequate, knowledgeable and skillful representation for those who could not otherwise afford to retain counsel in pursuit of their legitimate claims. Class actions provide a forum for the redress of grievances, and, through the notice process, advise individuals that they may have been the victims of latent injury or fraud. Class actions tend to clarify the issues for the court, which can better see both the significance of the claims and the consequenc-

---

224   "Modern society seems increasingly to expose men to group injuries for which individually they are in a poor position to seek legal redress, either because they do not know enough or because such redress is disproportionately expensive. If each is left to assert his rights alone if and when he can, there will at best be a random and fragmentary enforcement, if there is any at all. The result is not only unfortunate in the particular case, but it will operate seriously to impair the deterrent effect of the sanctions which underlie much contemporary law. The problem of fashioning an effective and inclusive group remedy is thus a major one." Kalven and Rosenfield, Function of Class Suit, 8 U.Chi.L.Rev. 684, 686 (1941).

es of imposing liability. Class actions are often the only means for assuring that a corporation which has harmed many individuals will not benefit from its wrongful conduct. And lastly, class actions ensure consistent results in litigation, where individual cases permit the defendant to play the odds in many jurisdictions.

In a class action, one single case is prosecuted on behalf of an identifiable group of people who have similar rights with respect to one or several defendants who have caused them harm. The "class" is defined by a series of traits which are outlined by attorneys when they draft the lawsuit, and in relation to one or several litigants who serve as "representatives" of the class. Anyone who could be considered a member of that class is bound by the court's decision in the event of loss, and is entitled to share in the recovery if the suit is successful. Persons who do not wish to have their rights litigated as a part of the class action suit are generally afforded the opportunity to "opt out" of the litigation. The courts are given wide latitude in structuring or further defining the class, and in approving the lawsuit for the trial of certain issues alone.[225] The courts are also afforded wide latitude in such actions to approve all settlements, and to make sure that all of the class-members' rights are protected. Through the adoption of this procedure, the class action accomplishes two important goals. First, it makes the court system more efficient and promotes judicial economy by consolidating the litigation of potentially thousands of different claims in one forum. More importantly, the class action procedure

---

[225] Where a defective product is alleged to have caused a wide range of injuries to a wide number of people, for example, the class action can be certified for the limited purpose of establishing whether the product is, in fact, defective. Class-members, if successful, could then conduct small individual trials, to prove damages. Alternatively, the court can adopt "pilot" cases, bellwether trials, sub-classification by injury, the use of a special master, or other administrative procedures for the ultimate adjudication of claims. See generally: Manual for Complex Litigation, Third §§30.17,33.28 (1995); Newberg on Class Actions §§4.26,9.51-9.70 (3rd ed. 1992).

enables people to enforce their rights, and hold wrong-doers accountable, in proceedings which would not otherwise be economically viable.[226]Take, for instance, the example of Company X, an exploration company which has acquired thousands of mineral leases across the state for drilling purposes. Having received large settlements from natural gas producers, Company X then cheats all of the individual property owners out of their royalties. The average loss to each landowner is only $1,000, but it will cost an attorney at least $30,000 to file suit, circumvent defense delay tactics, and prove liability. No attorney is going to spend three years of his life and $30,000 of his own money to recover $667 dollars for his client, and $333 dollars for himself. An attorney might, on the other hand, spend $30,000 and three years of his life for the chance to earn $250,000, while recovering $750,000 for the landowners who otherwise could not afford to enforce their claims.[227]

In this way, the attorney who represents the class members serves in the capacity of a "private attorney general" who holds wrongdoers accountable for their actions while protecting the rights of the class members who have been wronged. Despite these benefits, both social and econom-

[226]   The United States Supreme Court, for example, has described the class action as "an evolutionary response to the existence of injuries unremedied by regulatory action of government." The Court, in so doing, recognized that "a significant benefit to claimants who choose to litigate their individual claims in a class-action context is the prospect of reducing their costs of litigation, particularly attorney's fees, by allocating such costs among all members of the class who benefit from any recovery. For better or worse, the financial incentive that class actions offer to the legal profession is a natural outgrowth of the increasing reliance on the 'private attorney general' for the vindication of legal rights. Where it is not economically feasible to obtain relief within the traditional framework of a multiplicity of small individual suits for damages, aggrieved persons may be without any effective redress unless they may employ the class action device." Deposit Guaranty National Bank v. Roper, 445 U.S. 326, 338-339 (1980).

[227]   In a class action lawsuit, the plaintiffs' attorneys are generally awarded 25% to 30% of the recovery, as opposed to the customary 33% to 40% contingency fee. See, for example: In re Catfish Antitrust Litigation, 939 F. Supp. 493, 500 (N.D. Miss. 1996) (benchmark of 25%); In re Activision Sec. Litig., 723 F. Supp. 1373, 1375 (N.D. Cal. 1989) (benchmark of 30%).

ic, to consumers and to the public at large, the class action device has been subject to a battery of recent attacks, both publicly and by the judiciary. The most prevalent attack is not without some justification. Occasionally, attorneys have pursued what may be considered collusive bargains with corporations in various attempts to collect a substantial fee, while achieving very little benefit for the members of the class. These deals are very attractive to corporate defendants, who can cheaply insulate themselves from further liability, and are most often consummated in the form of "coupon cases" which entitle the class members to a $25 reduction in air fare, a free box of Cheerios, or a $400 coupon towards the purchase of a new car. While, in some cases, these criticisms are certainly well-founded,[228] it is ultimately the responsibility of the Court to protect the interests of the class members, and to ensure that they are being treated fairly.[229] As noted by Arthur Bryant, of

[228] A lawyer named John Deakle, for example, was recently involved in three very suspicious and apparently collusive commercial class actions in Mississippi. The first involved Deposit Guaranty National Bank, which was sued on a collateral-protection insurance fraud scheme, and was able to limit its liability to a fraction of what the plaintiffs were entitled, while paying Deakle off with a considerable fee. Despite a flurry of criticism, Mr. Deakle went on to engineer yet another suspect and apparently collusive settlement with BankAmerica. This case, which arises out of the forced-placement of mortgage insurance, resulted in a tentative settlement which, again, provided the classmembers with only a fraction of their damages, while entitling Mr. Deakle to a 74% contingency fee. The preliminary settlement was challenged by Trial Lawyers for Public Justice, a public interest law firm which protects consumers from corporate, governmental, and other abuse. As a result of this challenge, the class members ultimately received a total benefit of $7.4 million, (rather than the $2 million Deakle negotiated), while the fee was reduced to $2 million, (i.e. 27%), from the $5.4 million fee Deakle had originally claimed. Mr. Deakle "went to the well" a third time with Tower Loan of Mississippi, relating to a credit life insurance scheme. When he couldn't reach a quick settlement, Deakle sought to abandon the case. The bank moved to disqualify him, and to have the court appoint competent counsel to represent the interests of the class. The very next day, however, the attorneys reached an agreement under which most of the class members would receive no money, while Deakle would recover a $900,000 fee, irrespective of whether the settlement was approved. Again the settlement was challenged by Trial Lawyers for Public Justice, and thrown out by Judge Pickering. See generally: Starkman, "Lawyer Fees Assailed in BankAmerica Pact" Wall Street Journal, April 10, 1997, p.B-2; Chen, "Counsel Take Less in Fees, B of A Plaintiffs Get More" Daily Journal, April 21, 1997, p.1; "TLPJ Defeats Settlement" Public Justice Winter 1998, p.3.

[229] Federal Rule of Civil Procedure 23(e) provides that the settle-

Trial Lawyers for Public Justice, "the single best way to
stop class action abuse is for judges to take seriously their
fiduciary duty to protect class members and their rights.
Judges must make sure that the class action rules and the
Constitution are satisfied; that any proposed settlement
truly is fair, reasonable, and adequate; and that attorneys
fees are properly based on the recovery actually obtained
for the class. If they want justice to be done" he adds,
"judges must also certify class actions when the legal criteria are met. The solution to class action abuse is not
to eliminate class actions. The problem is not class actions; it's class action abuse."[230]More suspect criticisms,
advanced primarily by a conservative judiciary in support
of big business and industry, argue that the institution of
a class action will commonly place an insurmountable
pressure on the defendant to settle, due to the high level of exposure the defendant faces, and in this way constitutes a form of "judicial blackmail". These criticisms,
however, fail to take into consideration the fact that the
exposure is created ultimately not by the class action lawsuit, but by the defendant's conduct or omissions, which
have injured, or damaged, or defrauded, a wide number

---

ment of a class action must be approved by the court. The court will establish a
procedure by which class members are notified of the terms of the settlement, and are
afforded the right to object to the settlement, or, in most cases, to opt out of the settlement, if they so desire. A fairness hearing is then conducted by the court, at which
time the parties, as well as any objectors, will be heard. The court, in deciding whether
to approve the settlement, considers such things as the stage of the proceedings and
the amount of discovery completed; the factual and legal obstacles to prevailing on
the merits; the complexity, expense, and likely duration of trial; the possible range
of recovery; and the respective opinions of the participants, including class counsel,
class representatives, and absent class members. If it appears that the settlement is a
product of fraud or collusion, or is otherwise unreasonable, inadequate, or unfair, the
court can, and should, strike down the settlement, and, in the case of collusion or fraud,
disqualify the attorneys that were representing the class.

230   "Class actions are absolutely essential to the achievement of
justice" added Mr. Bryant in this regard. "In many circumstances, including where
large numbers of people have suffered small amounts of damage or require injunctive
relief, they are the only way that justice can be obtained. If class actions cannot be
brought, then widespread wrongdoing will often go uncorrected, unpunished, and undeterred." Arthur Bryant, Public Justice, Winter 1998, p.2.

of people. Such arguments likewise fail to consider the extortion that a corporation can exact on its consumers, who, absent the class action device, are powerless to seek any remedy through the courts. With respect to those infrequent class actions which are, in fact, baseless attempts to exact "judicial blackmail" from defendants, it is, again, ultimately the responsibility of the courts to evaluate these lawsuits on a case-by-case basis, and to impose sanctions on attorneys or litigants who are engaged in such abuse. Finally, there is the criticism advanced by Judge Posner in the now infamous *Rhone-Poulenc* decision, in which he asserts that society cannot trust the fate of an entire industry to a single jury. As disturbing as this prospect might be to some, it pales by comparison to the much more frightening alternative of entrusting the health and safety of the American public to the officers and directors of corporations such as Philip Morris and RJR.

The fates of families, the fates of accident victims, the fates of victims of fraud, the fates of mom-and-pop operations, and the fates of people accused of capital offenses who could be put to death, are all entrusted to the decisions of a single jury. Why, then, is the tobacco industry, or the pharmaceutical industry, or the chemical industry, entitled to any greater protection?[231] In reaction to the sentiments expressed by Judge Posner in the *Rhone-Poulenc* decision, Judge Spiegel, in a different case, felt compelled to comment that "it causes this Court pause that one of the nation's most respected jurists has lost faith in the very system in which he participates."[232]

---

231   Judge Posner's remarks, in this regard, are reminiscent of a comment by attorney Alfred Lee Felder of McComb, Mississippi. "The law lets you kill people in this country" he said, "but it'll be god-damned if it'll let you kill a corporation."

232   "While Judge Posner's economic theories and distrust of juries may carry weight in the Seventh Circuit, we are still bound by the Federal Rules of Civil Procedure." Judge Arthur Spiegel, In re Telectronics, 168 F.R.D. 203, 210 (S.D.Ohio 1996).

The true question, in the decision whether to certify a case as a class action, revolves around the size of the claims at issue, and the manageability of the class. In the case of bank or insurance fraud, for example, there will generally be computer or other records from which the identity of each and every potential class member can be readily ascertained. The individualized notice of virtually all of the class members will eliminate any Due Process concerns with respect to the plaintiffs, while the defendants will have a clear understanding of the number of potential claimants and the extent of exposure they face. In most of these cases, moreover, the records will provide the basis for a damage calculation which can be derived from a common formula, eliminating the need for an individualized determination. In cases where such records exist, class certification will rarely be inappropriate.[233] The other principal factor which guides the determination of whether a case can be maintained as a class action is the monetary value of the individual claims.[234]

---

234   The hallmark of class certification, in this respect, is manageability. As a practical matter, each plaintiff will receive notice at his or her last known address. Additional record searches can be made to locate plaintiffs whose notices are returned or unclaimed. The class members are then given the opportunity to opt out of the class by filing a request for exclusion, but are not required to take any affirmative action in order to preserve their claims. In the event of judgment or settlement in the class' favor, the recovery for each class member is calculated from the available records and derived from a common formula, and a check is issued in his name.

In the typical class action alleging a product defect, by contrast, notice is generally made by publication in newspapers and radio/television ads, providing people with a 1-800 number or an address in the event that they wish to assert a claim. Individuals who believe that they have been injured or defrauded as a result of the purchase or use of the product in question then have to assert their rights by providing a claim form with the pertinent information to the parties involved. In the event of a judgment or settlement, the court must then find some way to screen the cases, and to determine the amount of damages, if any, to which each claimant is entitled. This generally requires the appointment of a special master, who has to review the affidavit and supporting documentation provided by each claimant, or conduct a series of individual, consolidated, bellwether, pilot, or other, hearings or trials.

234   The hallmark of class certification, in this respect, falls with "the interest of members of the class in individually controlling the prosecution or defense of separate actions." Fed. Rule Civ. Pro. 23(b)(3)(A).

Where the damages to the prospective class members are significant enough to justify the time and expense of an individual lawsuit, a class action will likely lead to an ineffective or inadequate resolution of the claims. When, by contrast, the damages to each class member do not warrant individual prosecution, the class action is generally an effective way, if not the exclusive way, for consumers to enforce their rights when they have been wronged. While the above determination will generally serve as a pretty good litmus test for the maintenance of a class action, strict adherence to this approach fails to recognize what can sometimes be enormous burdens associated with the prosecution of product liability and other complex litigation, and the significant drain on judicial resources. In the context of tobacco litigation, for example, a class action would seem to be inappropriate, due to the significant damages suffered by the victims of emphysema, lung cancer, and other associated disease. Yet the cigarette companies have nevertheless been able to avoid virtually all civil liability for the sale of their products by making lawsuits against them prohibitively expensive. The tobacco industry, in this regard, has hired teams of high-priced attorneys, with large staffs, to manage millions of documents and other research materials. They can afford to hire a litany of experts, take hundreds of depositions, and spend thousands on document production, copying costs, and filing fees. In the *Cipollone* case, for example, the Liggett Group and other defendants filed over 100 pre-trial motions, and deposed one of the plaintiff's experts for 22 days. The verdict, before it was reversed on appeal, was $400,000, but the plaintiff's attorneys had spent $500,000 in out-of-pocket expenses and over $2 million in attorney and paralegal time. The tobacco industry, at the same time, spent an estimated $50 million in attorney's fees. "The aggressive posture we have taken regarding depositions and discovery" wrote one RJR attorney, "continues to make cases extremely burdensome and expensive to plaintiffs' lawyers, particularly solo practitioners. To paraphrase General Patton, the way we won these cases was not by spending all of our money, but by making that other son of a bitch spend all his."[235] Even where damages are significant, therefore, it is not always clear that the victim will have an economically viable claim. The conduct of the tobacco companies, and the defects in tobacco products, moreover, are common to all claims. It does not make sense for either the individual plaintiffs or the court system to be burdened with the discovery and admission of hundreds of thousands of documents and repetitive expert testimony to establish liability in millions and millions of trials. The

---

235   "All too often" noted the Court, "discovery practices enable the party with greater financial resources to prevail by exhausting the resources of the weaker opponent. The mere threat of delay or unbearable expense denies justice to many actual or prospective litigants." Haines v. Liggett, 814 F.Supp. 414, 423-424 (D.N.J. 1993). Almost a quarter of a century earlier, Judge Fox expressed similar sentiments following the conclusion of a trial involving the widow of a lung cancer victim against the same tobacco company. "The individual before the court was, in essence," he wrote, "asserting a claim for violation of the right to life and liberty. The central issue, namely the health hazards connected with the use of defendant's product, is of crucial public importance. It affects the lives of millions of Americans. When defendant manufacturer displays such colossal disregard for dangers to life as the evidence in this case indicated, the court cannot ignore such conduct. This case further demonstrates that a single individual human being – injured, aggrieved and disadvantaged – cannot afford the cost of protracted and multiple trials, petitions for writs of mandamus and prohibition, and appeals in complicated cases. The facts themselves mock the mandatory jury instruction that individuals and corporate institutions are always equal before the law. The court is convinced that the magnitude of the impact of the disparity in resources between these parties, plus the sophisticated and calculated exploitation of the situation by defendant, approach a denial of due process which would compel the granting of a new trial. This question, unfortunately, is now moot because plaintiff cannot afford further proceedings." The court reprinted the letter from plaintiff's counsel, informing the court that: "Although we are convinced that the law would have entitled plaintiff to a new trial, the prohibitive costs already incurred have prevented further post trial options, and we are closing our file." Judge Fox then expressed the opinion that a class action might be a better approach to such litigation. "The case of *Thayer v. Liggett & Myers* has ended" he concluded. "The observations made in this opinion, however, and the implications they contain for the development of justice, in fact and appearance, transcend the facts of any single case. It is hoped that they may aid in furthering 'a new world of law, where the strong are just and the weak are secure.'" Thayer v. Liggett & Myers, No. 5314 (W.D.Mich. Feb. 19, 1970).

class action procedure, on the other hand, is largely inadequate, when there must be an individual adjudication
of causation, damages, and apportionment of fault, with
respect to each individual claim.[236]

The question, at some point, becomes a question of
policy. And it is in this respect that the legislative process
and the judicial process sometimes collide.

Judicial vs. Legislative Roles

The resolution of a class action sometimes raises significant questions regarding the proper role of the judiciary in shaping social and economic policy. In many cases,
a class action judgment or settlement becomes, in effect,
the "law" with respect to that product, business practice,
or class. Whether the issue is nation-wide tobacco consumption, or a company's hiring and promotional practices, or a challenge to the parking meter system, or the
service of minorities in restaurants and in bars, the class
action effectively allows a few people to establish public
policy on behalf of a wide community of interests, without representation.[237]The legislative process, on the oth-

236   Of course, it is not absolutely necessary to have a particularized
adjudication of causation and damages for each individual claim. The courts can employ sample or "pilot" cases among plaintiffs who are grouped, (i.e. "sub-classed"),
according to the type of injury, the timing and length of exposure, or other factors,
where the results of pilot cases would serve as models or benchmarks from which
causation can be determined, and from which damages and an apportionment of fault
can be applied. The courts are nevertheless reluctant to employ such methods, particularly where there is a wide variance of individual factors, because they tend to deprive
both plaintiffs and defendants of their day in court.

237   Professor Coffee argues, for example, that class actions are
converting trial judges "from neutral umpires, adjudicating factual disputes, into prob-
lem-solving bureaucrats dispensing social justice. What does the court believe is a fair
and sensible solution to some pressing mass tort crisis (asbestos, Agent Orange, breast
implants) ? Does it believe that compensation should be denied to those with lesser
injuries in order to reserve the fund's limited resources for those with critical injuries?
How important is it to preserve the solvency of the corporate defendant and avert
bankruptcy? These are heady policy questions for federal judges, ones that vastly
increase their discretion – but in a manner not contemplated by the Constitution. The
task of crafting solutions to complex social problems properly belongs to the legislature." John C. Coffee, Jr., "The Corruption of the Class Action" Wall Street Journal,
Sept. 7, 1994.

er hand, is not bound to any body of factual evidence of wrongful conduct or injury, and is not obligated to afford any remedy to those who have been injured or wronged. The decision-making process would likely be influenced by anecdotal evidence, grandstanding by the lawmakers, campaign contributions, political motivations, and lobbying techniques, rather than the common sense and fair-mindedness of twelve ordinary citizens who have been assembled at random for a democratic cause. This tension between the roles of the legislature and the judiciary is highlighted by two recent court decisions involving the global resolution of asbestos litigation in the context of a settlement class. The U.S. Third Circuit Court of Appeals refused to approve a global class action settlement, suggesting that such action was an issue of public policy and should therefore be resolved by the legislature.[238] The U.S. Fifth Circuit, on the other hand, found that the reasonable settlement of a complex landscape of social and economic issues through hard-fought negotiations was an appropriate resolution of the various claims.[239] The U.S. Supreme Court adopted the former approach. "The argument is sensibly made" the Court noted, "that a nationwide administrative claims processing regime would provide the most secure, fair, and efficient

---

238   "Reform must come from policy-makers, not the courts. Congress, after appropriate study and review, might authorize the kind of class action that would facilitate the global settlement sought here. In a different vein, Congress might enact compensation-like statutes dealing with particular mass torts. Alternatively, Congress might enact a statute that would deal with choice of law in mass tort cases, and provide that one set of laws would apply to all cases within a class, at least on issues of liability." Georgine v. Amchem Products, 83 F.3d 610, 634 (3rd Cir. 1996), aff'd, 117 S.Ct. 2231 (1997).

239   "The global settlement offers all sides the best solution possible by eliminating costly disputes between Fiberboard, its insurers, and asbestos claimants and insuring an equitable distribution to asbestos claimants. The $1.5 billion global settlement was a major accomplishment by all parties concerned and no one seriously challenges its adequacy or the desirability of avoiding another bankruptcy of a vigorous American company." Flanagan v. Ahearn (In re Asbestos Litigation), 90 F.3d 963, 993 (5th Cir. 1996), vacated, 117 S.Ct. 2503 (1997), on remand, 134 F.3d 668 (5th Cir. 1998).

means of compensating victims of asbestos exposure. Congress, however, has not adopted such a solution." And the existing class action structure, the Court concluded, was not sufficient to enable the courts to do so.

The Civil Redress of Criminal Activity

By expanding the potential range of recovery, punitive damages, like class actions, promote the vindication of rights by providing an economic incentive for the pursuit of small, yet legitimate, claims. More importantly, however, the recovery of punitive damages enables the community to hold corporate wrongdoers accountable for indifference to personal safety and fraud.

Because corporate decisions are made by a committee of officers and directors, rather than individual actors, there tends to develop within the corporate environment a form of mob mentality, which tends to breed a wanton and often callous indifference to the safety and financial well-being of society as a whole.[240]

Elected officials, nevertheless, are naturally reluctant to prosecute wealthy and powerful corporations, or their

---

240   "Did you expect a corporation to have a conscience, when it has no soul to be damned and no body to be kicked?" - Edward Thurlow.

"Corporations cannot commit treason, nor be outlawed, nor excommunicated, for they have no souls." Sir Edward Coke, Case of Sutton's Hospital, 5 Rep. 303, 10 Rep. 326 (1612).

"A corporation cannot blush. It has a body, it is true; it certainly has a head – a new one every year; arms it has and very long ones, for it can reach at anything; a throat to swallow the rights of the community, and a stomach to digest them! But who ever yet discovered, in the anatomy of any corporation, either bowels or a heart?" - Howell Walsh (1825).

"Corporate bodies are more corrupt and profligate than individuals, because they have more power to do mischief, and are less amenable to disgrace or punishment." - William Hazlitt.

"The notion that a business is clothed with a public interest and has been devoted to public use is little more than a fiction intended to beautify what is disagreeable to the sufferers." Oliver Wendell Holmes, dissenting, in Tyson & Brother v. Banton, 273 U.S. 418, 446 (1927).

wealthy and powerful officers and directors, who provide jobs to the electorate, belong to the same country clubs, and contribute to their political campaigns. In the event of prosecution, the officers and directors who are responsible can always hide behind the collaborative process, protesting that "I didn't do it, I didn't know, I didn't realize, or I was just fulfilling my legal and fiduciary obligations to act in the best interests of the company." While, as a technical matter, in some jurisdictions, these protestations may not serve as legally recognizable defenses, as a practical matter, due to the cooperative and therefore ultimately anonymous decision-making structure of the corporation, such defenses will virtually always be sufficient to defeat the proof of a *mens rea* requirement, by creating a reasonable doubt.[241]   In the event of a conviction, moreover, the sentences, with respect to the officers and directors, or the fines and penalties, with respect to the company, tend to be small. It is nearly impossible, therefore, by these methods, to drive a corporation into bankruptcy. And you can't put a corporation in jail. The threat of punitive damages, therefore, may be the only effective means to deter a corporation from engaging in harmful or deceptive conduct. At the very least, an assessment of punitive damages can be employed to disgorge the corporation of its ill-gotten gains. In the *Gore vs. BMW* case, for example, the plaintiff's car was damaged during shipping, and then touched-up with new paint, and sold for full price, even though the damage in shipping had lowered by $4,000 the value of the car. The plaintiff showed, further, that BMW did this to about 1,000 other vehicles around the country, and had therefore profited to the tune of about $4 million by its fraud. The jury, therefore, quite logically awarded

---

241   *Mens rea,* which is used to denote willful, reckless, malicious, or fraudulent conduct, is an essential element of criminal responsibility, which requires proof that the defendant has acted with criminal intent, or a "guilty mind". See Black's Law Dictionary (6th ed. 1990), pp. 373, 985.

$4 million in punitive damages to divest the corporation of its ill-gotten gains. BMW, nevertheless, complained that this was unfair.[242]The first objection to the recovery of punitive damages is the fact that it creates a "windfall" for the plaintiffs. Why does Stella Liebeck, for example, deserve $2.7 million? Why do Smith and Holmes, who were defrauded by Trustmark in a CPI scheme, deserve $38 million? Why does Dr. Gore deserve $4 million? The absence of punitive damages, on the other hand, will often give rise to a windfall for the guilty parties. Why, in this regard, does McDonald's deserve to save millions of dollars by burning its customers while cheating them out of free refills? Why does Prudential deserve to keep the millions it has made by defrauding people through CPI? And why does BMW deserve to keep the millions of dollars it made by selling people damaged automobiles? Why does Angus Chemical Company deserve to keep $190 million in insurance proceeds for blowing up its plant and killing its workers? Why should Ford profit from the sale of the Pinto, or Philip Morris from the sale of cigarettes, or A.H.

---

242   BMW's complaints were recognized by the Supreme Court, which reversed, in part, the punitive damage award. The Court reasoned that principles of state sovereignty and comity among the states prevent one state from imposing economic sanctions on the violators of its laws with the intent of changing the wrongdoer's conduct in other states. Justice Scalia, joined by Justice Thomas, dissenting, noted that "at the time of the adoption of the Fourteenth Amendment, it was well understood that punitive damages represent the assessment by the jury, as the voice of the community, of the measure of punishment the defendant deserved." With respect, specifically, to the majority's opinion concerning state sovereignty and comity among the states, they responded that while a person cannot be held liable to be punished on the basis of a lawful act, "if a person has been held subject to punishment because he committed an unlawful act, the degree of his punishment assuredly can be increased on the basis of any other conduct that displays his wickedness, unlawful or not. Why could the Supreme Court of Alabama not consider lawful (but disreputable) conduct, both inside and outside Alabama, for the purpose of assessing just how bad an actor BMW was?" Finally, the dissenters concluded that the Due Process Clause is not "a secret repository of substantive guarantees against 'unfairness' – neither the unfairness of an excess civil compensatory award, nor the unfairness of an 'unreasonable' punitive award. What the 14th Amendment's procedural guarantee assures is an opportunity to contest the reasonableness of a damages judgment in state court; but there is no federal guarantee a damages award actually *be* reasonable." Justice Scalia, joined by Justice Thomas, dissenting, BMW v. Gore, 116 S.Ct. 1589, 1610-1613 (1996).

Robbins from the sale of the Dalkon Shield? Certainly, as between the wanton, reckless, or intentional corporate wrongdoer, and the innocent victim, it is better that there be a "windfall" for the plaintiff than that the corporation be permitted to profit from the harm it has caused.[243]

In several states, moreover, punitive damage awards are divided among the successful parties and the state, which places the money in educational or charitable or other administrative funds. Corporate and defense interests, (who, ironically, are the same people complaining about the windfall to the plaintiffs), have generally argued against such measures, on the basis that they might encourage juries to use such a system to accomplish a redistribution of the wealth, by granting more frequent and larger punitive damage awards.

Corporations also complain about the standard of proof as to causation, which is merely a preponderance of the evidence or clear and convincing standard, as opposed to the higher standard of beyond a reasonable doubt. It must be remembered, however, that the purpose of punitive damages is not to compensate the plaintiff for injuries which may have been caused by the defendant's conduct, but to deter corporations and other would-be defendants from acting with malice, or recklessness, or callous disregard. In the assessment of punitive damages, therefore, causation should not even be required.[244] When a person pulls out a gun and fires it at someone else, that person is guilty of attempted murder, even if the bullet misses the target and causes no harm. When a company knowingly places a potentially dangerous product on

---

243   "Such a harsh, and to some absurd, result is tolerated as a price of private achievement of a public goal, not because it provides a windfall to individual plaintiffs. The award is not the plaintiff's, but society's." <u>Allen v. R&H Oil</u>, 63 F.3d 1326, 1334 (5th Cir. 1995).

244   Judge Posner has noted, for example, that "society could allow whomever the law was intended to protect to sue for punitive damages." Richard Posner, <u>An Economic Theory of Criminal Law</u> 85 Colum.L.Rev. 1193, 1201 (1995).

the market, likewise, that company is guilty of a callous disregard for public safety, even if the product ultimately causes no harm. An award of punitive damages against the makers of silicone implants therefore may be warranted, irrespective of whether it is ever determined that such implants lead to connective tissue or other disease.[245] We, as a society, want to deter Dow Corning and other manufacturers from knowingly placing potentially dangerous products into the stream of commerce without fully explaining the risks, because they are in a superior position to know and to learn of the potential dangers, and because people can often not afford to wait until science and medicine have developed an adequate basis of knowledge and technology in order to judge.[246]The most widespread complaint, finally, with respect to the recovery of punitive damages, is that the awards are arbitrary, unpredictable, and without bounds. The truth is, however, that pu-

---

[245]   Despite Dow Corning's claims that the implants would "last a lifetime", it has been found that one-third to one-half of all implants rupture or leak silicone gel within 10 years, and that, after 10 years, the number increases between 64% and 96%. Allegations of rare connective tissue disease notwithstanding, it is undisputed that implants cause capsular contraption and other local problems, including infection, destruction of nipple tissue, and chronic pain. Twenty-four percent of women require additional surgery to replace ruptured implants or correct other problems. And the implants limit cancer detection by compromising, (by 25% to 35%), the effectiveness of a mammography.

[246]   After Dow Corning offered to establish a $4.2 billion fund to compensate women with breast implants, the Mayo Clinic released a study by comparing the medical records of 749 women who had received breast implants with the records of 1,498 women who had not. The researchers found "no association between breast implants and the connective tissue diseases that were studied." However, the researchers also noted their limited ability to detect an increased risk of rare connective tissue diseases, which would require a sample of 62,000 women with implants and 124,000 without them – 83 times the sample that was studied. Due to the flaws in this and other studies, the FDA released an exhaustive report in 1996 in which it was concluded that "no implant study has ruled out an increased risk of connective tissue disease." Harvard researchers then conducted a study which included a sample of 10,830 women with breast implants, which revealed a 24 percent increase in lupus, scleroderma, and rheumatoid arthritis. "This increase is small by statistical standards, but the real figure could be higher because, like other researchers, this group looked only for classic symptoms, not the atypical connective tissue disease that many women with implants have reported." Michael Castlema, "Implanted Evidence" Mother Jones, Jan/Feb 1998, p.25.

nitive damages are generally reasonable, when awarded, and that awards of punitive damages are rare.[247]Limits or caps on punitive damages, moreover, severely compromise their deterrent effect, by allowing the corporation to perform a cost/benefit analysis to determine whether it can profit from intentionally harmful conduct or fraud. If Ford, for example, knows that it will cost $100 million to manufacture a gas-tank safely; that, with faulty gas-tanks, there will be approximately 35 explosions resulting in approximately 75 deaths; that the average compensatory damage award for a wrongful death is $200,000; and that punitive damages are limited to three times the compensatory award; then the manufacturer can reasonably predict that the overall exposure will be limited to an average of $800,000 per person, at a total cost of $60 million to the company. There is no economic incentive in this case to correct the problem, because the car-maker can save $40 million by killing 75 of its customers.[248]In

247   A study of verdicts in the 45 largest counties in the U.S. found that punitive damages were awarded in just 6% of the cases where plaintiffs were successful, (i.e. only 3% of all trials). "Unless the case involves an intentional tort or a business-related tort (such as employment claims)" the study's author concluded, "punitive damages will almost never be awarded." The study found a strong correlation between compensatory and punitive damages, (with punitive verdicts generally running about 40% higher than compensatory awards), and noted that the absence of any large, headline-grabbing awards in such a broad sample "suggests that the punitive damage cases emphasized in the media are newsworthy precisely because they are so rare, and because they depart from an explicable underlying pattern of awards." Theodore Eisenberg, The Predictability of Punitive Damages (1996). In another recent study, it was found that juries awarded punitive damages in only 4% of cases in which the defendant was found liable, (i.e. around 2% of cases overall), and that $38,000 was the median punitive damage award. National Center for State Courts, Examining the Work of State Courts, 1994 Pub. No. R-178 (1996). In the 25 years between 1965 and 1990, only 355 punitive damage awards were rendered in product liability cases. Excluding asbestos cases, which accounted for 25% of these awards, there were an average of only 11 awards per year. See Rustad, Demystifying Punitive Damages in Products Liability Cases, The Roscoe Pound Foundation, p.23 (1991). Most punitive damages were awarded in intentional tort and business cases, which account for over 80% of all punitive damage awards. Product liability cases, by contrast, account for only 5% of all punitive damage awards. Erik Moller, Trends in Jury Verdicts Since 1985, Rand Institute for Civil Justice (1996).

248   The actual calculations were as follows: Ford set the value of a human life at $200,000, a burn injury at $67,000, and an incinerated Pinto at $700. The

support of his decision to vote against a bill to limit punitive damages in product liability cases in 1996, Senator John Breaux recognized that the threat of a $250,000 award to the family of a child that is burned to death by pajamas that aren't flame-retardant likely wouldn't be enough to force the company executives to recall a whole warehouse full of defective clothing. As even the smallest of Fortune 500 companies have assets of around $4 billion, the proposed cap of $250,000 would amount to less than .01% of the assets of the corporation. "Does anybody think a maximum fine that is .00625 percent of that corporation's assets is going to have any effect on their social behavior?"[249]In a case involving purely economic damages, it is even easier for the corporation to benefit from fraudulent business practices. In the CPI cases, for example, it is reasonable for the banks and the insurance companies to anticipate that only 10% of the customers whom they have defrauded will ever seek redress through the court system, or even discover that they have been the victims of fraud. If punitive damages, therefore, are limited to three times compensatory damages, there will be a maximum exposure of only 40% of the excessive and unauthorized premiums taken, and the defendants will profit from 60% of the fraud.

Some degree of unpredictability in jury verdicts, therefore, is a desirable feature of the justice system. Aside from the obvious deterrent effect, the jury system also serves to "make the difficult and uniquely human judgments that defy codification and that build discretion, eq-

---

company estimated that the corrections would prevent 180 deaths, 180 burn injuries, and around 2,100 incinerated vehicles per year, for a total cost of $49.5 million. Ford then estimated that it would cost $11 per auto to meet the propose standards, at a cost of $137 million. Grugh and Sauby, Ford Department of Environmental and Safety Engineering, <u>Fatalities Associated with Crash Induced Fuel Leakage and Fires</u>. See Mark Dowie, "Pinto Madness" <u>Mother Jones</u>, Sept/Oct 1977.

249   Senator John Breaux, quoted in Bruce Alpert, "Senate Oks Capping Damage Settlements" <u>Times Picayune</u> March 22, 1996, p.A-8.

uity, and flexibility into the legal system."[250] The question is which legal system, civil or criminal, do punitive damages serve.

The Confusion of Civil and Criminal Law

The civil law and the criminal law, while alike in some ways, are vastly different in design. The civil law, even in personal injury cases, operates on an economic basis – *i.e.* the repayment of a debt that is owed. The criminal law, by contrast, operates on a social level, with the objective of physical restraint. The criminal law is at its essence injunctive, while the civil law remedial. As a practical matter, the civil law tends to generate just results, because the fact-finder is able to look into the past, see what harm has evolved from a given course of conduct or activity, and redress the injured party for that harm. With the injection of punitive damages, however, the process becomes hindered by the guess-work that is naturally associated with any attempt to predict future conduct based on events lying solely in the past. Due to the compromise system which devolves from these two origins, the process, and its results, are often dissatisfying both to the wrongdoers and to those who have been wronged.[251]

The Private Attorney General

The formalization of the Private Attorney General into a quasi-public body could produce significant benefits for the legal system, and to society at large. A three-judge panel could be elected to preside over the litigation, which

---

250   Justice Scalia, concurring, Pacific Mutual Life Insurance v. Haslip, 499 U.S. 1, 41 (1991).

251   It should be pointed out that the above criticism of punitive damages has been described as an "overly formal distinction, which ignores the close theoretical ties between criminal law and tort law, and has, in the words of one commentator, 'resoundingly collapsed in American legal thought.'" David Owen, A Punitive Damages Overview: Functions, Problems, and Reform, 39 Vill.L.Rev. 363, 382 (1994).

would be initiated by private attorneys, or others, seeking to correct a perceived injustice through the courts.[252] The action would be initiated by petition, similar to a bill of information, outlining the suspected violations, and the factual support thereof. The panel would consider the petition, similar to a probable cause determination, and decide whether to authorize the attorneys to proceed with the case.[253] Similar petitions arising out of the same alleged conduct could be consolidated, and the attorneys could work together in pursuit of the claims.[254]The defendants would be afforded all constitutional protections, including the right to appointed counsel, the right to trial by jury, the right against self-incrimination, and proof beyond a reasonable doubt.[255]   By requiring the court to instruct the jury as to the results of any other private attorney general action or actions arising from the same

252   The basis of the action would be any wanton, reckless, or intentionally harmful conduct which creates a substantial risk to public health and safety, or any fraudulent act or omission which is employed for economic gain.

253   In so doing, the panel would be licensing or "deputizing" the lawyers as private attorney generals to act on behalf of the State.

254   In the event of too many or competing attorneys, the panel would appoint lead counsel, liaison counsel, and a steering committee, to organize and effectuate the prosecution of the litigation. At some point, the determination would be made that enough private attorneys were pursuing the matter, and no more law firms would be permitted to join. See generally: Manual for Complex Litigation, Third §§20.22,33.24 (1995); Newberg on Class Actions §§9.31-9.36 (3rd ed. 1992).

255   With respect to the right against self-incrimination, the defendant would not be required to submit to a deposition, nor to give oral testimony at trial, but documents and other tangible evidence would be discoverable, as in ordinary criminal cases. The initial determination allowing the case to go forward would also initiate the discovery process, similar to the application of a search warrant in a criminal case. With respect to the heightened burden of proof, the private attorney general would only have to prove, beyond a reasonable doubt, that the corporation engaged in wanton, reckless, or intentionally harmful conduct which created a substantial risk to public health and safety, or a fraudulent act or omission employed for economic gain. The attorney would not be required to prove, beyond a reasonable doubt or otherwise, that the conduct actually resulted in some physical injury or harm to the environment, or that the fraudulent conduct actually resulted in harm to the consumer, or economic gain. With respect to the *mens rea* requirement, the private attorney general would not have to prove that any particular officer or director acted wantonly, recklessly, intentionally, or with callous disregard, but only that such knowledge and intent is attributable to the corporation.

or similar conduct, (as well as any criminal or administrative sanctions or fines), the defendant would also be protected against double jeopardy. Where appropriate, the panel would be authorized to approve a class action for the distribution of restitution to the aggrieved parties, particularly where such victims are readily ascertainable, or in the case of a limited fund. The panel would also be required to approve any settlement, in order to protect the interests of the community, and to ensure that justice is done. In the event of a settlement or judgment against the defendant, the attorneys would be entitled to anywhere from 15% to 30% of the recovery, (plus out-of-pocket expenses), depending on the complexity of the case, the time and money expended, the quality of the work, and other well-accepted guidelines for the determination of an appropriate award.[256] The remainder of the funds could be divided among the court system, other public programs, the victims, where appropriate, or traditional *cy pres* awards.[257]

---

256   Under the equitable "common fund" doctrine, attorneys who obtain, protect, preserve, or make available a substantial benefit to a class of persons are entitled to an attorney's fee based upon the value of the benefit to the class. Boeing v. Van Gemert, 444 U.S. 472 (1980); Trustees v. Greenough, 105 U.S. (15 Otto) 527 (1882). At the same time, an attorney's fee must be reasonable, in light of the time and the money expended, the novelty and complexity of the claims, the likelihood of recovery, the skill and reputation of the attorneys, the fact that the fee is contingent, attorney's fees in other similar cases, and the results obtained. See generally: Professional Rule 1.5; Johnson v. Georgia Highway Express, 488 F.2d 714 (5th Cir. 1974); Lindy Brothers v. American Radiator, 487 F.2d 161 (3rd Cir. 1973), aff'd, in part, vacated, in part, 540 F.2d 102 (3rd Cir. 1976) ("Lindy II"). While the use of an hourly or "lodestar" method in common fund cases has been roundly criticized, in favor of a percentage-of-benefit award, (generally 25% to 30% of the fund), the above approach would combine the two methods to achieve an appropriate award. See generally: Manual For Complex Litigation, Third §24.12 (1995).

257   The cy pres doctrine allows the court to apply trust proceeds or other funds to an "as near as possible" use, when such funds cannot be distributed. In the context of class action law, class members will inevitably relocate or die during the pendency of the claim, or, for some other reason, cannot be found at the time of distribution. In other cases, the damages suffered by each class member may be too small to warrant distribution. Under the cy pres doctrine, such funds can be employed for some charitable or other purpose which furthers the policies that underlie the plaintiffs' claims. In this way, the funds can provide indirect benefits to the

The time, money and effort required to prosecute these cases would be shifted from over-worked, under-staffed, under-equipped, and under-paid public agencies, to private attorneys, who would bear all of the risks of litigation, as well as the costs. Such privatization of criminal enforcement would advance limited government, free-market ideals, and would produce substantial economic benefits for society at large. Such a system would also encourage vigorous enforcement of the standards which are necessary to maintain integrity in business transactions, and to protect the public and its environment from harm.

---

absent class members. See generally: Black's Law Dictionary (6th ed. 1990), p.387; Stewart Shepherd, Damage Distribution in Class Actions: The Cy Pres Remedy, 39 U.Chi.L.Rev. 448 (1972); Patricia Sturdevant, "Using the Cy Pres Doctrine to Fund Consumer Advocacy" Trial, Nov. 1997, p.80.

The Betrayed Profession

The legal profession has been said to function at the "friction points" of society. People only come to lawyers when they have a problem. Plaintiffs generally feel that they have been wronged by defendants, while defendants feel that they have been dragged into court for no good reason. They resent the fact that they need lawyers, they resent the fact that they have to pay lawyers, and they tend to blame lawyers for their problems, their frustrations, and the delay. People, naturally, therefore, will always have a certain amount of ambivalence and resentment for the legal profession. Yet, in recent years, there have been additional developments, both within the profession and without, which have resulted in increased attacks upon lawyers, particularly plaintiff's lawyers, who have, in many ways, become the betrayed profession.

Attorney Advertising
Like other forms of commercial speech, lawyer advertising has the potential to provide the public with valuable information about products which are harmful, about frauds which may have been committed without their knowledge, about their rights, about the vindication of those rights, and about the ways in which those rights may become limited or prescribed.

As a practical matter, however, lawyer advertising in virtually all cases fails to meet such goals. The ads do not provide the public with any substantive information, but merely encourage people to go to a particular lawyer for the evaluation of his or her potential claim.

Lawyer advertising also cheapens the profession. It turns lawyers into merchants and salesmen, and turns the pursuit of justice into a mechanical administration of claims. While only a very very small fraction of attorneys advertise on television, those are the attorneys that everyone sees. Those are the attorneys with whom the public identifies. And those are the attorneys which therefore become representative, in the public psyche, of the entire profession. The ads themselves, unfortunately, are generally cheap, distasteful, and wholly unprofessional, which leads the public to form such an impression of all attorneys, despite the fact that the overwhelming majority of attorneys do not in any way resemble the lawyers who advertise on tv.

While the First Amendment, and the anti-trust laws, a free-market economy, and various other factors militate against a prohibition on lawyer advertising, the bar association, as a profession, should be able to place reasonable restrictions on the style and the content of lawyer advertising, which would permit an attorney to communicate information and offer his or her legal services in an honest, respectable, and professional way.

The Fee

If your business were to burn down, and you suffered a $75,000 loss, but your insurance company were only willing to pay you $40,000, you would naturally resent having to pay an attorney thirty-three or forty percent of the remaining $35,000, when you are legally entitled to get that money in the first place. Defendants, likewise, who generally feel that they have been sued without cause, naturally resent having to hire an attorney to defend themselves, when they haven't done anything wrong.

Yet such resentment, while understandable, is ultimately misplaced. It is the insurance company, not the plaintiff's attorney, who refuses to honor its policy. It is the plaintiff, not the defense attorney, who drags the defendant into court.

The practice of law, moreover, is expensive. While, to the public, the business of law is mostly service-oriented and transactional, there are office spaces, library expenses, secretaries, paralegals, telephones, faxes, word processors, computer research, on-line services, investigators, court reporters, copying expenses, depositions, experts, computer animation, medical exhibits, court costs, and filing fees. Particularly, therefore, in a contingency fee situation, there is a great amount of risk and expense which is assumed for the costs of litigation.[258] People, at the same time, do not need an attorney in order to file a lawsuit or to defend a claim. Everyone has the right to represent his or her own interests *pro se*. There are public legal libraries, provided by the courts, or law schools, or other institutions, where the litigant can do his or her legal research, and get forms which will demon-

258   In one case, for example, 13 children in a small working-class town in Massachusetts all developed leukemia in a short period of time. Eight families sued W.R. Grace and Beatrice Foods for the illegal dumping of carcinogenic trichloroe-thylemen (TCE). After years of grueling and extremely expensive litigation, the EPA had identified the defendants as the sources, whistleblowers testified that Grace workers dumped TCE into the ground above the aquifers, and experts conducted endless medical and geological tests to show how the TCE permeated the wells and subsequently affected the children. The defendants, nevertheless, continued to stonewall and delay, and, with the help of hired experts, constructed a defense which challenged the conclusions of the residents, their experts, and the EPA. Due to the time, money, and risk involved, plaintiffs were forced to settle with W.R. Grace for a fraction of what the case was worth, while Beatrice was absolved of any fault by the jury. After the settlement, the EPA discovered that Beatrice had suppressed information, and that both Grace and Beatrice had polluted the wells. Grace, in addition, ultimately plead guilty to lying about its illegal dumping activities. In the meantime, however, the plaintiffs' lawyer, who had spent $2.6 million, recovered a mere $30,000, and had been forced into bankruptcy. See generally: Jonathan Harr, A Civil Action (1995).

strate how to prepare pleadings, motions, and briefs. In some cases, moreover, the court will allow the litigant to proceed *in forma pauperis,* and all of the court costs will be waived.In cases where an attorney is retained by the client, the attorney›s fee is subject to scrutiny and review by the court. If a litigant, therefore, believes that the fee is unreasonable or excessive, (even in cases where the client has contractually agreed to that fee), the client can, in most instances, force the attorney to place the disputed amount into the registry of the court. The court will then review the matter, and make some determination as to the fee, based upon the time and labor expended by the attorney, the novelty and complexity of the case, the experience and reputation of the attorney, the nature and length of the professional relationship with the client, whether the fee is fixed or contingent, fees in other similar cases, the amount at issue, and the results obtained.

Ultimately, however, attorneys' fees are a product of the marketplace. Litigants, in this respect, are certainly free to negotiate a lower fee with their attorney, or to go to another lawyer who will handle the case for less. Hourly fees may run anywhere from $50 to $1,000 per hour, while plaintiffs' attorneys will work on a contingency fee basis of anywhere from 25% to 50%. Certainly, with the glut of lawyers, and the number of unemployed lawyers, people should be able to find an attorney who will work for a reasonable fee. Fortunately, we live in a capitalistic society, with a free market economy, where Michael Jordan can make $37 million to play basketball, where Jim Carrey can make $20 million to star in a motion picture, and where Bill Gates can make $18 billion inventing new software technology. Attorneys should not be punished for trying to be good businessmen. We should celebrate, rather, the opportunity of everyone, including attorneys, to profit from their talents, hard work, and the value of the services they provide.

Placing a Money Value on Life, Liberty, and the Pursuit of Happiness

It is impossible to place a monetary value on someone's life. Or sadness. Or physical pain and suffering. It's strange, and in some ways distasteful, and in many ways arbitrary. But as a practical matter, nevertheless, we really don't have any choice. We can't bring a loved one back, or repair a physical handicap, or give the litigant happiness, or relieve the litigant's pain.

Business interests argue that because the court system cannot effectively compensate people for physical and emotional injury, they should not be permitted to recover at all. They talk about "non-economic damages" as if they are somehow less real. As if the loss of a loved one, or an arm, or a person's happiness, were for some reason less worthy of compensation.

Consider, however, the example of a five year-old girl who loses her reproductive organs at the hands of a negligent physician after going into the hospital for an emergency appendectomy. This girl has no economic damages. She has not been rendered medically dependent on subsequent health care services, nor deprived of her ability to earn a living, nor the ability to perform an everyday physical task. Yet her life has been potentially destroyed. She is going to be miserable, for example, in high school, when she develops awkwardly due to the unnatural hormone levels. She may have a more difficult time forming a meaningful relationship, or finding a husband. And, most significantly, she can never have a child. Society, of course, cannot put a price on that loss. Society cannot put a price on that pain and suffering. Society cannot put a price on that injury.[259] And the defendant will argue that, because we cannot compensate her adequately for such injury, she should get nothing at all. Maybe our system of awarding somewhat arbitrary values of money in an attempt to compensate physical and emotional injury isn't perfect. But it is, after all, the best that we can do. Money can, in some circumstances, bring happiness. Money has the potential to empower. Money can bring comfort, and security. And money, moreover, is the reason, in many instances, why the person was harmed. Companies, in many cases, are negligent, or reckless, or even intentionally fraudulent or destructive in an attempt to save money. Companies frequently place an economic value on human life. Ford, for example, in the Pinto case, was perfectly willing to place a value on human life.[260] Why is a jury, it may be asked, not qualified to do the same.

Representation

People, in general, do not like the idea that lawyers are "hired guns" who advocate for their clients without regard to their own personal beliefs. Obviously, we want lawyers to stay within ethical limits. We want lawyers to exhibit candor towards a tribunal, and to present evidence which is credible, reliable, and material to the merits of the claim. But within those ethical bounds, attorneys must be free to advocate for clients with whom they disagree. Because otherwise, the client would have no access to the courts. And ultimately, after all, it is the cause of the client, and not the cause of the lawyer, which must be heard.

The attorney-client model, therefore, ensures that people who are controversial, or unpopular, or who have controversial or unpopular social, political, or religious beliefs, nevertheless have the ability to have their action prosecuted or defended by an attorney, where, otherwise,

would be making that choice.

260   Ford determined that a human life was worth $200,000, a serious burn injury $67,000.

the litigant would have to search for one – and there might
not be one – who finds the litigant likeable, or personable,
or who shares the litigant's social, political, or religious
background or beliefs.As long as the cause or defense has
merit, and as long as the attorney does not misrepresent
the truth or hide things from the court, the attorney must,
and the public must demand, that he step into the shoes
of the client, and argue the client's cause, rather than his
own.

Politically Motivated Betrayal of Lawyers and the Law

While much resentment of lawyers stems from features
and dynamics, such as the foregoing, which are inherent
to the profession, an equal or greater amount of "lawyer
bashing" is generated by political forces, which seek to
profit by limiting the power of the jury, and removing the
access of people to the courts.

Businesses cannot, for obvious reasons, attack the injured, the innocent, or the disenfranchised victims of their
wrongdoing, so they attack the attorneys, who are depicted as greedy plaintiff's lawyers, trying to hit the jackpot
with a bunch of frivolous claims.[261]

They attack, for example, the plaintiff's attorneys as a
powerful lobbying force in Washington, which places undue influence on lawmakers to protect their own interests,
to the prejudice of the public good. They point out that

261   With respect to the Norplant litigation, for example, attorney
Chris Parks noted that "it's impossible to form a public relations campaign to blame
50,000 women, so you blame their lawyers." See Cohen, "Norplant Sales Fall Due
to Lawsuits" Times Picayune Oct. 1, 1995. Representative Dick Armey, likewise,
recently wrote a letter to the members of the House, advocating for the passage of a
nationalized universal no-fault auto insurance plan. Despite the fact that no-fault has
failed in the states which have adopted it; that bad drivers would not be accountable
for even the most serious and debilitating injuries; that a national auto insurance plan
violates principles of states' rights and Federalism. Nevertheless, says Armey: "The
Trial Lawyers Are Against It. It Must Be A Good Idea." Letter from Congressman
Armey to Members of the House, Oct. 1, 1997. See also: Garland, "Chamber of Commerce Battle Cry: Kill All the Lawyers" Business Week, March 2, 1998, p.53

between 1989 and 1994, the Association of Trial Lawyers of America made a total of $40 million in Congressional campaign contributions. But fail to point out that, during that same time period, the Product Liability Alliance and the American Tort Reform Association made a total of $62 million in contributions to Congressional campaigns.[262] This does not include, of course, all of the corporate interests, such as Ford, and Allstate, and R.J.R. Nabisco, which give separately and independently to lawmakers, and who overtly and expressly support measures of tort reform. It is commonly said, in this regard, that plaintiff's attorneys are one of the ten strongest lobbying interests in Washington. Yet, even assuming the truth of this assertion, the other nine strongest lobbying forces are corporate interests, defense interests, and the interests of big business. Which means that, while 10% of the lobbying interest in Washington might be fighting for due process, trial by jury, and access to the courts, 90% of the lobbying interests are fighting against them.[263]One technique commonly employed by big business to achieve such lobbying efforts is the creation of "grass roots" groups, such as People For A Fair Legal System, Citizens Against Law-

262   When a national Products Liability Act was vetoed by President Clinton, Bob Dole attacked him for submitting to "enormous pressure from the wealthiest and most powerful special-interest group in America: the trial lawyers." Yet, at least one reporter noted that "a coalition of businesses supporting limits on jury awards donated $4.8 million to federal candidates during the first half of 1995, according to the Center for Responsive Politics. The political action committee for the Association of Trial Lawyers of America gave only $191,850 during that same period." Bruce Alpert, "Senate Okays Capping Damage Settlements" Times Picayune March 22, 1996, p.A-8.

263   For the first half of 1997, for example, the AMA topped the list of organizations, with $8.5 million in campaign contributions, followed by the Chamber of Commerce, with $7 million, Philip Morris, with $5.9 million, GM, with $5.2 million, Edison Electric, with $5 million, Pfizer, with $4.6 million, United Technologies, with $4.1 million, and GE, with $4.1 million. Other big spenders include Ford, Exxon, Texaco, Citicorp, Boeing, the Christian Coalition, AARP, the American Hospital Association, the Association of American Railroads, and the Pharmaceutical Research and Manufacturers Association. The Association of Trial Lawyers of America is not even on the list. See "Doctors Lobby Tops List of 30 Biggest Spenders" Times Picayune, March 7, 1998, p.C-8.

suit Abuse, and the American Tort Reform Association,
which serve as fronts for insurance, tobacco, chemical,
and other industries.[264] "If State Farm or Nationwide is
the leader of the coalition" explains Neal Cohen of Apco
Associates, "you're not going to pass the bill. It is not
credible."[265] So they hire a Washington firm, like Apco
Associates, to organize a coalition of small businesses,
nonprofit groups, and individuals, in order to put a sympathetic face on the proposed measures, while the large
companies who are really calling the shots recede into the
background.[266] Like their advertisements which obscure
the issues behind rhetoric about "greedy" trial lawyers,
these coalitions camouflage the greedy corporate interests they serve.[267] Attacks on "frivolous" lawsuits, likewise, because they are politically motivated and therefore

----

[264]   The vice-President and general counsel of the American Tort
Reform Association ("ATRA") is a former top executive and attorney for RJR. AT-
RA's other members include Aetna, GEICO, Nationwide Insurance, Transamerica,
Eli Lilly, Exxon, Mobil, Dow, Philip Morris, Johnson & Johnson, Monsanto, Pfizer,
Union Carbide, the Amercian Hospital Association, the American Nurses Association,
the AMA, Boeing, Cooper, Litton, and GE.

[265]   State Farm, for example, has contributed $3.6 million to People
For A Fair Legal System. See Steven Griffith, "State Farm's Motives Are Less Than
Saintly" Times Picayune, June 26, 1996, p.B-6. See also: Jane Fritsch, "Sometimes,
Lobbyists Strive to Keep Public In the Dark" New York Times, March 19, 1996, p.A-
1.

[266]   "In 1993, Cohen began a blitzkrieg public attack on 'greedy'
trial lawyers, on behalf of a coalition he called 'Mississippians for a Fair Legal System'. He advertised for members with an 800 number on billboards carrying slogans
like 'Fairness, Yes. Greed, No.' It cost nothing to join. 'You just sign your name on a
form that said you're a member.' The effort took Mississippi lawyers completely by
surprise. 'They didn't really know who was at the heart of everything, and there were
no reporting requirements.' In the end, Cohen said, 'we have 1,500 Mississippians
mixed in with who our clients were.'" Jane Fritsch, "Sometimes, Lobbyists Strive to
Keep Public In the Dark" New York Times, March 19, 1996, p.A-1.

[267]   ATRA calls itself a broad-based national coalition of local organizations, large and small businesses, school boards and others. "But the legislation
that will go to the Senate floor will do little for those in the coalition, like the School
Board or the Little League Team afraid of being sued. The legislation would limit only
product liability lawsuits, claims that a poorly manufactured or dangerous product has
caused an injury. So if the bill becomes law, the victors will largely be tobacco companies, manufacturers, and insurance companies." Jane Fritsch, "Sometimes, Lobbyists
Strive to Keep Public In the Dark" New York Times, March 19, 1996, p.A-1.

one-sided, always tend to focus on the institution of law-suits, and never seem to focus on costly and inappropriate defense tactics, such as the assertion of frivolous defenses, third-party actions, counter-claims, cross-claims, and reconventional demands, not to mention common discovery abuses, abuse of the attorney-client privilege, or other methods resulting in needless expenditure and delay.[268]Attacks on "ambulance chasing", similarly, focus solely on the improper conduct of plaintiff's lawyers, who rush to the scene of a disaster to solicit clients, while completely disregarding the fact that defense attorneys, insurance adjusters and investigators are virtually always on the scene of the incident, confiscating evidence, taking statements, and trying to get injured workers and their relatives to sign a quick settlement or release. Such criticisms also disregard the solicitation of corporate clients by defense firms, with expensive dinners, tickets to the ballgame, and golf outings at the club.

Attacks on attorney's fees, in this manner, are exclusively attacks on the plaintiff's contingency fee arrangement.[269] No one is complaining, by contrast, about a defense attorney that earns $500 or $600 an hour.[270]In the

268   GM's attorneys, for example, recently engaged in "willful and intentional disobedience" in a case where the plaintiffs alleged that 22 year-old Sharon Bishop, who died in a 1993 fire, was killed as a result of a design defect in GM's pick-up truck. The conduct of the defense attorneys during discovery was so egregious that the judge prevented GM from introducing any exhibits at trial. See Benjamin Weiser, "Judge Imposes a Rare Sanction in GM Upcoming Pick-up Truck Trial" Washington Post, Sept. 10, 1995, p.A.-9.

269   These attacks, of course, do not emanate from the consumers who are entering into such contingency fee agreements, but from defense interests, whose only intention could be to limit the institution or effectiveness of plaintiff suits. The Rand Corporation, for example, in a study that was conducted for the U.S. Department of Heath, Education and Welfare, concluded that: "Ceilings on the contingency fee percentage may significantly reduce the number of hours an attorney will spend on a case and effectively bar certain cases from trail. Such a restriction could be expected to deter low and middle-income plaintiffs from filing even meritorious suits." See Drivon, The Civil War on Consumer Rights, p.64 (1990).

270   Nor is there criticism of the contingent fees earned by corporate attorneys representing large companies as plaintiffs in commercial and other litigation.

tobacco litigation, for example, plaintiffs' attorneys have spent millions of dollars out of their own pocket, and thousands of hours of their time, honestly and ethically, on the side of the consumer, with very little prospect of winning, and absolutely no guarantee of even recouping their costs. Defense attorneys, by contrast, have concealed evidence, abused the attorney-client privilege, and abused the litigation process with frivolous and expensive delay tactics, while helping the tobacco companies to manufacture, sell, lie about, and shield themselves from responsibility for a product that kills 400,000 people every year. These attorneys have assumed absolutely no risk, nor out-of-pocket expense, and have profited to the tune of $500 per hour, or $600 million per year. Yet now, when the plaintiffs' attorneys have apparently been successful in achieving a potential $368.5 billion result on behalf of the American people, everyone from defense interests, to defense attorneys, to lawmakers, to radio talk show hosts, have rushed to limit their fees to just $100 dollars per hour, or less than 0.1% of the results obtained.[271] The CEO

Compare, for example, the reaction of journalists, politicians, and the public at large, to the prospect of plaintiffs' attorneys earning multi-million dollar fees in tobacco litigation, with the public reaction, or lack thereof, to the prospect of Wachtell Lipton earning a $3 billion-plus fee, (assuming a 33% contingent fee), in Philip Morris' $10 billion defamation suit against ABC and *Day One*.

Consider the irony: When smokers institute a $5 billion lawsuit for medical monitoring, cessation programs, and cancer research funds, due to the harmful additives in cigarettes, people are outraged and offended. But when a tobacco company institutes a $10 billion lawsuit against a television network for reporting, truthfully, on a massive fraud on the public, with drastic health consequences, no one is concerned.

271   The plaintiffs' attorneys, by and large, have agreed to have their fees arbitrated by a independent panel, based on the time and money invested, the complexity of the cases, the likelihood of success, the results achieved, the fact that the fee is contingent, the preclusion of other employment, the reputation and skill of the lawyers, and the other factors provided in the Professional Rules. The fee would not come out of the $368.5 billion which is intended for cessation programs, medical monitoring, cancer research, the federal government, and the states, but would be paid over and above by the tobacco industry. Despite the enormous time and expense dedicated to this litigation, the enormous novelty and complexity of the litigation, the minimal prospects of prevailing when the litigation started, and the monumental results obtained, not to mention the fact that most common fund awards fall between 25% and 30%, and that the attorneys, in many cases, have anywhere from 10% to 40%

of a tobacco company can get paid as much as $23.8 million for riding around in corporate jets, and playing golf, while his company kills thousands and thousands of its most loyal customers. The CEO of an insurance company can get paid as much as $67 million for collecting premiums, denying claims, and arguing for legislative reforms. But when a plaintiff's lawyer goes out to fight for the little guy, who has been injured or defrauded or otherwise wronged, that plaintiff's attorney is portrayed as a greedy person, an economic parasite, who doesn't deserve to get paid one cent, for making the country a little bit safer, a little bit freer, and a little bit better for us all.

---

contingency fee contracts with their clients, the overall claim made by the majority of attorneys is for a mere 2%-3% of the fund.

"I do not understand how conservatives could suggest that the Federal Government mandate the fees that attorneys would receive" said Republican Senator Orrin Hatch, Chairman of the Judiciary Committee, when the issue was recently debated in the Senate. "It's as bad a setting prices" he said, while noting that "many of the wrongs in our society would not have been righted" had it not been for attorneys willing to accept cases on a contingency fee basis. See Daily Monitor, May 20, 1998.

What the Future Holds

There is a general belief in this country that if everyone were willing to work, and if everyone were able to
work, there would be something profitable for everyone
to do. Democrats generally believe that it is society's role,
through education and other assistance, to achieve such a
level of self-sufficiency. The Republicans generally believe that such achievement should be left solely to the
province of the individual. The reality is, however, that
even if everyone were willing to work, and even if everyone were able to work, there would not be enough productive things for everyone to do.[272]

---

272   "Modern industrialism came into being in a world very different from the one we live in today: fewer people, less material well-being, plentiful
natural resources. As a result of the successor industry and capitalism, these conditions have now reversed. Today, more people are chasing fewer natural resources. But
industry still operates by the same rules, using more resources to make fewer people
more productive." Paul Hawken, "Natural Capitalism" Mother Jones March 1997,
p.40.

There are, of course, many who reject this notion. Marc Levinson, for example,
points out that "while Americans fret about the demise of the good jobs they remember, the economy is creating millions of new ones that once we would never have
dreamed of." Levinson, "Not Everyone is Downsizing" Newsweek, March 18, 1996,
p.42. See also: Robert Samuelson, "Down-Sizing for Growth" Newsweek, March 25,
1996, p.45.

Gene Koretz reports, on the other hand, that the pattern of job creation on the
heels of downsizing appears to be swinging into reverse. See Korentz, "Will Downsizing Ever Let Up?" Business Week Feb. 16, 1998, p.26. Others point out that, despite
a 5.4% U.S. unemployment rate, "of the 127 million working, 38 million work part
time, and 35 million have full-time work that doesn't pay enough to support a family.
Then there are the actual unemployed, who number 7.4 million, as well as another 7

There are countless people in this country with college degrees, with law degrees, with business degrees, and even medical degrees, who are willing and able to work, but can't find anything profitable to do.

In some ways, we are too efficient. We are too productive. It doesn't take 250 million people to provide goods and services for 250 million people. We can produce more than we can consume. And we are getting more efficient all the time. The motto of the post-Reagan *Wall Street* era seems to be that we have too many people who don't produce anything; who just live off the buying and selling of others. But, really, the last thing we need is more things. We have too many things. Cheap, plastic, lifeless, temporary, consumable, non-consumable parts, soon to become trash, and garbage, and waste. What we need is not things, but, on the contrary, a way of getting rid of things. We need to be less efficient, in some ways. We need more middlemen. We need more brokers. We need more consultants. We need more service and information providers. We need more people who just live off the buying and selling of others.

The Democrats

The Democrats often cling blindly to social programs that are culturally or economically flawed. With respect to public assistance programs, for example, it makes sense to help out the five percent of the population, maybe, who find themselves temporarily down and out, or who can't take care of themselves. But as the ratio shifts, more and more, and the number rises from five percent to ten percent to twenty percent, so that we have less and less people putting into the system and more and more taking out, such policies tend to become impractical and arcane.

million who are discouraged, forcibly retired, or work as temps. Nineteen million people work in retain and earn less than $10,000 per year, usually without health or retirement benefits. For the majority of workers, wages are no higher today than they were in 1973." Paul Hawken, "Social Waste" Mother Jones, March 1997, p.46.

The other problem with the Democratic Party, in this respect, is a reliance on moral ideals for the justification of policy, when, truly, the advancement of moral causes is not a legislative role. The government is established in order to provide common and essential services for the good of all: army, navy, police, fire, education, sanitation, parks, and roads. If we, as a society, determine that we want to be charitable towards various persons or causes, we can certainly choose to do so. But the government has no "duty" to provide the basic necessities, nor does any individual have a "right" to basic health care, food, shelter, and clothes.

We should view such programs, rather, as an investment, for the benefit of all. We, as a society, have to invest in our children. We have to invest to protect the elderly. We have to invest to improve the lives of the poor. Or we will beget sickness. We will beget violence. We will beget destruction, and poverty, and decay. Yet we need to be careful, at the same time, about setting up broad, long-term programs, upon which people become dependent, and upon which the government becomes obligated, year in and year out, without regard to the economic climate, and the level or surplus or debt.

The Republicans

The Republicans often cling blindly to the American Dream mentality. They give us anecdotes, of modern day Horatio Alger stories, with the message that, if X can do it, then Y can do it, and the opportunity is there for us all. The fallacy of this argument is that there are only so many Xs and so many Ys. There are only so many Pet Rocks, or Lefty & Lorado's Salsas, or PJ's Coffee Houses. For every X that succeeds, there are a hundred Ys that fail. And, to some extent, the success of X will tend to diminish the success of A, B and C. If, for example, Lefty & Lorado's salsa takes off, it's not likely going to generate more overall revenue. More people aren't going to go out and buy large quantities of salsa. Whatever gains they make are just going to cut into the profits of Old El Paso, and Ortega, and Pace.

The other problem is that Republicans, like the Democrats, attempt to place a moral spin on their legislative agenda. It is perfectly acceptable, in this respect, to argue that society does not have a duty to provide assistance to the poor. But you can't say that it's "Christian" or "moral". There is nothing moral about turning a blind eye. There is nothing Christian about tough love.[273]

All-Or-Nothing and Either/Or

The problem with America's two-party system is that it forces the people to make choices between two competing policies, when often, each is only half right, or both are completely wrong.[274] This either/or mindset prevents

273   "Heal the sick" Jesus said to his disciples, "raise the dead, cleanse lepers, cast out demons. You received without paying, give without pay." MATTHEW 10:8.

"And when it grew late, his disciples came to him and said, 'This is a lonely place, and the hour is now late; send them away, to go into their country and villages round about and buy themselves something to eat.' But He answered them, 'You give them something to eat.'" MARK 6:35.

"And a ruler asked him, 'Good Teacher, what shall I do to inherit eternal life?' And Jesus said to him, 'Why do you call me good? No one is good but God alone. You know the commandments: Do not commit adultery, Do not kill, Do not steal, Do not bear false witness, Honor your father and mother.' And he said, 'All these I have observed from my youth.' And when Jesus heard it, He said to him, 'One thing you still lack. See all that you have and give it to the poor, and you will have treasure in heaven.'" LUKE 18:18.

274   In a piece on the legacy of Adam Smith in our two-party system, Robert Samuelson, for example, notes that: "Democrats are so protective of government that they cannot concede the great power of Smith's 'invisible hand'. Self-interest is not simply greed, selfishness or narcissism. If properly constrained, it is an immense force for social good, and much human progress stems from the independent exertions and creative energies of individuals and enterprises. Democrats recoil at this notion because it deprives them of the power, social status and psychological gratification of seeming to deliver (through government) all the trappings of a good society. Meanwhile, Republicans are so contemptuous of government that they can-

people from looking for other available alternatives, and often results in either a dead-lock,[275] or a deeply flawed compromise.[276]

A perfect example of this overly-constrictive either/or mindset is embodied in the ongoing debate that surrounds the issue of crime. Republicans generally argue that the solution to the crime problem lies in law enforcement, while Democrats generally argue that the solution lies primarily in prevention. The public, therefore, is constantly asked to make a choice between these two methods of crime-fighting, as if they were mutually exclusive.[277] And despite the obvious wisdom of combining

not admit that it is often more than a necessary evil. It creates the legal and political framework without which tolerably free markets could not survive. It also supplies the collective services – from defense to roads – that the private market doesn't and deals with the market's unwanted 'excesses'. Smith realized that government produced these benefits, but many Republicans who cite him seem oblivious to their existence or importance.... The antagonists talk past each other. Smith combined a lofty vision of a decent society with an exacting analysis of the means for attaining it. Our modern luminaries often assume that their means are always up to their ends." Samuelson, "The Spirit of Adam Smith" Newsweek, Dec. 2, 1996, p.63.

275   The either/or mindset resulting in dead-lock was highlighted by a recent article addressing the campaign finance system: "All we have to do is mix ingredients from two radically different proposals, one from the political left, and one from the political right. Such a reform won't solve every flaw in the system. But that's also why it would work: By realistically avoiding the problems that can't be solved, it gives us a chance to resolve the ones that can." Jonathan Rauch, "Give Pols Free Money, No Rules" U.S. News & World Report, Dec. 29, 1997, p.54.

276   Quoting Margaret Thatcher, George Will describes the system as "a process of abandoning all beliefs, principles, values and policies in search of something in which no one believes, but to which no one objects; the process of avoiding the very issues that have to be solved, merely because you cannot get agreement on the way ahead." George Will, "Consensus and Ladders" Newsweek, May 12, 1997, p.92. Gregg Easterbrook, on the other hand, describes the compromise process as ultimately successful, though not without partisan hurdles along the way: "First, all sides condemn the new idea: Environmental advocates say it isn't enough; some business executives say it will be impossibly expensive. Next comes a phase of general unhappiness in which lawyers rule. Then innovations occur – such as the invention of the catalytic converter, which made automobile smog control practical – and efficiencies result. Ten years later both pollution and costs are declining, though this never prevents the same institutional parties from making the same gloomy predictions about the next round of reforms." Easterbrook, "Greenhouse Common Sense" U.S. News & World Report, Dec. 1, 1997, p.58.

277   An example: "For the past two years, academics have engaged in a spirited debate over how much credit police should be given for the city's dramatic drop in crime, more than 35 percent overall since 1993. At stake is 40 years of

both efforts, legislation which includes both law enforcement and preventative measures is always portrayed as
a compromise, rather than an appropriate solution. The
problem with the two-party system is further compounded by the fact that the laws are so complex, and so complicated, that the people can never evaluate such proposals
for themselves. The Democrats say, for example, that the
proposal includes Medicare cuts. The Republicans argue
that the measures are not cuts, but merely a diminution in
the level of yearly increases. If you accept either premise,
that party is right. But there is no way for you, as a citizen, to know which side is telling the truth. The result is a
political age of sound-bytes, where proposals that, when
reduced to their simplest form, seem good, win. Because
the other side does not have the opportunity to explain
why a measure that seems fair might actually be unfair, or
why something which seems good might actually be bad.
The impact is lost. When you have a good bumper-stick-
er, a treatise cannot compete.[278]

Judgment

The existing rules of evidence are codified principles
sociological research, most of which concludes that crime rates are driven primarily
by social conditions, not police tactics. Some researchers give full credit to the New
York police, calling their approach nothing short of a revolution in law enforcement.
Others say police have merely piggybacked on a crime rate that was already falling
because of an improving economy, favorable demographics and the waning popularity
of crack cocaine." Michael Perlstein, "New Crime Strategy Clashes With Research"
Times Picayune, April 21, 1997, p.A-7.

[278]   A perfect example of this is the new movement for a national
sales tax. Supporters of this proposal argue that "rich people spend more money, so
they will pay more taxes" and hence the proposal is eminently fair. It requires more
airtime to explain that such a system is actually quite unfair, because it is so regres-
sive, to the middle and lower classes. Poor and middle class people generally spend
100% of the money they earn, because they need every cent just to get by. Wealthier
people, by contrast, are able to save and invest a greater proportion of what they earn.
If, therefore, the income tax is replaced by a flat 19% sales tax, lower and middle class
families will likely be taxed on a full 19% of what they earn, while wealthier people
will have effective tax rates of only 10% or 15%. In addition, wealthier people are
much more likely to pay for professional and other services, such as attorneys, accountants, personal trainers, gardeners, drivers, or maids. If, therefore, the tax is a strict
sales tax, on goods, and not services, the disparity will be even greater.

that were, for the most part, deeply rooted in the common law tradition. They are the result of centuries of experience and experimentation into the search for justice and truth in a court of law. They also can provide a useful roadmap for the judgment of issues, events, and courses of action, which arise in our daily lives.

First, the rules teach us that the most reliable information is personal knowledge, or that which can be empirically observed. That we should be resistant to and skeptical of rumor, and gossip, and other hearsay evidence, which is acquired second-hand.[279]

Next, the rules of evidence teach us not to accept, as conclusive, the lay opinions of others, which are, after all, no more credible or valid than the conclusions we are able to reach on our own.[280]

The rules of evidence also teach us that each issue, fact, event, or course of action, must be judged according to its own merits, and not based on the character, or intelligence, or record, of either its critics or its supporters. Stupid people are right, sometimes, even if only by accident. Smart people are wrong. Bad people support things which might be good, (maybe for the wrong reasons). And good people support things which might be bad, (maybe they are just mistaken).[281]One commonly

[279]   The rules of evidence provide that testimony should be based upon personal knowledge, and that hearsay, which is defined as any out-of-court statement offered to prove the truth of the matter asserted, is generally not admissible in a court of law. Federal Rules of Evidence 602, 801(c), and 802.

[280]   "If the witness is not testifying as an expert, the witness' testimony in the form of opinions or inferences is limited to those opinions or inferences which are (a) rationally based on the perception of the witness, and (b) helpful to a clear understanding of the witness' testimony or a determination of a fact in issue." Federal Rule of Evidence 701.

[281]   "Evidence of other crimes, wrongs, or acts is not admissible to prove the character of a person in order to show action in conformity therewith." Federal Rule of Evidence 404(b). "Ill Kings make many good laws." - Proverb. "It is a fair summary of history to say that the safeguards of liberty have frequently been forged in controversies involving not very nice people." Justice Frankfurter, United States v. Rabinowitz, 339 U.S. 56, 69 (1950). "I abhor averages. I like the individual case. A man may have six meals one day and none the next, making an average of

employed fallacy in this area is the statement of a universal truth, and then the use of that statement as a premise for a proposed change or solution, without examining the merits of the alternative. By doing so, the proponent instills confidence in the listener, who will then agree with the "solution" even though the causal link is missing. A simple example of this type of fallacy can be found in the following: "America should be a place where children can grow up free from violence, perversion, moral bankruptcy, and decay. Therefore, I propose a constitutional amendment mandating prayer in public schools." In this case, everyone universally agrees that America should be a place where children can grow up free from violence, perversion, moral bankruptcy, and decay; but there is no indication, much less explanation, of how prayer in the public schools could possibly transform America into that place. Another example often recited by Republicans is: "If you tax people too much, they will become less productive, because it isn't worth their time. Therefore, we need tax cuts." A logical cause and effect can be drawn between high taxes and decreased productivity. But that doesn't make it true. It is just as likely, in fact, that if you tax people more, they will become more productive, because they have to earn more money just to maintain the same standard of living.[282]

It is also commonly argued that if you lower taxes on
three meals per day, but that is not a good way to live." - Justice Lewis Brandeis. "It makes no difference whether a good man has defrauded a bad man or a bad man has defrauded a good man, or whether a good or bad man has committed adultery; the law can look only to the amount of damage done." Aristotle, Nicomachean Ethics. "The business of the court is to try the case and not the man; a very bad man may have a very righteous cause." Thompson v. Church, 1 Root 312 (1791).

282   Another similar example often recited by Republicans goes: "If we give single mothers more welfare for each additional child, they will have more illegitimate children." Well, that's rational. It's logical. It makes sense. But that doesn't mean that it's true. There is a logical connection that can be drawn, but that doesn't necessarily imply that there is an actual causal connection between the two. It is likely, rather, that, in many cases, single women are having illegitimate babies for deeply-rooted reasons wholly unrelated to their welfare checks, or anything economic at all.

the wealthy, they will invest more, which will create more jobs, and more business, which, in turn, will be taxed, and you will actually end up with more revenue. Well, that's rational. It's logical. But it is just as logical to say that if you give money to the lower classes, they will spend it, which will create more business, and more jobs, and more taxes, and ultimately you will end up with more revenue. [283]Finally, it has recently been suggested that we should adopt a national sales tax so that we can abolish the IRS. In this case, many people will agree that the IRS should be abolished. But what is the alternative? Specifically, how are these national sales taxes going to be collected? Isn't such tax collection going to be particularly difficult with respect to small, family-owned, all-cash businesses? Isn't there going to have to be some king of a body, or office, or agency, responsible for conducting audits and ensuring that the sales taxes are being paid? It is important, therefore, to always test the causal mechanisms at work, and to consider the alternatives. It is further important to judge facts, events, issues, and courses of action, based upon their own merits, and not the personality, history or character of the parties involved. Finally, it is important to make judgments according to first-hand or empirical observations of the events in question, while resisting rumor, gossip, and opinions that are uneducated and uninformed.

Standing

There is a legal requirement known as "standing" which is intended to ensure that a person who institutes a

---

283   Actually, it is logical to predict that you will generate more revenue, due to the "consumption function" and the "multiplier" which will together give you a greater return on your investment. Ultimately, however, there is a level at which the economy will reach a point of diminishing returns. At some point, the tax level will be so high that all productivity will be stifled; while, at some other point, the tax level will be too low to generate meaningful revenue. The goal, therefore, is to determine that optimal point in the middle, (which appears to be somewhere between 17% and 21%), where both productivity and revenue can be generated in a mutually beneficial way.

lawsuit has an actual and real interest in the outcome, and will truly be affected by the result. While the requirement of standing is strictly a judicial principle, America would do well to adopt such a philosophy regarding other issues of social or political concern.

On a basic level, there are too many people making too many decisions without standing. They vote for or against measures, not out of their own interests and positive motivations, but out of resentment, or prejudice, or spite.

Jessie Helms, for example, has no standing to tell two homosexuals in Denver, Colorado, that they can't get married or have sexual relations. He doesn't even have standing to tell that to two people in North Carolina. Their relationship does not affect him. He has no vested interest in the outcome. He's just acting out of spite.

Lower and middle class people who want to impose inheritance taxes, likewise, have no standing to strip upper class families of their wealth, (which has already been taxed), in order to "level the playing field". They are not acting out of their own self-interest. They are just acting out of spite. This is not to suggest that people do not have a right to engage in the political process. Within constitutional limits, everyone, in a democracy, has the right to participate in the formulation of law. But decisions, generally, should be made by those who are most directly affected. And people should support programs based upon their own interests, and for the good of the public, not out of some motivation, whether expressly or subconsciously, to cause another inconvenience or harm.

Focusing on Tomorrow's Solutions
There is no point in solving today's problems. We can't. It's too late. Today's problems were created five, or ten, or even fifty years in the past; just as the things that

we do now will determine the problems, and the solutions, of the year 2000, and 2050, and beyond. Those are the problems that we should be trying to solve. Those are the only ones that we can.

The Democratic Goal

With today's technology, we do not need a representative government. With the computer systems and phone systems and other communication and information networks, everyone could vote. We could elect lawmakers who would do just that: Make laws. Propose them, draft them, and explain them. But they would be voted on by the people.

This would force laws to be universal, simple, and fair. It would solve all of the budget problems, by getting rid of pork-barrel and special interest spending.[284] People would only vote to fund things that have a benefit for all. Army, navy, police, fire, education, sanitation, parks, and roads. With a broad consensus, the people could choose to fund other social programs, but without loopholes, or favors, or special guarantees. Local problems would be solved on a local level. As it should be. Yet such a democratic effort would, of course, require a renewed faith in the vision of America. Faith in people. Faith in the individual. Faith in democracy. Faith in ourselves.

---

284   Nobody outside of the Southeast, for example, is going to vote for a tobacco farm subsidy. Nobody outside of Colorado is going to vote for a tax exemption for Colorado silver mines. And nobody that's not a shareholder in Friskies cat food company is going to vote to spend their tax dollars marketing that product overseas.

A Few Lines for the Trial Lawyer

Across the Acres and the Aprils and the Fields,
the waning afterglow of what remained
Does make its way along the vast horizon.

The Titans or the Captains who did
forge our paths in steel and blood
Have now diminished or retreated

Yet defeated not in spirit, nor the Mind
of once what said we might have been.

And in that silent ringing from the Hill
you hear a voice; a human plea
that keeps you climbing: onward, upward

On the errant quest against
the lies and mountaintops and gold,
To speak for Her, and not be silenced!

Acknowledgments

I would like to thank all of my teachers, mentors, role models, and supporters, particularly Justice Harry T. Lemmon, Jim Kitchens, Howard Twiggs, Maury Herman, Sid Cotlar, Morton Katz, Matt Chenevert, Jim Klick, Lenny Davis, Steve Lane, Jeff Ellinport, Brian Katz, Rich King, Isaac and Lilian Kirshbom, MawMaw, PawPaw, Grandma, Penny, Liz, Mom, Dad, and Karen.

BIBLIOGRAPHY OF SOURCESAND ADDITIONAL REFERENCES

I. Chapter One:
Holding Wrongdoers Accountable

For the historical origins of civil liability, and a summary of the distinction between fault-based and strict liability, see generally: Oliver Wendell Holmes, "Early Forms of Liability" The Common Law Lecture I (Little Brown & Co. 1881) (Legal Classics Library 1982); Stone, Louisiana Civil Law Treatise Tort Doctrine §123 (West 1977); Prosser and Keeton, The Law of Torts (5th ed. 1984) §§ 69, 75; Posner, Economic Analysis of the Law (4th ed. 1992) pp.206-211; Geistfeld, Implementing Enterprise Liability 67 N.Y.U.L.Rev. 1157 (1992); Hanson & Logue, The First-Party Insurance Externality: An Economic Justification for Enterprise Liability 76 Cornell.L.Rev. 129 (1990); Fletcher, Fairness and Utility in Tort Theory, 85 Harv.L.Rev. 537 (1972); Olsen v. Shell Oil, 365 So.2d 1285, 1291-1292 n.13 (La. 1978).

"He who derives the advantage ought to sustain the burden." Legal Maxim. (Shrager & Frost, The Quotable Lawyer (New England Publishing 1986) p.61). Where two innocent parties must suffer a loss at the hands of another, that loss should be borne by the party who has most contributed to the injury by allowing it to occur. Flatte v.

Nichols, 96 So.2d 477, 480 (La. 1957); Trumbull Chevrolet Sales Company v. F.S. Maxwell, 142 So.2d 805, 806 (La. App. 2nd Cir. 1962).

Tort reform promises to "reduce the threat of runaway jury verdicts, promote settlements, and promote certainty in commercial transactions by establishing reasonable boundaries for awards." Newt Gingrich, Dick Armey, and House Republicans, Contract With America (Times Books 1994) p.154.

Less than 1% of the Federal Budget is dedicated to the entire Federal Court System. Johnson, "Federal Judiciary's Budget is Scrutinized" Wall Street Journal June 20, 1995, p.B-4. Less than 0.5% of the annual budget of the state of Louisiana in 1994 was dedicated to the judiciary. Annual Report of the Judicial Council of the Supreme Court of Louisiana, pp.22,30 (1995). In all, the entire court system, including judges, prosecutors, public defenders, courthouse operations and maintenance, requires only three-fifths of one percent of all government expenditures. Sol Linowitz, The Betrayed Profession (Charles Scribner's Sons 1994) p.222.

On secrecy agreements and protective orders generally, see: Hare, Gilbert & Ollanik, Full Disclosure: Combating Stonewalling and Other Discovery Abuses (ATLA Press 1994); Russ M. Herman, "No More Dirty Secrets in Court" Trial, Oct. 1989, p.4; Arthur Miller, Confidentiality, Protective Orders, and Public Access to the Courts, 105 Harv.L.Rev. 427 (1991); Alan Morrison, Protective Orders, Plaintiffs, Defendants and the Public, 24 U.Rich.L.Rev. 109 (1990); Hare, Gilbert & Remine, Confidentiality Orders (1988). See also: Thayer v. Liggett & Myers No. 5314 (W.D.Mich. Feb. 19, 1970), 1.2 TPLR

2.63, 2.67-2.68 (1986); Walsh & Weiser, "Court Secrecy Masks Safety Issues: Key GM Fuel Tank Memo Kept Hidden in Auto Crash Suit" Washington Post Oct. 23, 1988. The statutory authority for protective orders with respect to "trade secrets" stems from Federal Rule of Civil Procedure 26(c)(7), and similar provisions in the several states. See, for example: Cal. Code Civ. Pro. §2030(e)(6); Fla. Rule Civ. Pro. 1.280(c)(7); La. Code Civ. Pro. art. 1426; Ohio Civ. Rule 26(c)(7); Penn. Rule Civ. Pro. 4012(a)(9).

On the dangers associated with the use of ATVs, see generally: "Consumer Product Safety Commission's Response to Hazards of Three-Wheel All-Terrain Vehicles" 40th Report by the Committee on Government Operations (July 16, 1986); Brienza, "ATV Deaths Decline, But Danger Still Present" Trial July 1996, p.106; Yaworsky, Products Liability: All-Terrain Vehicles (ATV's) 83 A.L.R.4th 70 (1991); Antley v. Yamaha Motor Corp., 539 So.2d 696 (La. App. 3rd Cir. 1989).

Proof of industry knowledge concerning the dangers of asbestos is contained in: Letter from Ms. Rossiter, editor of "ASBESTOS" to S. Simpson, President of Rayoestos-Manhattan, Inc., Sept. 25, 1935; Letter from S. Simpson to Vaniver Brown, an attorney with Johns-Manville, Oct. 1, 1935; Letter from Vandiver Brown to S. Simpson, Oct. 3, 1935; Matthew Swetonic, Why Asbestos? Asbestos Textile Institute, June 7, 1973. See also: "Asbestos Danger Known Long Ago, Expert Testifies" Times Picayune, Oct. 7, 1995, p.B-5.

Proof of knowledge on the part of A.H. Robins with respect to the dangers associated with the Dalkon Shield is contained in: R.W. Nickless, Dalkon Shield: Orientation Report, June 29, 1970; Walt Schoenberger, Medical Department, A.H. Robins, Dalkon "String" March 26,

1971. See generally: Richard Sobol, Bending the Law (University of Chicago Press 1991).

The United States Supreme Court held that protective orders did not violate the First Amendment in Seattle Times v. Rhinehart, 467 U.S. 20, 104 S.Ct. 2199, 81 L.Ed.2d 17 (1984). The Court noted that "a litigant has no First Amendment right of access to information solely for purposes of trying his suit." Seattle Times, 467 U.S. at 32, 104 S.Ct. at 2207; Zemel v. Rusk, 381 U.S. 1, 16-17, 85 S.Ct. 1271, 1280-1281, 14 L.Ed.2d 179 (1965). Commentators have noted, however, that some information might be "so significant to the preservation of the process of self-governance... that it would violate the first amendment to keep the press and the public from that knowledge." Arthur Miller, Confidentiality, Protective Orders, and Public Access to the Courts, 105 Harv.L.Rev. 427, 441 (1991); Cohen, Access to Pretrial Documents Under the First Amendment, 84 Colum.L.Rev. 1813, 1833 (1984). See also, generally: FREEDOM OF INFORMATION ACT, 5 U.S.C. §552; U.S. Dept. of Justice v. Julian, 486 U.S. 1, 108 S.Ct. 1606, 100 L.Ed.2d 1606 (1988); Brown & Williamson v. FTC, 710 F.2d 1165 (6th Cir. 1983); Westchester General Hospital v. Dept. of Health, 464 F.Supp. 236, 239 (M.D.Fla. 1979); Fla. Stat. §69.081(3),(4); Tex. Rule Civ. Pro. 76(a); La. Const. Art. XII, §3; La. Rev. Stat. 42:1169; La. Rev. Stat. 44:31; La. Code Civ. Pro. art. 1426(c)-(e); Title Research v. Rausch, 450 So.2d 933, 936 (La. 1984); Kammerer v. Sewerage & Water Board, No. 93-1232, 633 So.2d 1357, 1362 (La. App. 4th Cir. 3/15/94) (Waltzer, J., concurring).

"Reports, surveys, schedules, lists, and data compiled or collected for the purpose of identifying, evaluating, or planning the safety enhancement of potential accident sites, hazardous roadway conditions, or railway-highway crossings... should not be subject to discovery or admitted into evidence in a Federal or State court proceeding or considered for any other purposes in any action for damages arising from any occurrence at a location mentioned or addressed in such reports...." 23 U.S.C. §409.

"'The power to create and enforce a legal code, both civil and criminal' is one of the quintessential functions of a State." Diamond v. Charles, 476 U.S. 54, 65, 106 S.Ct. 1697, 1705, 90 L.Ed.2d 48 (1986); Alfred L. Snapp v. Puerto Rico, 458 U.S. 592, 601, 102 S.Ct. 3260, 3265, 73 L.Ed.2d 995 (1982). See also: Hillsborough County v. Automated Medical Labs, 471 U.S. 707, 719, 105 S.Ct. 2371, 2378, 85 L.Ed.2d 714 (1985). It is "extraordinary for Congress to attempt to proscribe procedural rules for *state* courts." Allied-Bruce Terminix Cos. v. Dobson, 513 U.S. 265, 286, 115 S.Ct. 834, 846, 130 L.Ed.2d 753 (1995) (Thomas, joined by Scalia, dissenting). See also: L&L Kempwood v. Omega, 972 S.W.2d 819 (Tex. App. Corpus Christi 1998).

For information on Environmental Audit Bills, see generally: Hecker and Dolan, "A Shield Against Disclosure Just Might Kill Us" Legal Times Vol.XVIII, No.2, May 29, 1995. In particular, see: Ark. Stat. §§8-1-301 to 8-1-312; Colo. Rev. Stat. §13-25-126.5; Ill. Stat. §415:5/52.2; Ind. Rev. Stat. §§13-10-3-1 to 13-10-3-12; Ken. Rev. Stat. §224.01-040; Minn. Stat. §§ 114C.22, 114C.26; Miss. Code §49-2-71; Tex. Civ. Stat. Art. 4447cc; Utah Code §§ 19-7-105, 19-7-106, 19-7-107; Vir. Stat. §10.1-1198; Wyo. Stat. §35-11-1105. (In Louisiana, Proposed Louisiana Environmental Audit Bill HB-2085 was defeated in 1995, while HB-967 and SB-777 were defeated in 1997.) With respect to similar privileges for

banking institutions, at least one state's law provides that
the results of any "self-determination, self-assessment,
self-testing, or self corrections, and any notes, reports,
or work product derived therefrom, whether prepared by
internal or by outside attorneys, accountants, or consultants, shall be deemed privileged from all purposes and
shall not be subject to discovery in any private civil action brought against the bank or other financial institution alleging noncompliance with or violation of... state
and federal banking laws and regulations." La. Rev. Stat.
6:336. A "self-critical analysis privilege" has also been
recognized by some courts, even in the absence of specific legislation, to protect minutes and reports of hospital
staff on how to improve hospital standards, in the context
of a medical malpractice case, for example, or to protect
reports on the progress of advancement opportunities for
minorities and women, in the context of an employment
discrimination case. See, for example: Bredice v. Doctor's Hospital, 50 F.R.D. 249 (D.D.C. 1970), aff'd, 479
F.2d 920 (D.C. Cir. 1973); EEOC v. General Telephone,
885 F.2d 575, 578 (9th Cir. 1989); Coates v. Johnson &
Johnson, 756 F.2d 524, 551-552 (7th Cir. 1985); Banks
v. Lockheed-Georgia, 53 F.R.D. 283 (N.D.Ga. 1971);
Troupin v. Metropolitan Life, 169 F.R.D. 546 (S.D.N.Y.
1996); Todd v. South Jersey Hosp. System, 152 F.R.D.
676, 683 (D.N.J. 1993); Hardy v. New York News, 114
F.R.D. 633, 641-642 (S.D.N.Y. 1987); In re LTV Securities Litigation, 89 F.R.D. 595, 619 (N.D.Tex. 1981);
Leonard, Codifying A Privilege for Self-Critical Analysis
25 Harv.J.Legis. 113 (Winter 1988); Wallach, Reider &
Ginetto, "Self-Critical Analysis Privilege Has Been Recognized As Federal Common Law" Legal Times June
16, 1997, p.B-9. But see: University of Pennsylvania v.
EEOC, 493 U.S. 182, 110 S.Ct. 577, 107 L.Ed.2d 571
(1980); United States v. Nixon, 418 U.S. 683, 709, 94

S.Ct. 3090, 3108, 41 L.Ed.2d 1039 (1974); Branzburg v. Hayes, 408 U.S. 665, 92 S.Ct. 2646, 33 L.Ed.2d 626 (1972); Adams v. St. Francis Regional Medical Center, 264 Kan. 144, 173, 955 P.2d 1169, 1187 (1998); Hartson v. Campbell County Memorial Hospital, 913 P.2d 870 (Wyo. 1996); Greenwood v. Wierdsma, 741 P.2d 1079 (Wyo. 1987); Linder v. Smith, 193 Mont. 20, 629 P.2d 1187 (1981); M v. K, 186 N.J. Super. 363, 452 A.2d 704 (1982); In re Grand Jury, 541 F.2d 373, 382 (3rd Cir. 1976); Dowling v. American Hawaii Cruises, 971 F.2d 423 (9th Cir. 1992); Spencer Savings Bank v. Excell, 960 F.Supp. 835 (D.N.J. 1997); Jolly v. Superior Court, 540 P.2d 658, 662-663 (Ariz. 1975); Nazareth Literary & Benevolent Inst. v. Stephenson, 503 S.W.2d 177, 178-179 (Ky. App. 1973); Davison v. St. Paul, 248 N.W.2d 433, 440-442 (Wis. 1977); McNab, Criticizing the Self-Criticism Privilege, 1987 U.Ill.L.Rev. 675 (1987); Flanagan, Rejecting a General Privilege for Self-Critical Analyses, 57 Geo.Wash.L.Rev. 551 (1983).

A private citizen has the right to comment truthfully, (or even falsely, without malice), on a matter of public concern. Garrison v. State of Louisiana, 379 U.S. 64, 73, 85 S.Ct. 209, 215, 13 L.Ed.2d 125 (1964); New York Times v. Sullivan, 376 U.S. 254, 269, 84 S.Ct. 710, 720, 11 L.Ed.2d 686 (1964); Rosenbloom v. Metromedia, 403 U.S. 29, 43-44, 91 S.Ct. 1811, 1819-1820, 29 L.Ed.2d 296 (1971). See also: Pickering v. Board of Education, 391 U.S. 563, 88 S.Ct. 1731, 20 L.Ed.2d 811 (1968); Frazier v. King, 873 F.2d 820, 825-826 (5th Cir. 1989); La. R.S. 42:1169.

II. Chapter Two: The Million-Dollar Cup of Coffee

Liebeck v. McDonald's, No. CV-93-02419 (2nd JDC, Benanillo County, N.M.).

"The truth is that the news is the reporting of aberrant behavior. It's different. If it's the same, and it goes on every day, then it doesn't get reported." Walter Cronkite, Interview on CNN, Sept. 23, 1994.

For the *Smith v. Ireland* Michigan custody battle, see generally: "Sonya Live" CNN, Aug. 16, 1994; United Press International, "Appeals Court Hears Baby Maranda Case" May 3, 1995.

Girl Scouts have to sell 87,000 boxes of cookies just to pay liability insurance. See, for example: George Will, "Consensus and Ladders" Newsweek, May 12, 1997, p.92; Bob Eaton, "No Joking Matter" Newsweek, Sept. 23, 1996, p.20. There are over 2.5 million Girl Scouts, according to information provided at: http://www. gsusa/organization, http://girlscoutstotam.org/funding.htm, and http://www.gsusa. org/organization/cookiesales.htm, as of March 4, 1998.

On the myth of the liberal media, see generally: Peter Laufer, Inside Talk Radio (Birch Lane Press 1995) pp.208-220.

Disney purchased ABC for $19 billion. Geraldine Fabrikant, "It's No Mickey Mouse Deal: Walt Disney Buying ABC" Times Picayune, Aug. 1, 1995, p.A-1. (See also: Stevens, "Mouse*ke*fear" Brill's Content, Dec. 1998, p.95.) CBS was purchased by Westinghouse for $5.4 billion. Geraldine Fabrikant, "CBS Sold in Second Network Takeover" Times Picayune, Aug. 2, 1995, p.A-1.

Newspapers report plaintiff victories in punitive damage cases 20 times more often than defendant victories, and the reduction of such awards on appeal is rarely reported. "Punitive Damages 'Crisis' a Myth, Scholars Say" Trial, Dec. 1996, p.14. "Punitive damage cases emphasized in the media are newsworthy precisely because they are so rare." Theodore Eisenberg, The Predictability of Punitive Damages (1996) (published in the *Journal of Legal Studies,* Vol.26, p.623 (1997)).

In the 1980s, Penzoil sued Texaco for interfering with a merger agreement, and was awarded $3 billion in punitive damages, over and above a $7.53 billion compensatory damage award. "Penzoil Win $10.53 Billion in Texaco Suit" L.A. Times, Nov. 19, 1985. In another commercial oil and gas lawsuit in Texas, the plaintiff corporation was awarded $263 million in compensatory and punitive damages. "Local Firm Wins Big Oil Case" Times Picayune, July 25, 1992, p.C-1.

"Headlines like: 'WOMAN WINS $200,000 FOR SLIP ON A BANANA PEEL' appear frequently, usually with little or no explanation of what actually happened or what the woman's real injuries were." Laurence E. Drivon, The Civil War on Consumer Rights (Conari Press 1990) pp.41-42. See generally: Galanter, An Oil Strike in Hell: Contemporary Legends About the Civil Justice System, 40 Ariz.L.Rev. 717 (1998); Rustad, Nationalizing Tort Law: The Republicans Attack on Women, Blue Collar Workers and Consumers, 48 Rutgers L.Rev. 673 (1996); Galanter, Real World Torts: An Antidote to An-

ecdote, 55 Md.L.Rev. 1093 (1996); "Punitive Damages
'Crisis' a Myth, Scholars Say" Trial, Dec. 1996, p.14;
Theodore Eisenberg, The Predictability of Punitive Dam-
ages (1996) (published in the *Journal of Legal Studies,*
Vol.26, p.623 (1997)); Jane Fritsch, "Sometimes, Lobby-
ists Strive to Keep Public In the Dark" New York Times,
March 19, 1996, p.A-1; Griffith, "State Farm's Motives
Are Less Than Saintly" Times Picayune, June 26, 1996,
p.B-6; Ivins, "Clinton Earns a Reprieve for Quashing Tort
Reform" Seattle Times, March 25, 1996, p.B-5; Daniels,
"The Question of Jury Competence and the Politics of
Civil Justice Reform: Symbols, Rhetoric, and Agenda
Building" Law and Contemporary Problems, Vol.52,
p.269 (1989); "Grassroots 'Weeds' Need to be Clipped,
Say Angry Activists" O'Dweyer's PR Service Reporter
(June 1996); Guerry, "Corporate Ads Attack Civil Justice
System" Louisiana Advocates, Feb. 1999, p.2; "Follow
the Money... And the Anti-Trial Lawyer Rhetoric" Loui-
siana Advocates, Feb. 1999, p.12. Examples include the
following:

A man is injured when drunk driver crashed into a
telephone booth and California Chief Justice Rose Bird
rules that the company that designed the booth is liable." – The editorial, which appeared in *The Wall Street
Journal,* (like the remarks of Ronald Reagan, see Public
Papers of the Presidents of the United States, May 30,
1986), did not inform the reader, however, that the phone
booth was only fifteen feet from the highway; that it had
been hit and destroyed, and then replaced in the very
same spot, just twenty months earlier; and that it had a
door which jammed shut, so that when the man using the
telephone saw the drunk driver bearing down on him, he
was trapped inside. The California Supreme Court, moreover, did not hold that the telephone company was liable;
the court, rather, in a 6-1 decision, merely found that it

was improper for the judge to dismiss the case without giving the plaintiff his day in court. (See <u>Bigbee v. Pacific Telephone and Telegraph Co.</u>, 665 P.2d 947 (Cal. 1983). See also: <u>Brown v. Michigan Bell</u>, 572 N.W.2d 33 (Mich. App. 1997).) The parties subsequently reached a settlement prior to trial, and the defendants requested a protective order from the court to prevent disclosure of its terms.

"41-year-old body builder entered a footrace with a refrigerator strapped to his back to prove his prowess. During the race, he alleged, one of the straps came loose and the man was hurt. He sued everyone in sight, including the maker of the strap. Jury award: $1 million." – The plaintiff, in fact, was Franco Columbo, a world-champion body builder, who was approached by television producers to participate in a "World's Strongest Man" television show. The show provided him with a written contract which guaranteed that all of the equipment had been tested for his safety. The rack on which Mr. Columbo's refrigerator was mounted, however, was centered too low, and he suffered total knee displacement, requiring extensive surgery. The chief engineer for the defendant admitted that the equipment had never been tested for anyone of Mr. Columbo's size, that the equipment was never tested by anyone who had to run with it, and that he had personally informed the promoters of the event that he did not think that either the equipment nor the race itself was safe. The jury accordingly found that the promoters of the event had breached their contract with Mr. Columbo, resulting in serious injury. With respect to the maker of the strap, the plaintiff never alleged that the strap had broken, and the manufacturer of the strap was never sued. (For the "horror story" see Burt Solomon, "Finger-Pointing Distinguishes Attempts to Fix Blame for Liability Crisis" <u>National Journal</u> Feb. 15, 1986, p.378; "A World

Without Insurance" Forbes July 15, 1985, p.40. For the real facts, see John Gannon, Tort Deform - Lethal Bedfellows, Essential Information, 1995.)

An Oregon jury awarded $1.5 million in damages to the estate of a woman who was killed when a horse fell through the roof of her 1980 Ford Pinto. The horse had been spooked by wolves or coyotes and broke through the triple-strand, barbed-wire fence onto the highway. The horse was hit head-on by the woman's car, was knocked into the air and fell down onto the hood and roof of the car. Although Ford argued that the accident was a 'one in a million accident' and that no car could ever withstand the impact of a horse, the jury found Ford liable."
– In fact, Mr. Green was driving his 20 year-old wife and their newborn baby home from the hospital, when a horse darted out into the road. The animal slid across the windshield, and then up onto the roof, which collapsed, and Mrs. Green was killed. Contrary to Ford's claims that this was a 'one-in-a-million accident', Oregon transportation records show that a horse is involved in a collision with an automobile every three days. The National Transportation Safety Board, moreover, requires that a vehicle withstand 5,000 pounds of impact. The evidence proved that the Pinto could only withstand about 3,800 pounds. Ford employees, moreover, admitted that records of vehicles which had failed safety tests had been destroyed. Whether the threat to a passenger is presented by a rollover, or by the weight of a horse, millions of people depend on the crashworthiness of their cars.
    "Back in 1979, a $2 million product liability suit topped by a $3 million punitive damage award almost put this factory out of business." – Walter Cronkite, Liability: Injustice for All, Manhattan Institute, 1991. What Mr. Cronkite failed to explain was that a compressor, designed

to last 60-100 years, yet assembled improperly, even by 1942 standards, blew up, resulting in the shattering of one worker's leg, (six surgeries could not repair damage), and the loss of a foot of another. A mechanical engineer testified that the wrong type of safety valve had been installed in the wrong place, facing the wrong direction. The jury agreed, and awarded the two families a total of $4.7 million, which was $1.7 million more than the $3 million they asked for. Contrary to Cronkite's report, no punitive damages were assessed, nor even requested. In addition, the plaintiffs did not collect the full award, but agreed to a $1.65 million post-trial settlement. The defendant, Gardner-Denver, interestingly enough, is a subsidiary of Cooper industries, which, (though not acknowledged on the videotape), contributed $50,000 for *Liability's* production. See generally: John Gannon, Tort Deform - Lethal Bedfellows Essential Information, 1995; Saundra Torry, "Walter Cronkite Video Helps Stir Up Debate Over Tort Reform" Washington Post, Sept. 14, 1992, p.F-5.

Examples of truly frivolous lawsuits involving corporations suing other businesses, (which occurs at a rate of 10 times that of businesses being sued by injured consumers), include:

The Walt Disney Company sued the Academy of Motion Picture Arts and Sciences over a dance routine on the Oscars featuring Snow White.

The Italian maker of Baretta guns sued General Motors, charging that GM's Beretta would "dilute" the gunmaker's good family name.

Kellogg hit rival Raisin Bran maker General Mills with a $100 million lawsuit, arguing that Post Natural Raisin Bran was not, in fact, natural, because it was coated with coconut oil.

Hormel Foods, the maker of SPAM, sued Jim Henson Productions to stop the company from merchandising a movie character named "Spa'am." Hormel claimed that the character represented "an unclean grotesque boar" that would call into question the purity of its meats and that SPAM sales would drop if the product were linked with "evil in porcine form." After a full trial, a Federal Judge rejected Hormel's claim. Hormel appealed, but lost again. See <u>Hormel Foods v. Jim Hnson Productions</u>, 73 F.3d 497 (2nd Cir. 1996).

Scott Paper's Canadian division sued Procter & Gamble in 1995, alleging that it had exaggerated the performance of its Bounty paper towels by comparing an 11-inch-long Bounty sheet with the 9-inch sheet generally used in Canada. "P&G, Scott Paper Unit Set Accord in Canada", <u>Wall Street Journal</u>, Dec. 20, 1995.

Mattel sued MCA Records when the record company released a CD that included a song called "Barbie Girl", in which Barbie is referred to as a "blond bimbo girl in a fantasy world." The court denied Mattel's request for an injunction, noting that the song is a parody, and not likely to confuse consumers or harm the Barbie product line. See <u>Mattel v. MCA Records</u>, 46 U.S.P.Q.2d 1407 (C.D. Cal. 1998).

See generally: "Spam v. The Muppets and Other Strange Stories of Corporate Lawsuit Abuse" <u>Business Wire</u>, Sept. 17, 1997; Leshne, "Shedding New Light" <u>Trial</u> Oct. 1998, p.32.

Incomplete, misleading accounts of the *Stella Liebeck v. McDonald's* verdict include: "We live in a litigious society. Every day there seems to be another story about an

unbelievable multimillion-dollar award. Who can forget
the woman awarded $2.7 million from a jury after she
spilled coffee on her lap?" Amanda Walmac, "Don't Settle for Less: Protect Your Assets from a Lawsuit" Conti-
nental April 1998, p.64. "A jury awarded a woman $2.9
million in a lawsuit against McDonald's. She spilled coffee in her lap while sitting in her car and claimed that it
was too hot." American Tort Reform Association, Coffee.
"Is it fair to get a couple million dollars from a restaurant
just because you spilled your hot coffee on yourself? Of
course not. It's ridiculous. But it happened." U.S. Chamber of Commerce Radio Ad. "Nearly $3 million awarded
to a customer who spilled coffee on herself." Mobil Oil
Ad, New York Times, Feb. 16, 1995. See also: Rosen,
"Coffee and $2.9 Million to Go" Denver Post, Aug. 26,
1994, p.B-11; "Hot Coffee and a Paint Job" Washington
Post, Oct. 18, 1995, p.A-18; "A Nation of Lawyers" Oakland Tribune, May 5, 1995, p.A-14; Saundra Torry, "Tort
and Retort: The Battle Over Reform Heats Up" Washington Post, March 6, 1995, p.F-7.

For the real facts of the *Stella Liebeck v. McDonalds*
case, see: Eric Press, Ginny Carroll, Steven Waldman,
"Are Lawyers Burning America?" Newsweek, March
20, 1995, p.32; "McDonald's Scalding Coffee Case:
The Real Facts" Commercial Litigation Vol.II, No.1, p.1
(1997); Howard Twiggs, "How Civil Justice Saved Me
From Getting Burned" Trial, June 1997, p.9; Rustad, Nationalizing Tort Law: The Republicans Attack on Women,
Blue Collar Workers and Consumers, 48 Rutgers L.Rev.
673 (1996); John Gannon, Tort Deform - Lethal Bedfellows, Essential Information, 1995; Bogus, "Tort 'Reform'
Should Be Kept Out of Contract" Palm Beach Post, July
16, 1995, p.1-F; Ralph Nader and Wesley J. Smith, No
Contest (Random House 1996), pp.266-273.

For the facts and the holding of the Eugene Frazier case, see Campbell v. DOTD, No. 94-1052, 648 So.2d 898 (La. 1/17/95).

III. Chapter Three: Making the Case Against Cigarettes

On the history of tobacco litigation generally, see: Robert L. Rabin, A Sociolegal History of Tobacco Tort Litigation, 44 Stan.L.Rev. 853 (1992); Tucker S. Player, After the Fall: The Cigarette Papers, the Global Settlement, and the Future of Tobacco Litigation, 49 S.C.L.Rev. 311 (1998); Glen Collins, "A Tobacco Case's Legal Buccaneers" New York Times, March 6, 1995, p.C-3; Richard Kluger, Ashes to Ashes (Knopf 1996); Philip Hilts, Smoke Screen (Addison-Wesley 1996); Glantz, Slade, Bero, Hanauer & Barnes, The Cigarette Papers (University of California Press 1996); J.D. Lee, The Settlement (Hyde-Muehler 1997); Peter Pringle, Cornered: Big Tobacco at the Bar of Justice (Marian Wood 1998); Mollenkamp, Levy, Menn, Rothfeder, The People vs. Big Tobacco (Bloomberg Press 1998); Thayer v. Liggett & Myers, No. 5314 (W.D.Mich. Feb. 19, 1970), 1.2 TLPR 2.63 (1986); Haines v. Liggett, 814 F.Supp. 414 (D.N.J. 1993); Bothwell v. Republic Tobacco, 912 F.Supp. 1221 (D.Neb. 1995); Patricia Gray, "Tobacco Firms Defend Smoker Liability Suits With Heavy Artillery" Wall Street Journal, April 29, 1987; Charles Strum, "Major Lawsuit on Smoking is Dropped" New York Times, Nov. 6, 1992; Alison Frankel, "Was Budd Larner Another Smoking Victim?" New Jersey Law Journal, July 12, 1993; John Schwartz and Saundra Torry, "Anti-Tobacco Activists Hope to Put Industry's Legal Tactics on Trial" Washington Post, Sept. 26, 1995.

The original nation-wide class action instituted against the tobacco industry was Castano v. The American Tobacco Company, 160 F.R.D. 544 (E.D.La. 1995), *rev'd,*

84 F.3d 734 (5th Cir. 1996).

Tobacco products kill an estimated 420,000 Americans every year. See, among other sources: Institute of Medicine, Growing Up Tobacco Free: Preventing Nicotine Addiction in Children and Youths (1994) p.5; Center for Disease Control and Prevention, "Cigarette Smoking - Attributable Mortality and Years of Potential Life Lost - United States, 1990" Morbidity and Morality Weekly Report Vol.42, No.33, Aug. 27, 1993, pp.645-49; Bartecchi, MacKenzie & Schrier, "The Global Tobacco Epidemic" Scientific American, May 1995, p.45. One in every six Americans will die of a tobacco-related illness. "Smoking remains the single most important preventable cause of death in our society." U.S. Dept. of Health and Human Services, Reducing the Health Consequences of Smoking: 25 Years of Progress DHHS Publication No. CDC 89-8411 (1989).

"The nicotine alters the state of the smoker by becoming a neurotransmitter and a stimulant.... Nicotine mimics the body's most important neurotransmitter, acetylcholine (ACH), which controls the heart rate and message sending within the brain." Cigarettes and other tobacco products are "nicotine delivery devices"; the smoker "learns to control the delivery of nicotine." Philip Morris, Table (cir. 1992). See also: U.S. Dept. of Health and Human Services, The Health Consequences of Smoking: Nicotine Addiction: A Report of the Surgeon General DHHS publication CDC 88-8406 (1988); Alix M. Freedman, "Philip Morris Memo Likens Nicotine to Cocaine" Wall Street Journal, Dec. 8, 1995.

A 1946 Lorillard letter expresses the possibility that tobacco use contributes to cancer; a 1956 Philip Morris memorandum recognizes a potential health hazard; a 1961 memorandum from Arthur Little acknowledges cancer causing elements in cigarette tobacco; and a 1961 report concedes that smoking may be a cause of cancer and lists particular compounds in cigarette smoke which were known to be carcinogens. See Haines v. Liggett Group, 140 F.R.D. 681, 693 n.9 (D.N.J. 1992), *vacated,* 975 F.2d 81 (3rd Cir. 1992).

With respect to the Tobacco Institute, CTR, the *Frank Statement,* and the "siphoning off" of scientific research into a "special projects" program protected by claims of attorney-client privilege, see generally: Haines v. Liggett Group, 140 F.R.D. 681, 696 (D.N.J. 1992), *vacated,* 975 F.2d 81 (3rd Cir. 1992); Hanauer, Slade, Barnes, Bero, and Glantz, "Lawyer Control of Internal Scientific Research to Protect Against Products Liability Lawsuits" Journal of the American Medical Association Vol.274, No.3, July 19, 1995, p.234; Bero, Barnes, Hanauer, Slade, and Glantz, "Lawyer Control of the Tobacco Industry's External Research Program" Journal of the American Medical Association Vol.274, No.3, July 19, 1995, p.241; Charles Strum, "Judge Cites Possible Fraud in Tobacco Research" New York Times, Feb. 8, 1992.

"Carbon monoxide will become increasingly regarded as a serious health hazard for smokers.... lithium hydroxide reduced CO substantially but is coupled with an increase in tumorigenic activity." Green, Notes on the Group Research & Development Conference, Jan. 12, 1974. See also: Glantz, Barnes, Bero, Hanauer, and Slade, "Looking Through a Keyhole at the Tobacco Industry" Journal of the American Medical Association Vol.274, No.3, July 19, 1995, p.221.

The Tobacco Institute represented that "there is still no basic answer to why people who smoke fall victim to some diseases in greater numbers than people who don't smoke." See "Studies Show That Nonsmokers Live 2 Years More By Heading Alerts" <u>New York Times</u>, Sept. 22, 1979, p.A-6. "Science does not yet know enough about any suspected factors to judge." A Tobacco Industry Research Committee organization and policy document from 1967 refers to such representations contained in a public relations statement from 1963. See Glantz, "Looking Through a Keyhole at the Tobacco Industry" <u>Journal of the American Medical Association</u> Vol.274, No.3, July 19, 1995, p.221. Brown & Williamson represented that there is "sound evidence to conclude that 'cigarettes cause cancer' is not a statement of fact *but merely a hypothesis.*" Brown & Williamson, <u>Project Truth: The Smoking Health Controversy: A View From the Other Side</u> (1971). Phillip Morris represented that, with respect to "the lack of research on the 'harmful' effects of smoking, the fact is there is good reason to doubt the culpability of cigarette smoking in coronary heart disease." See Millhiser, "In Defense of Smoking" <u>New York Times</u>, Jan. 12, 1978, p.A-19.

An industry advertisement told the public that new headlines about tobacco smoke had appeared "because several eminent biostatisticians have found an apparent statistical error in the Japanese calculations – raising serious questions about the study.... If you'd like to know more about these developments, write Scientific Division, The Tobacco Institute, 1875 I St., N.W., Washington, D.C. 20006. **BEFORE YOU BELIEVE HALF THE STORY, GET THE WHOLE STORY.**" See Barnes, Hanauer, Slade, Bero, and Glantz, "Environmental Tobacco Smoke" <u>The Journal of the American Medical Association</u>, July, 19, 1995, p. 252.

"Chronic intake of nicotine tends to restore the normal physiological functioning of the endocrine system, so that ever-increasing dose levels of nicotine are necessary to maintain the desired action.... This unconscious desire explains the addiction of the individual to nicotine." Haselbach and Libert, Tentative Hypothesis on Nicotine Addiction, British American Tobacco Company (1963). See also: Geissbuhler and Haselbach, The Fate of Nicotine in the Body (1963). A 1969 Phillip Morris document stated that the craving for nicotine was so powerful that it "will even pre-empt food in times of scarcity on the smoker's priority list." It continued that "the ultimate explanation for the perpetuated cigarette habit resides in the pharmacological effect of smoke upon the body of the smoker." Before the Health and Environmental Subcommittee, however, the president of Phillip Morris testified that: "I really don't accept that smoking is addictive." See John Leland, Michael Isikoff & Mark Hosenball, "A Whiff of Smoking Guns" Newsweek, Aug. 7, 1995, p.66. "I do not believe that nicotine is addictive... nicotine is a very important constituent in the cigarette smoke for taste." Thomas Sandefur, Chairman and CEO of Brown & Williamson, testifying before the Health and Environment Subcommittee, Energy and Commerce Committee, U.S. House of Representatives, June 23, 1994.

For information concerning the dangers of "low-tar" and "light" cigarettes, and the effects of compensation, see generally: U.S. Dept. of Health and Human Services, The Health Consequences of Smoking: The Changing Cigarette: A Report of the Surgeon General (1981); U.S. Dept. of Health, Education and Welfare, Smoking and Health: A Report of the Surgeon General (1979); Glantz, "Looking Through a Keyhole at the Tobacco Industry" Journal of the American Medical Association Vol.274,

No. 3, July 19, 1995, p. 220; David Segal, "The Unfiltered Truth" Washington Monthly, Sept. 1993, (condensed in Reader's Digest, April 1994, p.121); Alix M. Freedman, "Impact Booster: Tobacco Firm Shows how Ammonia Spurs Delivery of Nicotine" Wall Street Journal, Oct. 18, 1995, p.A-1; Alix M. Freedman, "Brown & Williamson Report Says Philip Morris Fine-Tunes Marlboro" Wall Street Journal, Oct. 18, 1995, p.A-6.

"The addition of nicotine to SM [substitute materials] was considered, and it was recommended that nicotine per se, should not be use inside any tobacco factory. However, high nicotine content tobacco extract might be added. So long as SM remains a blend constituent, it would not be considered desirable for the supplier to include nicotine in the formulation. Nevertheless, for purposes of laboratory experimentation under suitable controls, nicotine-containing materials offered by suppliers may be used." British American Tobacco Company, Summary and Conclusions: BAT Group Research Conference (1970).

With respect to allegations that the cigarette companies have been manipulating the levels of nicotine, see generally: Alix Freedman and Suein Hwang, "Why Don't Low-Tar Cigarettes Have Lower Nicotine?" Wall Street Journal, July 14, 1995, p.B-1; Alix M. Freedman, "Impact Booster: Tobacco Firm Shows how Ammonia Spurs Delivery of Nicotine" Wall Street Journal, Oct. 18, 1995, p.A-1; Alix M. Freedman, "Brown & Williamson Report Says Philip Morris Fine-Tunes Marlboro" Wall Street Journal, Oct. 18, 1995, p.A-6; David Segal, "The Unfiltered Truth" Washington Monthly, Sept. 1993, (condensed in Reader's Digest, April 1994, p.121).

The tobacco industry in America takes in approximately 48 billion dollars in revenue each year. See, among other sources, Shannon Brownlee and Steven Roberts, "Should Cigarettes Be Outlawed?" U.S. News & World Report, April 18, 1994, p.35.

The sale of tobacco products creates billions in heath care costs, accounts for approximately $8.4 billion dollars of corporate loss due to smoke-related employee absenteeism, and results in the loss of one work-month of cigarette breaks per smoker employee each year. Brownlee and Roberts, "Should Cigarettes Be Outlawed?" U.S. News and World Report, April 18, 1994, p.35. The University of California and the Center for Disease Control have reported an estimated $50 billion per year in total health care costs, with the Federal Government spending $20 billion each year on Medicare and Medicaid alone. Based on these and other figures, it has been estimated that the United States economy loses a total of $100 billion due to cigarette consumption each year. See Bartecchi, MacKenzie, and Schrier, "The Global Tobacco Epidemic" Scientific American, May 1995, p.46; Glantz, Fox and Lightwood, "Tobacco Litigation: Issues of Public Health and Public Policy" Journal of the American Medical Association, Vol.277, No.9, March 5, 1997, p.752; Center for Disease Control and Prevention, "Medical Care Expenditures Attributable to Cigarette Smoking–U.S." Morbidity and Mortality Weekly Reporter, Vol. 43, pp.469-472 (1994); Anthony Lewis, "Just Say No" New York Times, Oct. 16, 1995.There are over three million smokers under the age of eighteen in this country, who consume over a billion packs of cigarettes each year. The average smoker begins smoking when 14.5 years old. 91.3% of all smokers are addicted by their twentieth birthday. See Center for Disease Control and Prevention, "Changes in the Cigarette Brand Preferences of Adolescent Smokers – United States, 1989-1993" Morbidity and Mortality Weekly Re-

272 STEPHEN J. HERMAN

port, Vol.43, No.32, Aug. 14, 1994, p.577; Wayne Hearn, "Adolescence and Addiction: War on Smoking Has New Front" Times Picayune, March 5, 1995, p.D-12; Brownlee and Roberts, "Should Cigarettes Be Outlawed?" U.S. News & World Report, April 18, 1994, p.38.

It is generally reported that the tobacco companies spend over $5 billion each year on advertising. See, for example, Philip J. Hilts, "Teen Smoking on the Rise Again, Poll Finds" Times Picayune July 20, 1995, p.A-12. Varying accounts report the annual expenditures to be anywhere from $4 billion to $6 billion. The FTC reported, for example, expenditures of $4 billion in 1990. See U.S. Dept. of Health and Human Services, Preventing Tobacco Use Among Young People: A Report of the Surgeon General, Feb. 24, 1994, p.160. In 1992, the industry spent a reported total of $5.2 billion. See Federal Trade Commission, Report to Congress Pursuant to the Federal Cigarette Labeling and Advertising Act p.3 (1992); Pierce and Gilpin, "Looking for a Market Among Adolescents" Scientific American, May 1995, p.50. And Shankar Vedantam, in an article entitled, "Ads, Not Peers, Recruit Young Smokers, Study Says" Times Picayune, Oct. 18, 1995, p.A-10, reported expenditures of $6 billion per year.

91% of all six year-olds know Joe Camel. 69% of all teen smokers smoke Marlboro, the most advertised brand. Fisher, Schwartz, Richards, Goldstein & Rojas, "Brand Logo Recognition by Children Aged 3 to 6 Years, Mickey Mouse, and Old Joe the Camel" Journal of the American Medical Association Vol.266, No.22, pp.3145-48 (1991); John Slade, "Adolescent Nicotine Use and Dependence" Adolescent Medicine Vol.4, No.2, June 1993, p.309; Mizerski, Straughn & Feldman, The Relationship Between Cartoon Character Recognition and Product Category Attitudes in Young Children, May 13, 1994. One in five eighth graders smoke on a monthly basis, which is a 30% increase from 1991, with almost ten percent of all eighth graders smoking daily. This rise was accompanied by 20% increase among tenth graders, with over a quarter of all tenth graders admitting that they had smoked in the past thirty days, and almost fifteen percent of all tenth graders smoking daily. Among seniors, occasional smoking increased from 27.8% to 31.2% since 1991, with almost one in every five seniors smoking cigarettes on a daily basis. See Philip J. Hilts, "Teen Smoking on the Rise Again, Poll Finds" Times Picayune July 20, 1995, p.A-12.

"However intriguing smoking was at 11, 12 or 13, by the age of 16 or 17 many regretted their use of cigarettes for health reasons and because they feel unable to stop smoking when they want to." Kwechansky Marketing Research, for Imperial Tobacco, Project 16, Oct. 18, 1977. "Starters no longer disbelieve the dangers of smoking, but they almost universally assume these risks will not apply to themselves because they will not become addicted.... The desire to quit seems to come earlier, than before, even before the end of high school.... However, the desire to quit, and actually carrying it out, are two quite different things." Kwechansky Marketing Research, for Imperial Tobacco Limited, Project Plus/Minus, May 7, 1982. Most adolescent smokers either plan to quit before they reach adulthood but fail, or have already attempted to kick the habit unsuccessfully. 64% of adolescent smokers have tried to quit, and 70% regret their decision to start smoking. 85% of high school seniors who smoked believed that they would not be smoking in five years, but five years later, only half of the occasional smokers had managed to quit, while almost 40% had actually increased their consumption; 70% of those who were heavy smokers in high school were still going through at least a pack a day. See Wayne Hearn, "Adolescence and Addiction: War on Smoking Has New Front" Times Picayune, March 5, 1995, p. D-12. See also: "Cigarette Smoking Among Adults in the United States" Journal of American Medical Association, Vol.273, pp.369-370 (1996); Slade, "Adolescent Nicotine Use and Dependence" Adolescent Medicine, Vol.4, No.2, June 1993, pp.308-309. "While experimenting with high-risk behavior is part of growing up for most children and adolescents, it's the addictive nature of nicotine that makes smoking experimentation particularly dangerous. Skateboarding behind a truck, for example, may be more immediately dangerous to one's health, but it's an activity unlikely to hook someone for life." Wayne Hearn, "Adolescence and Addiction: War on Smoking Has New Front" Times Picayune, March 5, 1995, p. D-13. See also: Suein Hwang, "Letter From a Tobacco Company to an Art Professor, August 1970" Wall Street Journal, July 21, 1995, p.B-1; Leland, Isikoff & Hosenball, "A Whiff of Smoking Guns" Newsweek, Aug. 7, 1995, p.66.

98% of all cigarette smokers are addicted, with only 2% smoking occasionally, (compared with 2% of people who drink alcohol and are dependent on it). Dr. M.A.H. Russell, Meeting of Experimental Pathology Club, at the Imperial Cancer Research Fund, London, June 27, 1975. The majority of people who drink are not dependent on alcohol, while as many as 90 percent of smokers are addicted. See Carl Sherman "Kicking Butts" Psychology Today Vol.27, No.5, p.40 (Sept. 1994). Alcoholism affects between 6% and 10% of the population. See Margaret Munro, "New Drug For Alcoholics Takes Buzz Out of Booze" The Vancouver Sun Jan. 24, 1996, p.A-1. Ten percent of drinkers will become alcoholics, (6% of the population in Washington State). See Warren King, "The Puzzle of Alcoholism" Seattle Times, July 2, 1990, p.A-6. 70%-80% of the population uses alcohol, with an abuse rate of 5%-6%. Professor Michael Gazzaniga, "The Federal Drugstore" National Review, Feb. 5, 1990, p.34. The National Institute of Alcohol Abuse and Alcoholism reported that 1.7% of the American people are "alcohol dependent". Nancy Shute, "The Drinking Dilemma" U.S. News and World Report, Sept. 8, 1997, p.58. The 1996 Report of the University of Connecticut research Center reported that 5% are "alcohol dependent". Shute, "The Drinking Dilemma" U.S. News and World Report, Sept. 8, 1997, p.58. Even among people who drink heavily, only 25% actually become alcoholics. Shute, "The Drinking Dilemma" U.S. News and World Report, Sept. 8, 1997, p.58. 7% of the adult population is addicted to alcohol. See Charles Taylor, "First Year Crucial for Reformed Alcoholics" United Press International, Dec. 21, 1981.

"I was ultimately convinced of the propriety of this strategy based primarily upon two factors: the addiction of kids and the deadliness of the addiction. That, I think, distinguishes the tobacco industry from virtually any other industry that produces consumer products in America." Dennis Vacco, "Vacco: Tobacco Deal Unique" National Law Journal, Sept. 8, 1997, p.A-6.

IV. Chapter Four: The English Rule

Civil filings have decreased a total of 6% over the past three years. "Painful Decisions" ABA Journal, Aug. 1995, p.67. In Louisiana, civil filings decreased in 1994 by 3.7%, while civil jury trials decreased by 13.6%. Annual Report of the Judicial Council of the Supreme Court of Louisiana (1995). The volume of tort filings in state courts, nationwide, has declined since 1990. National Center for State Courts, Examining the Works of State Courts, 1994 Pub. No. R-178 (1996) pp.7,34. In the Eastern District of Louisiana, civil filings have decreased by 45% since 1984. See Bruce Alpert, "Federal Bench Is Case Poor" Times Picayune, March 7, 1996, p.A-1. In the Eastern District of Louisiana, civil filings have decreased by 43% since 1983. See Bruce Alpert, "Leave Seat on Court Vacant, Judge Says" Times Picayune, Dec. 21, 1995, p.A-1. Filings in Federal Court nation-wide have decreased by 36% from 1985-1991. See Marc Galanter, "Public View of Lawyers" Trial, April 1992, p.72. There are no more civil lawsuits per capita today than there were in 1959. See Gerry Spence, With Justice for None (Penguin 1989) p.195; Peterson and Priest, The Civil Jury: Trends in Trials and Verdicts, The Rand Institute for Civil Justice (1982). The "litigation explosion" was largely attributable to suits involving one product – asbestos. With the exception of asbestos cases, product liability filings in federal court decreased dramatically during the 1980s. American Bar Association, Facts About the American Civil Justice System, p.2; General Accounting Office, Product Liability: Extent of "Litigation Explosion" in Federal Courts Questioned Pub. No. GAO/HRD-88-36BR (1988). In 1994, federal product liability lawsuits constituted less than three tenths of one percent,

(0.025%), of the total state/federal caseload. Facts About the American Civil Justice System, p.3 (based on data from the Administrative Office of U.S Courts). From 1978 to 1984, there was a 9% increase in tort filings, which directly corresponded with a 9% increase in the population over that same period of time. National Center for State Courts, A Preliminary Examination of Available Civil and Criminal Trend Data in State Trial Courts for 1978, 1981, and 1984 (1986). From 1970 to 1986, tort cases filed in federal court increased by 70%, compared with a 200% increase in contract disputes, a 180% increase in statutory actions, and a 290% increase in civil rights cases. Dungworth and Pace, Statistical Overview of Civil Litigation in the Federal Courts Rand Institute for Civil Justice (1990). From 1984 to 1994, the civil caseload increased only 24%, while criminal filings increased 35%, juvenile cases 59%, and domestic cases 65%. In 1994, civil filings comprised only 22% of the total caseload in state courts, while juvenile (2.2%), criminal (15.6%), and traffic and municipal cases (60.2%), made up the rest. Tort cases comprised only 6.2% of civil filings, while domestic relations (25%), property (17.2%), small claims (20.5%), contract (8.6%), and other (22.5%), made up the rest. See American Bar Association, Facts About the American Civil Justice System, p.1; Donald Dilworth, "Court Statistics Confirm No Litigation Explosion" Trial May 1996, p.19; National Center for State Courts, Examining the Works of State Courts, 1994, Pub. No. R-178 (1996). In 1992, tort suits represented less than ten percent of all civil filings, the other 91% percent the result of domestic relations disputes (35%), small claims cases (11%), property rights (9%), wills and estates (9%), mental health cases (1%), civil appeals (1%), contract disputes (11%), and miscellaneous suits (14%). National Center for State Courts, 1992 Annual Report of the Na-

tional Center for State Courts (1994); "Someone Hear
An Explosion?" Newsweek, March 20, 1995, p.34. From
1985 to 1991, almost half of all federal lawsuits involved
businesses suing other businesses. "Suits by Firms Exceed Those By Individuals" Wall Street Journal, Dec. 3,
1993. "While critics are talking about ambulance-chasing
lawyers and bulging civil dockets, the California Judicial
Council is releasing figures showing a dramatic drop in
statewide tort claims. The decline is particularly steep for
the mother lode of civil litigation – automobile-related
claims. The number of such lawsuits filed in California
superior courts dropped nearly 50% between 1988 and
1995." Reuben,"Putting the Brakes on Torts" ABA Journal Jan. 1997, p.39. See also, generally: Ostrom & Kaud-
er, Examining the Work of State Courts, 1996: A National
Perspective From the Court Statistics Project, National
Center for State Courts (1997); Galanter, The Day After
the Litigation Explosion, 46 Md.L.Rev. 3 (1986); "The
Litigation Explosion is a Myth" Business Week, March
10, 1986.

A definitive study conducted in 1990 determined that
the principal factors affecting the U.S.'s competitiveness
in world markets were capital costs, the quality of human resources, and lack of technology in small and medium sized companies, (not the tort liability system). See
Congressional Office of Technology Assessment, Making
Things Better: Competing in Manufacturing, Pub. No.
OTA-ITE-443 (1990).

A study conducted by the Civil Trial Court Network
in 1991, which was sponsored by the Justice Department,
indicates that 23.7% of tort cases are dismissed summarily by the courts. 73.4% are settled by the parties. Only
2.9% go to trial. See "The Big Picture" ABA Journal,
Aug. 1995, p.65. See also: National Center for State
Courts, Examining the Work of State Courts, 1994 Pub.

No. R-178 (1996).

A study conducted by Tillinghast-Towers Perrin shows that more than 50% of all pain, suffering and economic loss goes uncompensated, and that the gross annual costs of tort suits have not increased in proportion to the general growth of the economy since 1985. Robert Sturgis, who conducted the study, concluded that "both the propensity to sue and the willingness of defendants to settle questionable liability claims have actually declined." Jay Matthews, "Payment Rates Ease in Jury Awards and Liability Settlements, Survey Shows" Washington Post, Nov. 13, 1995, p. A-5. See also: Tillinghast-Towers Perrin, 1995 Cost of Risk Survey (1995); Gene Koretz, "A Malpractice Conundrum: Actually, Too Few Claims are Filed" Business Week, March 27, 1995, p.28; Richard Perez-Pena, "U.S. Juries Grow Tougher on Plaintiffs in Lawsuits" New York Times June 17, 1994; Sally Roberts, "Plaintiffs Winning Fewer Personal Injury Suits" Business Insurance, March 28, 1994; Deborah Hensler, Compensation for Accident Injuries in the U.S., Rand Corporation (1991); Michael Saks, Do We Really Know Anything About the Behavior of the Tort Liability System – And Why Not? 140 Penn.L.Rev. 1287 (1992); Terence Dunworth and Joel Rogers, Corporations in Court: Big Business Litigation in U.S. Federal Courts, 1971-91 (1995); Vidmar, The Performance of the American Civil Jury: An Empirical Perspective, 40 Ariz.L.Rev. 849 (1998); Hans, Illusions and Realities in Jurors' Treatment of Corporate Defendants (1998); Hans, The Contested Role of the Civil Jury in Business Litigation 79 Judicature 242 (1996); Hans, "The Jury's Response to Business and Corporate Wrongdoing" Law and Contemporary Problems, Vol.52, p.177 (1989); Hans & Erman, "Responses to Corporate Versus Individual Wrongdoing" Law and Behavior, Vol.13, p.151 (1989); Hans & Lofquist, "Jurors' Judgment of Business Liability in Tort Cases" Law and Society Review, Vol.26, p.85 (1992); Evidence on the Deep Pocket Hypothesis: Jury Awards for Pain and Suffering in Medical Malpractice Cases, 43 Duke.L.J. 217 (1993); Rustad, Nationalizing Tort Law: The Republicans Attack on Women, Blue Collar Workers and Consumers, 48 Rutgers L.Rev. 673 (1996); Hans & Vidmar, Judging the Jury (1996); Abel, The Real Tort Crisis - Too Few Claims, 48 Ohio St. L.J. 443 (1987); Daniels & Martin, Civil Juries and the Politics of Reform (1995); Galanter, Real World Torts: An Antidote to Anecdote, 55 Md.L.Rev. 1093 (1996); Ostrom, Rottmann & Hanson, "What Are Tort Awards Really Like" Law and Policy Vol.14, pp.77,83 (1992);Valerie Hans and William Lofquist, "Perceptions of Civil Justice: The Litigation Crisis Attitudes of Civil Juries" Behavioral Sciences and the Law Vol.12, p.181 (1994); Hager and Miltenberg, "Punitive Damages and the Free Market: A Law and Economics Perspective" Trial, Sept. 1995, p.30; Hensler, "Taking Aim at the American Legal System" Judicature, Vol.75, No.5, Feb. 1992, pp.244-250; Daniels, "We Are Not a Litigious Society" Judges Journal (Spring 1985); Galanter, Reading the Landscape of Disputes: What We Know and Don't Know (And Think We Know) About Our Allegedly Litigious Society, 31 UCLA.L.Rev. 4 (1983); Quick Facts on Products Liability (1995).

Two-thirds of the world's lawyers live in America, which accounts for only 6% of the world's population; there were 355,000 lawyers in 1970, doubling by 1990, and growing steadily at a rate of approximately 40,000 per year; amounting to 2.67 lawyers for every thousand people, with one lawyer for every 60 people in Washington D.C. See Gerry Spence, With Justice for None (Penguin 1989) p.27; Lawrence Wrightsman, Psychology and the Legal System (1987); Richard Greene, "Lawyers vs. the Marketplace" Forbes, Jan. 16, 1984; Lawrence M. Friedman, Total Justice (Russell Sage Foundation 1985). Other statistics show that American lawyers, in fact, make up only 25 to 35% of the world's attorneys, including judges, in-house counsel, and government employees. This is roughly proportionate to the United States' share of the world's gross national product, and far less than the U.S. expenditures on scientific research and development. See Marc Galanter, "Pick a Number, Any Number" Legal Times, Feb. 17, 1992; Marc Galanter The Debased Debate on Civil Justice University of Wisconsin-Madison Law School Disputes Processing Research Program (1992), pp.10-17; "The Public View of Lawyers" Trial April 1992, p.71. While Japan has only 16,000 licensed lawyers, public prosecutors, and judges, it also has around 70,000 unlicenced legal professionals performing work that, in America, would be performed by lawyers. Marc Galanter, "Pick a Number, Any Number" Legal Times, Feb. 17, 1992. "The number of lawyers in a country seems to relate directly to the level of individual rights and freedoms their citizens possess. China's 1.1 billion people have a mere 50,000 lawyers, almost all of whom work for the government. East Germany, with 16.6 million people, had about 3,500 lawyers and judges, only 600 of them private attorneys. The Soviet Union, with more than 280 million people, had only 230,000 lawyers, most, again, working for the government. There are few, if any, lawyers in Rwanda." American Bar Association, Facts About the American Civil Justice System, p.4. See also, generally: Lawrence M. Friedman, Total Justice (Russell Sage Foundation 1985).

Less than 1% of the Federal Budget is dedicated to the entire Federal Court System. Constance Johnson, "Federal Judiciary's Budget is Scrutinized" Wall Street Journal June 20, 1995, p. B4. Less than 0.5% of the annual budget of the state of Louisiana in 1994 was dedicated to the judiciary. Annual Report of the Judicial Council of the Supreme Court of Louisiana (1995). In all, the entire court system, including judges, prosecutors, public defenders, courthouse operations and maintenance, requires only three-fifths of one percent of all government expenditures. See Sol Linowitz, The Betrayed Profession (Charles Scribner's Sons 1994) p.222.

"If our tort system is expensive, it's because we have lots of torts. We should be thinking of ways to reduce the number of torts, not the number of recoveries." Professor Richard Abel, "Public Discontent" ABA Journal, Aug. 1995, p.71. See also: Abel, The Real Tort Crisis - Too Few Claims, 48 Ohio St. L.J. 443 (1987). See also: "Sellers of Unsafe Products Are Treated as Criminals" Times Picayune, Aug. 15, 1995, p.C-3.

Big businesses are overwhelmingly the winners in lawsuits, whether plaintiffs or defendants. When they are plaintiffs, they win 79% of the time, compared to an overall average of 62%. As defendants, they win 62% of the time, compared with an overall average of 38%. Terence Dunworth and Joel Rogers, Corporations in Court: Big Business Litigation in U.S. Federal Courts, 1971-91 (1995). See also: Hans, Illusions and Realities in Jurors' Treatment of Corporate Defendants (1998). Individuals win only half the time against corporations, while over 60% of the time against other individuals. The average jury verdict is only somewhere between $19,000 and $30,000. Stephen J. Adler, The Jury (Doubleday 1994) pp.147-148, 257-258. The average bodily injury claim payment under an auto liability policy is only around $8,000. Leslie Scism, "Auto-Insurance Premiums Are Declining" Wall Street Journal, Jan. 20, 1998, p.A-2 (with data from Bureau of Labor Statistics, Insurance Services

Office, National Association of Independent Insurers, and National Independent Statistical Service). The median award for plaintiffs who won at jury trials is around $51,000. Million-dollar awards are awarded in only 8% of jury trials won by plaintiffs, (one-tenth of one percent of tort cases). Juries awarded punitive damages in only 4% of cases in which the defendant was found liable. The median punitive damage award was $38,000. National Center for State Courts, Examining the Work of State Courts, 1994 Pub. No. R-178 (1996); Donald Dilworth, "Court Statistics Confirm No Litigation Explosion" Trial May 1996, p.19. See also: Daniels and Martin, Civil Juries and the Politics of Reform (1995). In the 25 years between 1965 and 1990, only 355 punitive damage awards were rendered in product liability cases. Excluding asbestos cases, which accounted for 25% of these awards, there were an average of only 11 awards per year. See Rustad, Demystifying Punitive Damages in Products Liability Cases, The Roscoe Pound Foundation, p.23 (1991). Most punitive damages were awarded in intentional tort and business cases, which accounted for over 80% of all punitive damage awards. Products liability cases, by contrast, accounted for only 5% of all punitive damage awards. Erik Moller, Trends in Jury Verdicts Since 1985, Rand Institute for Civil Justice (1996). See generally: Galanter and Luban, Poetic Justice: Punitive Damages and the Public Trust Am.U.L.Rev. Vol.42 (1993); Theodore Eisenberg, The Predictability of Punitive Damages (1996) (published in the *Journal of Legal Studies,* Vol.26, p.623 (1997)); Rustad and Koenig, "Punitive Damages in Products Liability" Products Liability law Journal, Vol.3, No.2 (Feb. 1992); Peterson, Sarma & Shanley, Punitive Damages, Empirical Findings, Rand Institute for Civil Justice (1987); Hensler and Moller, Trends in Punitive Damages: Preliminary Data From Cook County, Illinois,

and San Francisco, California, Rand Institute for Civil
Justice (March 1995); Hans, Illusions and Realities in
Jurors' Treatment of Corporate Defendants (1998); Hans
& Lofquist, "Jurors' Judgment of Business Liability in
Tort Cases" Law and Society Review, Vo.26, p.85 (1992);
Ostrom, Rottmann & Hanson, "What Are Tort Awards
Really Like" Law and Policy Vol.14, pp.77,83 (1992);
Daniels and Martin, Empirical Patterns in Punitive Dam-
age Cases: A Description of Incidence Rates and Awards,
American Bar Foundation Paper No. 8705 (1987); Dan-
iels and Martin, Myth and Reality in Punitive Damages,
75 Minn.L.Rev. 1 (1990).

Only 26% of trial verdicts in medical malpractice cases
run in favor of the plaintiff. "The Big Picture" ABA Journal, August 1995, p.65. See also: American Bar Association, Facts About the American Civil Justice System, p.6
(doctors win approximately 70% of their lawsuits); Erik
Moller, Trends in Civil Jury Verdicts Since 1985, Rand
Institute for Civil Justice, p.17 (1996) (plaintiffs win
only 44% of products liability suits). See also: Richard
Perez-Pena, "U.S. Juries Grow Tougher on Plaintiffs in
Lawsuits" New York Times June 17, 1994; Sally Roberts,
"Plaintiffs Winning Fewer Personal Injury Suits" Busi-
ness Insurance, March 28, 1994.

80% of people suffering injuries serious enough to
require medical attention never even considered trying
to collect money from someone else; of the remaining
20%, only half take any action, (e.g. talking to an attorney, threatening to sue), while only one-fifth, (i.e. 2 in
100), actually filed suit. If workplace injuries and auto
accidents are excluded, less than 3% make even an in-
formal demand against an insurance company. See Deborah Hensler, Compensation for Accidental Injuries in
the U.S., Rand Corporation (1991); Hensler, "Taking

Aim at the American Legal System" Judicature, Vol.75, No.5, Feb. 1992, pp.244-250. See also: Daniels, "We Are Not a Litigious Society" Judges Journal (Spring 1985); Galanter, Reading the Landscape of Disputes: What We Know and Don't Know (And Think We Know) About Our Allegedly Litigious Society, 31 UCLA.L.Rev. 4; Jay Matthews, "Payment Rates Ease in Jury Awards and Liability Settlements, Survey Shows" Washington Post, Nov. 13, 1995, p.A-5; Michael Saks, Do We Really Know Anything About the Behavior of the Tort Liability System – And Why Not? 140 Penn.L.Rev. 1287 (1992); Richard Perez-Pena, "U.S. Juries Grow Tougher on Plaintiffs in Lawsuits" New York Times June 17, 1994; Sally Roberts, "Plaintiffs Winning Fewer Personal Injury Suits" Business Insurance, March 28, 1994; Paul Weiler, Medical Malpractice on Trial (1991); Valerie Hans and William Lofquist, "Perceptions of Civil Justice: The Litigation Crisis Attitudes of Civil Juries" Behavioral Sciences and the Law Vol.12, p.181 (1994); Ostrom, Rottmann & Hanson, "What Are Tort Awards Really Like" Law and Policy Vol.14, pp.77,83 (1992); Hager and Miltenberg, "Punitive Damages and the Free Market: A Law and Economics Perspective" Trial, Sept. 1995, p.30; Galanter, Reading the Landscape of Disputes: What We Know and Don't Know (And Think We Know) About Our Allegedly Litigious Society, 31 UCLA.L.Rev. 4 (1983); Quick Facts on Products Liability (1995).

A recent study conducted by Harvard University concluded that only one out of every 7 or 8 hospital patients who are injured as a result of malpractice actually file malpractice claims, while only half of these claimants actually recover. The legal system, therefore, is paying just 1 malpractice victim for every 15 or 16 torts committed by hospitals and physicians. The Report of the Harvard Medical Practice Study to the State of New York. Doctors and Lawyers: Medical Injury, Malpractice Litigation, and Patient Compensation in New York (Harvard University 1990). See also: Brennan, Leape, Laird, et al, "Incidence of Adverse Events and Negligence in Hospitalized Patients: Results of the Harvard Medical Practice Study II" New England Journal of Medicine, Feb. 7, 1991, p.370; Weiler, Hiatt, Newhouse, et al, A Measure of Malpractice: Medical Injury, Malpractice Litigation and Patient Compensation (Harvard University Press 1993); Gene Koretz, "A Malpractice Conundrum: Actually, Too Few Claims are Filed" Business Week, March 27, 1995, p.28; U.S. Congress Office of Technology Assessment, Impact of Legal Reforms on Medical Malpractice Costs OTA-BP-H-119 (Oct. 1993); U.S. Congress Office of Technology Assessment, Defensive Medicine and Medical Malpractice, OTA-H-602 (July 1994); Congressional Budget Office, Economic Implications of Rising Health Care Costs (1992); General Accounting Office, Health Care Spending – Nonpolicy Factors Account for Most State Differences (1992); National Insurance Consumer Organization, Medical Malpractice Insurance: 1985-1991 Calender Year Experience (1993); J. Robert Hunter, Medical Malpractice Insurance, Consumer Federation of America (Sept. 1995); A.M. Best, Aggregates and Averages (1995); Minnesota Attorney General, Medical Malpractice Reform and Healthcare Costs (1996); Forbes, Jan. 17, 1994; McGinley, "Lawsuits Have Little Effect on Premiums" Wall Street Journal, July 8, 1998, p.B-6; Golz, "HMO Disputes Less Than Expected" Austin Am-Statesman, July 14, 1998, p.D-1; Kinney, Granfien & Gannon, Indiana's Medical Malpractice Act: Results of a Three-Year Study, 24 Ind.L.Rev. 1275 (1991); "Lawyers Write About What's Wrong With the System" The Times Picayune, June 9, 1995, p.E-5; Ralph Warner and Stephen Elias, Fed Up With the System (1995); Harvey

Wachsman and Steven Alschuler, <u>Lethal Medicine: The Epidemic of Medical Malpractice in America</u> (Henry Holt & Co. 1993); Localio, "Variations on $962,258: The Misuse of Data on Medical Malpractice" <u>Law, Medicine and Health Care</u> (June 1985); Paul Weiler, <u>Medical Malpractice on Trial</u> (1991); Neil Vidmar, <u>Medical Malpractice and the American Jury: Confronting the Myths About Jury Incompetence, Deep Pockets, and Outrageous Damage Awards</u> (1995).

In a front-page article sub-titled "Frivolous Suits Hurt Business", a staff writer explains that, if your tree falls on a neighbor's car, the courts can hold you responsible for the damage, even if you weren't aware of the harm. Finch, "Foster Seeking to Limit Liability" <u>Times Picayune</u>, March 20, 1996, p.A-1.

"He who derives the advantage ought to sustain the burden." Legal Maxim. (Shrager & Frost, <u>The Quotable Lawyer</u> (New England Publishing 1986) p.61).

Ford calculated that the cost to society of allowing people to become injured and killed by defective gas-tanks would be $49.5 million, (at $200,000 for a death – estimated at 180 annually – and $67,000 for a burn injury – 180 annually – and $700 for damaged vehicles – 2,100 annually), while the cost of correcting the problem, (at $11 per vehicle – although a different memo estimated that the cost would only be $5.08 to $9.95 per vehicle), would have been $137 million. Grush and Saunby, Ford Department of Environmental and Safety Engineering, <u>Fatalities Associated with Crash Induced Fuel Leakage and Fires</u>. See also: Dowie, "Pinto Madness" <u>Mother Jones</u>, Sept/Oct 1977; Walsh & Weiser, "Court Secrecy Masks Safety Issues: Key GM Fuel Tank Memo Kept Hidden in Auto Crash Suit" <u>Washington Post</u> Oct. 23, 1988; Nader and Smith, <u>No Contest</u> (Random House 1996) pp.70-73.Where two innocent parties must suffer a loss at the hands of another, that loss should be borne by the party who has most contributed to the injury by allowing it to occur. Flatte v. Nichols, 233 La. 171, 96 So.2d 477, 480 (1957); Trumbull Chevrolet Sales Company v. F.S. Maxwell, 142 So.2d 805, 806 (La. App. 2nd Cir. 1962).

Joint and several liability has been modified or abolished in 41 states. "Status of States" ABA Journal, Aug. 1995, p.59.

"Reallocation" avoids the unfairness of the traditional common law rules of joint and several liability, which would cast the total risk of uncollectibility upon the solvent defendants, and of a rule abolishing joint and several liability, which would cast the entire risk of uncollectibility upon the plaintiff. Uniform Comparative Fault Act, §2(a) (1977).

The English "no longer believe that you can achieve civil justice, changes in unsafe products, safe workplaces, and a clean environment, without the American-style contingent fee system where people have access to the courts." G. Marc Whitehead, "Public Discontent" ABA Journal, Aug. 1995, p.71.

Litigants and attorneys may be sanctioned for the prosecution of frivolous lawsuits. Fed. Rule of Civ. Pro. 11. See also, for example: Ariz. Rule Civ. Pro. 11; Cal. Code Civ. Pro. §128.7; La. Code Civ. Pro. art. 863; Mass. Rule Civ. Pro. 11; Mich. Civ. Rule 2.114; Ohio Civ. Rule 11; Tex. Civ. Rule 13; Vir. Stat. §8.01-271.1.

"In many cases, defendants know that the suit would not stand on its own merits, but agree to settle out of court just to avoid the endless and expensive claim and appeal

process." Newt Gingrich, Dick Armey, and House Republicans, Contract With America (Times Books 1995)
p.145.

23.7% of all tort cases are dismissed by summary
judgment, default judgement, involuntary dismissal, directed verdict, etc. See "The Big Picture" ABA Journal,
Aug. 1995, p.65.

"We cannot accept the notion that it is always better
for a person to suffer a wrong silently than to redress it by
legal action." Bates v. State Bar of Arizona, 433 U.S. 350,
376, 97 S.Ct. 2691, 2705, 53 L.Ed.2d 810 (1977). "Over
the course of centuries, our society has settled upon civil
litigation as a means for redressing grievances, resolving
disputes, and vindicating rights when other means fail.
There is no cause for consternation when a person who
believes in good faith and on the basis of accurate information regarding his legal rights that he has suffered a
cognizable injury turns to the courts for a remedy.... That
our citizens have access to their civil courts is not an evil
to be regretted; rather, it is an attribute of our system
of justice in which we ought to take pride." Zauderer v.
Office of Disciplinary Counsel, 471 U.S. 626, 643, 105
S.Ct. 2265, 2277, 85 L.Ed.2d 652 (1985)."The fear that
courts may be flooded with litigation is not a sufficient
justification to disallow those claims that are legitimate.
It is the duty of the courts to discern valid claims from the
fraudulent ones." LeJune v. Rayne Branch Hospital, 556
So.2d 559, 563 (La. 1990); Waldrop v. Vistron Corp., 391
So.2d 1274, 1278 (La. App. 1st Cir. 1980); Brauninger v.
Ducote, 381 So.2d 1246, 1249 (La. App. 4th Cir. 1979)
(Lemmon, J., concurring). "Most frivolous and vexatious
litigation is terminated at the pleading stage or on sum-
mary judgment, with little if any personal involvement

by the defendant.... Moreover, the threat of sanctions provides a significant deterrent to litigation directed at the President in his unofficial capacity for purposes of political gain or harassment." Clinton v. Jones, No. 95-1853, 117 S.Ct. 1636, 1651, 137 L.Ed.2d 945 (May 27, 1997).

The direct costs of medical malpractice litigation, (including settlements/awards, insurance premiums, self-insurance costs, attorneys fees, and costs of litigation), account for only 1% of total health care expenditures. Minnesota Attorney General, Medical Malpractice Reform and Healthcare Costs (1996); U.S. Congress Office of Technology Assessment, Impact of Legal Reforms on Medical Malpractice Costs OTA-BP-H-119 (Oct. 1993), p.5; Forbes, Jan. 17, 1994. See also: Congressional Budget Office, Economic Implications of Rising Health Care Costs (1992) p.27; National Insurance Consumer Organization, Medical Malpractice Insurance: 1985-1991 Calender Year Experience (1993) (premiums totaled a mere 0.6% of all health care costs); Jones v. State Board of Medicine, 97 Idaho 859, 555 P.2d 399 (1976) (insurance less than 2% of all health costs); "Medical and Hospital Professional Liability" Texas Bar Journal, Vol.55, No.9 (insurance less than 1% of all health costs); Insurers made 40% profits on medical malpractice lines in 1990. See Jamie Court "Malpractice Reform is Harmful" San Diego Union-Tribune, Aug. 24, 1994. Awards and settlements to medical malpractice victims account for only 45 cents of every premium dollar, with the insurance companies pocketing the other 55%. Patrick Salvi, "Malpractice Award Limits Hurt Victims" Chicago Tribune, Oct. 12, 1993, p.18. *Per capita* health costs approximately doubled in every state of the union between 1982 and 1990, irrespective of whether the state had adopted caps on damages, or other legal reforms. General Accounting Office, Health Care Spending – Nonpolicy Factors Account for Most State Differences (1992). According to data from the National Association of Insurance Commissions, profits from medical malpractice insurance increased in almost every state, between 1985 and 1992, regardless of whether there was a cap on damages. Wencl and Brizzolara, "Medical Negligence: Survey of the States" Trial, May 1996, p.22. Six of the top ten states in medical malpractice insurance profitability did not have caps on damages, and two of the states which have implemented some of the most limiting restrictions on damages, (California and Indiana), have enjoyed no comparative savings in health care expenditures. Wencl and Brizzolara, "Medical Negligence: Survey of the States" Trial, May 1996, p.22; General Accounting Office, Health Care Spending – Nonpolicy Factors Account for Most State Differences (1992); American Bar Association, Facts About the American Civil Justice System, p.8. A neurosurgeon at Sloan-Kettering recently took the wrong person's diagnostic films into the operating room, and began searching through the healthy part of his patient's brain. Another surgeon, in Long Beach, California, recently performed an operation which sought to remove Harry Jordan's cancerous kidney, but the doctor removed Mr. Jordan's healthy kidney instead. See Larry McShane, "Doctor Goofs in Brain Surgery" Times Picayune, p.A-10; Public Citizen, "Republican Medicare Plan: Profit-Driven 'Managed Care' and Tort Law Restrictions Are a 'Lethal Combination' for Consumers" Sept. 25, 1995. For other incidents of malpractice, see: Pamela Liapakis, "The Medical Malpractice Epidemic" Trial, Feb. 1996; Ellyn Spragins, "To Sue or Not to Sue" Newsweek, Dec. 9, 1996, p.50. Medical malpractice is estimated to cost the country around $60 billion annually, (compared with total insurance premiums of $4.9 bil). See Dr. Troyen

Brennan, Harvard School of Public Health, before Subcommittee on Health and Environment, Nov. 10, 1993.
An exhaustive study conducted by Harvard Medical
School concluded that less than 5% of medical malpractice victims receive any type of compensation, and those
who do wait an average of seven years to collect a single
cent. The Report of the Harvard Medical Practice Study
to the State of New York. Doctors and Lawyers: Medical
Injury, Malpractice Litigation, and Patient Compensation
in New York (Harvard University 1990); Brennan, Leape,
Laird, et al, "Incidence of Adverse Events and Negli-
gence in Hospitalized Patients: Results of the Harvard
Medical Practice Study II" New England Journal of Medicine, Feb. 7, 1991, p.370; Weiler, Hiatt, Newhouse, et al,
A Measure of Malpractice: Medical Injury, Malpractice
Litigation and Patient Compensation (Harvard University
Press 1993). See also, generally: "Lawyers Write About
What's Wrong With the System" Times Picayune, June 9,
1995, p.E-5; Gene Koretz, "A Malpractice Conundrum:
Actually, Too Few Claims are Filed" Business Week,
March 27, 1995, p.28; U.S. Congress Office of Tech-
nology Assessment, Impact of Legal Reforms on Medi-
cal Malpractice Costs OTA-BP-H-119 (Oct. 1993); U.S.
Congress Office of Technology Assessment, Defensive
Medicine and Medical Malpractice, OTA-H-602 (July
1994); Congressional Budget Office, Economic Implica-
tions of Rising Health Care Costs (1992); General Ac-
counting Office, Health Care Spending – Nonpolicy Fac-
tors Account for Most State Differences (1992); National
Insurance Consumer Organization, Medical Malpractice
Insurance: 1985-1991 Calender Year Experience (1993);
J. Robert Hunter, Medical Malpractice Insurance, Con-
sumer Federation of America (Sept. 1995); A.M. Best,
Aggregates and Averages (1995); Minnesota Attorney
General, Medical Malpractice Reform and Healthcare

Costs (1996); McGinley, "Lawsuits Have Little Effect on Premiums" Wall Street Journal, July 8, 1998, p.B-6; Golz, "HMO Disputes Less Than Expected" Austin Am-Statesman, July 14, 1998, p.D-1; Kinney, Granfien & Gannon, Indiana's Medical Malpractice Act: Results of a Three-Year Study, 24 Ind.L.Rev. 1275 (1991); Cleckley & Hariharan, A Free Market Analysis of the Effects of Medical Malpractice Damage Caps: Can We Live With Inefficient Doctors?, 94 W.Va.L.Rev. 11 (1991); Ralph Warner and Stephen Elias, Fed Up With the System (1995); Harvey Wachsman and Steven Alschuler, Lethal Medicine: The Epidemic of Medical Malpractice in America (Henry Holt & Co. 1993); Localio, "Variations on $962,258: The Misuse of Data on Medical Malpractice" Law, Medicine and Health Care (June 1985); Paul Weiler, Medical Malpractice on Trial (1991); Neil Vidmar, Medical Malpractice and the American Jury: Confronting the Myths About Jury Incompetence, Deep Pockets, and Outrageous Damage Awards (1995).

In 1992, the President of CIGNA earned $7.5 million, the president of Philip Morris earned $23.8 million, and the president of Travelers earned $67.6 million. American Almanac of Jobs and Salaries (ed. John W. Wright) 1994-1995. In 1995, the CEO of Travelers reaped $41 million in stock options alone. "Options for Everyone" Business Week, July 22, 1996, p.81. In 1997, Allstate's CEO was paid $2.7 million in salary and bonuses, (a 131% increase from 1996), while the president of the company was paid $2.6 million, (up 160%); CIGNA's CEO earned $3.27 million; Progressive's CEO earned $2.78 million; Travelers' CEO made $9.25 million. See "Executive Pay" Wall Street Journal, April 9, 1998, p.R-17; Wall Street Journal, March 16, 1998. USA Today reported that Travelers' CEO actually earned $227.7 million in 1997, with the inclusion of stock options. "Travelers CEO Rakes in $228 M" USA

Today, March 5, 1998.

Auto insurers experienced five years of profits before beginning to pass any savings along to their customers. These savings are attributed primarily to cautious driving among aging baby boomers, safer cars, increases in seatbelt usage, and stricter enforcement of drunk driving laws. Leslie Scism, "Auto-Insurance Premiums Are Declining" Wall Street Journal, Jan. 20, 1998, p.A-2. In 1989, the majority of the ten states with the highest premiums were no-fault states, while seven of the ten states with the lowest premiums were not. In 1993, the average insurance premium in no-fault states was $792, while only $667 in states with traditional tort liability. In 1994, the premiums in no-fault states were an average of 15% higher than those with fault-based systems, while four of the five states with the highest insurance premiums, (New Jersey, Hawaii, Connecticut, and Massachusetts), were states which adopted no-fault schemes. In Georgia, premiums decreased 9-10% after the repeal of no-fault in 1991. National Association of Insurance Commissioners, State Average Expenditures for Personal Auto Insurance in 1994 (1996); National Association of Insurance Commissioners, Auto Insurance Database Report (1993); Howard Twiggs, "No-Fault Means No Choice and No Savings" Trial March 1997, p.9; Robert Manard, "No-Fault's A Failed System that Doesn't Work" Times Picayune, Jan. 26, 1997, p.B-8; Robert Fineberg, "Before Blaming Lawyers, Think About Giving Up Your Right to Sue" The Star Ledger, Sect.10, p.1; Insurance Research Council, Trends in Auto Injury Claims (1994); Auto Injuries: Claiming Behavior and its Impact on Insurance Costs (1994); Wencl and Vacante, "No-Fault Auto Insurance: Great Pain – No Gain" Trial, Oct. 1996, p.48; Mass. Academy of Trial Lawyers, The New Auto Insurance Debate: Choice No-Fault vs. Real Change, B14(a).

From 1984-1988, the number of claims per dollar of product liability insurance premiums fell by almost 50% nationwide. General Accounting Office, U.S. General Accounting Office Products Liability Rate Levels and Claim Payments in the 1970s and 1980s, Pub. No. GAO/ HRD-91-108 (1991). The total cost of product liability insurance premiums ($2.8 bil) in 1993 was less than the country spent on cat food, ($3 bil). See Nye, "The Faces of Product Liability" Public Citizen, Nov. 1992, p.20. Products liability litigation accounts for only 26 cents of every $100 of retail sales. See J. Robert Hunter, Product Liability Insurance Experience 1984-1993 Consumer Federation of America (1995). In 1991, products liability premiums represented just 0.14% of retail sales. National Insurance Consumer Organization, First Ever Insurance Data on Product Liability (1992). Insurance costs represented only 0.6% of the annual gross receipts of large businesses, and around 1% for small businesses. U.S. General Accounting Office, Product Liability Verdicts and Case Resolution in Five States Pub. No. GAO/ HRD-89-99 (1989). In sum, it appears safe to conclude that products liability costs, including the costs of defending litigation and various prevention activities, probably amounts to much less than 1% of retail sales revenue. Designing Safer Products: Corporate Responses to Product Liability Law and Regulation, The Rand Institute for Civil Justice (1983) p.121. See also: Peter Reuter, The Economic Consequences of Expanded Corporate Liability: An Exploratory Study, Rand Institute for Civil Justice (1988); Tillinghast-Towers Perrin, 1995 Cost of Risk Survey (1995); Ellen Schultz, "Large Employers Are Carrying Lighter Loads of Liability Costs" Wall Street Journal, Dec. 12, 1995; Schultz, "U.S. Firms are Spending Less to Guard Against Risk for the First Time in Years" Wall

Street Journal, April 25, 1995.

State Farm Fire and Casualty's total assets increased by 28.1% (from $10.3 billion to $13.2 billion), State Farm Mutual Auto Insurance Company's by 34.2% (35.4 bil - 47.5 bil), and Allstate Insurance Company's by 42.7% (19.9 bil - 28.4 bil), from 1989 to 1993. Standard & Poor's Property/Casualty Insurance Solvency Review (1994-1995), pp. 62-63, 616-617. CIGNA earned $234 million, Progressive earned $267 million, and The Travelers earned $950 million in 1993. Forbes, April 25, 1995, p.264. Property and casualty insurers, as a whole, experienced a 127% increase in total assets, (and a 163% increase in policyholder surplus), between 1982 and 1991. Even after adjusting for inflation, the industry experienced a 61% increase in total assets and an 86% increase in policyholder surplus over that same period of time. The Fact Book: Property/Casualty Insurance Facts, Insurance Information Institute, (1993) pp.17-18. In 1995, property and casualty insurers experienced an 85% increase in profits in 1995, with a net income of $20.1 billion. Times Picayune March 27, 1996, p.C-1. "'Allstate's stock has more than tripled the past three years, outperforming both the S&P 500 and the S&P property and casualty insurance index by wide margins, and in 1997 the company earned a record $3.1 billion on revenues of $25 billion.' The question that comes to mind, of course, is: Why aren't insurance premiums dropping dramatically?" See "More Investigations of Allstate" Advocate, Vol.24, No.6, Aug. 1998, p.1; "A Tornado of a Turnaround" Business Week, March 30, 1998, p.182.

In 1995, the Dow Jones rose 33.5%, the S&P 500 rose 34.1%, the NASDQ composite rose 39.9%, and the NYSE composite rose 31.3%, while the bond markets jumped by over 25%. See Bill Sessums, U.S. News & World Report, Dec. 25, 1995, p.104; Manny Alessadra,

"The Charge of '95" <u>Times Picayune</u>, Dec. 31, 1995, p.F-1. Wages and benefits in 1995 rose just 2.8%, the smallest increase since 1981. See "State of the Union" <u>U.S. News & World Report</u>, Dec. 25, 1995, p.64. Mobil, which earned $523 million in the fourth quarter of 1994, cut 500 jobs in January, while ATT, which earned $2.82 billion during the first quarter of 1995 and whose stock is up 46.3% from its yearly low, will cut 40,000. See John Keller, "ATT Will Eliminate 40,000 jobs" <u>Wall Street Journal</u>, Jan. 3, 1996, p.A-2; John Keller, "ATT Cuts Are Just First Shot in Telecom Wars" <u>Wall Street Journal</u>, Jan. 4, 1996, p.A-2; Leslie Cauley, "Baby Bells Face a Tough Balancing Act" <u>Wall Street Journal</u>, Jan. 4, 1996, p.A-2. 85,000 manufacturing jobs were lost in July 1995. See Lucinda Harper, <u>Wall Street Journal</u>, Aug. 7, 1995, p.A-2. Firms laid off 41,335 jobs in October. See Kirstin Downey Grimsley, <u>Washington Post</u>, Nov. 7, 1995, p.C-3. October saw 10,000 additional losses in the apparel industry. See Carol Emert, <u>WWD</u>, Nov. 6, 1995, p.2. The Union Bank Merger in California lost 850 jobs. See Michael Liedtke, <u>Knight-Ridder/Tribune Business News</u>, Sept. 29, 1995. U.S. job losses rose by 43% in August. <u>L.A. Times</u>, September 6, 1995, p.D-2. In addition to the 40,000 ATT cuts, the baby bells have cut an additional 130,000 jobs since 1984, plus 20,000 more by GTE, and with an additional 50,000 more projected over the next year. See Leslie Cauley, "Baby Bells Face a Tough Balancing Act" <u>Wall Street Journal</u>, January 4, 1996, p.A-2; John Keller, "ATT Will Eliminate 40,000 jobs" <u>Wall Street Journal</u>, January 3, 1996, p.A-2; John Keller, "ATT Cuts Are Just First Shot in Telecom Wars" <u>Wall Street Journal</u>, January 4, 1996, p.A-2. In all, despite the economic recovery, IBM has cut 100,000 jobs, GM 74,000, Sears 50,000, and Digital 20,000, since 1993. <u>Time</u>, Sept. 4, 1995, p.21. See also: Tyson, "Why the Wage Gap Just Keeps Getting Bigger" Business Week, Dec.14, 1998, p.22.

The average physician spends $15,000 on malpractice insurance premiums each year. "Malpractice Costs/ Tort Reform Missing in Health Care Debate" San Diego Union-Tribune, Sept. 12, 1994, p.B-6; The Report of the Harvard Medical Practice Study to the State of New York. Doctors and Lawyers: Medical Injury, Malpractice Litigation, and Patient Compensation in New York (Harvard University 1990).

"The Nation had been rid of human slavery – fortunately, as now we all feel – but the conviction was universal that the country was in real danger from another kind of slavery thought to be fastened on the American people, namely, the slavery that would result from aggregations of capital in the hands of a few individuals and corporations controlling, for their own profit and advantage exclusively, the entire business of the country, including the production and sale of the necessaries of life. Such a danger was thought to be then imminent, and all felt that it must be met firmly and by such statutory regulations as would adequately protect the people against oppression and wrong." Standard Oil v. The United States, 221 U.S. 1, 83-84, 31 S.Ct. 502, 525, 55 L.Ed. 619 (1910) (Harlan, concurring). See also: United States v. Columbia Steel Co., 334 U.S. 495, 536, 68 S.Ct. 1107, 1128, 92, L.Ed. 1533 (1948) (Douglas, dissenting).

On tort reform generally, see: Rustad, Nationalizing Tort Law: The Republicans Attack on Women, Blue Collar Workers and Consumers, 48 Rutgers L.Rev. 673 (1996); Lawrence Drivon, The Civil War On Consumer Rights (Conari Press 1990); Gerry Spence, With Justice for None (Penguin 1989); Tort Law and the Public Interest (ed. by Peter Schuck, W.W. Norton & Company 1991); Ralph Nader and Wesley J. Smith, No Contest:

Corporate Lawyers and the Perversion of Justice in America (Random House 1996) pp.256-319; Rahdert, Covering Accident Costs: Insurance, Liability, and Tort Reform (1996); Daniels and Martin, Civil Juries and the Politics of Reform (1995); Lawrence M. Friedman, Total Justice (Russell Sage Foundation 1985); Ralph Warner and Stephen Elias, Fed Up With the Legal System (1995); Paul Weiler, Medical Malpractice on Trial (1991); John Gannon, Tort Deform - Lethal Bedfellows Essential Information (1995); J. Minos Simon In Search of a Creed (1996); Galanter, Real World Torts: An Antidote to Anecdote, 55 Md.L.Rev. 1093 (1996); "Are Lawyers Burning America?" Newsweek, March 20, 1995, p.32; "Someone Hear An Explosion?" Newsweek, March 20, 1995, p.34; Jane Bryant Quinn, "Losing Your Right to Sue?" Newsweek, June 26, 1995, p.43; Leshne, "Shedding new Light" Trial Oct. 1998, p.32; Thompson, "Letting the Air Out of Tort Reform" ABA Journal May 1997, p.64; Gary Hengstler, "At the Seat of Power" ABA Journal, April 1995, p.70; Rhonda McMillion, "Congress Speeds Legal Changes" ABA Journal, June 1995, p.111; Henry Reske, "A Classic Battle of Lobbyists" ABA Journal, June 1995, p.22; Martha Middleton, "A Changing Landscape" ABA Journal, Aug. 1995, p.56; Mark Hansen, "Changes Put Goals of Tort Law in Doubt" ABA Journal, Aug. 1995, p.64; "The Big Picture" ABA Journal, Aug. 1995, p.65; Laura Duncan, "Painful Decisions" ABA Journal, Aug. 1995, p.66; "By the Numbers" ABA Journal, Aug. 1995, p.67; Hope Viner Samborn, "Plaintiffs Often Pay a Price for Reform" ABA Journal, Aug. 1995, p.68; "Public Discontent" ABA Journal, Aug. 1995, p.70; Mark Hager and Ned Miltenberg, "Punitive Damages and the Free Market: A Law and Economics Perspective" Trial, Sept. 1995, p.30; Jonathan Massey, "Why Tradition Supports Punitive Damages" Trial, Sept. 1995, p.19.

On the Tenth Amendment and the principles of Federalism generally, see: Printz v. U.S., No. 95-1478, 117 S.Ct. 2365, 138 L.Ed.2d 914 (1997); U.S. v. Lopez, 514 U.S. 549, 115 S.Ct. 1624, 131 L.Ed.2d 626 (1995); New York v. United States, 505 U.S. 144, 112 S.Ct. 2408, 120 L.Ed.2d 120 (1992); Gregory v. Ashcroft, 501 U.S. 452, 458, 111 S.Ct. 2395, 115 L.Ed.2d 410 (1991); Carter v. Carter Coal, 298 U.S. 238, 308-309, 56 S.Ct. 855, 871-872, 80 L.Ed. 1160 (1936); James Madison, The Federalist Papers, No.45 (1788); James Madison, The Federalist Papers, No. 51 (1788); Alexander Hamilton, The Federalist Papers, No.17 (1788); Alexander Hamilton, The Federalist Papers, No.28 (1788).

The United States Supreme Court has recognized that the specific guarantees in the Bill of Rights have "penumbras" which emanate from such personal freedoms, and which give them the life and substance they require. Griswold v. Connecticut, 381 U.S. 479, 85 S.Ct. 1678, 14 L.Ed.2d 510 (1965); Roe v. Wade, 410 U.S. 113, 93 S.Ct. 705, 35 L.Ed.2d 147 (1973).

On the right of access to the courts, see generally: Bounds v. Smith, 430 U.S. 817, 822, 97 S.Ct. 1491, 1494-95, 52 L.Ed.2d 72 (1977); California Transport v. Trucking Unlimited, 404 U.S. 508, 510-13, 92 S.Ct. 609, 611-13, 30 L.Ed.2d 642 (1971); Boddie v. Connecticut, 401 U.S. 371, 374-75, 91 S.Ct. 780, 784, 28 L.Ed.2d 113 (1971); NAACP v. Button, 371 U.S. 415, 429-31, 83 S.Ct. 328, 336, 9 L.Ed.2d 405 (1963); Chambers v. Baltimore & Ohio Railroad, 207 U.S. 142, 148, 28 S.Ct. 34, 35, 52 L.Ed. 143 (1907); Marbury v. Madison, 5 U.S. (1 Cranch) 137, 163, 2 L.Ed. 60 (1803); John Locke, Second Treatise on Government, Chapter. II, §§10-11 (1681); Blackstone, Commentaries on the Laws of England, Vol.I, pp.120-137

(1765); Magna Carta (1215). See also: Penn. Cont. Art. I,
§11; Fla. Const. Art. I, §21; Ill. Const. Art. I, §12; La.
Const. Art. I, §22; Ohio Const. Art. I, §16; N.H. Const. Pt.
I, Art. 14; R.I. Const. Art. I, §5; Va. Const. Art. III, §17.
Jones v. City of New Orleans, No. 94-0172 (La. App.
4th Cir. Dec. 15, 1994). See also: Kammerer v. Sewerage
& Water Board, 633 So.2d 1357, 1362 (La. App. 4th Cir.
1994) (Waltzer, J., concurring).

On the right to trial by jury generally, see: J. Kendall
Few, In Defense of Trial by Jury (American Jury Trial
Foundation 1993); Railroad Co. v. Stout, 84 U.S. 657,
664, 21 L.Ed. 745 (1873); Maxwell v. Dow, 176 U.S.
581, 609, 20 S.Ct. 448, 44 L.Ed. 597 (1900) (Harlan, J.,
dissenting); Theil v. Southern Pacific, 328 U.S. 217, 227,
66 S.Ct. 984, 989, 90 L.Ed. 1181 (1946) (Frankfurter, J.,
dissenting); Parklane Hosiery v. Shore, 439 U.S. 322,
340-344, 95 S.Ct. 645, 656-658, 58 L.Ed.2d 552 (1979)
(Renquist, J., dissenting); McKlesky v. Kemp, 481 U.S.
279, 311, 107 S.Ct. 1756, 1777, 95 L.Ed.2d 262 (1987);
Pacific Mutual v. Haslip, 499 U.S. 1, 40-41, 111 S.Ct.
1032, 1055, 113 L.Ed.2d 1 (1991) (Scalia, J., concurring);
Dimick v. Schiedt, 293 U.S. 474, 486, 55 S.Ct. 296, 79
L.Ed. 603 (1935); Thomas Jefferson, Letter to Pierre S.
DuPont, (April 4, 1816); James Madison, In Defense of
Trial by Jury, Vol. I, p. 8 (1789); Thomas Jefferson, The
Writings of Thomas Jefferson (1788), p.41; Alexander
Hamilton, The Federalist Papers, No.83 (1788); Alixis de
Tocqueville, Democracy in America (1835-1840); John
Wigmore, To Ruin Jury Trial in the Federal Courts 19
Ill.L.Rev. 98 (1924); Henry Hallam, The Constitutional
History of England (1827); Winston Churchill, A History
of English Speaking Peoples, Vol.I, pp.218-19 (1956).

Silkwood v. Kerr-McGee, 464 U.S. 238, 104 S.Ct.

615, 78 L.Ed.2d 443 (1984); Gerry Spence, With Justice for None (Penguin 1989) p.81.

"All power tends to develop into a government in itself. Power that controls the economy should be in the hands of elected representatives of the people, not an industrial oligarchy. Industrial power should be decentralized. It should be scattered into many different hands so that the fortunes of people will not be dependent on the whim or caprice, the political prejudices, the emotional stability of a few self-appointed men." United States v. Columbia Steel Co., 334 U.S. 495, 536, 68 S.Ct. 1107, 1128, 92, L.Ed. 1533 (1948) (Douglas, dissenting). See also: Standard Oil v. The United States, 221 U.S. 1, 83-84, 31 S.Ct. 502, 525, 55 L.Ed. 619 (1910) (Harlan, concurring).

On Separation of Powers Doctrine, and the protection of individual freedoms through a system of checks and balances, see generally: Aristotle, Politics, Books VI, XIV; John Locke, Second Treatise on Civil Government §141 (1690); Montesquieu, Spirit of the Laws, Book XI (1748); James Madison, The Federalist Papers, No. 51 (1788); Alexander Hamilton, The Federalist Papers, No.28 (1788); Durr and Whiteside, "Delegata Potestas Non Potest Delegari" Selected Essays on Constitutional Law, Vol. IV, pp.291-316 (1938).

The Supreme Court of Illinois recently held that a cap of $500,000 in general damages was unconstitutional, because it was an improper intrusion upon the judiciary's power to ensure that damage awards are reasonable, as well as the jury's careful deliberative assessment of damages according to the facts of each case. Best v. Taylor Machine Works, 179 Ill.2d 367, 689 N.E.2d 1057 (1997).

See also: Carson v. Maurer, 424 A.2d 825, 837 (N.H. 1980); Lucas v. United States, 757 S.W.2d 687 (Tex. 1988); Smith v. Department of Insurance, 507 So.2d 1080 (Fla. 1987).

"The Fifth Amendment's guarantee that private property shall not be taken for public use without just compensation was designed to bar the Government from forcing some people alone to bear public burdens which, in all justice and fairness, should be borne by the public as a whole." Dolan v. City of Tigard, 512 U.S. 374, 114 S.Ct. 2309, 2316, 129 L.Ed.2d 304 (1994); Armstrong v. U.S., 364 U.S. 40. 49, 80 S.Ct. 1563, 1569, 4 L.Ed.2d 1554 (1960).

"If by the mere force of numbers a majority should deprive a minority of any clearly written constitutional right, it might, in a moral point of view, justify revolution." Abraham Lincoln, First Inaugural Address, March 4, 1961.

Whitnell v. Menville, No. 93-2468, 646 So.2d 989 (La. App. 4th Cir. 11/4/94), rev'd, No. 95-0112, 686 So.2d 23 (La. 12/6/96).

The most common form of malpractice occurs when a doctor fails to diagnose breast cancer. There have been around 2,450 reported cases of such failure to diagnose since 1985. The failure to follow-up physical examinations or inconclusive mamograms was found to be present in over 30% of the cases. See Lauren Neergaard, "Breast Cancer Victims Sue Most" Times Picayune, June 3, 1995, p.A-6.

V. Chapter Five: Clear and Present Danger

On the right of free speech generally, see: John Stuart Mill, On Liberty (1859); James Madison, Annals of Congress, Vol.4, p.934 (1794); Abrams v. United States, 250 U.S. 616, 630, 40 S.Ct. 17, 63 L.Ed. 1173 (1919) (Holmes, J., joined by Brandeis, dissenting); Whitney v. California, 274 U.S. 357, 376-377, 47 S.Ct. 641, 648-649, 71 L.Ed. 1095 (1927) (Brandeis, J., joined by Holmes, concurring); United States v. Associated Press, 52 F.Supp. 362, 372 (S.D.N.Y. 1943), aff'd, 326 U.S. 1, 65 S.Ct. 1416, 89 L.Ed. 2013; U.S. v. Dennis, 183 F.2d 201, 212 (2nd Cir. 1950), aff'd, 341 U.S. 494, 71 S.Ct. 857, 95 L.Ed. 1137; Cantwell v. Connecticut, 310 U.S. 296, 310, 60 S.Ct. 900, 906, 84 L.Ed. 1213 (1940); York Times v. Sullivan, 376 U.S. 254, 84 S.Ct. 710, 11 L.Ed.2d 686 (1964); Gertz v. Robert Welch, Inc., 418 U.S. 323, 339-340, 94 S.Ct. 2997, 3007, 41 L.Ed.2d 789 (1974); Central Hudson v. Public Service Commission, 447 U.S. 557, 100 S.Ct. 2343, 65 L.Ed.2d 341 (1980); Virginia Board v. Virginia Citizens, 425 U.S. 748, 96 S.Ct. 1817, 48 L.Ed.2d 346 (1976); Texas v. Johnson, 491 U.S. 397, 414, 109 S.Ct. 2533, 2545, 105 L.Ed.2d 342 (1988); Stanley v. Georgia, 394 U.S. 557, 565, 89 S.Ct. 1243, 1248, 22 L.Ed.2d 542 (1969); United States v. Reidel, 402 U.S. 351, 356, 91 S.Ct. 1410, 1412, 28 L.Ed.2d 813 (1971); Osborne v. Ohio, 495 U.S. 103, 139-145, 110 S.Ct. 1691, 1712-1715, 109 L.Ed.2d 98 (1990) (Brennan, joined by Marshall and Stevens, dissenting).

"If the First Amendment guarantee means anything, it means that, absent clear and present danger, government has no power to restrict expression because of the effect of its message is likely to have on the public."

Central Hudson v. Public Service Commission, 447 U.S. 557, 575, 100 S.Ct. 2343, 2356, 65 L.Ed.2d 341 (1980) (Blackmun, joined by Brennan, concurring). "If there is a bedrock principle underlying the First Amendment, it is that the government may not prohibit the expression of an idea merely because society itself finds the idea itself offensive or disagreeable." Texas v. Johnson, 491 U.S. 397, 414, 109 S.Ct. 2533, 2545, 105 L.Ed.2d 342 (1988).

On the cartoon characters Beavis and Butthead, see: Leland, "Battle for Your Brain" Newsweek Oct. 11, 1993, pp.50-51; Hamilton and Peyser, "Cartoon Culprits" Newsweek Oct. 18, 1993, p.10. More recently: "As to your request for 'TV experts' to take responsibility – who exactly are these experts, or is that a code word for censors? We are all the TV experts. If the viewers do not like a show, they don't watch. That is called democracy (also protected by the First Amendment – you can look it up." John Murphy, "'South Park' 1: 'We Are All TV Experts'" Times Picayune: TV Focus, April 12, 1998, p.5. "Last time I checked, both television and cable boxes are equipped with remote controls. Are your fingers broken?!!! If you don't like the kids of 'South Park', change the channel." Melissa Savoie, "'South Park' 1" TV Focus, p.5. "I'm starting to get a little sick and tired of all of this. It strikes me as a repeat of the 'Beavis and Butthead' controversy of years ago. Both shows carry warnings their content is not suitable for young children. Both are aired at times when young children should be in bed and at least one working parent should be home. The lament of parents who can't monitor their children 24 hours a day is well founded, but it is ridiculous to claim a regularly-scheduled program cannot be monitored. On a recent TV news report I heard a mother complaining that she couldn't know what her daughter was watching at the time because she had her own TV in her room. Wouldn't it be easier for her to peek in her daughter's room once in awhile than to change the TV lineup?" Greg London, "'South Park' 3: 'Who's the Boss'" Times Picayune: TV Focus, April 12, 1998, p.5.

On Hegel and the Dialectic, see Julian Marias, The History of Philosophy (Dover 1967), pp.17-329.

William Wordsworth, Ode: Intimations of Immortality from Recollections of Early Childhood (1802-1804).

"Commercial expression not only serves the economic interest of the speaker, but also assists consumers and furthers the societal interest in the fullest possible dissemination of information." Central Hudson v. Public Service Commission, 447 U.S. 557, 561, 100 S.Ct. 2343, 2349, 65 L.Ed.2d 341 (1980). "Normally, the availability of greater information can only benefit economically rationally individuals – the more information individuals have, the more knowledgeably they can define their ends, calculate their means, and plan their actions." Daniel A. Farber, Free Speech Without Romance: Public Choice and the First Amendment 105 Harv. L. Rev. 554, 558 (1991). "That is, the benefits of information cannot be restricted to direct purchasers but inevitably spread to larger groups. The production of information often produces positive externalities–that is, benefits to third parties. because the producer does not consider these benefits in his production decision, less information is produced than is socially optimal. There are people who, if they had to, would be willing to pay for the benefits of additional information, but the additional information is not produced because the market is unable to translate those individuals' preferences into an incentive for the producer. Market demand reflects only benefits to purchasers, not benefits to free riders. According to this analysis, if the government intervenes in the market at all, it should *subsidize* speech rather than limit it." Daniel A. Farber, <u>Free Speech Without Romance: Public Choice and the First Amendment</u> 105 Harv.L.Rev. 554, 559 (1991). The nature of a Democracy is designed to assume "that information is not in itself harmful, that people will perceive their own best interests if only they are well enough informed, and that the best means to that end is to open the channels of communication rather than to close them." <u>Virginia Board v. Virginia Citizens</u>, 425 U.S. 748, 770, 96 S.Ct. 1817, 1829, 48 L.Ed.2d 346 (1976). See also: <u>Rubin v. Coors Brewing Company</u>, 514 U.S. 476, 115 S.Ct. 1585, 1597, 131 L.Ed.2d 532 (1995) (Stevens, J., concurring).

"Though all the winds of doctrine were let loose to play upon the earth, so Truth be in the field, we do injuriously by licensing and prohibition, to misdoubt her strength. Let her and falsehood grapple; who ever knew Truth put to worse, in a free and open encounter?" John Milton, <u>Areopagitica</u> (1644). "If there be any among us who would wish to dissolve this Union or change its republican form, let them stand undisturbed as monuments of the safety with which error of opinion may be tolerated where reason is left free to combat it." Thomas Jefferson, <u>First Inaugural Address</u> (1801). "I believe that unarmed truth and unconditional love will have the final word in reality. That is why right temporarily defeated is stronger than evil triumphant." Dr. Rev. Martin Luther King, Jr., <u>Acceptance of the Nobel Peace Prize</u>, (Dec. 11, 1964).

The Federal Government prohibits the transmission of language which is obscene, indecent, and profane. 18 U.S.C. §§ 1461, 1464. The government's power to prohibit obscene and indecent communication through radio and television stems from: (a) the individual's right to be left alone in the privacy of his own home, and (b) the protection of children. FCC v. Pacifica, 438 U.S. 726, 98 S.Ct. 3026, 57 L.Ed.2d 1073 (1978). See generally: Congressional Research Service, The Constitution of the United States: Analysis and Interpretation (Killian ed. 1987) pp.1090-1093.

Emerging evidence that violent and sexually explicit expression can have a real and actual effect on the psychological development and ultimately therefore the actions of children includes: (a) Leonard Eron and Rowell Huesmann of the University of Michigan found, in a 22-year study following kids from third grade through adulthood, that the single biggest predictor of later aggression (more than poverty, grades, or a single-parent home) was tv violence; (b) Brandon S. Centerwall asserts that there would be 10,000 fewer murders per year without television, 70,000 fewer rapes, and 700,000 fewer assaults; (c) George Gerbner found that, because of the way in which men are victimizers and the way in which women and minorities are victimized, some kids see themselves as more likely to become victimized, and develop a vulnerability, while others see themselves as more likely to perpetrate violence without consequences, and develop a greater sense of aggression; (d) a Time/CNN poll from June 1995, revealed that 76% believe that violence in movies and on television numbs people to violence so that they're insensitive to it, 75% believe that it inspires young people to violence, and 71% believe that it tells people that violence is acceptable. See Lynn Elber, "TV-Violence Study Hits Kid Shows" Times Picayune Sept. 20, 1995, p.A-7; Richard Lacayo, Time June 12, 1995, p.26. See also: John Leland, "Violence, Reel to Real" Newsweek Dec. 11, 1995, p.46.

On the regulation of television and radio broadcasting, see National Broadcasting Company v. United States, 319

U.S. 190, 213, 226, 63 S.Ct. 997, 1008, 1014, 87 L.Ed. 1344 (1943); Reno v. American Civil Liberties Union, No. 96-511, 117 S.Ct. 2329, 2344, 138 L.Ed.2d 874 (June 26, 1997). See also: Howard Stern, Private Parts (Simon & Schuster 1993) pp.415-437; Mark Lorando, "V-chip Clouds the Future of Television" Times Picayune, Aug. 13, 1995, p.A-6; Richard Schickel, "No, But He Reads the Polls" Time June 12, 1995, p.29.

"Obscene" material is material which, taken as a whole, the average person, applying contemporary community standards, would find appeals to the prurient interest; describes, in a patently offensive way, sexual conduct specifically defined by statute; and, taken as a whole, lacks serious literary, artistic, political, or scientific value. Miller v. California, 413 U.S. 15, 93 S.Ct. 2607, 37 L.Ed.2d 419 (1973).

A study conducted by the Libel defense Resource Center revealed that, from 1990-1994, defendants ultimately prevailed on summary judgment in 78.6% of libel cases. Defendants won 45.5% of the jury trials in 1992-1993, with awards exceeding one million dollars in only 18.2% of the cases. In the ten years from 1984-1994, only 28.3% of all libel awards were affirmed in their entirety, with 30.7% reversed, in part, and 41% reversed entirely. See "A Winning Record for Libel Defendants" ABA Journal, Jan. 1996, p.21.

"Actual malice" is present when a statement is made with the knowledge that the statement is false, or with reckless disregard as to whether the statement is true. New York Times v. Sullivan, 376 U.S. 254, 279-280, 84 S.Ct. 710, 726, 11 L.Ed.2d 686 (1964).

Many state constitutions guarantee the right of free speech, but at the same time make it clear that people are responsible for the abuse of that right. See, for example: N.Y. Const. Art. I, §8; La. Const. Art. I, §7; Ohio Const. Art. I, §11; Penn. Const. Art. I, §7; Texas Const. Art. I, §8.

"Newspapers, magazines, and broadcasting companies are businesses conducted for profit and often make very large ones. Like other enterprises that inflict damage in the course of performing a service highly useful to the public, they must pay the freight; and injured persons should not be relegated to remedies which make collection of their claims difficult or impossible unless strong public policy considerations demand." Curtis Publishing Company v. Butts, 388 U.S. 130, 147, 87 S.Ct. 1975, 1987, 18 L.Ed.2d 1094 (1967); quoting, Buckley v. New York Post, 373 F.2d 175, 182 (2nd Cir. 1967). "Accountability, like subjection to law, is not necessarily a net subtraction from liberty.... The First Amendment was intended to guarantee free expression, not to create a privileged industry." Commission on Freedom of the Press, A Free and Responsible Press (1947), pp.81,130. See also: Gertz v. Robert Welch, 418 U.S. 323, 369-404, 94 S.Ct. 2997, 3022-3038, 41 L.Ed.2d 789 (1974) (White, J., dissenting). "I think we will all agree on certain core propositions. First, as a general matter, the States have a perfectly legitimate interest, exercised in a variety of ways, in redressing and preventing careless conduct, no matter who is responsible for it, that inflicts actual, measurable injury upon individual citizens. Secondly, there is no identifiable value worthy of constitutional protection in the publication of falsehoods. Third, although libel law provides that truth is a complete defense, that principle, standing alone, is insufficient to satisfy the constitutional interest in the freedom of speech." Rosenbloom v. Metromedia, 403 U.S. 29, 64, 91 S.Ct. 1811, 1830, 29 L.Ed.

296 (1971) (Harlan, J., dissenting). See also, generally: Lidsky, <u>Prying, Spying and Lying: Intrusive Newsgathering and What the Law Should Do About It</u>, 73 Tul.L.Rev. 173 (1998).

VI. Chapter Six: The O.J. Simpson Trial

See generally: Ellis Cose, "Getting Past the Myths" Newsweek Feb. 17, 1997, p.36; Carrizosa, "Critics Call for Ban on Cameras in the Courts" L.A. Daily Journal, Jan. 9, 1996, p.1; Dilworth, "California Task Force Reviews Cameras in the Courts" Trial March 1996, p.79; Michael Fleeman, "In a Civil Trial, 2 Jurors Say, They'd Have Convicted O.J." Times Picayune, Jan. 17, 1996, p.A-6; Barry Scheck, "Tried and True" Newsweek Feb. 17, 1997; Booth, "Legal Experts Cite Many Factors as Making Difference in Simpson Verdicts" Washington Post, Feb. 6, 1997, p.A-6.

"Evidence of other crimes, wrongs, or acts is not admissible to prove the character of a person in order to show action in conformity therewith."   Federal Rule of Evidence 404(b). "Ill Kings make many good laws." Proverb. (Thomas Fuller, Gnomologia (1732)). "It is a fair summary of history to say that the safeguards of liberty have frequently been forged in controversies involving not very nice people." Justice Frankfurter, United States v. Rabinowitz, 339 U.S. 56, 69 (1950). "I abhor averages. I like the individual case. A man may have six meals one day and none the next, making an average of three meals per day, but that is not a good way to live." Justice Brandeis (A.T. Mason, Brandeis: A Free Man's Life (1946)). "It makes no difference whether a good man has defrauded a bad man or a bad man has defrauded a good man, or whether a good or bad man has committed adultery; the law can look only to the amount of damage done." Aristotle, Nicomachean Ethics. "The business of the court is to try the case and not the man; a very bad man may have a very righteous cause." Thompson v.

Church, 1 Root 312 (1791).

State v. Van Winkle, No. 93-843, 635 So.2d 1177 (La. App. 5th Cir. 3/16/94), *rev'd, in part, on other grounds,* No. 94-0947, 658 So.2d 198 (La. 6/30/95).

STEPHEN J. HERMAN

VII. Chapter Seven: The Oklahoma City Bombing

See generally: Alter, "Jumping to Conclusions" Newsweek, May 1, 1995, p.55; Alter, "Toxic Speech" Newsweek, May 8, 1995, p.4; Limbaugh, "Blame the Bombers Only" Newsweek, May 8, 1995, p.39; Raspberry, "Words Can Push Some Over Edge" Times Picayune April 27, 1995, p.B-7; "Hollywood Brushes Off Attacks by Dole" Times Picayune, June 2, 1995, p.A-9; Cal Thomas, "Is the Problem Really Hollywood?" Times Picayune June 8, 1995, p.B-7; Schickel, "No But He Reads the Polls" Time, June 12, 1995; Lacayo, "A Moment of Silence" Time, May 8, 1995, p.47.

"The power to proscribe particular speech on the basis of a noncontent element (*e.g.* noise) does not entail the power to proscribe the same speech on the basis of a content element." RAV v. City of St. Paul, 505 U.S. 377, 386, 112 S.Ct. 2538, 2544, 120 L.Ed.2d 305 (1992). "What they mean is that these forms of speech can, consistent with the First Amendment, be regulated *because of their constitutionally proscribable content* (obscenity, defamation, etc.) – not that they are categories of speech entirely invisible to the Constitution, so that they may be made the vehicles of content discrimination unrelated to their distinctively proscribable content. Thus, the government may proscribe libel; but it may not make the further content discrimination of proscribing *only* libel critical of the government." RAV, 505 U.S. at 383-384, 112 S.Ct. at 2543. "Fighting words are thus analogous to a noisy sound truck: Each is, as Justice Frankfurter recognized, a 'mode of speech'; both can be used to convey an idea, but neither has, in and of itself, a claim upon the First Amendment. As with the sound truck, so also with fighting words: The government may not regulate based on hostility – or favoritism – towards the underlying message expressed." RAV, 505 U.S. at 386, 112 S.Ct. at 2545.

"In the classic definition of 'liberal,' *The Economist* concludes that everyone in the mainstream of American politics is liberal: 'Bill Clinton, Bob Dole and (yes) Newt Gingrich, are all liberals.' They are liberal in that they 'all three share a belief in society that provides a constitutional government (rule by laws, not men) and freedom of religion, thought, expression and economic interaction; a society in which infringements on individual liberty must be justified.' In America the use of the word 'liberal' by politicians has been used in the same degree of reverence as 'child-molester' to mean a person who believes in big government, lots of taxes and public spending, someone who is willing to infringe economic liberties in pursuit of the common good. In Europe, the word means just the opposite. A European liberal, says *The Economist,* 'will favour limited government and give freedom priority over the supposed interests of society.... So it seems that in America 'liberal' has become detached from its proper meaning and attached to the opposite." Pike, "The European Take on 'Liberalism'" Times Picayune, Jan. 1, 1997, p.B-7. See also: George Will, "Big Stick Conservatism" Newsweek, Nov. 11, 1996, p.96.

On the events of Waco and Ruby Ridge, see generally: "The Echoes of Ruby Ridge" Newsweek, Aug. 28, 1995, p.24; Jess Walter, "Every Knee Shall Bow" Newsweek, Aug. 28, 1995, p.28; Jess Walter, Every Knee Shall Bow (1995).

See also, generally: Morris Dees, Gathering Storm: America's Militia Threat (Harper Collins 1996).

On the trial of Terry Nichols, see generally: Thomas, "FBI: Prints Incriminate Nichols" <u>Times Picayune</u>, Nov. 15, 1997, p.A-17; Serrano, "Right-wing Gun Collector Testifies Against Nichols" <u>Times Picayune</u>, Nov. 19, 1997, p.A-10; Thomas, "Prosecutors: Nichols Built Bomb With McVeigh" <u>Times Picayune</u>, Nov. 26, 1997, p.A-4; Shore, "Prosecutors Hammer Away at Witnesses" <u>Times Picayune</u>, Dec. 4, 1997, p.A-15; Thomas, "Nichols' Wife Helps Tie Him to McVeigh" <u>Times Picayune</u>, Dec. 12, 1997, p.A-4; Thomas, "Bombing Trial Winds Down With Attorneys on the Attack" <u>Times Picayune</u>, Dec. 16, 1997, p.A-1.

VIII. Chapter Eight: The Social Contract

On the Social Contract generally, see: Hobbes, Leviathan, Part I, Chpt. 13 (1651); Locke, Second Treatise on Government, Chpt. VIII, §95 (1681); Rousseau, The Social Contract, Chpt. 4 (1762).

On the limits of the social contract, and the authority of the State over the individual, see generally: John Stuart Mill, "Of the Limits of Authority of Society Over the Individual" On Liberty (1859); Olmstead v. United States, 277 U.S. 438, 478, 48 S.Ct. 564, 572, 72 L.Ed. 944 (1928) (Brandeis, J., dissenting); Griswold v. Connecticut, 381 U.S. 479, 488-489, 85 S.Ct. 1678, 1684, 14 L.Ed.2d 510 (1965) (Goldeberg, J., concurring).

"If Congress deems it appropriate to afford the President stronger protection, it may respond with appropriate legislation. As petitioner notes in his brief, Congress has enacted more than one statute providing for the deferral of civil litigation to accommodate important public interests. See, e.g., 11 U.S.C. §362 (litigation against debtor stayed upon filing of bankruptcy litigation); Soldiers' and Sailors' Civil Relief Act of 1940, 50 U.S.C. §§501-525 (provisions governing tolling or stay of civil claims during course of active duty). If the Constitution embodied the rule that the President advocated, Congress, of course, could not repeal it. But our holding today raises no barrier to a statutory response to these concerns." Clinton v. Jones, No. 95-1853, 117 S.Ct. 1636, 1652, 137 L.Ed.2d 945 (May 27, 1997).

The United States "is not governed by one constitution, but by fifty-one." Stephen Griffin, The Problem of Constitutional Change, 70 Tul.L.Rev. 2121, 2140 (1996). Our constitution establishes a dual sovereignty wherein the power of the Federal Government is coexistent with the powers of the respective States. Like the separation of powers among the three branches of the Federal Government, a bifurcation of power between the States and the Federal Government would prevent an accumulation of excessive power in any one body, thereby reducing the risk of tyranny, and promoting the preservation and advancement of individual liberties. U.S. v. Lopez, 514 U.S. 549, 115 S.Ct. 1624, 131 L.Ed.2d 626 (1995); Gregory v. Ashcroft, 501 U.S. 452, 457-459, 111 S.Ct. 2395, 2399-2400, 115 L.Ed.2d 410 (1991); Garcia v. San Antonio Metropolitan Transit, 469 U.S. 528, 105 S.Ct. 1005, 83 L.Ed.2d 1016 (1985); James Madison, The Federalist Papers, No. 51 (1788); Alexander Hamilton, The Federalist Papers, No.28 (1788). Within this framework, the powers of the States are numerous and indefinite, while the powers of the Federal Government are few and defined. U.S. v. Lopez, 115 S.Ct. at 1626; James Madison, The Federalist Papers, No. 45 (1788). Each state is an independent sovereign, with the inherent power to create and enforce a legal code, both civil and criminal. Diamond v. Charles, 476 U.S. 54, 65, 106 S.Ct. 1697, 1705, 90 L.Ed.2d 48 (1986); Alfred L. Snapp v. Puerto Rico, 458 U.S. 592, 601, 102 S.Ct. 3260, 3265, 73 L.Ed.2d 995 (1982). See also: Hillsborough County v. Automated Medical Labs, 471 U.S. 707, 719, 105 S.Ct. 2371, 2378, 85 L.Ed.2d 714 (1985). Accordingly, the consideration of issues arising under the Supremacy Clause always begins and ends with presumption that the historic police powers of the States are not pre-empted by a Federal statute, unless it is the clear and manifest purpose of Congress. Medtronic v. Lohr, 518 U.S. 470, 116 S.Ct. 2240, 135 L.Ed.2d 700 (1996); Cipollone v. Liggett Group, 505 U.S. 504, 518, 112 S.Ct. 2608, 2617, 120 L.Ed.2d 407 (1992). See also: Restatement, Third, of Torts: Products Liability §4(b)

(1997).

The courts have recognized three types of preemption: (i) express preemption, where Congress explicitly provides that State law is to be preempted by Federal statute; (ii) implied preemption, where the scheme of Federal regulation is sufficiently comprehensive to reasonably infer that Congress has "left no room" for supplementary regulations by the States; and, (iii) implied preemption, where there is an actual conflict between the Federal legislation and incompatible State regulation or law. California Federal Savings & Loan Association v. Guerra, 479 U.S. 272, 107 S.Ct. 683, 93 L.Ed.2d 613 (1987).

"We need a traffic safety agency and we need to research our problem from end to end, but we don't need to relieve the manufacturer of his natural responsibility for the performance of his product. You may think that the manufacturer is afraid of Government regulation but the cry you are hearing may be, 'Brer Fox, please don't throw me into the briar patch.' If the Government assumes the responsibility of safety design in our vehicles, the manufacturers will join together for another 30-year snooze under the veil of Government sanction and in thousands of courtrooms across the Nation wronged individuals will encounter the stone wall of, 'Our product meets Government standards,' and an already compounded problem will be recompounded." Tom Triplett, Hearings Before the Committee on Interstate and Foreign Commerce of the House of Representatives, 89th Congress, 2nd Sess. Part 2, 1249 (1966). See also: Kennedy v. Collagen Corp., 67 F.3d 1453, 1459-1460 (9th Cir. 1995), cert. denied, 116 S.Ct. 2579, 135 L.Ed.2d 1094 (1996); Attorney General Dennis Vacco, "Medtronic v. Lohr: Important But Incomplete" New York State Trial Lawyers

Institute, p.10 (1996); Ford Bronco II, 909 F.Supp. 400, 409 (E.D.La. 1995).

Adam Smith believed in three vital roles for the state: (1) a national defense, (2) ensuring justice and protecting property, and (3) building canals, harbors, and roads. Smith also supported universal education, as an antidote to the numbing effects of economic specialization. Adam Smith, An Inquiry into the Nature and Causes of the Wealth of Nations (1776); Robert Samuelson, "The Spirit of Adam Smith" Newsweek, Dec. 2, 1996, p.63.

The doctrine of "sovereign immunity" was judicially established in the European monarchies such as England, founded upon the ancient principle that the King can do no wrong. Black's law Dictionary (6th ed. 1990) p.1396.

The authors of the *Contract With America* claim to "restore accountability" to the government. Gingrich, Armey, and House Republicans, Contract With America (Times Books 1995) p.14. The authors of the *Contract* propose, for example, that a new right of action be created in favor of corporation that is investigated by a Federal Agency, so that the corporation can recover damages from the United States. Contract With America, p.134.

"The Fifth Amendment's guarantee that private property shall not be taken for a public use without just compensation was designed to bar the Government from forcing some people alone to bear public burdens which, in all justice and fairness, should be borne by the public as a whole." Dolan v. City of Tigard, 512 U.S. 374, 114 S.Ct. 2309, 2316, 129 L.Ed.2d 304 (1994); Armstrong v. U.S., 364 U.S. 40. 49, 80 S.Ct. 1563, 1569, 4 L.Ed.2d 1554 (1960). See also: Jean Jacques Rousseau, The Social Contract, Chapter 4 (1762).

IX. Chapter Nine: Crime and Punishment

On the limits of the State's authority over the individual, see John Stuart Mill, On Liberty (1859). See also: Ronald Rychlak, Society's Moral Right to Punish 65 Tul.L.Rev. 299 (1990); Kansas v. Hendricks, No. 95-1649, 117 S.Ct. 2072, 2080, 138 L.Ed.2d 501 (1997); Hansen, "Danger v. Due Process" ABA Journal, Aug. 1997, p.43.

On the history and development of the exclusionary rule generally, see: John Wasowicz, "Exclusionary Rule: A 20th Century Invention" Trial, p.79 (Feb. 1998); McCormick on Evidence (Clearly ed. 1978) p.365; U.S. Dept. of Justice, The Effects of the Exclusionary Rule: A Study In California (1982); Mapp v. Ohio, 367 U.S. 643, 81 S.Ct. 1684, 6 L.Ed.2d 1081 (1961); Weeks v. U.S., 232 U.S. 383, 34 S.Ct. 341, 58 L.Ed. 652 (1914).

On the costs of the "War on Drugs", see generally: Jim Harrigan, "More Than Just Saying No" L.A. Times, Aug. 27, 1997, p.B-6; John Leone, "A Partnership Blind to Corruption" L.A. Times March 17, 1997, p.B-5. See also: Michael Hedges, "War On Drugs May End" Chicago Sun Times Feb. 9, 1997, p.36; Headden, "Guns, Money & Medicine" U.S. News & World Report, July 1, 1996, p.31.

The Nineteenth Century scribe, William Hazlitt, once noted that "corporate bodies are more corrupt and profligate than individuals, because they have more power to do mischief, and are less amenable to disgrace or punishment – they neither feel shame, remorse, gratitude nor good-will." See Earle Lasseter, "Power Play Incorporated" ABA Journal, May 1997, p.112. "Did you expect a corporation to have a conscience, when it has no soul to be damned and no body to be kicked?" Edward Thurlow, (Wilberface, Life of Thurlow (1775)). "Corporations cannot commit treason, nor be outlawed, nor excommunicated, for they have no souls." Sir Edward Coke, Case of Sutton's Hospital, 5 Rep. 303, 10 Rep. 326 (1612). "A corporation cannot blush. It has a body, it is true; it certainly has a head – a new one every year; arms it has and very long ones, for it can reach at anything; a throat to swallow the rights of the community, and a stomach to digest them! But who ever yet discovered, in the anatomy of any corporation, either bowels or a heart?" Howell Walsh (1825) (Shrager & Frost, The Quotable Lawyer (1986) p.27). "The notion that a business is clothed with a public interest and has been devoted to public use is little more than a fiction intended to beautify what is disagreeable to the sufferers." Tyson & Brother v. Banton, 273 U.S. 418, 446, 47 S.Ct. 426, 434, 71 L.Ed. 718 (1927) (Holmes, dissenting). See also: Standard Oil v. The United States, 221 U.S. 1, 83-84, 31 S.Ct. 502, 525, 55 L.Ed. 619 (1910) (Harlan, concurring); United States v. Columbia Steel Co., 334 U.S. 495, 536, 68 S.Ct. 1107, 1128, 92, L.Ed. 1533 (1948) (Douglas, dissenting).

David and Melissa Baucus studied of the effects of corporate crime in the *Academy of Management Journal*. In an analysis of 256 major corporations from 1974 to 1983, the researchers looked at the stock price of 68 companies that were convicted of employment discrimination, antitrust violations, or the sale of harmful products, and found that, despite slightly lagging performance, the stock price of most convicted companies kept pace with the market over the five years following a conviction. It was only the stocks of corporations that were assessed with punitive damages in product liability cases that took a relative bath. See Gene Koretz, "Does Corporate Crime Pay?" <u>Business Week</u> April 14, 1997, p.30.

See also, generally: Posner, <u>An Economic Theory of Criminal Law</u> 85 Colum.L.Rev. 1193 (1995); Hager and Miltenberg, "Punitive Damages and the Free Market" <u>Trial</u> Sept. 1995, p.30.

X. Chapter Ten: A Nation of Victims

From 1985 to 1991, almost half of all federal lawsuits involved businesses suing other businesses. "Suits by Firms Exceed Those By Individuals" Wall Street Journal, Dec. 3, 1993. See also: "Spam v. The Muppets and Other Strange Stories of Corporate Lawsuit Abuse" Business Wire, Sept. 17, 1997. Big businesses are overwhelmingly the winners in lawsuits, whether plaintiffs or defendants. When they are plaintiffs, they win 79% of the time, compared to an overall average of 62%. As defendants, they win 62% of the time, compared with an overall average of 38%. Terence Dunworth and Joel Rogers, Corporations in Court: Big Business Litigation in U.S. Federal Courts, 1971-91 (1995). Individuals win only half the time against corporations, while over 60% of the time against other individuals. The average jury verdict is only somewhere between $19,000 and $30,000. Stephen J. Adler, The Jury (Doubleday 1994) pp.147-148, 257-258. See also: Daniels and Martin, Myth and Reality in Punitive Damages 75 Minn.L.Rev. 1 (1990); Ostrom, Rottmann & Hanson, "What Are Tort Awards Really Like" Law and Policy Vol.14, pp.77,83 (1992); Richard Perez-Pena, "U.S. Juries Grow Tougher on Plaintiffs in Lawsuits" New York Times June 17, 1994; Sally Roberts, "Plaintiffs Winning Fewer Personal Injury Suits" Business Insurance, March 28, 1994; Vidmar, The Performance of the American Civil Jury: An Empirical Perspective, 40 Ariz.L.Rev. 849 (1998); Hans, Illusions and Realities in Jurors' Treatment of Corporate Defendants (1998); Hans and Lofquist, "Perceptions of Civil Justice: The Litigation Crisis Attitudes of Civil Juries" Behavioral Sciences and the Law Vol.12, p.181 (1994); Hans & Lofquist, "Jurors' Judgment of Business Liability in Tort Cases" Law and Society Review, Vol.26, p.85 (1992).

On the "Nation of Victims" generally, see: Newt Gingrich, "Renewing America" Newsweek, July 10, 1995, p.26; Gingrich, To Renew America (1995); Robert Wright, "Newt the Blameless" Time July 17, 1995, p.64.

In 1995, the Republican-controlled Congress handed out $12 billion in farm subsidies, (including $42 million to tobacco growers), $600 million in merchant marine fleet subsidies, $750 million on Amtrak, over $500 million on power plants, $40 million to GE, Westinghouse and Asea Brown for research and development, $35 million to purchase land from McDonnell Douglas, $2.4 billion to General Dynamics for the construction of a Wolf submarine, an $840 million increase in highway expenditures, and an excess of $6 billion to the Defense Department over and above what the Pentagon asked for. See Goodgamen, "Her Comes the Pork" Time May 17, 1995, p.18; Samuelson, "Surviving the Guillotine" Newsweek, Nov. 20, 1995, p.65. In 1996, such outlays continued, including, for example, $2 billion to subsidize electric power in Aspen and Hilton Head, $3 million per vessel to cargo ship owners, and $110 million to promote Uncle Ben's Rice, V8 Juice and Friskies overseas, (a budget which is almost 30% higher than it was in 1995). In all, the government spends an estimated $75 billion a year to various business interests, almost half of the Federal deficit. Tumulty, "Why Subsidies Survive" Time, March 25, 1996, p.46. See also: Bartlett & Steele, "Corporate Welfare" Time, Nov. 9, 1998, p.34.

In 1995, the Dow Jones rose 33.5%, the S&P 500 rose 34.1%, the NASDQ composite rose 39.9%, and the NYSE composite rose 31.3%, while the bond markets jumped by over 25%. See Bill Sessums, U.S. News &

World Report, Dec. 25, 1995, p.104; Manny Alessadra, "The Charge of '95" Times Picayune, Dec. 31, 1995, p.F-1. Wages and benefits in 1995 rose just 2.8%, the smallest increase since 1981. See "State of the Union" U.S. News & World Report, Dec. 25, 1995, p.64. Mobil, which earned $523 million in the fourth quarter of 1994, cut 500 jobs in January, while ATT, which earned $2.82 billion during the first quarter of 1995 and whose stock is up 46.3% from its yearly low, will cut 40,000. See John Keller, "ATT Will Eliminate 40,000 jobs" Wall Street Journal, Jan. 3, 1996, p.A-2; John Keller, "ATT Cuts Are Just First Shot in Telecom Wars" Wall Street Journal, Jan. 4, 1996, p.A-2; Leslie Cauley, "Baby Bells Face a Tough Balancing Act" Wall Street Journal, Jan. 4, 1996, p.A-2. 85,000 manufacturing jobs were lost in July 1995. See Lucinda Harper, Wall Street Journal, Aug. 7, 1995, p.A-2. Firms laid off 41,335 jobs in October. See Kirstin Downey Grimsley, Washington Post, Nov. 7, 1995, p.C-3. October saw 10,000 additional losses in the apparel industry. See Carol Emert, WWD, Nov. 6, 1995, p.2. The Union Bank Merger in California lost 850 jobs. See Michael Liedtke, Knight-Ridder/Tribune Business News, Sept. 29, 1995. U.S. job losses rose by 43% in August. L.A. Times, Sept. 6, 1995, p.D-2. In addition to the 40,000 ATT cuts, the baby bells have cut an additional 130,000 jobs since 1984, plus 20,000 more by GTE, and with an additional 50,000 more projected over the next year. See Leslie Cauley, "Baby Bells Face a Tough Balancing Act" Wall Street Journal, Jan. 4, 1996, p.A-2; John Keller, "ATT Will Eliminate 40,000 jobs" Wall Street Journal, Jan. 3, 1996, p.A-2; John Keller, "ATT Cuts Are Just First Shot in Telecom Wars" Wall Street Journal, Jan. 4, 1996, p.A-2. In all, despite the economic recovery, IBM has cut 100,000 jobs, GM 74,000, Sears 50,000, and Digital 20,000, since 1993. Time, Sept. 4, 1995, p.21. In the recent Wells Fargo takeover of First Interstate Bank in California, the institution has promised to cut 9,000 jobs, as opposed to First Bank of Minneapolis, which only wanted to get rid of 6,000. "This was probably the first big takeover battle ever decided by how many people Wall Street thought each bidder could fire.... Interstate stock closed Friday at more than $40 above its price of $106 before Wells pounced. Wells stock was up almost $20 from its pre-offer price of $207. First Bank has made $190 million. The losers? Guess who? The Interstate and Wells employees who will lose their jobs when the banks are combined. Meanwhile, Wall Street's blood lust for job cuts rages on, looking for its next set of victims." Allan Sloan, "Take This Job and Cut It" Newsweek, Feb. 5, 1996, p.47. In 1992, the Chairman and CEO of HCA received $127 million in total compensation, which is enough to: (a) reduce by 10% the hospital bills of over a quarter of a million patients, (b) pay the full hospital bills of 25,400 patients, or (c) pay the salary of about 6,500 Columbia/HCA employees. "Health Care Costs: Executive Compensation" Health Letter, Vol.12, No.4 (April 1996). Sanford Weill, CEO of Travelers, reaped $41 million in 1995 in stock options alone. "Options for Everyone" Business Week, July 22, 1996, p.81. In 1996, the average total compensation for top execs at big companies rose 54%, to $5.8 million, while ordinary Americans saw pay raises in the area in the 3% to 5% range. See Reingold, "Even Executives Are Wincing at Executive Pay" Business Week, May 12, 1997, p.40. In 1995, the annual total compensation of top executives included: $8.1 million for the CEO of Aetna, $4.8 million for the CEO of CIGNA, $11 million for the CEO of Transamrica, $27.4 million for the CEO of GE, $10.8 million for the CEO of Pfizer, and $9.9 million for the CEO of Exxon. "Executive Pay" The Wall Street Journal, April 11, 1996, pp.R16-R17. Ford's CEO

STEPHEN J. HERMAN

saw his compensation rise 27% in 1996, to $7 million. See Carrig, "Ford CEO Pay" USA Today, April 8, 1997, p.B-1. In 1995, there was 42% gain in corporate profits, which translated to a 10.4% increase in CEO compensation, yet only a 2.9% increase in wages and benefits for the average worker, which was the smallest increase in 14 years. The heads of major companies received 212 times the compensation of the average employee. "Executive Pay" Wall Street Journal, April 11, 1996, p.R1. See also: Tyson, "Why the Wage Gap Just Keeps Getting Bigger" Business Week, Dec.14, 1998, p.22. Disney's CEO received over $100 million in total compensation in 1997. "Why the CEO May Be Worth $100 Million" Business Week, March 2, 1998, p.6. In 1997, the CEO of CIGNA earned $3.27 million in total compensation; the CEO of Progressive earned $2.78 million; the CEO of Travelers $9.5 million; the CEO of Pfizer $3.8 million; the CEO of Philip Morris $3.2 million; the CEO of RJR $2.7 million; the CEO of GE $8 million; the CEO of American Home Products $2.7 million; and Allied Signal $5 million. See "Executive Pay" Wall Street Journal, April 9, 1998, pp.R14-R17. USA Today reported that the CEO of Travelers earned $227.7 million in 1997, including stock options; that the CEO of Disney earned $565 million; and the CEO of Health South earned $106 million. "Travelers CEO Rakes in $228 Million" USA Today, March 5, 1998. The CEO of Conseco earned $119 million. "Conseco's Chairman Hilbert Receives $119 Million in Direct Compensation" Wall Street Journal, April 16, 1998. See also: Sparks, "The Mother of All Stock Option Plans" Business Week, Nov.23, 1998, p.158. In 1997, Philip Morris earned over $6.3 billion. The insurance industry earned almost $20 billion in 1997, including $3.1 billion for Allstate, up 50% from 1996, $1.2 billion for Travelers, up 216% from 1996, $1 billion for CIGNA, $1.3 billion for

The Hartford, and $3.3 billion for the American International Group. "Corporate Scoreboard" Business Week March 2, 1998, pp.110-128. "'Allstate's stock has more than tripled the past three years, outperforming both the S&P 500 and the S&P property and casualty insurance index by wide margins, and in 1997 the company earned a record $3.1 billion on revenues of $25 billion.' The question that comes to mind, of course, is: Why aren't insurance premiums dropping dramatically?" See "More Investigations of Allstate" Advocate, Vol.24, No.6, Aug. 1998, p.1; "A Tornado of a Turnaround" Business Week, March 30, 1998, p.182.

The Winston man once noticed that none of the corporate executives at R.J. Reynolds seemed to smoke. "We don't smoke that shit" one executive told him. "We reserve that right to the young, the poor, the black, and the stupid." See Davis, "Winston Man Repents: He's Now a Tobacco Critic" Times Picayune, Dec. 3, 1995, p.D-16.

"The median, two-paycheck family last year ($52,000 in income) paid Uncle Sam 9.5%, down from 11.5% in 1985, says economist Arthur Hall of the Tax Foundation.... there was no Reagan miracle, says Herbert Stein, senior fellow of the American Enterprise Institute. Total output in the 1980s ran a tad above that of the 1970s but well below the fat 1950s and 1960s, when marginal tax rates were much higher. Compared with other countries, America is lightly taxed. All levels of government collected 31.5 percent of GDP in 1994, compared with 32.3% in Japan and 46.5% in Germany." Jane Bryant Quinn, "Politics: Fable vs. Fact" Newsweek, April 1, 1996, p.62. See also: "Profit Taxes: Crying Wolf" Business Week, July 2, 1996, p.26.

The "multiplier effect" is a "theoretical concept, formulated by John Maynard Keynes, of the effect on national income or employment by an adjustment in overall demand." Websters New World Encyclopedia (College Edition 1993) p.727. It is an "increase in national income divided by the increase in expenditure generating that income. In simple models, the size of the multiplier depends upon the marginal propensity to consume. For example, if the government increased its investment expenditure by L100, this sum would be paid out in wages, salaries, and profits of the suppliers. The households and firms receiving these incomes and profits will, in turn, save a proportion and spend the remainder. These expenditures will in turn again generate further incomes and profits and so on." The Penguin Dictionary of Economics (5th ed. 1992) pp.297-298. The "accelerator-multiplier model" is a model of economic growth which incorporates the effects of both the accelerator principle and the multiplier. "An increase in government expenditure, says, raises consumers' incomes which through the multiplier leads o an increase in out put, which, in turn, through the accelerator, raises investment. This increase in expenditure, in the latter, itself raises incomes and the process is repeated." The Penguin Dictionary of Economics (5th ed. 1992) pp.9-10. "As income increases, other things being equal, consumption will increase, though not at the same rate as income. As income rises, consumers tend to save proportionately more and spend proportionately less and the reverse happens when income falls." Penguin Dictionary of Economics (5th ed. 1992) p.86.

On the tyranny of the corporation, see generally: Standard Oil v. The United States, 221 U.S. 1, 83-84, 31 S.Ct. 502, 525, 55 L.Ed. 619 (1910) (Harlan, concurring); United States v. Columbia Steel Co., 334 U.S. 495, 536, 68 S.Ct. 1107, 1128, 92, L.Ed. 1533 (1948) (Douglas, dissenting); Tyson & Brother v. Banton, 273 U.S. 418, 446, 47 S.Ct. 426, 434, 71 L.Ed. 718 (1927) (Holmes, dissenting); <u>Case of Sutton's Hospital</u>, 5 Rep. 303, 10 Rep. 326 (1612); Lasseter, "Power Play Incorporated" <u>ABA Journal</u> May 1997, p.112; Shrager & Frost, <u>The Quotable Lawyer</u> (1986) p.27.

Bill Richards, "Shareholder Law Raises Hurdle for Top Killer of Class Actions" <u>Wall Street Journal</u>, Jan. 4, 1996, p.B-1.

The *Contract* seeks to restrict the average person's access to the courts by placing economic and substantive legal barriers, such as caps on damages, abrogation of joint and several liability, giving preemptive effect to the presence or lack of government regulation, interference with the contingency fee arrangement, and the imposition of a loser pay rule. See generally: Newt Gingrich, Dick Armey, and House Republicans, <u>Contract with America</u> (Times Books 1994) pp.143-155. "Americans spend an estimated $300 billion a year in needlessly higher prices for products and services as a result of excessive legal costs." <u>Contract with America</u>, p.143. The $300 billion figure in the *Contract* is manipulated and exaggerated from another assertion by former vice-President Dan Quayle, which was itself erroneous, misleading, and never supported by any social or economic study, summary, or report. See Marc Galanter, "The Public View or Lawyers" <u>Trial</u> April 1992. In fact, the total cost of all litigation, including judgments and settlements, attorneys fees on both sides, court costs, and the value of time litigants spend dealing with lawsuits, is somewhere between $28 billion and $35 billion per year. Testimony of James S. Kalalik, Rand Corporation Institute for Civil Justice, before the Joint Economic Committee, United States Congress, July 29, 1986.Not only does the *Contract* actually seek to expand a corporation's access to the courts to challenge government regulation, but also affords the corporation a right of action against the government, to collect damages incidental to agency investigation. See generally: Newt Gingrich, Dick Armey, and House Republicans, Contract with America, pp.125-141 (1994); Sharon Begley, "Of Helmets & Hanburger" Newsweek July 24, 1995; Anthony Lewis, "Are Americans Looking Up to the Radical Reality?" Times Picayune, Aug. 1, 1995, p.B-5.

"Though a company is typically richer and more powerful than the individual, its wealth provides it no particular advantage before a jury that is randomly picked from the community. The company can't buy the jury's protection, as it conceivably might buy the loyalty of an elected state judge who's dependent on campaign contributions. And it can't benefit from social connections at the top of society that's shared by corporate and judicial officials but not by the average juror." Stephen J. Adler, The Jury (Doubleday 1994) p.146. See also: Pacific Mutual v. Haslip, 499 U.S. 1, 40-41, 111 S.Ct. 1032, 1055, 113 L.Ed.2d 1 (1991) (Scalia, concurring); Parklane Hosiery v. Shore, 439 U.S. 322, 343-344, 99 S.Ct. 645, 657-658, 58 L.Ed.2d 552 (1979) (Renquist, dissenting); Oliver Wendell Holmes, Collected Legal Papers (1920) p.237; Theil v. Southern Pacific, 328 U.S. 217, 227, 66 S.Ct. 984, 989, 90 L.Ed. 1181 (1946) (Frankfurter, dissenting); Railroad Company v. Stout, 84 U.S. 657, 664, 21 L.Ed. 745 (1873); John F. Geeting, 69 Albany Law Journal 134 (1907); Delphin Delmas, The Democracy of Justice - The Jury 6 Ken.L.J. 245, 249-250 (1918). "One bad Federal Judge can do a lot more damage than a jury who goes crazy in one case." Judge Martin Feldman, Eastern District of Louisiana, It' the Law Oct. 23, 1995. Judge Feldman also noted that, in thirteen years on the bench, he has only disagreed with the jury on two occasions.

Network, © Copyright 1976, by Metro-Goldwyn-Meyer and United Artists, written by Paddy Chayefsky, produced by Howard Gottfried, and directed by Sidney Lumet.

The Verdict, © Copyright 1982 by 20th Century Fox, written by David Mamet, based on the novel by Barry Reed, produced by Richard Zanuck & David Brown, and directed by Sidney Lumet.

XI. Chapter Eleven: The Private Attorney General

The class action serves an important function in our system of civil justice. Gulf Oil v. Bernard, 452 U.S. 89, 99, 101 S.Ct. 2193, 2199, 68 L.Ed.2d 693 (1981). The right to file a class action originated in equity, with the objective of addressing small wrongs that otherwise might go unredressed. Over the years, the device has developed as an effective means of both protecting consumers and promoting judicial economy. Class actions prevent duplicative proceedings and endless repetition of common issues. Class actions allow plaintiffs to combine their efforts and resources, and thereby obtain adequate, knowledgeable and skillful representation for those who could not otherwise afford to retain counsel in pursuit of their legitimate claims. Class actions provide a forum for the redress of grievances, and, through the notice process, advise individuals that they may have been the victims of latent injury or fraud. Class actions tend to clarify the issues for the court, which can better see both the significance of the claims and the consequences of imposing liability. Class actions are often the only means for assuring that a corporation which has harmed many individuals will not benefit from its tortious conduct. And class actions ensure consistent results in litigation, whereas individual cases permit the defendant to play the odds in many jurisdictions. See generally: Phillips Petroleum Co. v. Shutts, 472 U.S. 797, 809, 105 S.Ct. 2965, 2973, 86 L.Ed.2d 628 (1985); Deposit Guaranty National Bank v. Roper, 445 U.S. 326, 338-339, 100 S.Ct. 1166, 1174, 63 L.Ed.2d 427 (1980); Sterling v. Velsicol Chemicals, 855 F.2d 1188, 1196-1197 (6th Cir. 1988); Phillips v. Joint Legislative Committee, 637 F.2d 1014 (5th Cir. 1981); Eisen v. Carlisle & Jacquelin, 391 F.2d 555, 560 (2nd Cir.

1968); Montgomery Ward v. Langer, 168 F.2d 187 (8th Cir. 1948); In re "Agent Orange" Products Liability Litigation, 597 F.Supp. 740, 841-842 (E.D.N.Y. 1984), aff'd, 818 F.2d 145 (2nd Cir. 1987), cert. denied, 484 U.S. 1004 (1988); Sala v. National Railroad Passenger Corp., 120 F.R.D. 494, 499 (E.D. Pa. 1988); Vasquez v. Superior Court, 4 Cal.3d 800, 807-808, 484 P.2d 964, 968-969, 94 Cal.Rptr. 796 (1971); Fletcher v. Security Pacific National Bank, 23 Cal.3d 442, 451-452, 591 P.2d 51, 57, 153 Cal.Rept. 28 (1979); In re Cadillac V8-6-4 Class Action, 93 N.J. 412, 426 (1983); Riley v. New Rapids Carpet Center, 61 N.J. 218, 225 (1972); McCastle v. Rollins Environmental Services, 456 So.2d 612, 618 (La. 1984); Eshaghi v. Hanley Dawson Cadillac, 574 N.E.2d 760 (Ill. App. 1st Dist. 1991). "Modern society seems increasingly to expose men to... group injuries for which individually they are in a poor position to seek legal redress, either because they do not know enough or because such redress is disproportionately expensive. If each is left to assert his rights alone if and when he can, there will at best be a random and fragmentary enforcement, if there is any at all. The result is not only unfortunate in the particular case, but it will operate seriously to impair the deterrent effect of the sanctions which underlie much contemporary law. The problem of fashioning an effective and inclusive group remedy is thus a major one." Kalven and Rosenfield, Function of Class Suit, 8 U.Chi.L.Rev. 684, 686 (1941). "The use of the class-action procedure for litigation of individual claims may offer substantial advantages for named plaintiffs; it may motivate them to bring cases that for economic reasons might not be brought otherwise.... A significant benefit to claimants who choose to litigate their individual claims in a class-action context is the prospect of reducing their costs of litigation, particularly attorney's fees, by allocating such costs among all members of the class who benefit from any recovery.... For better or worse, the financial incentive that class actions offer to the legal profession is a natural outgrowth of the increasing reliance on the "private attorney general" for the vindication of legal rights.... [It] is an evolutionary response to the existence of injuries unremedied by regulatory action of government. Where it is not economically feasible to obtain relief within the traditional framework of a multiplicity of small individual suits for damages, aggrieved persons may be without any effective redress unless they may employ the class action device." De-posit Guaranty v. Roper, 445 U.S. at 338-339, 100 S.Ct. at 1174. See also: Phillips Petroleum v. Shutts, 472 U.S. at 809, 105 S.Ct. at 2973. The alternatives, (including joinder, intervention, consolidation, and the use of a test case), often do not sufficiently protect the legal rights of the aggrieved parties, because they "presuppose a group of economically powerful parties who are obviously able and willing to take care of their own interests individually through individual suits." Vasquez, 4 Cal.3d at 808, 484 P.2d at 968; Doglow v. Anderson, 43 F.R.D. 472, 484 (E.D.N.Y. 1968). "To permit the defendants to contest liability with each claimant in a single, separate suit, would, in many cases give defendants an advantage which would be almost equivalent to closing the door of justice to all small claimants. This is what we think the class suit practice was to prevent." Roper v. Conurve, Inc., 578 F.2d 1106, 1114-1116 (5th Cir. 1978), aff'd, 445 U.S. 326, 100 S.Ct. 1166, 63 L.Ed.2d 427 (1980); Hohmann v. Packard Instrument, 399 F.2d 711, 715 (7th Cir. 1968); Weeks v. Bareco Oil Company, 125 F.2d 84, 90 (7th Cir. 1941).

A class action can be certified for the limited purpose of resolving some, but not all issues, which may be common to the class. Basic liability on the part of the defendant, for example, may be established on a class-wise basis. Then, the class members, if successful, may conduct small individual trials, to prove causation and damages. Alternatively, the court can adopt "pilot" cases, bellwether trials, sub-classification by injury (or other factors), the use of a special master, and/or other administrative procedures for the ultimate adjudication of claims. See generally: Fed. Rule Civ. Pro. 23(c)(4); Manual for Complex Litigation, Third (Federal Judicial Center 1995) §§30.17,33.28; Newberg on Class Actions §§ 4.26, 9.51-9.70 (3rd ed. 1992).

The fee awarded in class actions in generally 25% to 30% of the recovery, (as opposed to the ordinary 33% to 40% contingency fee in individual cases). See generally: Manual For Complex Litigation, Third (Federal Judicial Center 1995) §24.12 (courts have generally awarded 25%-30% of the fund); In re Catfish Antitrust Litigation, 939 F. Supp. 493, 500 (N.D. Miss. 1996) (benchmark of 25%); In re Activision Securities Litigation, 723 F. Supp. 1373, 1375 (N.D. Cal. 1989) (benchmark of 30%). See also: In re Warner Communications Securities Litigation, 618 F. Supp. 735, 749-750 (S.D.N.Y. 1995), aff'd, 798 F.2d 35 (2nd Cir. 1996).

On attorney John Deakle and what appear to be collusive abuses of the class action device to protect big business, on the one hand, and to generate attorneys fees, on the other, at the expense of the class, see: Starkman, "Lawyer Fees Assailed in BankAmerica Pact" Wall Street Journal, April 10, 1997, p.B-2; Chen, "Counsel Take Less in Fees, B of A Plaintiffs Get More" Daily Journal, April 21, 1997, p.1; "TLPJ Defeats Settlement" Public Justice Winter 1998, p.3.

The settlement of any class action must be approved by the court. Fed. Rule Civ. Pro 23(e). The court, in deciding whether to approve the settlement, considers such things as: the stage of the proceedings and the amount of

discovery completed; the factual and legal obstacles to
prevailing on the merits; the complexity, expense, and
likely duration of trial; the possible range of recovery;
and the respective opinions of the participants, including class counsel, class representatives, and absent class
members. Parker v. Anderson, 667 F.2d 1204, 1209 (5th
Cir. 1982); Pettway v. American Cast Iron, 576 F.2d 1157
(5th Cir. 1978).

"Class actions are absolutely essential to the achievement of justice. In many circumstances, including where
large numbers of people have suffered small amounts of
damage or require injunctive relief, they are the only way
that justice can be obtained. If class actions cannot be
brought, then widespread wrongdoing will often go uncorrected, unpunished, and undeterred.... The single best
way to stop class action abuse is for judges to take seriously their fiduciary duty to protect class members and
their rights. Judges must make sure that the class action
rules and the Constitution are satisfied; that any proposed
settlement truly is fair, reasonable, and adequate; and that
attorneys fees are properly based on the recovery actually obtained for the class. If they want justice to be done
judges must also certify class actions when the legal criteria are met. The solution to class action abuse is not to
eliminate class actions. That only hurts the class members
in a different way.... The problem is not class actions; it's
class action abuse." Arthur Bryant, Public Justice, Winter
1998, p.2.

For Judge Posner's concerns about a jury's ability to
hold the fate of an entire industry in the palm of its hand,
see In the Matter of Rhone-Poulenc Rorer, 51 F.3d 1293,
1299-1300 (7th Cir. 1995). But see: In re Copley, 161
F.R.D. 456, 460 n.4 (D.Wyo. 1995) ("Judge Posner's ap-

prehension... is simply not a legal basis to deny certification. This reasoning also shows a profound mistrust in the jury system."); In re Telectronics, 168 F.R.D. 203, 210 (S.D.Ohio 1996) ("It causes this Court pause that one of the nation's most respected jurists has lost faith in the very system in which he participates.... While Judge Posner's economic theories and distrust of juries may carry weight in the Seventh Circuit, we are still bound by the Federal Rules of Civil Procedure").

In the determination of whether a class action is superior to other available methods of adjudication, the court considers: (a) the interest of the class members in individually controlling the litigation, (b) the nature and extent of existing litigation by putative class members, (c) the desirability of concentrating the litigation in the particular forum, and (d) the difficulties likely to be encountered in the management of the class. Fed. Rule Civ. Pro. 23(b)(3). Many courts have indicated that, because class actions were principally designed to allow for the aggregation of otherwise unenforceable claims, the appropriateness of class certification is largely determined by the first factor – *i.e.* the value of the individual claims. See, for example: Amchem v. Windsor, 117 S.Ct. 2231, 2246, 138 L.Ed.2d 689 (1997).

On the tremendous costs associated with the prosecution of products liability litigation against the tobacco industry, see: Thayer v. Liggett & Myers, No. 5314 (W.D. Mich. Feb. 19, 1970), 1.2 TLPR 2.63 (1986); Haines v. Liggett, 814 F.Supp. 414 (D.N.J. 1993); Bothwell v. Republic Tobacco, 912 F.Supp. 1221 (D.Neb. 1995); Patricia Gray, "Tobacco Firms Defend Smoker Liability Suits With Heavy Artillery" Wall Street Journal, April 29, 1987; Charles Strum, "Major Lawsuit on Smoking is Dropped"

<u>New York Times</u>, Nov. 6, 1992; Alison Frankel, "Was Budd Larner Asnother Smoking Victim?" <u>New Jersey Law Journal</u>, July 12, 1993; Glen Collins, "A Tobacco Case's Legal Buccaneers" <u>New York Times</u>, March 6, 1995, p.C-3; Schwartz and Torry, "Anti-Tobacco Activists Hope to Put Industry's Legal Tactics on Trial" <u>Washington Post</u>, Sept. 26, 1995; Rabin, <u>A Sociolegal History of Tobacco Tort Litigation</u>, 44 Stan.L.Rev. 853 (1992); Tucker S. Player, <u>After the Fall: The Cigarette Papers, the Global Settlement, and the Future of Tobacco Litigation</u>, 49 S.C.L.Rev. 311 (1998).

On the potential conflicts between legislative and judicial roles in the resolution of broad social problems, such as the injury and death caused by exposure to asbestos, see generally: John C. Coffee, Jr., "The Corruption of the Class Action" <u>Wall Street Journal</u> Sept. 7, 1994; <u>Georgine v. Amchem Products</u>, 83 F.3d 610, 634 (3rd Cir. 1996), *aff'd,* <u>Amchem v. Windsor</u>, 117 S.Ct. 2231, 138 L.Ed.2d 689 (1997); <u>Flanagan v. Ahearn (In re Asbestos Litigation)</u>, 90 F.3d 963, 993 (5th Cir. 1996), *vacated,* 117 S.Ct. 2503 (1997), *on remand,* 134 F.3d 668 (5th Cir. 1998); <u>Report of the Judicial Conference Ad Hoc Committee on Asbestos Litigation</u> (March 1991). See also: Higgins, "Mass Tort Makeover?" <u>ABA Journal</u>, Nov.1998, p.53.

"Did you expect a corporation to have a conscience, when it has no soul to be damned and no body to be kicked?" Edward Thurlow, (Wilberface, <u>Life of Thurlow</u> (1775)). "Corporations cannot commit treason, nor be outlawed, nor excommunicated, for they have no souls." Sir Edward Coke, <u>Case of Sutton's Hospital</u>, 5 Rep. 303, 10 Rep. 326 (1612). "A corporation cannot blush. It has a body, it is true; it certainly has a head – a new one every year; arms it has and very long ones, for it can reach at anything; a throat to swallow the rights of the community, and a stomach to digest them! But who ever yet discovered, in the anatomy of any corporation, either bowels or a heart?" Howell Walsh (1825) (Shrager & Frost, The Quotable Lawyer (1986) p.27). "Corporate bodies are more corrupt and profligate than individuals, because they have more power to do mischief, and are less amenable to disgrace or punishment." William Hazlitt, (Earle Lasseter, "Power Play Incorporated" ABA Journal, May 1997, p.112.) "The notion that a business is clothed with a public interest and has been devoted to public use is little more than a fiction intended to beautify what is disagreeable to the sufferers." Tyson & Brother v. Banton, 273 U.S. 418, 446, 47 S.Ct. 426, 434, 71 L.Ed. 718 (1927) (Holmes, dissenting). "Corporate bodies are more corrupt and profligate than individuals, because they have more power to do mischief, and are less amenable to disgrace or punishment." William Hazlitt, (Lasseter, "Power Play Incorporated" ABA Journal May 1997, p.112). See also: Standard Oil v. The United States, 221 U.S. 1, 83-84, 31 S.Ct. 502, 525, 55 L.Ed. 619 (1910) (Harlan, concurring); United States v. Columbia Steel Co., 334 U.S. 495, 536, 68 S.Ct. 1107, 1128, 92, L.Ed. 1533 (1948) (Douglas, dissenting).

On the fraud perpetrated by BMW and a history and analysis of the assessment of punitive damages, see BMW v. Gore, 517 U.S. 559, 116 S.Ct. 1589, 134 L.Ed.2d 809 (1996).Despite Dow Corning's claims that the implants would "last a lifetime", it has been found that one-third to one-half of all implants rupture or leak silicone gel within 10 years, and that, after 10 years, the number increases between 64% and 96%. Allegations of rare connective tissue disease notwithstanding, it is undisputed that implants cause capsular contraption and other local problems, including infection, destruction of nipple tissue, and chronic pain. Twenty-four percent of women require additional surgery to replace ruptured implants or correct other problems. And the implants limit cancer detection by compromising, (by 25% to 35%), the effectiveness of a mammography. After Dow Corning offered to establish a $4.2 billion fund to compensate women with breast implants, the Mayo Clinic released a study by comparing the medical records of 749 women who had received breast implants with the records of 1,498 women who had not. The researchers found "no association between breast implants and the connective tissue diseases that were studied." However, the researchers also noted their limited ability to detect an increased risk of rare connective tissue diseases, which would require a sample of 62,000 women with implants and 124,000 without them – 83 times the sample that was studied. Due to the flaws in this and other studies, the FDA released an exhaustive report in 1996 in which it was concluded that "no implant study has ruled out an increased risk of connective tissue disease." Harvard researchers then conducted a study which included a sample of 10,830 women with breast implants, which revealed a 24 percent increase in lupus, scleroderma, and rheumatoid arthritis. "This increase is small by statistical standards, but the real figure could be higher because, like other researchers, this group looked only for classic symptoms, not the atypical connective tissue disease that many women with implants have reported." Michael Castlema, "Implanted Evidence" Mother Jones, Jan/Feb 1998, p.25.

A study of verdicts in the 45 largest counties in the U.S. found that punitive damages were awarded in just 6% of the cases where plaintiffs were successful, (i.e. only 3% of all trials). "Unless the case involves an intentional tort or a business-related tort (such as employment claims)" the study's author concluded, "punitive damages will almost never be awarded." The study found a strong correlation between compensatory and punitive damages, (with punitive verdicts generally running about 40% higher than compensatory awards), and noted that the absence of any large, headline-grabbing awards in such a broad sample "suggests that the punitive damage cases emphasized in the media are newsworthy precisely because they are so rare, and because they depart from an explicable underlying pattern of awards." Theodore Eisenberg, The Predictability of Punitive Damages (1996) (published in the *Journal of Legal Studies*, Vol.26, p.623 (1997)). See also: Erik Moller, Trends in Jury Verdicts Since 1985, Rand Institute for Civil Justice (1996); Galanter and Luban, Poetic Justice: Punitive Damages and the Public Trust Am.U.L.Rev. Vol.42 (1993); Theodore Eisenberg, The Predictability of Punitive Damages (1996) (published in the *Journal of Legal Studies*, Vol.26, p.623 (1997)); Rustad and Koenig, "Punitive Damages in Products Liability" Products Liability law Journal, Vol.3, No.2 (Feb. 1992); Peterson, Sarma & Shanley, Punitive Damages, Empirical Findings, Rand Institute for Civil Justice (1987); Hensler and Moller, Trends in Punitive Damages: Preliminary Data From Cook County, Illinois, and San Francisco, California, Rand Institute for Civil Justice (March 1995); "Punitive Damages 'Crisis' is a Myth, Scholars Say" Trial, Dec. 1996, p.14; Mark Thompson, "Applying the Brakes to Punitives: But Is There Anything to Slow Down?" ABA Journal, Sept. 1997, p.68; Ostrom, Rottmann & Hanson, "What Are Tort Awards Really Like" Law and Policy Vol.14, pp.77,83 (1992); Daniels and Martin, Empirical Patterns in Punitive Damage Cases: A Description of Incidence Rates and Awards, American Bar Foundation Paper No. 8705 (1987); Daniels and Martin, Myth and Reality in Punitive Damages, 75 Minn.L.Rev. 1 (1990); National Center for State Courts, Examining the Work of State Courts, 1994, Pub. No. R-178 (1996); Rustad, Demys-

344   STEPHEN J. HERMAN

tifying Punitive Damages in Products Liability Cases,
Roscoe Pound Foundation (1991); Stephen Daniels and
Joanne Martin, Civil Juries and the Politics of Reform
(1995); Bureau of Justice Statistics Special Report: Civil
Justice Survey of State Courts, 1992 (1995); Shanley and
Peterson, Comparative Justice, Civil Jury Verdicts in San
Francisco and Cook Counties 1959-1980, Rand Corpora-
tion (1983); Peterson and Priest, The Civil Jury, Trends
in Trials and Verdicts, Cook County, Illinois, 1960-1979,
Rand Corporation (1982).

Ford calculated that a death would cost $200,000, (180
deaths annually), a burn injury $67,000, (180 annually),
and damaged vehicles $700, (2,100 annually), for a to-
tal cost of $49.5 million, while the cost of correcting the
problem, (at $11 per vehicle – although a different memo
estimated that the cost would only be $5.08 to $9.95 per
vehicle), would have been $137 million. Grush and Saun-
by, Ford Department of Environmental and Safety Engineering, Fatalities Associated with Crash Induced Fuel
Leakage and Fires. See also: Dowie, "Pinto Madness"
Mother Jones, Sept/Oct 1977; Walsh & Weiser, "Court
Secrecy Masks Safety Issues: Key GM Fuel Tank Memo
Kept Hidden in Auto Crash Suit" Washington Post Oct.
23, 1988; Nader and Smith, No Contest (Random House
1996) pp.70-73.

Senator John Breaux, quoted in Bruce Alpert, "Senate Oks Capping Damage Settlements" Times Picayune
March 22, 1996, p.A-8.

"Our legal tradition is one of progress from fiat to ra-
tionality. The evolution of the jury illustrates this principle. From the 13th or 14th century onward, the verdict
of the jury found gradual acceptance not as a matter of
ipse dixit, the basis for verdicts in trial by ordeal which
the jury came to displace, but instead because the verdict

was based on rational principles. Elements of whim and
caprice do not predominate when the jury reaches a consensus based upon arguments of counsel, the presentation
of evidence, and instructions from the trial judge, subject
to review by the trial and appellate courts. There is a prin-
cipled justification too in the composition of the jury, for
its representative character permits its verdicts to express
the sense of the community.... 'It is not surprising that
such collective judgments are often difficult to explain.
But the inherent unpredictability of jury decisions does
not justify their condemnation. On the contrary, it is the
jury's function to make the difficult and uniquely human
judgments that defy codification and that build discretion,
equity, and flexibility into the legal system.'" Pacific Mutual v. Haslip, 499 U.S. 1, 40-41, 111 S.Ct. 1032, 1055,
113 L.Ed.2d 1 (1991) (Scalia, J., concurring); McKlesky
v. Kemp, 481 U.S. 279, 311, 107 S.Ct. 1756, 1777, 95
L.Ed.2d 262 (1987); Kalven & Zeisel, The American Jury
(1966) p.498; Plucknett, A Concise History of the Common Law (5th ed. 1956) pp.120-131. "The day of manipulating a jury is over, if there ever was such a day. Cases
are won through preparation, dragging the facts into the
courtroom. The lawyer excavates the facts, and the more
he digs, the more certain he is to win; and then he can
pound upon the facts and an emotional appeal – that's the
way of persuasion. But to play clever with a jury when
you don't have the facts leaves them cold. They resent
it." Louis Nizer, San Francisco Examiner, May 29, 1974.
See also: Parklane Hosiery v. Shore, 439 U.S. 322, 343-
344, 99 S.Ct. 645, 657-658, 58 L.Ed.2d 552 (1979) (Renquist, dissenting); Oliver Wendell Holmes, Collected Legal Papers (1920) p.237; Theil v. Southern Pacific, 328
U.S. 217, 227, 66 S.Ct. 984, 989, 90 L.Ed. 1181 (1946)
(Frankfurter, dissenting); Railroad Company v. Stout, 84
U.S. 657, 664, 21 L.Ed. 745 (1873); John F. Geeting, 69

Albany Law Journal 134 (1907); Delphin Delmas, The Democracy of Justice - The Jury 6 Ken.L.J. 245, 249-250 (1918).

For the legal, social, historical, philosophical, and economic theories underlying the recovery of punitive damages, see generally: Jonathan Massey, "Why Tradition Supports Punitive Damages" Trial, Sept. 1995, p.19; Pacific Mutual v. Haslip, 499 U.S. 1, 111 S.Ct. 1032, 113 L.Ed.2d 1 (1991); BMW v. Gore, 517 U.S. 559, 116 S.Ct. 1589, 134 L.Ed.2d 809 (1996); David Owen, A Punitive Damages Overview: Functions, Problems, and Reform, 39 Vill.L.Rev. 363 (1994); Posner, An Economic Theory of Criminal Law 85 Colum.L.Rev. 1193 (1995); Philip Ackerman, Some Don't Like It Hot: Louisiana Eliminates Punitive Damages for Environmental Torts, 72 Tul.L.Rev. 327 (1997); Hager and Miltenberg, "Punitive Damages and the Free Market: A Law and Economics Perspective" Trial, Sept. 1995, p.30.

The State of California has incorporated a private attorney general component into its Business and Professions Code, which permits a private plaintiff who has himself suffered no injury to bring an action to enforce the law and obtain relief on behalf of the public at large. See generally: Cal. Bus. and Prof. Code §17200, *et seq.;* Stop Youth Addiction v. Lucky Stores, 17 Cal.4th 553, 731 P.2d 1086, 71 Cal.Rptr.2d 731 (1998); Committee on Children's Television v. General Foods, 35 Cal.3d 197, 673 P.2d 660, 197 Cal.Rptr. 783 (1983).

For the management of consolidated, class action, or other complex litigation, through the appointment of lead counsel, liaison counsel, and/or a plaintiffs' steering committee, see generally: Manual for Complex Litigation, Third (Federal Judicial Center 1995) §§20.22,33.24;

Newberg on Class Actions §§9.31-9.36 (3rd ed. 1992).

Under the equitable "common fund" or "common benefit" doctrine, counsel whose efforts obtain, protect, preserve or make available a substantial benefit to a class of persons are entitled to an attorney's fee based upon the worth of the benefit to the class. Boeing Co. v. Van Gemert, 444 U.S. 472, 100 S.Ct. 745, 62 L.Ed.2d 676 (1980); Trustees v. Greenough, 105 U.S. 527, 26 L.Ed. 1157 (1881). See also: "Common Fund and Substantial Benefit" Awarding Attorneys' Fees and Managing Fee Litigation (Federal Judicial Center 1995) pp.49-85. The "lodestar" approach, by contrast, is achieved by multiplying the number of hours expended by the attorneys times each attorney's customary hourly rate. The court then adjusts the lodestar upward or downward, depending on the respective weight of the twelve factors outlined in the Rules of Professional Conduct, Rule 1.5, and Johnson v. Georgia Highway Express, Inc., 488 F.2d 714 (5th Cir. 1974). See generally: Lindy Bros. v. American Radiator & Standard, ("Lindy I"), 487 F.2d 161 (3rd Cir. 1973), aff'd, in part, vacated, in part, 540 F.2d 102 (3rd Cir. 1976) ("Lindy II"); Kerr v. Screen Extras Guild, 526 F.2d 67 (9th Cir. 1975), cert. denied, 425 U.S. 951, 96 S.Ct. 1726, 48 L.Ed.2d 195 (1976). Courts have noted that, for many reasons, the percentage-of-benefit method is preferable in complex actions, particularly in "common fund" cases, where the attorneys' fee is awarded from the class' recovery, (i.e. the common fund), as opposed to a statutory fee award, (such as an anti-trust case, for example), where the attorneys' fee is ordered to be paid by the defendant, over and above the damages recovered by the class. The trend, therefore, is to award a percentage of the benefits obtained on behalf of the class members, which is generally 25% - 30% of the fund. See generally: Manual For Complex Litigation, Third (Federal Judicial

Center 1995) §24.12; <u>Swedish Hospital Corp. v. Shalala</u>, 1 F.3d 1261, 1269 (D.C. Cir. 1993); <u>In re Catfish Antitrust Litigation</u>, 939 F. Supp. 493, 500 (N.D. Miss. 1996); <u>In re Warner Communications</u>, 618 F.Supp 735 (D.C.N.Y. 1985), *aff'd,* 798 F.2d 35 (2nd Cir. 1996); <u>Longden v. Sunderman</u>, 979 F.2d 1095, 1099 n.9 (5th Cir. 1992).

With respect to the *cy pres* doctrine, see generally: <u>Black's Law Dictionary</u> (6th ed. 1990) p.387; Stewart Shepherd, <u>Damage Distribution in Class Actions: The *Cy Pres* Remedy</u>, 39 U.Chi.L.Rev. 448 (1972); Patricia Sturdevant, "Using the *Cy Pres* Doctrine to Fund Consumer Advocacy" <u>Trial</u>, Nov. 1997, p.80

XII. Chapter Twelve: The Betrayed Profession

The Betrayed Profession, by Sol Linowitz, (Charles Scribner's Sons 1994).

Attorneys fees must be reasonable, in light of the time and labor expended by each attorney, as well as the novelty and difficulty of the questions involved, the skill requisite to perform the legal service properly, the preclusion of other employment by the attorney due to acceptance of the case, the limitations imposed by the clients and the circumstances, the amount involved and the results obtained, the experience and reputation and abilities of the attorneys, the nature and length of the professional relationship with the client, and fees in similar cases. See ABA Model Rules of Professional Conduct Profession Rule 1.5.

Jonathan Harr, A Civil Action (Vintag 1995); Sharon Begley, "A Lawsuit Toxic to Justice" Newsweek, Oct. 2, 1995, p.89.

Ford determined that a human life was worth $200,000, a burn injury $67,000. Grush and Saunby, Ford Department of Environmental and Safety Engineering, Fatalities Associated with Crash Induced Fuel Leakage and Fires. See also: Dowie, "Pinto Madness" Mother Jones, Sept/ Oct 1977; Walsh & Weiser, "Court Secrecy Masks Safety Issues: Key GM Fuel Tank Memo Kept Hidden in Auto Crash Suit" Washington Post Oct. 23, 1988; Nader and Smith, No Contest (Random House 1996) pp.70-73.
"It's impossible to form a public relations campaign to blame 50,000 women, so you blame their lawyers." Attorney Chris Parks, quoted in Sharon Cohen, "Norplant

Sales Fall Due to Lawsuits" Times Picayune Oct. 1, 1995.
See also: Letter from Congressman Dick Armey to Members of the House, Oct. 1, 1997; Susan Garland, "Chamber of Commerce Battle Cry: Kill All the Lawyers" Business Week, March 2, 1998, p.53; Terry Carter, "A Lesson Learned" ABA Journal, May 1998, p.70.

Between 1989 and 1994, the Association of Trial Lawyers of America ("ATLA") made a total of $40 million in Congressional campaign contributions. During that same time period, the American Tort Reform Association ("ATRA") and the Product Liability Alliance made a total of $62 million in contributions to Congressional campaigns. Henry Reske, "A Classic Battle of Lobbyists" ABA Journal June 1995, p.22. When a national Products Liability Act was vetoed by President Clinton, Bob Dole attacked him for submitting to "enormous pressure from the wealthiest and most powerful special-interest group in America: the trial lawyers." Yet, "big money interests on both sides of the issue contributed heavily to lawmakers. A coalition of businesses supporting limits on jury awards donated $4.8 million to federal candidates during the first half of 1995, according to the Center for Responsive Politics. The political action committee for the Association of Trial Lawyers of America gave only $191,850 during that same period." Bruce Alpert, "Senate Okays Capping Damage Settlements" Times Picayune March 22, 1996, p.A-8. For the first half of 1997, the AMA topped the list of organizations, with $8.5 million in campaign contributions, followed by the Chamber of Commerce, with $7 million, Philip Morris, with $5.9 million, GM, with $5.2 million, Edison Electric, with $5 million, Pfizer, with $4.6 million, United Technologies, with $4.1 million, and GE, with $4.1 million. Other big spenders include Ford, Exxon, Texaco, Citicorp, Boeing, the Christian Coalition, AARP, the American Hospital Association, the Association of American Railroads, and the Pharmaceutical Research and Manufacturers Association. ATLA is not even on the list. See "Doctors Lobby Tops List of 30 Biggest Spenders" Times Picayune, March 7, 1998, p.C-8. See also: Jim Drinkard, "Lobbyists Spend $1.2 Billion, Study Shows" Times Picayune, March 7, 1998, p.C-8; The Advocate, March 7, 1998.

The vice-President and general counsel of the American Tort Reform Association ("ATRA") is a former top executive and attorney for RJR. ATRA's other members include Aetna, GEICO, Nationwide Insurance, Transamerica, Eli Lilly, Exxon, Mobil, Dow, Philip Morris, Johnson & Johnson, Monsanto, Pfizer, Union Carbide, the Amercian Hospital Association, the American Nurses Association, the AMA, Boeing, Cooper, Litton, and GE. See John Gannon, Tort Deform - Lethal Bedfellows Essential Information (1995). "If State Farm or Nationwide is the leader of the coalition" explains Neal Cohen of Apco Associates, "you're not going to pass the bill. It is not credible." So they hire a Washington firm, like Apco Associates, to organize a coalition of small businesses, nonprofit groups, and individuals, in order to put a sympathetic face on the proposed measures, while the large companies who are really calling the shots recede into the background. "In 1993, Cohen began a blitzkrieg public attack on 'greedy' trial lawyers, on behalf of a coalition he called 'Mississippians for a Fair Legal System.' He advertised for members with an 800 number on billboards carrying slogans like 'Fairness, Yes. Greed, No.' It cost nothing to join. 'You just sign your name on a form that said you're a member.' The effort took Mississippi lawyers completely by surprise. 'They didn't really know who was at the heart of everything, and there were no reporting requirements.' In the end, Cohen said, 'we have 1,500 Mississippians mixed in with who our clients were.'" ATRA calls itself a broad-based national coalition of local organizations, large and small businesses, school boards and others. "But the legislation that will go to the Senate floor will do little for those in the coalition, like the School Board or the Little League Team afraid of being sued. The legislation would limit only product liability lawsuits, claims that a poorly manufactured or dangerous product has caused an injury. So if the bill becomes law, the victors will largely be tobacco companies, manufacturers, and insurance companies." Jane Fritsch, "Sometimes, Lobbyists Strive to Keep Public In the Dark" New York Times, March 19, 1996, p.A-1. State Farm has contributed $3.6 million to People for a Fair Legal System. See Steven Griffith, "State Farm's Motives Are Less Than Saintly" Times Picayune, June 26, 1996, p.B-6. See also, generally: Chesebro, Galileo's Report: Peter Huber's Junk Scholarship, 42 Am.U.L.Rev. 1637 (1993); Galanter, An Oil Strike in Hell: Contemporary Legends About the Civil Justice System, 40 Ariz.L.Rev. 717 (1998); Rustad, Nationalizing Tort Law: The Republicans Attack on Women, Blue Collar Workers and Consumers, 48 Rutgers L.Rev. 673 (1996); Ivins, "Clinton Earns a Reprieve for Quashing Tort Reform" Seattle Times, March 25, 1996, p.B-5; Daniels, "The Question of Jury Competence and the Politics of Civil Justice Reform: Symbols, Rhetoric, and Agenda Building" Law and Contemporary Problems, Vol.52, p.269 (1989); "Grassroots 'Weeds' Need to be Clipped, Say Angry Activists" O'Dweyer's PR Service Reporter (June 1996); Guerry, "Corporate Ads Attack Civil Justice System" Louisiana Advocates, Feb. 1999, p.2; "Follow the Money... And the Anti-Trial Lawyer Rhetoric" Louisiana Advocates, Feb. 1999, p.12.

Benjamin Weiser, "Judge Imposes a Rare Sanction in

GM Upcoming Pick-up Truck Trial" Washington Post, Sept. 10, 1995, p.A.-9.

The law firm of Wachtell, Lipton earned $1.4 million per partner in 1994, while the Cravath law firm earned $1.2 million per partner, and Skadden, Arps earned over $800,000. Amy Stevens, "Law Firms Regain Profit Margins" Times Picayune May 4, 1995, p.C-3. In-house general counsel for large corporations, in 1994, earned the following: General counsel for Merrill Lynch $2.8 million; Viacom $2.27 million; Time Warner $1.65 million; GE $1.4 million; Philip Morris $1.13 million; not including stock options or other additional compensation. See Fisk, "What Lawyers earn" National Law Journal, July 10, 1995. See also: Nader and Smith, "The Top-Grossing Law Firms in the United States" No Contest (Random House 1996), pp.371-376; "The Am Law 100" The American Lawyer, July/Aug 1995.

An example of the efforts to limit fees in tobacco cases can be found in Lester Brickman, "Congress Should Set Fees in this Unique Case" ABA Journal, Sept. 1997, p.75. Such arguments have been refuted by others, such as Professor Charles Silver, (in that same *ABA Journal* issue), and Senator Orrin Hatch, who was quoted in the Daily Monitor, May 20, 1998.In 1992, the President of CIGNA earned $7.5 million, the president of Philip Morris earned $23.8 million, and the president of Travelers earned $67.6 million. American Almanac of Jobs and Salaries (ed. John W. Wright) 1994-1995. In 1997, Allstate's CEO was paid $2.7 million in salary and bonuses, (a 131% increase from 1996), while the president of the company was paid $2.6 million, (up 160%); CIGNA's CEO earned $3.27 million; Progressive's CEO earned $2.78 million; Travelers' CEO made $9.25 million. See "Executive Pay" Wall Street Journal, April 9, 1998, p.R-17; Wall Street Journal, March 16, 1998. *USA Today* reported that Travelers' CEO actually earned $227.7 million in 1997, with the inclusion of stock options. "Travelers CEO Rakes in $228 M" USA Today, March 5, 1998. See also: Guerry, "Corporate Ads Attack Civil Justice System" Louisiana Advocates, Feb.1999, p.2.

For information concerning abuses of the legal system by corporate and defense attorneys, see generally: Ross E. Cheit, "Corporate Ambulance Chasers: The Charmed Life of Business in Litigation" Studies in Law Politics and Society (1991); Ralph Nader and Wesley Smith, No Contest: Corporate Lawyers and the Perversion of Justice in America (Random House 1996).

XIII. Chapter Thirteen: What the Future Holds

"Modern industrialism came into being in a world very different from the one we live in today: fewer people, less material well-being, plentiful natural resources. As a result of the successor industry and capitalism, these conditions have now reversed. Today, more people are chasing fewer natural resources. But industry still operates by the same rules, using more resources to make fewer people more productive." Paul Hawken, "Natural Capitalism" Mother Jones March 1997, p.40. "While Americans fret about the demise of the good jobs they remember, the economy is creating millions of new ones that once we would never have dreamed of." Levinson, "Not Everyone is Downsizing" Newsweek, March 18, 1996, p.42. See also: Robert Samuelson, "Down-Sizing for Growth" Newsweek, March 25, 1996, p.45. The pattern of job creation on the heels of downsizing appears to be swinging into reverse. See Korentz, "Will Downsizing Ever Let Up?" Business Week Feb. 16, 1998, p.26. Despite a 5.4% U.S. unemployment rate, "of the 127 million working, 38 million work part time, and 35 million have full-time work that doesn't pay enough to support a family. Then there are the actual unemployed, who number 7.4 million, as well as another 7 million who are discouraged, forcibly retired, or work as temps. Nineteen million people work in retain and earn less than $10,000 per year, usually without health or retirement benefits. For the majority of workers, wages are no higher today than they were in 1973." Paul Hawken, "Social Waste" Mother Jones, March 1997, p.46.

On the Christian principles of charity, see generally: MATTHEW 10:8. MARK 6:35. LUKE 18:18.

On the confusion, grid-lock, disconnection, and unre-
sponsiveness of the two-party system, see: Robert Samuelson, "Washington Disconnected" <u>Newsweek</u>, Jan.
11, 1999, p.41; Robert Samuelson, "The Spirit of Adam
Smith" <u>Newsweek</u>, Dec. 2, 1996, p.63; George Will,
"Consensus and Ladders" <u>Newsweek</u>, May 12, 1997,
p.92; George Will, "Big Stick Conservatism" <u>Newsweek</u>,
Nov. 11, 1996, p.96; Pike, "The European Take on 'Liberalism'" <u>Times Picayune</u>, Jan. 1, 1997, p.B-7; Michael
Perlstein, "New Crime Strategy Clashes With Research"
<u>Times Picayune</u>, April 21, 1997, p.A-7.

On the "Invisible Hand" which guides the free-market
economy, and basic functions of government in a capalist
system, see generally: Adam Smith, <u>An Inquiry into the
Nature and Causes of the Wealth of Nations</u> (1776).

"All we have to do is mix ingredients from two radically different proposals, one from the political left, and
one from the political right. Such a reform won't solve
every flaw in the system. But that's also why it would
work: By realistically avoiding the problems that *can't* be
solved, it gives us a chance to resolve the ones that can."
Jonathan Rauch, "Give Pols Free Money, No Rules"
<u>U.S. News & World Report</u>, Dec. 29, 1997, p.54. Con-
sensus is, as Margaret Thatcher once noted, "a process
of abandoning all beliefs, principles, values and policies
in search of something in which no one believes, but to
which no one objects; the process of avoiding the very
issues that have to be solved, merely because you cannot
get agreement on the way ahead." George Will, "Consensus and Ladders" <u>Newsweek</u>, May 12, 1997, p.92. "First,
all side condemn the new idea: Environmental advocates
say it isn't enough; some business executives say it will

be impossibly expensive. Next comes a phase of general unhappiness in which lawyers rule. Then innovations occur – such as the invention of the catalytic converter, which made automobile smog control practical – and efficiencies result. Ten years later both pollution and costs are declining, though this never prevents the same institutional parties from making the same gloomy predictions about the next round of reforms." Easterbrook, "Greenhouse Common Sense" U.S. News & World Report, Dec. 1, 1997, p.58.

"A witness may not testify to a matter unless evidence is introduced sufficient to support a finding that the witness has personal knowledge of the matter." Fed. Rul Evid. 602. Hearsay is any out-of-court statement offered to prove the truth of the matter asserted. Fed. Rule Evid. 801(c). Hearsay is generally not admissible in a court of law. Fed. Rule Evid. 802.

"If the witness is not testifying as an expert, the witness' testimony in the form of opinions or inferences is limited to those opinions or inferences which are (a) rationally based on the perception of the witness, and (b) helpful to a clear understanding of the witness' testimony or a determination of a fact in issue." Fed. Rule Evid. 701.

"Evidence of other crimes, wrongs, or acts is not admissible to prove the character of a person in order to show action in conformity therewith." Fed. Rule Evid. 404(b). "Ill Kings make many good laws." Proverb (Thomas Fuller, Gnomologia (1732)). "It is a fair summary of history to say that the safeguards of liberty have frequently been forged in controversies involving not very nice people." Justice Frankfurter, United States v. Rabinowitz, 339 U.S. 56, 69 (1950). "I abhor averages. I like the individual case. A man may have six meals one day and none the next, making an average of three meals per day, but that is not a good way to live." Justice Brandeis (A.T. Mason, Brandeis: A Free Man's Life (1946)). "It makes no difference whether a good man has defrauded a bad man or a bad man has defrauded a good man, or whether a good or bad man has committed adultery; the law can look only to the amount of damage done." Aristotle, Nicomachean Ethics. "The business of the court is to try the case and not the man; a very bad man may have a very righteous cause." Thompson v. Church, 1 Root 312 (1791).

The concept of "standing" requires that an individual must have some special, particular, individual interest, (*i.e.* something greater than the mere fact that the individual is a citizen or a taxpayer), in order to "champion a cause or subject-matter which pertains to the whole people in common" or to "enforce the performance of a duty which a public officer owes the public at large". See generally: Allen v. Wright, 468 U.S. 737, 104 S.Ct. 3315, 82 L.Ed.2d 556 (1984); City of Los Angeles v. Lyons, 461 U.S. 95, 103 S.Ct. 1660, 75 L.Ed.2d 675 (1983); Valley Forge v. Americans United, 454 U.S. 464, 102 S.Ct. 752, 70 L.Ed.2d 700 (1982); Schlesinger v. Reservists Committee, 418 U.S. 208, 94 S.Ct. 2925, 41 L.Ed.2d 706 (1974).

Additional References (General) :

For additional references and information concerning the road to justice in America, see generally: J. Kendall Few, In Defense of Trial by Jury (American Jury Trial Foundation 1993); Laurence E. Drivon, The Civil War on Consumer Rights (Conari Press 1990); Ralph Nader and Wesley J. Smith, No Contest: Corporate Lawyers and the Perversion of Justice in America (Random House 1996); Gerry L. Spence, With Justice for None (Penguin 1989); Lawrence M. Friedman, Total Justice (Russell Sage Foundation 1985); James Madison, Alexander Hamilton, and John Jay, The Federalist Papers (1787-1788); John Locke, Second Treatise on Government (1681); John Staurt Mill, On Liberty (1859).

About the Author

Steve Herman was born and raised in New Orleans, Louisiana, where he attended Isidore Newman School. He received a Bachelor of Arts degree from Dartmouth College, where he was awarded Citations of Excellence in the study of Milton and Shakespeare, and won the Eleanor Frost Playwriting Competition with his one-act play, *The Phoenix Sleeps Tonight.* Herman was then named Order of the Coif at Tulane Law School, where he graduated, *Magna Cum Laude,* in 1994. After graduating from Tulane, Herman clerked for Justice Harry T. Lemmon of the Louisiana Supreme Court, and developed a broad civil practice with the Herman Herman & Katz law firm. The recipient of numerous professional appointments and accolades, he teaches complex litigation at both Tulane and Loyola Law Schools, and served, among other things, as Lead Counsel in the BP Oil Spill/*Deepwater Horizon* Litigation. In addition to *America and the Law,* Herman is the author of three novels, *The Gordian Knot, The Sign of Four,* and *A Day in the Life of Timothy Stone,* as well as the recently published *My Life As a Spy.* He maintains a What's New in the Courts law blog at www.gravierhouse. com.

www.ingramcontent.com/pod-product-compliance
Lightning Source LLC
Chambersburg PA
CBHW022109210326
41521CB00028B/174